BOTSWANA

TAXATION LAWS AND REGULATIONS HANDBOOK

VOLUME 1

STRATEGIC INFORMATION AND REGULATIONS

International Business Publications, USA
Washington DC, USA- Botswana

BOTSWANA

TAXATION LAWS AND REGULATIONS HANDBOOK

VOLUME 1 STRATEGIC INFORMATION AND REGULATIONS

UPDATED ANNUALLY

We express our sincere appreciation to all government agencies and international organizations which provided information and other materials for this handbook

Cover Design: **International Business Publications, USA**

2017 Edition Updated Reprint International Business Publications, USA
ISBN 978-1-4330-7940-5

For additional analytical, business and investment opportunities information, please contact Global Investment & Business Center, USA at (703) 370-8082. Fax: (703) 370-8083. E-mail: ibpusa3@gmail.com
Global Business and Investment Info Databank - www.ibpus.com

Printed in the USA

BOTSWANA

TAXATION LAWS AND REGULATIONS HANDBOOK

VOLUME 1

STRATEGIC INFORMATION AND REGULATIONS

TABLE OF CONTENTS

BOTSWANA STRATEGIC & DEVELOPMENT PROFILES

STRATEGIC PROFILE

Capital and largest city	Gaborone 24°39.5′S 25°54.5′E24.6583°S 25.9083°E
Official languages	• English • Setswana
Ethnic groups	• 79% Tswana • 11% Kalanga • 3% Basarwa • 3% Kgalagadi • 3% White • 1% others
Demonym	• Batswana • Motswana
Government	Unitary parliamentary republic
- President	Ian Khama
- Vice-President	Ponatshego Kedikilwe
Legislature	National Assembly
Independence from the United Kingdom	
- Established (Constitution)	30 September 1966
Area	
- Total	581,730 km^2 (48th) 224,610 sq mi
- Water (%)	2.6
Population	
- 2014 estimate	2,155,784 (145th)
- 2011 census	2,038,228
- Density	3.4/km^2 (231st) 8.9/sq mi
GDP (PPP)	2014 estimate
- Total	$35.978 billion
- Per capita	$17,101
GDP (nominal)	2014 estimate
- Total	$16.046 billion
- Per capita	$7,627
Gini	63 very high
HDI (2013)	▼0.634 medium · 119th
Currency	Pula (BWP)
Time zone	Central Africa Time (UTC+2)
- Summer (DST)	not observed (UTC)
Drives on the	left
Calling code	+267
ISO 3166 code	BW
Internet TLD	.bw

Botswana officially the **Republic of Botswana** (Tswana: *Lefatshe la Botswana*), is a landlocked country located in Southern Africa. The citizens refer to themselves as *Batswana* (singular: *Motswana*). Formerly the British protectorate of Bechuanaland, Botswana adopted its new name after becoming independent within the Commonwealth on 30 September 1966. Since then, it has maintained a strong tradition as a stable representative democracy, with a consistent record of uninterrupted democratic elections.

Geographically, Botswana is flat, with up to 70 percent of its territory being the Kalahari Desert. It is bordered by South Africa to the south and southeast, Namibia to the west and north, and Zimbabwe to the northeast. Its border with Zambia to the north near Kazungula is poorly defined but at most is a few hundred metres long.

A mid-sized country of just over two million people, Botswana is one of the most sparsely populated nation's in the world. Around 10 percent of the population lives in the capital and largest city, Gaborone. Once one of the poorest countries in the world — with a GDP per capita of about US$70 per year in the late 1960s — Botswana has since transformed itself into one of the fastest-growing economies in the world, now boasting a GDP (purchasing power parity) per capita of about $16,400 per year as of 2013. Its high gross national income (by some estimates the fourth-largest in Africa) gives the country a modest standard of living and the second highest Human Development Index of continental Sub-Saharan Africa.

Botswana is a member of the African Union, the Southern African Development Community, the Commonwealth of Nations, and the United Nations. Despite its political stability and relative socioeconomic propserity, the country is among the hardest hit by HIV/AIDS epidemic, with around a quarter of the population estimated to be infected

BACKGROUND: Formerly the British protectorate of Bechuanaland, Botswana adopted its new name upon independence in 1966. Four decades of uninterrupted civilian leadership, progressive social policies, and significant capital investment have created one of the most dynamic economies in Africa. Mineral extraction, principally diamond mining, dominates economic activity, though tourism is a growing sector due to the country's conservation practices and extensive nature preserves. Botswana has one of the world's highest known rates of HIV/AIDS infection, but also one of Africa's most progressive and comprehensive programs for dealing with the disease.

GEOGRAPHY

Location:	Southern Africa, north of South Africa
Geographic coordinates:	22 00 S, 24 00 E
Map references:	Africa
Area:	total: 600,370 sq km land: 585,370 sq km water: 15,000 sq km
Area - comparative:	slightly smaller than Texas
Land boundaries:	total: 4,013 km border countries: Namibia 1,360 km, South Africa 1,840 km, Zimbabwe 813 km
Coastline:	0 km (landlocked)
Maritime claims:	none (landlocked)
Climate:	semiarid; warm winters and hot summers

Terrain:	predominantly flat to gently rolling tableland; Kalahari Desert in southwest

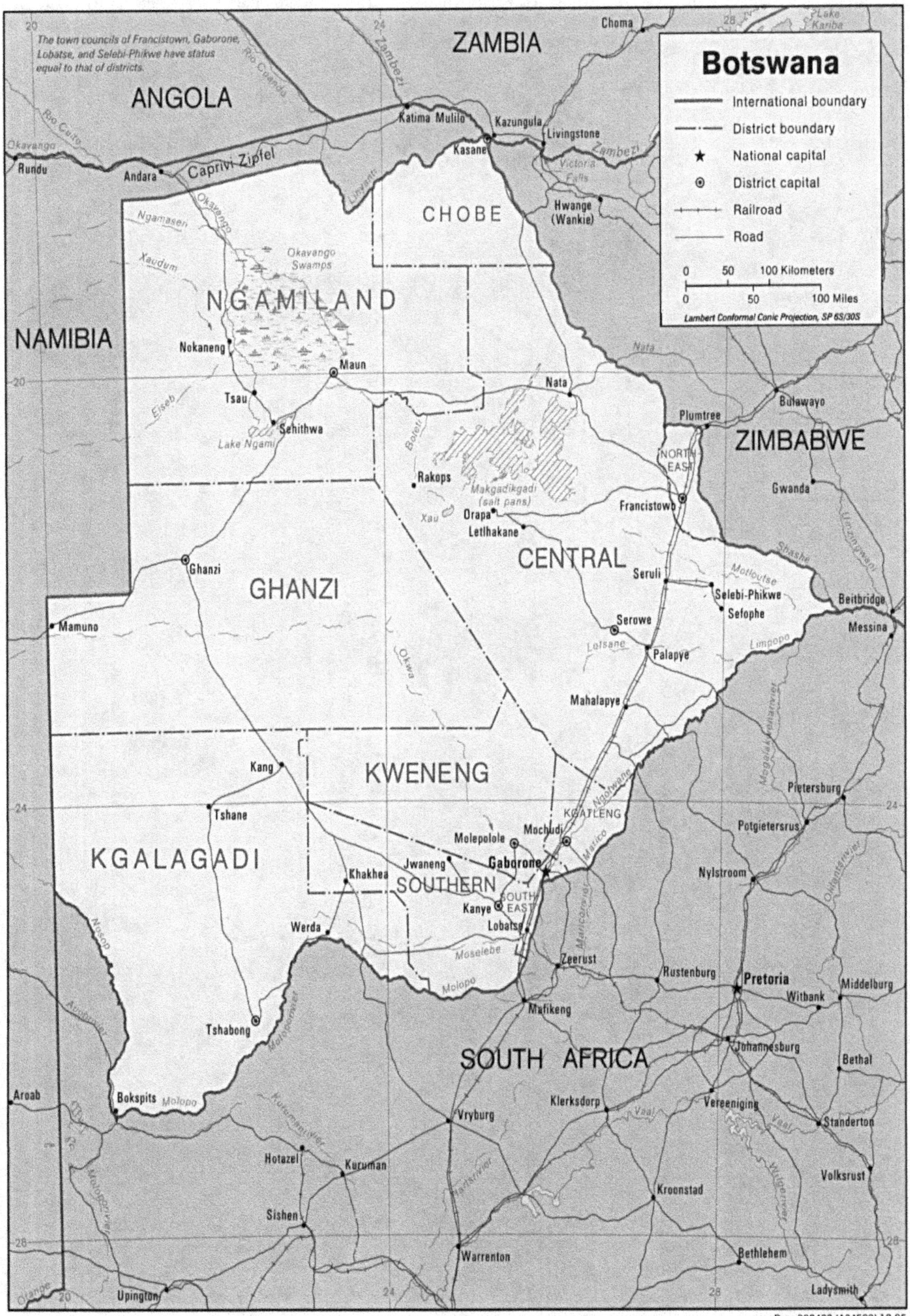

Base 802422 (A04503) 12-95

For additional analytical, marketing, investment and business opportunities information, please contact
Global Investment & Business Center, USA
(202) 546-2103. Fax: (202) 546-3275. E-mail: ibpusa3@gmail.com

Elevation extremes:	*lowest point:* junction of the Limpopo and Shashe Rivers 513 m *highest point:* Tsodilo Hills 1,489 m
Natural resources:	diamonds, copper, nickel, salt, soda ash, potash, coal, iron ore, silver
Land use:	*arable land:* 0.65% *permanent crops:* 0.01% *other:* 99.34%
Irrigated land:	10 sq km
Natural hazards:	periodic droughts; seasonal August winds blow from the west, carrying sand and dust across the country, which can obscure visibility
Environment - current issues:	overgrazing; desertification; limited fresh water resources
Environment - international agreements:	*party to:* Biodiversity, Climate Change, Climate Change-Kyoto Protocol, Desertification, Endangered Species, Hazardous Wastes, Law of the Sea, Ozone Layer Protection, Wetlands *signed, but not ratified:* none of the selected agreements
Geography - note:	landlocked; population concentrated in eastern part of the country

PEOPLE

POPULATION:	1,815,508 note: estimates for this country explicitly take into account the effects of excess mortality due to AIDS; this can result in lower life expectancy, higher infant mortality and death rates, lower population and growth rates, and changes in the distribution of population by age and sex than would otherwise be expected (July 2007 est.)
Age structure:	0-14 years: 35.8% (male 330,377/female 319,376) 15-64 years: 60.3% (male 549,879/female 545,148) 65 years and over: 3.9% (male 28,725/female 42,003)
Median age:	total: 20.9 years male: 20.7 years female: 21.1 years
Population growth rate:	1.503%
Birth rate:	23.17 births/1,000 population
Death rate:	13.63 deaths/1,000 population
Net migration rate:	5.49 migrant(s) /1,000 population note: there is an increasing flow of Zimbabweans into South Africa and Botswana in search of better economic opportunities
Sex ratio:	at birth: 1.03 male(s) /female under 15 years: 1.034 male(s) /female 15-64 years: 1.009 male(s) /female 65 years and over: 0.684 male(s) /female

	total population: 1.003 male(s) /female
Infant mortality rate:	total: 43.97 deaths/1,000 live births male: 45.02 deaths/1,000 live births female: 42.9 deaths/1,000 live births
Life expectancy at birth:	total population: 50.58 years male: 51.55 years female: 49.58 years
Total fertility rate:	2.73 children born/woman
HIV/AIDS - adult prevalence rate:	37.3%
HIV/AIDS - people living with HIV/AIDS:	350,000
HIV/AIDS - deaths:	33,000
Major infectious diseases:	degree of risk: high food or waterborne diseases: bacterial diarrhea, hepatitis A, and typhoid fever vectorborne disease: malaria (2007)
Nationality:	noun: Motswana (singular) , Batswana (plural) adjective: Motswana (singular) , Batswana (plural)
Ethnic groups:	Tswana (or Setswana) 79%, Kalanga 11%, Basarwa 3%, other, including Kgalagadi and white 7%
Religions:	Christian 71.6%, Badimo 6%, other 1.4%, unspecified 0.4%, none 20.6% (2001 census)
Languages:	Setswana 78.2%, Kalanga 7.9%, Sekgalagadi 2.8%, English 2.1% (official) , other 8.6%, unspecified 0.4% (2001 census)
Literacy:	definition: age 15 and over can read and write total population: 79.8% male: 76.9% female: 82.4%

GOVERNMENT

COUNTRY NAME:	conventional long form: Republic of Botswana conventional short form: Botswana local long form: Republic of Botswana local short form: Botswana former: Bechuanaland
Government type:	parliamentary republic
Capital:	name: Gaborone geographic coordinates: 24 45 S, 25 55 E time difference: UTC+2 (7 hours ahead of Washington, DC during Standard Time)
Administrative divisions:	9 districts and 5 town councils*; Central, Francistown*, Gaborone*, Ghanzi, Jwaneng*, Kgalagadi, Kgatleng, Kweneng, Lobatse*, Northeast, Northwest, Selebi-Pikwe*, Southeast, Southern
Independence:	30 September 1966 (from UK)
National holiday:	Independence Day (Botswana Day) , 30 September (1966)

Constitution:	March 1965, effective 30 September 1966
Legal system:	based on Roman-Dutch law and local customary law; judicial review limited to matters of interpretation; accepts compulsory ICJ jurisdiction, with reservations
Suffrage:	18 years of age; universal
Executive branch:	chief of state: President Seretse Khama Ian KHAMA (since 1 April 2008) ; Vice President Mompati MERAFHE (since 1 April 2008) ; note - the president is both the chief of state and head of government head of government: President Seretse Khama Ian KHAMA (since 1 April 2008) ; Vice President Mompati MERAFHE (since 1 April 2008) cabinet: Cabinet appointed by the president elections: president indirectly elected for a five-year term (eligible for a second term) ; election last held on 20 October 2009 (next to be held in October 2014) ; vice president appointed by the president election results: Seretse Khama Ian KHAMA elected president; percent of National Assembly vote - NA%
Legislative branch:	**description:** unicameral Parliament consists of the National Assembly (63 seats; 57 members directly elected in single-seat constituencies by simple majority vote, 4 nominated by the president and indirectly elected by simple majority vote by the rest of the National Assembly, and 2 ex-officio members - the president and attorney general; elected members serve 5-year terms); note - the House of Chiefs (Ntlo ya Dikgosi), an advisory body to the National Assembly, consists of 35 members - 8 hereditary chiefs from Botswana's principal tribes, 22 indirectly elected by the chiefs, and 5 appointed by the president; the House of Chiefs consults on issues including powers of chiefs, customary courts, customary law, tribal property, and constitutional amendments **elections:** National Assembly elections last held on 24 October 2014 (next to be held in October 2019) **election results:** percent of vote by party - BDP 46.5%, UDC 30.0%, BCP 20.4%, independent 3.1%; seats by party - BDP 37, UDC 17, BCP 3
Judicial branch:	High Court; Court of Appeal; Magistrates' Courts (one in each district)
Political parties and leaders:	Botswana Alliance Movement or BAM [Ephraim Lepetu SETSHWAELO]; Botswana Congress Party or BCP [Otlaadisa KOOSALETSE]; Botswana Democratic Party or BDP [Festus G. MOGAE]; Botswana National Front or BNF [Otswoletse MOUPO]; Botswana Peoples Party or BPP; MELS Movement of Botswana or MELS; New Democratic Front or NDF note: a number of minor parties joined forces in 1999 to form the BAM but did not capture any parliamentary seats - includes the United Action Party [Ephraim Lepetu SETSHWAELO]; the Independence Freedom Party or IFP [Motsamai MPHO]; the Botswana Progressive Union [D. K. KWELE]
Political pressure groups and leaders:	NA

International organization participation:	ACP, AfDB, AU, C, FAO, G-77, IAEA, IBRD, ICAO, ICCt, ICRM, IDA, IFAD, IFC, IFRCS, ILO, IMF, Interpol, IOC, IPU, ISO, ITU, MIGA, NAM, OPCW, SACU, SADC, UN, UNCTAD, UNESCO, UNIDO, UNMIS, UNWTO, UPU, WCO, WFTU, WHO, WIPO, WMO, WTO
Diplomatic representation in the US:	chief of mission: Ambassador Lapologang Caesar LEKOA chancery: 1531-1533 New Hampshire Avenue NW, Washington, DC 20036 telephone: (202) 244-4990 FAX: (202) 244-4164
Diplomatic representation from the US:	chief of mission: Ambassador Katherine H. CANAVAN embassy: address NA, Gaborone mailing address: Embassy Enclave, P. O. Box 90, Gaborone telephone: [267] 353982 FAX: [267] 312782
Flag description:	light blue with a horizontal white-edged black stripe in the center

ECONOMY

Botswana has maintained one of the world's highest economic growth rates since independence in 1966. However, economic growth was negative in 2009, with the industrial sector shrinking by 30%, after the global crisis reduced demand for Botswana's diamonds. Although the economy recovered in 2010, GDP growth has again slowed. Through fiscal discipline and sound management, Botswana transformed itself from one of the poorest countries in the world to a middle-income country with a per capita GDP of $16,400 in 2013. Two major investment services rank Botswana as the best credit risk in Africa. Diamond mining has fueled much of the expansion and currently accounts for more than one-third of GDP, 70-80% of export earnings, and about one-third of the government's revenues. Botswana's heavy reliance on a single luxury export was a critical factor in the sharp economic contraction of 2009. Tourism, financial services, subsistence farming, and cattle raising are other key sectors. According to official government statistics, unemployment reached 17.8% in 2009, but unofficial estimates run much higher. The prevalence of HIV/AIDS is second highest in the world and threatens Botswana's impressive economic gains. An expected leveling off in diamond production within the next two decades overshadows long-term prospects. A major international diamond company signed a 10-year deal with Botswana in 2012 to move its rough stone sorting and trading division from London to Gaborone by the end of 2013. The move may support Botswana's downstream diamond industry.

GDP (purchasing power parity):
$34 billion (2013 est.)
country comparison to the world: 111
$32.71 billion (2012 est.)
$31.4 billion (2011 est.)
note:data are in 2013 US dollars

GDP (official exchange rate):
$15.53 billion (2013 est.)

GDP - real growth rate:
3.9% (2013 est.)
country comparison to the world: 84

4.2% (2012 est.)
6.1% (2011 est.)

GDP - per capita (PPP):
$16,400 (2013 est.)
country comparison to the world: 82
$15,900 (2012 est.)
$15,500 (2011 est.)
note:data are in 2013 US dollars

Gross national saving:
33.7% of GDP (2013 est.)
country comparison to the world: 17
28.9% of GDP (2012 est.)
41.1% of GDP (2011 est.)

GDP - composition, by end use:
household consumption: 51.6%
government consumption: 18.3%
investment in fixed capital: 34.1%
investment in inventories: -1.2%
exports of goods and services: 47%
imports of goods and services: -49.8%
(2013 est.)

GDP - composition, by sector of origin:
agriculture: 1.9%
industry: 35.7%
services: 62.4% (2013 est.)

Agriculture - products:
livestock, sorghum, maize, millet, beans, sunflowers, groundnuts

Industries:
diamonds, copper, nickel, salt, soda ash, potash, coal, iron ore, silver; livestock processing; textiles

Industrial production growth rate:
7.2% (2013 est.)
country comparison to the world: 31

Labor force:
1.308 million (2013 est.)
country comparison to the world: 136

Labor force - by occupation:
agriculture: NA%
industry: NA%

services: NA%

Unemployment rate:
17.8% (2009 est.)
country comparison to the world: 156
7.5% (2007 est.)

Population below poverty line:
30.3% (2003)

Household income or consumption by percentage share:
lowest 10%: NA%
highest 10%: NA%

Distribution of family income - Gini index:
63 (1993)
country comparison to the world: 3

Budget:
revenues: $5.04 billion
expenditures: $4.952 billion (2013 est.)

Taxes and other revenues:
32.4% of GDP (2013 est.)
country comparison to the world: 79

Budget surplus (+) or deficit (-):
0.6% of GDP (2013 est.)
country comparison to the world: 32

Public debt:
17.9% of GDP (2013 est.)
country comparison to the world: 139
17.4% of GDP (2012 est.)

Fiscal year:
1 April - 31 March

Inflation rate (consumer prices):
6.1% (2013 est.)
country comparison to the world: 177
7.5% (2012 est.)

Central bank discount rate:
9.5% (31 December 2010 est.)
country comparison to the world: 27
10% (31 December 2009 est.)

Commercial bank prime lending rate:
10% (31 December 2013 est.)
country comparison to the world: 73
11% (31 December 2012 est.)

Stock of narrow money:
$1.517 billion (31 December 2013 est.)
country comparison to the world: 137
$1.358 billion (31 December 2012 est.)

Stock of broad money:
$8.293 billion (31 December 2013 est.)
country comparison to the world: 110
$7.635 billion (31 December 2012 est.)

Stock of domestic credit:
$1.38 billion (31 December 2013 est.)
country comparison to the world: 145
$2.111 billion (31 December 2012 est.)

Market value of publicly traded shares:
$4.588 billion (31 December 2012 est.)
country comparison to the world: 79
$4.107 billion (31 December 2011)
$4.076 billion (31 December 2010 est.)

Current account balance:
$1.375 billion (2013 est.)
country comparison to the world: 47
-$795.2 million (2012 est.)

Exports:
$7.569 billion (2013 est.)
country comparison to the world: 103
$6.011 billion (2012 est.)

Exports - commodities:
diamonds, copper, nickel, soda ash, meat, textiles

Imports:
$7.389 billion (2013 est.)
country comparison to the world: 112
$7.918 billion (2012 est.)

Imports - commodities:
foodstuffs, machinery, electrical goods, transport equipment, textiles, fuel and petroleum

products, wood and paper products, metal and metal products

Reserves of foreign exchange and gold:
$7.933 billion (31 December 2013 est.)
country comparison to the world: 79
$7.628 billion (31 December 2012 est.)

Debt - external:
$2.416 billion (31 December 2013 est.)
country comparison to the world: 141
$2.443 billion (31 December 2012 est.)

Exchange rates:
pulas (BWP) per US dollar -
8.732 (2013 est.)
7.6181 (2012 est.)
6.7936 (est.)
7.1551 (2009)
6.7907 (2008)

ENERGY

Electricity - production:
429.6 million kWh (est.)
country comparison to the world: 165

Electricity - consumption:
3.118 billion kWh (2011 est.)
country comparison to the world: 129

Electricity - exports:
0 kWh (2012 est.)
country comparison to the world: 102

Electricity - imports:
2.985 billion kWh (est.)
country comparison to the world: 46

Electricity - installed generating capacity:
132,000 kW (2011 est.)
country comparison to the world: 169

Electricity - from fossil fuels:
100% of total installed capacity (est.)
country comparison to the world: 6

Electricity - from nuclear fuels:

0% of total installed capacity (est.)
country comparison to the world: 45

Electricity - from hydroelectric plants:
0% of total installed capacity (est.)
country comparison to the world: 157

Electricity - from other renewable sources:
0% of total installed capacity (est.)
country comparison to the world: 155

Crude oil - production:
0 bbl/day (2012 est.)
country comparison to the world: 151

Crude oil - exports:
0 bbl/day (est.)
country comparison to the world: 81

Crude oil - imports:
0 bbl/day (est.)
country comparison to the world: 157

Crude oil - proved reserves:
0 bbl (1 January 2013 est.)
country comparison to the world: 105

Refined petroleum products - production:
0 bbl/day (est.)
country comparison to the world: 120

Refined petroleum products - consumption:
15,420 bbl/day (2011 est.)
country comparison to the world: 141

Refined petroleum products - exports:
0 bbl/day (est.)
country comparison to the world: 151

Refined petroleum products - imports:
19,360 bbl/day (est.)

country comparison to the world: 107

Natural gas - production:
0 cu m (2011 est.)
country comparison to the world: 100

Natural gas - consumption:
0 cu m (est.)
country comparison to the world: 119

Natural gas - exports:
0 cu m (2011 est.)
country comparison to the world: 62

Natural gas - imports:
0 cu m (2011 est.)
country comparison to the world: 157

Natural gas - proved reserves:
0 cu m (1 January 2013 est.)
country comparison to the world: 111

Carbon dioxide emissions from consumption of energy:
3.843 million Mt (2011 est.)

COMMUNICATIONS

Telephones - main lines in use:
160,500

country comparison to the world: 134

Telephones - mobile cellular:
3.082 million
country comparison to the world: 129

Telephone system:
general assessment: Botswana is participating in regional development efforts; expanding fully digital system with fiber-optic cables linking the major population centers in the east as well as a system of open-wire lines, microwave radio relays links, and radiotelephone communication stations
domestic: fixed-line teledensity has declined in recent years and now stands at roughly 7 telephones per 100 persons; mobile-cellular teledensity now pushing 140 telephones per 100 persons
international: country code - 267; international calls are made via satellite, using international direct dialing; 2 international exchanges; digital microwave radio relay links to Namibia, Zambia, Zimbabwe, and South Africa; satellite earth station - 1 Intelsat (Indian

Ocean)

Broadcast media:
2 TV stations - 1 state-owned and 1 privately owned; privately owned satellite TV subscription service is available; 2 state-owned national radio stations; 3 privately owned radio stations broadcast locally

Internet country code:
.bw

Internet hosts:
1,806
country comparison to the world: 163

Internet users:
120,000
country comparison to the world: 154

TRANSPORTATION

Airports:
74 (2013)
country comparison to the world: 71

Airports - with paved runways:
total: 10
over 3,047 m: 2
2,438 to 3,047 m: 1
1,524 to 2,437 m: 6
914 to 1,523 m: 1 (2013)

Airports - with unpaved runways:
total: 64
1,524 to 2,437 m: 5
914 to 1,523 m: 46
under 914 m:
13 (2013)

Railways:
total: 888 km
country comparison to the world: 93
narrow gauge: 888 km 1.067-m gauge

Roadways:
total: 17,916 km

country comparison to the world: 117
note:includes 8,916 km of Public Highway Network roads (6,116 km paved and 2,800 km unpaved) and other 9,000 km of District Council roads (2011)

MILITARY

Military branches:
Botswana Defense Force (BDF): Ground Forces Command, Air Wing Command, Defense Logistics Command, Special Forces Group (2013)

Military service age and obligation:
18 is the legal minimum age for voluntary military service; no conscription (2012)

Manpower available for military service:
males age 16-49: 557,647
females age 16-49: 531,095 (est.)

Manpower fit for military service:
males age 16-49: 340,949
females age 16-49: 302,332 (est.)

Manpower reaching militarily significant age annually:
male: 23,649
female: 23,063 (est.)

Military expenditures:
2.31% of GDP (2012)
country comparison to the world: 34
2.43% of GDP (2011)
2.31% of GDP (2010)

TRANSNATIONAL ISSUES

Disputes - international:
none

IMPORTANT INFORMATION ON BOTSWANA

PROFILE

OFFICIAL NAME: Republic of Botswana

Geography
Area: 582,000 sq. km. (224,710 sq. mi.) , about the size of Texas.
Cities (2001 census) : *Capital*--Gaborone (pronounced ha-bo-ro-neh) , pop. 186,007. *Other towns*--Francistown (83,023) , Selebi-Phikwe (49,849) , Molepolole (54,561) , Kanye (40,628) , Serowe (42,444) , Mahalapye (39,719) , Lobatse (29,689) , Maun (43,776) , Mochudi (36,962) .

Terrain: Desert and savanna.
Climate: Mostly subtropical.

People
Nationality: *Noun and adjective*--Motswana (sing.) , Batswana (pl.) .
Population : 1.76 million.
Annual population growth rate (2002) : 0.6%.
Ethnic groups: Tswana 79%; Kalanga 11%; Kgalagadi, Herero, Bayeyi, Hambukush, Basarwa ("San") , Khoi, whites 10%.
Religions: Christianity 70%, none 20%, indigenous beliefs 6%, other 4%.
Languages: English (official) , Setswana, Ikalanga.
Education: *Adult literacy*--81%.
Health (2004) : *Life expectancy*--33.9 years. *Infant mortality rate*--56/1,000.
Work force : 274,000.

Government
Type: Republic, parliamentary democracy.
Independence: September 30, 1966.
Constitution: March 1965.
Branches: *Executive*--president (chief of state and head of government) , cabinet. *Legislative*--popularly elected National Assembly; advisory House of Chiefs. *Judicial*--High Court, Court of Appeal, local and customary courts, industrial labor court.
Administrative subdivisions: Five town councils and nine district councils.
Major political parties: Botswana Democratic Party (BDP) --48 seats, Botswana National Front (BNF) --12 seats, Botswana Congress Party (BCP) --1 seat, Botswana Alliance Movement (BAM) , Botswana Peoples Party (BPP) --0 seats.
Suffrage: Universal at 18.

Economy
Natural resources: Diamonds, copper, nickel, coal, soda ash, salt, gold, potash.
Agriculture (2.1% of GDP, 2004/5) : *Products*--livestock, sorghum, white maize, millet, cowpeas, beans.
Industry: *Types*--mining (38% of GDP) : diamonds, copper, nickel, coal; tourism, textiles, construction, tourism, beef processing, chemical products production, food and beverage production.
Trade (2003/4) : *Exports*--$2.9 billion: diamonds, nickel, copper, meat products, textiles, hides, skins, and soda ash. *Partners*--EU, South Africa, Zimbabwe. *Imports*--$2.9 billion: machinery, transport equipment, manufactured goods, food, chemicals, fuels. *Major suppliers*--South Africa, EU, and U.S.

PEOPLE AND HISTORY

The Batswana, a term also used to denote all citizens of Botswana, refers to the country's major ethnic group (the "Tswana" in South Africa) , which came into the area from South Africa during the Zulu wars of the early 1800s. Prior to European contact, the Batswana lived as herders and farmers under tribal rule.

In the 19th century, hostilities broke out between the Batswana and Boer settlers from the Transvaal. After appeals by the Batswana for assistance, the British Government in 1885 put "Bechuanaland" under its protection. The northern territory remained under direct administration and is today's Botswana, while the southern territory became part of the Cape Colony and is now part of the northwest province of South Africa; the majority of Setswana-speaking people today live in South Africa.

Despite South African pressure, inhabitants of the Bechuanaland Protectorate, Basuotoland (now Lesotho) , and Swaziland in 1909 asked for and received British assurances that they would not be included in the proposed Union of South Africa. An expansion of British central authority and the evolution of tribal government resulted in the 1920 establishment of two advisory councils representing Africans and Europeans. Proclamations in 1934 regularized tribal rule and powers. A European-African advisory council was formed in 1951, and the 1961 constitution established a consultative legislative council.

In June 1964, Britain accepted proposals for democratic self-government in Botswana. The seat of government was moved from Mafikeng, in South Africa, to newly established Gaborone in 1965. The 1965 constitution led to the first general elections and to independence in September 1966. Seretse Khama, a leader in the independence movement and the legitimate claimant to traditional rule of the Bamangwato, was elected as the first president, re-elected twice, and died in office in 1980. The presidency passed to the sitting vice president, Ketumile Masire, who was elected in his own right in 1984 and re-elected in 1989 and 1994. Masire retired from office in 1998. The presidency passed to the sitting vice president, Festus Mogae, who was elected in his own right in 1999. Mogae won a second term in elections held October 30, 2004.

GOVERNMENT AND POLITICAL CONDITIONS

Botswana has a flourishing multiparty constitutional democracy. General elections are held every 5 years. Each of the elections since independence has been freely and fairly contested and has been held on schedule. The country's minority groups participate freely in the political process. The openness of the country's political system has been a significant factor in Botswana's stability and economic growth.

The president of Botswana is indirectly elected. The presidential candidate from the political party that wins the majority of the 57 seats in the National Assembly is sworn in as president. The cabinet is selected by the president from the National Assembly; it consists of a vice president and a flexible number of ministers and assistant ministers, currently 16 and 8, respectively. The National Assembly has 57 elected and 4 specially elected members; it is expanded following each census (every 10 years; the most recent was conducted in 2001) . The next census will be held in 2011.

There are three main parties and a number of smaller parties. In national elections held October 16, 2009, the Botswana Democratic Party (BDP) won 45 of 57 contested National Assembly seats, the Botswana National Front (BNF) won 6 seats, and the Botswana Congress Party (BCP) /Botswana Alliance Movement pact won 5 seats. For the first time in the history of the country, an independent candidate won a seat in parliament during this election. Individuals elected by the National Assembly hold an additional 4 seats; the ruling BDP currently holds all 4. The ruling BDP took all but one of the five constituencies in the city of Gaborone from the opposition. BDP now controls the city council.

The advisory House of Chiefs represents the eight principal subgroups of the Batswana tribes, five members specially elected by the president, and 22 members elected from designated regions. The elected members hold office for a period of only 5 years whereas the eight principal chiefs are members for life. A draft of any National Assembly bill of tribal concern must be referred to the House of Chiefs for advisory opinion. Chiefs and other leaders preside over customary traditional courts, though all persons have the right to request that their case be considered under the formal British-based legal system.

The roots of Botswana's democracy lie in Setswana traditions, exemplified by the Kgotla, or village council, in which the powers of traditional leaders are limited by custom and law. Botswana's High Court has general civil and criminal jurisdiction. Judges are appointed by the president and may be removed only for cause and after a hearing. The constitution has a code of fundamental human rights enforced by the courts, and Botswana has a good human rights record.

Local government is administered by nine district councils and five town councils. District commissioners have executive authority and are appointed by the central government and assisted by elected and nominated district councilors and district development committees. There has been ongoing debate about the political, social, and economic marginalization of the San (an indigenous tribal population) . The government's policies for the Basarwa (San) and other remote area dwellers continue to spark controversy.

Principal Government Officials

President--Lt. Gen. (ret.) Seretse Khama Ian Khama

Cabinet Ministers
Finance and Development Planning--Kenneth Mathambo
Foreign Affairs and International Cooperation--Phandu T.C. Skelemani
Environment, Wildlife and Tourism--Onkokame Kitso Mokaila
Infrastructure, Science and Technology--Johnny Swartz
Office of the President for Justice, Defense and Security--Dikgakgamatso R. Seretse
Office of the President for Public Administration--Lesego Motsumi
Trade and Industry--Dorcas Makgato-Malesu
Minerals, Energy and Water Resources--Ponatshego Kedikilwe
Lands and Housing--Nonofo E. Molefi
Local Government--Lebonamang T. Mokalake
Education and Skills Development--Pelononi Venson-Moitoi
Health--John Seakgosing
Transport and Communications--Frank Ramsden
Labour and Home Affairs--Peter L. Siele
Sports, Youth, and Culture--Shaw Kgathi
Agriculture--Christian De Graaff

Ambassador to the United States--L. Caesar Lekoa
Ambassador to the United Nations--Charles Ntwaagae

Botswana maintains an embassy at 1531-1533 New Hampshire Avenue NW, Washington DC 20036 (tel. 202-244-4990; fax 202-244-4164) . Its mission to the United Nations is at 103 E. 37th Street, New York NY 10017 (tel. 212-889-2277; fax 212-725-5061) .

ECONOMY

Rank	111th
Currency	Pula (BWP)
	Statistics
GDP	$34.0 billion (PPP, 2013)

	$15.53 billion (nominal, 2013)
GDP growth	3.9% (2013)
GDP per capita	▲$16,400(PPP, 2013)
GDP by sector	agriculture 1.9%, industry 35.7%, services 62.4% (2013 est.)
Inflation (CPI)	8.1%
Population below poverty line	20.0%
Labour force	1.31 million (2013 est.)
Unemployment	17.5%
Main industries	diamonds, copper, nickel, salt, soda ash, potash, livestock processing, textiles
Ease-of-doing-business rank	56th
	External
Exports	$5.127 billion f.o.b.
Export goods	diamonds, copper, nickel, soda ash, meat, textiles
Main export partners	European Free Trade Association (EFTA) 87%, Southern African Customs Union (SACU) 7%, Zimbabwe 4%
Imports	$3.931 billion f.o.b.
Import goods	foodstuffs, machinery, electrical goods, transport equipment, textiles, fuel and petroleum products, wood and paper products, metal and metal products
	Public finances
Public debt	5.1% of GDP
Revenues	$4.556 billion
Expenses	$4.127 billion
Economic aid	$73 million
Credit rating	A (Domestic) A- (Foreign) A+ (T&C Assessment) (Standard & Poor's)

Since independence, Botswana has had the highest average economic growth rate in the world, averaging about 9% per year from 1966 to 1999. Growth in private sector employment has averaged about 10% per annum over the first 30 years of independence. At the start of the 21st century, however, the **economy of Botswana** stagnated up until the early 2010s when it registered for the first time since the economic boom a GDP growth up above the 6-7% target. Botswana is also commended for the site of Africa's longest and among the world's longest economic booms (which almost surpassed that in Asia's largest economies). The relatively high quality of the country's statistics means that these figures are likely to be quite accurate. The government has consistently maintained budget surpluses and has extensive foreign exchange reserves.

Botswana's impressive economic record has been built on a foundation of diamond mining, prudent fiscal policies, international financial and technical assistance, and a cautious foreign policy. It is rated the least corrupt country in Africa, according to an international corruption watchdog, Transparency International. By one estimate, it has the fourth highest gross national income at purchasing power parity in Africa, giving it a standard of living around that of Mexico and Turkey.

Trade unions represent a minority of workers in the Botswana economy. In general they are loosely organized "in-house" unions, although the Botswana Federation of Trade Unions (BFTU) is consolidating its role as the sole national trade union centre in the country

Botswana has enjoyed one of the fastest growth rates in per capita income in the world since independence, although it has slowed considerably due to the global economic slowdown. Economic growth averaged 9% per year from 1967-2006, but slowed during 2007 and 2008 to only 3% before contracting by an estimated 4-5% in 2009. The government has maintained a sound fiscal policyand a negligible level of foreign debt. Foreign exchange reserves were estimated to be $9.2 billion in November 2009, representing approximately 20 months' cover of imports of goods and services. In the second quarter of 2009, imports remained in excess of exports, resulting in a trade deficit that was partially offset by the revenues from the Southern African Customs Union. Botswana's impressive economic record has been built on the foundation of wisely using revenue generated from diamond mining to fuel economic development through prudent fiscal policies and a cautious foreign policy. The government recognizes that HIV/AIDS will continue to affect the economy and is providing leadership and programs to combat the epidemic, including free anti-retroviral treatment and a nationwide Prevention of Mother-to-Child Transmission program.

Mining

Debswana (formed by the government and South Africa's DeBeers in equal partnership) is the largest mining operation in Botswana. Several other mining operations exist in the country, including the Bamangwato Concessions, Ltd. (BCL, also with substantial government equity participation) and Tati Nickel.

Since the early 1980s, the country has been the world's largest producer of gem-quality diamonds. Four large diamond mines have opened since independence. DeBeers prospectors discovered diamonds in northern Botswana in the late 1960s. The first mine began production at Orapa in 1972, followed by the smaller mines of Lethlakane and Damtshaa. What has become the single-richest diamond mine in the world opened in Jwaneng in 1982. The Orapa 2000 Expansion of the existing Orapa mine was opened in 2000. In December 2004, Debswana negotiated 25-year lease renewals for all four of its mines with the Government of Botswana. Diamond mining accounts for approximately one-third of Botswana's GDP and 70 percent of export earnings. However, the industry is capital intensive and accounts for less than 5 percent of private sector employment. The global economic crisis greatly reduced worldwide demand for diamonds, and the government reports that Botswana's diamond sales volume for 2009 was 37% lower than that of 2007.

Diamond mining will continue to be the mainstay of Botswana's economy, with known current reserves sufficient for at least the next 20 years. Exploration for additional kimberlite pipes continues. However, the current economic slowdown greatly impacts Botswana's diamond mining industry. As part of Botswana's drive to diversify and increase local value added within the mining sector, De Beers opened the Diamond Trading Center Botswana (DTCB) in 2008 to shift sorting, cutting, polishing, aggregating, and marketing to Gaborone from London. In 2009, the DeBeers group postponed moving its worldwide diamond aggregation from London to Botswana. However, the DTCB is currently responsible for sorting all stones mined in Botswana before they are sent for aggregation in London. In addition, DTCB receives packets of rough stones from DTC London which it is authorized to sell to sixteeen diamond cutting and polishing firms (known as "sightholders") which have opened factories in Gaborone, creating approximately 2,500 new jobs and helping to diversify Botswana's economy. .
BCL, which operates a copper-nickel mine at Selebi-Phikwe, has had a troubled financial history

but remains an important employer, although the life of the mine is expected to end in the next 5 to 10 years. Other copper-nickel mines include Tati Nickel near Francistown. Botash, the sole producer of soda ash in the region and supported by substantial government investment, produced 265,000 tons of soda ash in 2005.

Coal-bed methane gas has been discovered in the northeastern part of the country, estimated by the developers at a commercially viable quantity of 12 trillion cubic feet. Development of the gas fields has been slow, however.

Tourism
Tourism is an increasingly important industry in Botswana, accounting for approximately 6% of GDP. One of the world's unique ecosystems, the Okavango Delta, is located in Botswana. The country offers excellent game viewing and birding both in the Delta and in the Chobe Game Reserve--home to one of the largest herds of free-ranging elephants in the world. Botswana's Central Kalahari Game Reserve also offers good game viewing and some of the most remote and unspoiled wilderness in southern Africa.

Agriculture
More than one-half of the population lives in rural areas and is largely dependent on subsistence crop and livestock farming. Agriculture meets only a small portion of food needs and contributes a very small amount to GDP--primarily through beef exports--but it remains a social and cultural touchstone. Cattle raising in particular dominated Botswana's social and economic life before independence. The national herd is estimated between 2 and 3 million head, but the cattle industry is experiencing a protracted decline.

Private Sector Development and Foreign Investment
Botswana seeks to further diversify its economy away from minerals, which accounts for more than one-third of GDP. Foreign investment and management are welcomed in Botswana. Botswana abolished foreign exchange controls in 1999, has a low corporate tax rate (15%) , and no prohibitions on foreign ownership of companies. The government reports that the average year-on-year annual inflation rate dropped to 8.2 percent for 2009 as compared to 12.6 percent in 2008.

With its proven record of good economic governance, Botswana was ranked as Africa's least corrupt country by Transparency International in 2009 (37th out of 180 countries, ahead of many European and Asian countries) . Botswana is consistently ranked by international organizations as among the freest economies in sub-Saharan Africa. In the 2009 Economic Freedom of the World report, Botswana was ranked 60th overall and third-highest in Africa, while the Heritage Foundation's 2008 Index of Economic Freedom ranked Botswana at 69.7, making it second in sub-Saharan Africa. In 2010, the Moodys' credit rating agency downgraded Botswana's rating from an "A" grade to an "A-" but also revised its outlook from "negative" to "stable". However, Botswana remains one of the best credit risks in Africa and is on par with many countries in central Europe, East Asia, and Latin America.

U.S. investment in Botswana remains at relatively low levels. Major U.S. corporations, such as H.J. Heinz and AON Corporation, are present through direct investments, while others, such as Kentucky Fried Chicken and Remax, are present via franchise. The sovereign credit ratings by Moody's and Standard & Poor's clearly indicate that, despite continued challenges such as small market size, landlocked location, and cumbersome bureaucratic processes, Botswana remains one of the best investment opportunities in the developing world.

Because of history and geography, Botswana has long had deep ties to the economy of South Africa. The Southern Africa Customs Union (SACU) , comprised of Botswana, Namibia, Lesotho, Swaziland, and South Africa, dates from 1910, and is the world's oldest customs union. Under this arrangement, South Africa has collected levies from customs, sales, and excise duties for all five members, sharing out proceeds based on each country's portion of imports. The exact formula for sharing revenues and the decision-making authority over duties--held exclusively by the Government of South Africa--became increasingly controversial, and the members renegotiated the arrangement in 2001. A new structure was formally ratified and a SACU Secretariat was established in Windhoek, Namibia. Following South Africa's accession to the World Trade Organization (WTO, of which Botswana also is a member) , many of the SACU duties are declining, making American products more competitive in Botswana. Botswana signed an Economic Partnership Agreement with the European Union in December 2007, and, as a member of SACU, it signed a preferential trade agreement in 2004 with Mercosur.

Botswana's currency--the Pula--is fully convertible and is valued against a basket of currencies heavily weighted toward the South African Rand. Profits and direct investment can be repatriated without restriction from Botswana. The Botswana Government eliminated all exchange controls in 1999.

Botswana is a member of the 14-nation Southern African Development Community (SADC) , and Gaborone hosts the SADC Secretariat's headquarters. SADC has a broad mandate to encourage growth, development, and economic integration in Southern Africa. SADC's Trade Protocol, calls for the elimination of all tariff and non-tariff barriers to trade among the 12 signatory countries. However, implementation of the protocol has been slow and is not yet complete. Zimbabwe's membership has limited SADC's opportunities for cooperation with the United States.

Transportation and Communications

A sparsely populated, semi-arid country about the size of Texas, Botswana has nonetheless managed to incorporate many rural areas into the national economy. An "inner circle" highway connecting all major towns and district capitals is completely paved, and the all-weather Trans-Kalahari Highway connects the country (and, through it, South Africa's commercially dominant Gauteng Province) to Walvis Bay in Namibia. A fiber-optic telecommunications network has been completed in Botswana connecting all major population centers. The Civil Aviation Authority of Botswana (CAAB) has been established as a regulator of the air transport services to further enhance the transport system.

In addition to the government-owned newspaper and national radio network, there is an active, independent press (one daily and seven weekly newspapers) . Two privately owned radio stations began operations in 1999, and a third began operations in 2008. In 2000, the government-owned Botswana Television (BTV) was launched, which was Botswana's first national television station. GBC is a commercially owned television station that broadcast programs to the Gaborone area only. Foreign publications are sold without restriction in Botswana, and there are 22 commercial Internet service providers. Three cellular phone providers cover most of the country.

DEFENSE

The president is commander in chief of the Botswana Defense Force (BDF) . A defense council is appointed by the president. The BDF was formed in 1977 and has approximately 13,000 members.

The BDF is a capable and well-disciplined military force. Following positive political changes in South Africa and the region, the BDF's missions have increasingly focused on border control and anti-poaching activities. The United States has been the largest single contributor to the development of the BDF, and a large segment of its officer corps has received U.S. training. It is considered an apolitical and professional institution.

FOREIGN RELATIONS

Botswana puts a premium on economic and political integration in Southern Africa. It seeks to make SADC a working vehicle for economic development, and promotes efforts to make the region self-policing in terms of preventative diplomacy, conflict resolution, and good governance. Botswana joins the African consensus on most major international matters and is a member of international organizations such as the United Nations and the African Union (AU) .

U.S.-BOTSWANA RELATIONS

The United States considers Botswana an advocate of and a model for stability in Africa and has been a major partner in Botswana's development since its independence. The U.S. Peace Corps returned to Botswana in August 2002 with a focus on HIV/AIDS-related programs after concluding 30 years of more broadly targeted assistance in 1997. Similarly, the USAID phased out a longstanding partnership with Botswana in 1996, after successful programs emphasizing education, training, entrepreneurship, environmental management, and reproductive health. Botswana, however, continues to benefit along with its neighbors in the region from USAID's Initiative for Southern Africa. The Regional Center for Southern Africa (RCSA) , which implements the U.S. Agency for International Development's (USAID) Initiative for Southern Africa (ISA) , is headquartered in Gaborone as well. The United States International Board of Broadcasters (IBB) operates a major Voice of America (VOA) relay station in Botswana serving most of the African Continent.

In 1995, the Centers for Disease Control (CDC) started the BOTUSA Project in collaboration with the Botswana Ministry of Health in order to generate information to improve TB control efforts in Botswana and elsewhere in the face of the TB and HIV/AIDS co-epidemics. Under the 1999 U.S. Government's Leadership and Investment in Fighting an Epidemic (LIFE) Initiative, CDC through the BOTUSA Project has undertaken many projects and has assisted many organizations in the fight against the HIV/AIDS epidemic in Botswana. Botswana is one of the 15 focus countries for PEPFAR, the President's Emergency Plan for Aids Relief and began receiving funding and assistance under this program in January 2004. PEPFAR assistance to Botswana, which totaled $20 million in FY 2004 and doubled to $40 million in FY 2005, is contributing to HIV/AIDS prevention, treatment, and care interventions.

The Governments of Botswana and the United States entered into an agreement in July 2000 to establish an International Law Enforcement Academy (ILEA) in Gaborone. The academy, jointly financed, managed and staffed by the two nations, provides training to police and government officials from Southern Africa and eventually from across the continent. The academy's permanent campus, in Otse outside of Gaborone, opened March 2003. Over 1,500 law enforcement professionals from Sub-Saharan Africa have received training from ILEA since it began offering classes in 2001.

Principal U.S. Officials
Ambassador-- Earl R. Miller

Earl R. Miller was sworn in as the U.S. Ambassador to the Republic of Botswana on December 18, 2014. Ambassador Miller, a career member of the U.S. Senior Foreign Service, joined the Department of State in 1987. His previous assignment was Consul General at the U.S. Consulate General in Johannesburg, South Africa, from 2011 to 2014. Ambassador Miller has served in Washington, San Francisco, Miami and Boston and at U.S. embassies in El Salvador, Malaysia, Indonesia, Iraq, and India.

Deputy Chief of Mission--Scott Hamilton
Office of Security Cooperation--William Wyatt
Centers for Disease Control--Kathleen Toomey
International Board of Broadcasters--George Miller
International Law Enforcement Academy--James O. Smith
Peace Corps--Margaret McClure

The U.S. Embassy is on Embassy Drive off Khama Crescent--P.O. Box 90, Gaborone (tel. 267-353-982; fax 267-356-947) . USAID is located on Lebatlane Road. DAO and ODC are located at the embassy. CDC is located on Ditlhakore Way in Gaborone. ILEA is located in Otse, about 30 minutes outside of Gaborone. The IBB station is located in Selebi-Phikwe, about 400 kilometers northeast of Gaborone.

TRAVEL AND BUSINESS INFORMATION

COUNTRY DESCRIPTION: Botswana is a country in southern Africa with a stable democratic government and a growing economy. Facilities for tourism are widely available.

ENTRY/EXIT REQUIREMENTS: A passport with at least six months of validity remaining is required. U.S. citizens are permitted stays up to 90 days without a visa. For additional information on entry requirements, travelers may contact the Embassy of the Republic of Botswana, 1531-1533 New Hampshire Ave, N.W., Washington, D.C. 20036, telephone (202) 244-4990/1, fax (202) 244-4164 or the Permanent Mission of the Republic of Botswana to the United Nations, 103 E. 37th St., New York, NY, 10016, telephone (212) 889-2277, fax (212) 725-5061. There are also honorary consuls in Los Angeles, San Francisco and Houston. See our *Foreign Entry Requirements* brochure for more information on Botswana and other countries. Visit the Embassy of Botswana's web site at http://www.botswanaembassy.org/ for the most current visa information.

SAFETY AND SECURITY: Civil unrest and disorder are rare. U.S. citizens should avoid crowds, political rallies, and street demonstrations and maintain security awareness at all times.

For the latest security information, Americans traveling abroad should regularly monitor the Department's Internet web site, where the current Worldwide Caution Public Announcement, Travel Warnings and Public Announcements, can be found. Information can also be obtained from the American Citizen Services section of the U.S. Embassy's website at http://usembassy.state.gov/botswana/.

Up-to-date information on safety and security can also be obtained by calling 1-888-407-4747 toll free in the U.S. and Canada, or for callers outside the U.S. and Canada, a regular toll-line at 1-202-501-4444. These numbers are available from 8:00 a.m. to 8:00 p.m. Eastern Time, Monday through Friday (except U.S. federal holidays) .

The Department of State urges American citizens to take responsibility for their own personal security while traveling overseas. For general information about appropriate measures travelers can take to protect themselves in an overseas environment

CRIME: Violent crime is relatively infrequent in Botswana, but appears to be on the rise in urban centers. Prudent security measures such as house and car alarms and immobilizers should be used to deter residential burglaries and car theft. In addition, the increased instance of armed robbery and mugging in Botswana over the past two years warrants increased vigilance while walking in urban areas, particularly after dark and when traveling alone. Petty street crime and crimes of opportunity, primarily the theft of money and personal property, remain the most common forms of crime in Botswana. Visitors to Gaborone, as to any major city, should avoid walking at night in unfamiliar areas. U.S. Embassy personnel are advised against travel to the Kgale Hill area, a popular Gaborone hiking venue, and the area surrounding the Gaborone Dam because of multiple incidents of violent crime. American citizens are strongly urged to avoid these areas.

INFORMATION FOR VICTIMS OF CRIME: The loss or theft abroad of a U.S. passport should be reported immediately to the local police and the nearest U.S. Embassy or Consulate. If you are the victim of a crime while overseas, in addition to reporting to local police, please contact the nearest U.S. Embassy or Consulate for assistance. The Embassy/Consulate staff can, for example, assist you to find appropriate medical care, contact family members or friends and explain how funds could be transferred. Although the investigation and prosecution of the crime is solely the responsibility of local authorities, consular officers can help you to understand the local criminal justice process and to find an attorney if needed.

MEDICAL FACILITIES AND HEALTH INFORMATION: Medical facilities in Gaborone are adequate, but available facilities in other areas are limited. Well-equipped emergency rooms and trained physicians are available in the capital but services are rudimentary elsewhere. Professional private emergency rescue services operate air and ground ambulances throughout the country, but care is rendered only after a patient's ability to pay is established. Response times are often slow in less populated areas. Malaria is prevalent only in the north of the country, particularly around the Chobe and Okavango National Parks. Malaria prophylaxis is not required in Gaborone but is suggested for travel to the north. For advanced care Americans often choose to travel to South Africa. Most prescription drugs are available in Gaborone.

Information on vaccinations and other health precautions, such as safe food and water precautions and insect bite protection, may be obtained from the Centers for Disease Control and Prevention's hotline for international travelers at 1-877-FYI-TRIP (1-877-394-8747) or via the CDC's internet site at http://www.cdc.gov/travel. For information about outbreaks of infectious diseases abroad consult the World Health Organization's (WHO) website at http://www.who.int/en. Further health information for travelers is available at http://www.who.int/ith.

MEDICAL INSURANCE: The Department of State strongly urges Americans to consult with their medical insurance company prior to traveling abroad to confirm whether their policy applies overseas and whether it will cover emergency expenses such as a medical evacuation.

TRAFFIC SAFETY AND ROAD CONDITIONS: While in a foreign country, U.S. citizens may encounter road conditions that differ significantly from those in the United States. The information below concerning Botswana is provided for general reference only, and may not be totally accurate in a particular location or circumstance.

Traffic circulates on the left in Botswana, as elsewhere in the region. While the roads in major population centers in Botswana are generally good, travel by automobile outside of large towns may be dangerous. The combination of long, tedious stretches of two-lane highways, high speed limits, and poor lighting make driving at night on rural highways particularly hazardous. Free-range domestic animals and large numbers of pedestrians and hitchhikers in the roadways make fatal accidents a frequent occurrence. Traumatic injury is the second major cause of death in Botswana; motor vehicle accidents take the lead.

Please refer to our Road Safety page for more information. Visit the website of the country's national tourist office and national authority responsible for road safety at http://www.botswana-tourism.gov.bw.

AVIATION SAFETY OVERSIGHT: As there is no direct commercial air service between the United States and Botswana, the U.S. Federal Aviation Administration (FAA) has not assessed Botswana'sCivil Aviation Authority for compliance with International Civil Aviation Organization (ICAO) aviation safety standards. For more information, travelers may visit the FAA's Internet website at http://www.faa.gov/safety/programs_initiatives/oversight/iasa.

SPECIAL CIRCUMSTANCES: Botswana strictly enforces its laws controlling the trade in animal products. The hunting of lions is explicitly prohibited and leopards and elephants are covered under a strict quota regime. Botswana's Wildlife Conservation and National Parks Act makes illegal the possession or removal from Botswana, without a government permit of any living or dead animal or trophy from an animal. A trophy is any horn, ivory, tooth, tusk, bone, claw, hoof, hide, skin, hair, feather, egg, or other durable portion of an animal, whether the item has been processed or not. Curio shops and vendors throughout the country sell items such as animal skins, plain and decorated ostrich eggs and eggshells, and carved bones or teeth of animals protected by this law. All of the souvenirs, although widely sold, are subject to this Act. Travelers departing the country with a trophy must have a receipt from a store licensed to sell such items. Ivory and endangered rhinoceros horn products obtained in Botswana may not be removed from the country under any circumstances; elephant hair jewelry may be removed only with the appropriate license from the Department of Wildlife and National Parks. Trophies may not be taken from the wild without a permit. Violators are subject to arrest and may face a penalty of up to five years imprisonment and a substantial fine.

Wild animals pose may pose a danger to tourists. Tourists should bear in mind that, even in the most serene settings, the animals are wild and can pose a threat to life and safety. Tourists should use common sense when approaching wildlife, observe all local or park regulations, and heed all instructions given by tour guides. In addition, tourists are advised that potentially dangerous areas sometimes lack fences and warning signs. Exercise appropriate caution in all unfamiliar surroundings.

CRIMINAL PENALTIES: While in a foreign country, a U.S. citizen is subject to that country's laws and regulations, which sometimes differ significantly from those in the United States and may not afford the protections available to the individual under U.S. law. Penalties for breaking the law can be more severe than in the United States for similar offences. Persons violating Botswana laws, even unknowingly, may be expelled, arrested or imprisoned. Penalties for possession, use, or trafficking in illegal drugs in Botswana are severe, and convicted offenders can expect long jail sentences and heavy fines. Homosexual activity is illegal in Botswana. Engaging in sexual conduct with children or using or disseminating child pornography in a foreign country is a crime, prosecutable in the United States.

REGISTRATION / EMBASSY LOCATION: Americans living or traveling in Botswana are encouraged to register with the nearest U.S. Embassy or Consulate through the State Department's travel registration website so that they can obtain updated information on travel and security within Botswana. The U.S.

Embassy is located in Gaborone on Embassy Drive in the Government Enclave. The mailing address is P.O. Box 90, Gaborone, telephone +267 395-3982; fax +267 318-0232; email consulargaboro@state.gov, and the after-hours emergency telephone is +267 395-7111.

BOTSWANA ECONOMY - STRATEGIC INFORMATION AND DEVELOPMENTS

INSTITUTIONAL AND LEGAL FRAMEWORK

The Constitution of Botswana, which dates to 1966, established a parliamentary system.[9] The Parliament consists of the President and the National Assembly. The government is divided into three branches: the executive, the legislative and the judicial.

The executive branch consists of the President, the Vice-President, the Cabinet and the Attorney General. The President is the head of state and assumes office through elections that take place every 5 years. The President, who may hold office for a maximum of 2 consecutive periods, is elected by the National Assembly from amongst its members. The President appoints the Vice-President and the Cabinet from members of the National Assembly.[10] The Attorney General is also appointed by him.[11]

The legislative is comprised of the President and the National Assembly. The President is an ex officio member of Parliament and is entitled to speak and vote in all proceedings.[12] The National Assembly consists of 57 members elected by the people, and 4 that are specially elected.[13] These 4 members are elected by secret ballot from amongst 4 candidates nominated by the President and 4 candidates nominated by the elected members of the National Assembly. The core function of the legislative is to enact laws but it is also in charge of controlling public finances, through the approval of the National Budget, and of scrutinizing government.[14] In addition to the legislature, the *Ntlo ya Dikgosi* ("House of Chiefs"), which comprises 35 traditional leaders, advises the Parliament regarding traditional matters.

2.4. The judicial branch is composed of the High Court and the Court of Appeals.[15] There are also specialized parallel courts and other subordinate courts. The court of first instance is the High Court; it has unlimited original jurisdiction to hear and resolve any civil or criminal proceedings. The Court of Appeal is the highest court of the land.

Botswana's legal system consists of Roman-Dutch and customary law; the latter is administered by the customary courts. Botswana's legislation may take one of three forms: acts of parliament, delegated or subsidiary legislation, and autonomic legislation. Acts of parliament are the principal source of law in Botswana; they must be consistent with the Constitution, the supreme law of the country.[16] Acts are initiated through a bill drafted in the National Assembly at the request of the relevant ministry; thereafter the draft is submitted for discussion and if necessary amended. Once approved by the National Assembly, bills are presented to the President for assent, which he or she may withhold. If sanctioned it becomes an Act, but it needs to be gazetted to have the force of law.[17]

Subsidiary or delegated legislation is issued under the direction of subordinate bodies under specific powers delegated to them by Parliament. Subsidiary legislation is usually in the form of proclamations, regulations and orders. Autonomic legislation is issued by an autonomous, specialized body that has been given the power to create laws to regulate itself, for instance, the Law Society of Botswana.

For international agreements to be implemented they need to be approved by the Cabinet and by the National Assembly.

TRADE POLICY

The Ministry of Trade and Industry is responsible for the formulation and implementation of trade policy, along with other stakeholders, through the National Committee on Trade Policy and Negotiations (NCTPN), which consists of representatives of different ministries, parastatals, the private sector, academic and research institutions, and non-governmental organizations (Table 2.1) .[18] The NCTPN is supported by various technical committees in charge of trade policy formulation, which in turn have representatives of different ministries and the private sector. These committees meet on a quarterly basis and their recommendations are passed to the NCTPN. The NCTPN is in charge of coordinating the formulation and implementation of trade policy and of ensuring its consistency with Botswana's international commitments.[19] The private sector and public enterprises are represented in this process by the Botswana Confederation of Commerce, Industry and Manpower (BOCCIM) and the Botswana Exporters and Manufacturing Association (BEMA) .

Main institutions involved in trade policy formulation and implementation

Institutions	Trade related function
Development of policy	
Ministry of Trade and Industry	
National Committee on Trade Policy and Negotiations (NCTPN)	Provides a forum for consultations regarding the formulation of trade policy and of Botswana's position in trade negotiations
Department of International Trade	Develops, implements and monitors trade policy; Responsible for negotiation and implementation of multilateral, regional and bilateral trade agreements
Department of Industrial Affairs	Develops and reviews policies, programmes and strategies aimed at diversifying the economy, creating employment and stimulating local entrepreneurship
Cabinet	Approves and endorses trade policy
Implementation of policy	
Ministries (e.g. Ministry of Trade and Industry, Ministry of Agriculture and Ministry of Finance and Development Planning)	Implements trade policy and the trade agreements
Parastatals (e.g. Botswana Investment Trade Centre (BITC))	Implements trade policy by facilitating specific policy objectives (e.g. export promotion and FDI facilitation)
Evaluation and review	

Ministry of Trade and Industry National Committee on Trade Policy and Negotiations (NCTPN) Parliamentary Committee on Foreign Affairs, Trade and Security (PCFATS)	Reviews trade policy every five years or whenever it deems necessary

Source: Ministry of Trade and Industry (2009), *National Trade Policy for Botswana*, Gaborone, July. Viewed at:http://www.mti.gov.bw/webfm_send/182.

Botswana sees trade policy as a means to achieve its overall economic policy objective of sustainable growth, economic and export diversification, and social inclusion. More specifically, its overall trade objective is to increase and improve market access and international competitiveness for its exports through reduced transaction costs, investment in education and improved infrastructure. Botswana's trade policy is defined largely by its membership of SACU, as well as other regional arrangements, such as SADC. However, within the framework of these arrangements, Botswana has developed several policies which outline its national trade policy. These include: the National Development Plan 10 (NDP10), the National Trade Policy (2009), the Industrial Development Policy (2014), the Economic Diversification Drive (2011), the National Export Strategy (2010), the Special Economic Zones Policy (2010) and the Citizen Economic Empowerment Policy (2012) . All these instruments seem to share the same goals and objectives regarding trade and economic policy and in certain instances they overlap.

BOTSWANA GOVERNMENT 2016 BUDGET SPEECH[1]

I. INTRODUCTION

1. Madam Speaker, I have the honour this afternoon to present to the National Assembly budget proposals for the financial year 2016/2017.

2. Madam Speaker, the 2016/2017 budget marks the end of the tenth National Development Plan (NDP 10), whose implementation was characterised by slow growth in both the global and domestic economies. It is, therefore, an opportune time to reflect on our achievements during NDP 10, as well as determine how best to address the persistent development challenges facing this country such as unemployment and poverty.

3. Among the achievements by Government was the ability to support growth momentum in the domestic economy during NDP 10, despite the fact that the implementation of the Plan coincided with the global financial and economic crisis of 2008/2009. In the face of the crisis, this Government demonstrated its prudent stewardship in economic and financial management and acted decisively by adopting a proactive fiscal stance to support domestic economic activities. As a result, the average growth in the domestic economy over the Plan period is now expected to be around 4.5 percent, compared to the initial 3.3 percent forecast at the beginning of the Plan.

[1] By Honourable O.K. Matambo Minister of Finance and Development Planning Delivered to the National Assembly on 1st February 2016

4. Most importantly, the use of fiscal policy to support growth was done responsibly to ensure continued macroeconomic stability; with the average accumulated budget deficit during the Plan period now estimated at P4.7 billion or negative 3.1 percent of Gross Domestic Product (GDP), compared to P31.9 billion or negative 16.4 percent of GDP initially projected for the Plan. Monetary policy also remained supportive over the Plan period, with inflation decelerating towards the lower end of the Bank of Botswana's objective range of 3-6 percent, while the exchange rate policy resulted in a stable real effective exchange rate, which is a necessary condition for promoting competitiveness of domestic industries.

5. Despite the achievements in the macroeconomic area, the Government's effort to address development challenges facing this country was constrained by the continued weak recovery of the global economy. The prolonged depression of commodity prices, especially of diamonds, has further weakened the domestic economic prospects. In addition, the shortage of water and electricity, which are key inputs in driving economic activities, has also undermined domestic growth prospects.

6. Madam Speaker, the constraints I have just outlined led to a significant downwards revision of the domestic growth forecast for 2015, prompting Government to adopt the Economic Stimulus Programme (ESP) as a strategy to: boost growth, promote economic diversification, and create jobs. ESP is aimed at supporting domestic economic activities in the short term, while providing foundation for a sustainable growth path for the economy in the long term through investment in infrastructural development. In this regard, a strategic approach was adopted in the selection of sectors for interventions, based on their potential for growth and job creation. The implementation of the ESP is scheduled to start in earnest in 2016/2017 financial year. With the extension of NDP 10 by an additional year to end in 2016/2017, any new projects under the ESP will therefore be approved through this budget. The intention is to use the ESP to accelerate the implementation of these programmes and projects. I will return to some of the elements of this Programme in my presentation of the 2016/2017 budget proposals.

7. Madam Speaker, the preparation of the budget proposals for the 2016/2017 financial year was guided by priorities, as presented in the 2016/2017 Budget Strategy Paper. These priorities were discussed extensively during the Budget *diPitso* held with relevant stakeholders late last year. Among the top national priorities to be addressed through the 2016/2017 budget are: *economic growth; employment creation; and poverty eradication.* Accordingly, resources are proposed for allocation to: infrastructure development to address the challenges of inadequate water and electricity supply; social infrastructure to address existing backlogs of classrooms and health facilities; and land servicing to facilitate business opportunities.

8. In many respects, the 2016/2017 budget is a transitional budget, specifically from: NDP 10 to NDP 11; Vision 2016 to Vision 2036; and the United Nations Millennium Development Goals (MDGs) to Sustainable Development Goals (SDGs). Efforts were therefore made during the preparation of the 2016/2017 budget to ensure that it lays a sound foundation and expenditure path for NDP 11, while at the same time aligning its priorities with the emerging themes of both the Vision 2036, and the Sustainable Development Goals. The preparation of the Vision 2036 is underway, while the SDGs were adopted by the United Nations General Assembly in September 2015. A full alignment of the Vision 2036 and the SDGs with the annual budgets will be achieved through implementation of NDP 11, whose preparation is at an advanced stage and I hope to present its draft to this Honourable House in July this year.

9. At this juncture, Madam Speaker, I wish to review the global and domestic economic performance and outlook, which provide the context for the 2016/2017 budget proposals.

II. ECONOMIC REVIEW AND OUTLOOK

Global Economic Review

10. Madam Speaker, owing to declining commodity prices and increasing financial market volatility, the global economic performance for 2015 was characterised by an uneven economic performance. According to the World Economic Outlook released by the International Monetary Fund in January 2016, growth in the global economy was 3.1 percent in 2015. This is lower than a growth rate of 3.4 percent achieved in 2014. World output growth is however expected to improve slightly in 2016 to reach 3.4 percent.

11. Growth in advanced economies remained modest during 2015; registering 1.9 percent, from 1.8 percent recorded in 2014, and is expected to reach 2.1 percent in 2016. The outlook for 2016 is underpinned by strengthening of growth in emerging market and developing economies, which is expected to reach 4.3 percent. The downside risks to such forecast include: the continued slowdown in the growth of the Chinese economy, weaker growth in oil exporting countries, and declines in other commodity prices. Given that economies are to a large extent integrated, the weak global economic prospects impact negatively on the performance of sub-Saharan Africa, including Botswana. In the event, growth in these economies is expected to have declined to 3.5 percent in 2015, from 5.0 percent in 2014. However, in 2016, economic growth for sub-Saharan Africa is expected to strengthen to 4.0 percent, due to an expected modest recovery in oil prices, which will benefit large oil exporting economies in the region, particularly, Nigeria and Angola, as well as an improvement in the outlook of countries which were initially affected by Ebola.

Regional Economic Review

12. Madam Speaker, the economic performance of the Southern African Development Community (SADC) region mirrors that of the global outlook. The region's real GDP growth and inflation rate are expected to be on a downward trend, because of falling commodity prices and weak demand for exports. According to the recent World Economic Outlook of January 2016, only two Member States namely, Mozambique and Democratic Republic of Congo are expected to surpass the region's real GDP growth target of 7.0 percent in 2015. Much of the decline in the growth rate occurred within the Southern African Customs Union (SACU) Member States. Consequently, growth in the SADC region is expected to average 3.9 percent during 2015, compared to 4.6 percent recorded in 2014. Inflation in most SADC Member States eased in 2015, remaining below the region's target rate of 7.0 percent, with the exception of Malawi and Zimbabwe. In general, inflation within the region is expected to be stable at 5.6 percent during 2015; the same rate recorded in 2014.

Domestic Economic Review

ECONOMIC GROWTH

13. Madam Speaker, the continued slowdown of growth in the global economy, particularly in the major markets for our diamonds, has had profound impact on the domestic economy. The latest estimates from Statistics Botswana indicate that, the domestic economy declined by 3.5 percent in the third quarter of 2015. As a result, the growth estimate for the 2015 has been revised downwards from 2.6 percent to 1.0 percent. This compares to the growth rate of 3.2 percent recorded in 2014. Contributing to the slow growth in the domestic economy in 2015 was the mining sector, which declined by 14.0 percent in 2015, due to the reduction of diamond production. Water and Electricity sector also registered a decline of 104 percent, due to continued water and electricity supply challenges. Growth in other non-mining sectors is also estimated to slow down during the year, reflecting the effect of the water and electricity shortages on domestic economic activities.

14. However, a modest recovery in the domestic economy is expected in 2016 and 2017, with growth rates projected to be 4.2 percent and 4.3 percent, respectively, underpinned by recovery in both the mining and non-mining sectors. Mining sector, which accounts for a quarter of the domestic output, is forecast to grow by 0.6 percent in 2016, and a further 0.7 percent in 2017, compared to the decline of 14 percent in 2015. The non-mining sector, on the other hand, is forecast to grow by 4.7 percent and 4.9 percent in 2016 and 2017, respectively, compared to 3.9 percent achieved in 2015. These growth forecasts are based on the expected moderate recovery in the global economy, as well as the impact of the domestic policy initiatives such the Economic Stimulus Programme.

MONETARY POLICY AND INFLATION

15. Madam Speaker, to support growth, an accommodative monetary policy stance was maintained during 2015, with the Bank Rate being reduced from 6.5 percent at the beginning of the year to 6.0 percent in August 2015. This reduction was consistent with the inflationary outlook and was expected to reduce the cost of borrowing for investment in the country.

16. Over the twelve months to December 2015, annual inflation rate fell from 3.8 percent in 2014 to 3.1 percent in 2015. This was driven by the decrease in fuel prices, which were adjusted downwards in February, August and December 2015, following a decrease in crude oil prices worldwide. It is anticipated that this trend will continue, thus exerting downward pressure on domestic prices; with inflation remaining within the Bank of Botswana's objective range of 3 - 6 percent.

BALANCE OF PAYMENTS AND FOREIGN EXCHANGE RESERVES

17. Madam Speaker, the preliminary overall balance of payments for 2015 is estimated at P3.3 billion as at November 2015, a decrease from P11.4 billion recorded in 2014. The current account surplus is estimated to fall, from P22.9 billion in 2014 to P12.9 billion in 2015. The positive contribution of net inflows of receipts from the Southern African Customs Union (SACU) to the current account balance is expected to be offset by the trade deficit. Exports of goods and services are estimated to decrease by 18.6 percent in 2015, due to weak global demand for rough diamonds, while imports are also projected to decline by 8.1 percent in 2015.

18. The level of the country's foreign exchange reserves stood at P84.9 billion in December 2015, an increase of 7.3 percent from P79.1 billion in the previous year. Expressed in US dollar and Special Drawing Rights (SDR) terms, the foreign exchange reserves were equivalent to USD7.5 billion and SDR5.5 billion, respectively. This represents an equivalent of 19 months of import cover of goods and services. The increase in foreign exchange reserves in Pula terms was mainly due to the depreciation of the Pula against major international currencies.

19. Madam Speaker, of the total amount of reserves in December 2015, Government Investment Account, which is Government savings, amounted to P35.0 billion. While this portion of the reserves is available for Government use, it is important that the use of these reserves is restricted to investment in high impact projects, with potential to bolster economic growth, and thus, contribute to future budget surpluses needed to re-build depleted reserves.

EXCHANGE RATE DEVELOPMENTS

20. Madam Speaker, the exchange rate policy supports our export-oriented development strategy, as it ensures stability of the real effective exchange rate (REER). As an inflation-adjusted exchange rate, REER is used to measure the country's competitiveness; a rise in the REER implies that the country's exports are more expensive and imports are cheaper, while a fall in the REER makes a country's exports cheaper and its imports expensive. It is therefore important to ensure that the domestic currency is neither over nor undervalued for the country to remain competitive in international markets.

21. The annual review of the Pula exchange rate mechanism, which took place in December 2015, resulted in maintaining the current basket weights of 50 percent South African rand and 50 percent IMF's Special Drawing Rights (SDR), while the rate of crawl was changed from zero to an upward rate of 0.38 percent per annum for 2016. This in line with expected monetary developments in the country's major trading partners. In terms of the bilateral exchange rate movements in 2015, the Pula appreciated against the South African Rand by 13.6 percent, while it depreciated by 11.6 percent against the SDR.

22. Madam Speaker, it is important to note that while a country can achieve some competitiveness in the short term through the management of the exchange rate, a sustainable way to achieve robust international competiveness is through growth in productivity and improved efficiency among domestic economic entities. In this regard, Government will continue to implement public sector reforms, and undertake other structural reforms to improve productivity in the economy.

PERFORMANCE OF PUBLIC ENTERPRISES

23. Madam Speaker, parastatal organisations or state owned enterprises showed mixed performance in 2014 and 2015. While some State owned enterprises such as; Botswana Development Corporation, Botswana Telecommunications Corporation Limited, Botswana Communications Regulatory Authority, Botswana Housing Corporation, and Botswana Savings Bank, made profit, others, which include; Water Utilities Corporation, Air Botswana, National Development Bank, and Botswana Meat Commission, recorded operational losses. I will now give a brief overview of the performance of each of these selected parastatal organisations.

24. During 2015, BDC made a net profit of P202.2 million, after a net loss of P7.8 million in 2014. Similarly, Botswana Telecommunications Corporation Limited (BTCL) performed well, recording a net profit of P146.8 million in 2015, compared to P140 000 in 2014. The lower profit in 2014 for BTCL was attributed to the impairment charged for the significant drop in the value of the company, as a result of the transfer of some of its assets to BOFINET. Meanwhile, an Initial Public Offer (IPO) was launched in December 2015, which provided an opportunity for Batswana to own shares in BTCL. So far, the response from Batswana has been overwhelming. Eventually, the BTCL shares will be listed in the Botswana Stock Exchange to allow for their trading.

25. The Botswana Communications Regulatory Authority also recorded a net profit of P31.7 million in 2015, a decline from P48.1 million in 2014, mainly due to a fall in operating revenues owing to tariff reductions for essential services and a rise in operating expenses due to acquisition and replacement of network equipment as well as digital migration. The Botswana Housing Corporation recorded a net profit of P9.8 million in 2015, a decrease of 39.9 percent, from P16.3 million in 2014, as a result of its outreach programme that increased its staff costs and the construction of social housing projects. Botswana Savings Bank's net profit declined marginally to P12.2 million in 2015, compared to

P12.8 million in 2014, due to increased competition in the domestic banking sector.

26. Madam Speaker, the Water Utilities Corporation, recorded a net loss of P367.0 million in 2015 up from P361.0 million in 2014. The continued poor performance was due to prolonged drought spells which increased water transfer cost and provision of additional water sources. Air Botswana made a net loss of P165 million in 2015 compared to, P100 million in 2014, mainly due to high costs of maintenance of its old fleet of aircrafts.

27. The National Development Bank registered a net loss of P37.2 million in 2015 compared to a net loss of P86.3 million in 2014. The Botswana Meat Commission whose latest audited financial statements are for 2014, registered a net loss of P9.6 million in 2014, after registering a net profit of P25 million in 2013. This loss was partly due to measles outbreak during 2014, and inadequate supply of cattle to the Commission, resulting in its failure to supply beef to the lucrative European Union market.

DEVELOPMENT OF VISION 2036 AND ADOPTION OF SUSTAINABLE DEVELOPMENT GOALS

28. Madam Speaker, the year 2016 marks an important milestone in our journey as a nation; as the country will be celebrating its 50th anniversary of independence. The year also coincides with the end of Vision 2016. In this regard, the ongoing review of the Vision 2016 will provide an opportunity to assess our achievements as a country over the past five decades, as well as the challenges facing the country. Meanwhile, a process to develop the next vision – Vision 2036, has since been launched, with a Presidential Task Team appointed towards the end of 2015 to guide national consultations on the development of the new Vision. The Team is expected to conclude its task in April 2016, with the draft Vision 2036 scheduled for presentation to Parliament in June 2016. The new Vision is expected to be launched in September 2016 to coincide with celebrations for the country's 50th anniversary of independence.

29. Madam Speaker, the United Nations family adopted the Sustainable Development Goals (SDGs) that will guide development process for the next 15 years. The SDGs cover a wide spectrum of dimensions such as poverty, hunger, health, gender equality, energy, water, economy, income inequality, climate change and governance. A number of these goals are aligned to Botswana's national priorities and will be implemented as part of our normal planning process.

III. KEY THEMATIC AREAS FOR 2016/2017 FINANCIAL YEAR

30. Madam Speaker, as 2016/2017 is the last financial year of NDP 10, the proposed budget provides an opportunity to consolidate activities originally

planned for the Plan period; some of which were later postponed due to the global financial and economic recession of 2008/2009. The recently announced Economic Stimulus Programme also provides an opportunity to intensify backlog eradication efforts by accelerating the implementation of programmes and projects approved for NDP 10. In this respect, the proposed budget allocations for 2016/2017 cover key thematic areas of: *investing in infrastructural development; creating employment opportunities; strengthening human capital; enhancing national security; and strengthening local governance.* I shall briefly discuss the details of each of these thematic areas in turn:

INVESTING IN INFRASTRUCTURAL DEVELOPMENT

31. Madam Speaker, the importance of water and electricity, as key inputs into economic activities cannot be overemphasised. The country is currently faced with water and electricity supply shortages due to the drought situation and continued technical problems related to power supply, respectively. Shortages of such critical utilities do not only inconvenience the general public, but also undermine growth in the economy; as they adversely affect business operations. As such, all projects for water and electricity will be accorded high priority in the allocation of the budget in 2016/2017.

WATER

32. Madam Speaker, to address the water situation, Government has embarked on a number of projects in various districts to ensure security of water and improved waste water management. For the Greater Gaborone area, Government intends to meet water demands by, among others, increasing water storage capacities and construction of new primary water pipelines. Phase II of the North-South Carrier Water Scheme, which involves construction of a parallel pipeline to the existing line is underway. Other initiatives include exploring the possibilities of accessing water from Lesotho and the Chobe-Zambezi area.

33. In addition, initiatives are underway to reclaim waste water, as an alternative water resource. The construction of a waste water reclamation plant in Mahalapye is underway. This Plant will produce 3.9 million Cubic Meters of water per annum, with a potential to irrigate 40 hectares of agricultural land. It is expected that the reclaimed waste water initiative will reduce pressure on usage of portable water on agricultural production. Moreover, Government through Botswana Institute for Technology Research and Innovation, has set-up a world class Centre for Material Sciences that will assist in the development of new materials in the water purification sector and air filtration, amongst others.

ENERGY

34. Madam Speaker, to address power challenges, efforts continue to be made to address the technical issues facing the Morupule B Power Station. The plant's

reliability has been low due to major defects arising from the construction of the project. This has resulted in a financial burden for Botswana Power Corporation, which has to source power from, among others, the Emergency Diesel Power plants and import power at high costs. To improve on the power generation situation in the country, the Morupule A Power Station is being refurbished. The project scope includes overhauling and repairing various units, which should result in an additional output of 132 MW.

35. Despite the power challenges, Government remains committed to improving access to electricity within the country, with more villages planned for electrification through the rural electrification programme. In this regard, network extension in 24 villages is currently ongoing. The solar electrification programme is also ongoing in Government schools and associated facilities that are far away from the national power grid. Furthermore, the implementation of the National Electricity Standard Cost, which was established to reduce the burden of high connection cost for domestic consumers, is ongoing. In an effort to cut on costs, Government has adopted low cost solar technology for street lighting, and sensitised Government departments on its availability. Its use has been demonstrated in Gaborone, Ghanzi and Southern Kgalagadi Districts, with possible roll-out to other areas across the country.

CREATING EMPLOYMENT OPPORTUNITIES

36. Madam Speaker, unemployment, especially among the youth, is one of the development challenges facing this country. To address this, Government has resolved to, among others, use its spending power to boost economic growth and create jobs in the country. Therefore, in addition to seeking value-for-money in spending Government budget, efforts will be made to ensure that such expenditure, whether under recurrent or development budget, contributes to job creation in the country.

37. Some of the economic activities with potential for creating employment opportunities, which Government will be undertaking during 2016/2017 include: *infrastructure backlog eradication, road networks and maintenance, wildlife and tourism initiatives, continued implementation of EDD initiatives, creation of Special Economic Zones, as well as regulatory reforms and improving efficiency.*

Infrastructure Backlog Eradication

38. Madam Speaker, the global financial and economic crisis led to a number of projects being deferred, especially in the areas of social and economic infrastructure such as in education, health, and roads. In this regard, Government, through the ESP is embarking on fast-tracking backlog eradication, which covers construction of classrooms, staff quarters, and customary courts; upgrading of health facilities; and rural electrification. The implementation of the ESP will

create jobs especially in the construction sector and rural areas. In the same vein, youth owned construction companies and individual youths with vocational skills in maintenance should be given priority in the implementation of the ESP through the Youth Empowerment Reservation Programme. Currently, the Programme reserves 15 percent of minor maintenance budget of Government facilities for youth companies and youth with vocational skills in construction.

Road Networks and Maintenance

39. Madam Speaker, another potential area for employment creation is in the area of maintenance of the road network in the country. With better project designs and proper packaging of contracts, contractors can be encouraged to use more labour than machinery in the execution of the road maintenance programmes. A study commissioned in the 2013/2014 financial year to look at the condition of our road network as well as investment needs analysis revealed that about 90 percent of our roads are in good condition, while 10 percent require urgent maintenance. It is against this background that road maintenance interventions have been given priority to eradicate existing backlogs.

40. Some major maintenance works are ongoing in the following roads; Sefophe – Martin's Drift, Tsau – Nokaneng, Maun – Toteng, and Ghanzi (Junction 44) – Tsootsha. In addition, Notwane and Kazungula bridges are being constructed, while Platjan and Mohembo Bridges are at tendering stage. Civil works contracts for two (2) Output and Performance-based Road Contract (OPRC) packages covering a total of 335 km in the Southern region were signed in February 2014 and the rehabilitation works are underway. The implementation of these construction activities relating to road infrastructure will boost domestic economic growth and also create employment opportunities.

WILDLIFE AND TOURISM INITIATIVES

41. Madam Speaker, the tourism sector has potential to contribute positively to growth and job creation in the country. Hence, Government will continue to create an enabling environment for tourism businesses including encouraging joint partnerships between individuals, citizen companies and non-citizens. A number of initiatives are also being undertaken which include; the Dams Tourism project, the Gaborone Precinct project, which will showcase diverse tourism products under one roof, and the Kasane-Kazungula Redevelopment project currently under preparation. With the initiatives to grow tourism in the country, Botswana was voted the best destination country to visit in 2016 by Lonely Planet Publication, a global travel and tourism publication.

ECONOMIC DIVERSIFICATION DRIVE AND SPECIAL ECONOMIC ZONES

42. Madam Speaker, the Economic Diversification Drive (EDD) initiative and the establishment of Special Economic Zones are considered important in

promoting both domestic and foreign direct investments, thus boosting growth and creating the much needed employment opportunities in the country. Furthermore, these initiatives are consistent with other Government policies such as the Citizen Economic Empowerment, and initiatives to develop entrepreneurial culture among Batswana, especially the young emerging business entrepreneurs. This should, in turn, develop local capacity to diversify the economy.

43. The EDD initiative continues to be one of Government's priority areas in promoting domestic production, and consumption of local products. In December 2014, Government issued a Directive to reinforce EDD by instructing all Government and parastatal organisations to prioritise procurement of locally produced goods and services, in addition to awarding price preference to local enterprises.

44. Madam Speaker, as part of creating a conducive environment for private sector development in the country, a Special Economic Zones (SEZs) legislation was promulgated in August 2015. The implementation of the SEZ programme will be in three (3) phases. Phase I will include three sites namely: (i) the mixed-use near Sir Seretse Khama International Airport, comprising international diamond activities, auto components manufacturing, agro-processing, pharmaceuticals, and general manufacturing; (ii) Gaborone Fairgrounds' financial services; and (iii) Pandamatenga Integrated farming, agro business and food processing. Activities under this phase are at various stages of implementation and form part of the 2016/2017 financial year's budget. Phase II of the SEZs is planned for Francistown, Selebi Phikwe, and Lobatse areas, while Phase III will focus on the Tuli Block and Palapye areas. Government is in the process of establishing a Special Economic Zone Authority which will oversee the implementation of the SEZ programme.

REGULATORY REFORMS AND IMPROVING EFFICIENCY

45. Madam Speaker, creating employment opportunities requires rapid and sustained economic growth, which in turn depends on among others, the overall efficiency and productivity of the economy. In this connection, Government continues to undertake various measures to deregulate the goods and labour markets, with a view to improving efficiency. Specifically, Government has intensified the implementation of the reform roadmap and action plan for Doing Business in Botswana. Some of the initiatives in the roadmap include: reviewing of various pieces of legislation, public sector reforms to streamline processes for service delivery in the country, and leveraging on the information and communications technology to improve productivity in the economy.

Strengthening Human Capital

46. Madam Speaker, human capital development remains a high priority for Government as education and training are critical for capacity building, citizen economic empowerment, as well as social and economic development. In this regard, substantial resources will continue to be channelled towards education and training with emphasis on ensuring that the skills and qualifications offered and acquired are more responsive to the needs of the labour market.

Skills Development

47. Madam Speaker, in recognition of the importance of education to achieving inclusive growth, Government has, over the years, invested substantial resources in the development of skills for the country's workforce. Besides empowering the individual to make informed choices in life, education can contribute to sustainable economic growth through improved productivity of the workforce, as well as the ability to adopt technology. Concerned with the declining education performance, Government adopted the Education and Training Sector Strategic Plan (ETSSP) in 2015, whose implementation is expected to address the quality of existing Vocational Education and Training programmes as a way of equipping the youth with appropriate skills.

48. Furthermore, the ETSSP will also increase equitable access to education by intensifying the use of Information, Communication and Technology (ICT) in learning. Under the ETSSP, an Early Childhood Policy Framework will be developed in partnership with the United Nations Children's Fund to guide the implementation of Early Childhood Care and Development in the next five years. The acceleration of backlog eradication of classrooms and other education facilities under the ESP will help achieve some of these targets.

Health

49. Madam Speaker, as the old adage goes *"a healthy nation is a productive nation";* hence, Government is committed to investing in health not only to raise the standard of living in the country, but also to improve the productivity of the workforce. In this connection, Government will continue to pursue avenues to improve the standard of health by continuously reviewing the policies and processes of delivering health in the country. One such avenue will be the implementation, in 2016, of the Medicines and Related Products Supply Chain Strategy. The objective of the Strategy is to ensure regular availability and rational use of essential medicines, and provide quality assurance and security of health commodities throughout the supply chain.

Enhancing National Security

Combating Crime and Corruption

50. Madam Speaker, our continued ranking as the least corrupt country in Africa in the Transparency International Corruption Perception Index is commendable. However, there is no room for complacency, given the negative impact of crime and corruption in our individual lives, as well as on the economy. In this regard, Government regularly conducts audits in different areas such as: recruitment and promotions processes; acquisition and distribution of drugs; and procurement of medical equipment, with a view to identifying loopholes in the systems.

51. Efforts by Government in combating crime are yielding positive results as indicated by the recent decline in some categories of crime. However, the country continues to be susceptible to security challenges including cybercrime. In order to address these challenges, initiatives are being put in place, particularly through provision of capacity building in investigation, intelligence and forensics. In addition, the capacities of the various security agencies are being strengthened to respond to the emerging need for a secure environment. These include the recruitment of more security personnel, providing transport and logistics, and equipping them to, among others, undertake quality investigations and improve surveillance.

STRENGTHENING LOCAL GOVERNANCE

52. Madam Speaker, with their close proximity to the communities, Local Authorities play an important role in the delivery of services to the public. It is for this reason that Government is committed to strengthening and fostering their operations in providing local services and promoting local participation, as part of the efforts to create employment opportunities and alleviating poverty.

Local Economic Development

53. Madam Speaker, in order to strengthen local governance, Government continues to put in place policies and strategies to develop districts and urban centres. In this regard, Government developed the Local Economic Development (LED) Framework in 2015 in recognition of the potential for Local Authorities to drive economic growth. The LED initiative is intended to enable communities to: identify their development challenges and needs; understand their resource endowment; mobilise resources; and take action to grow and diversify their local economies. This initiative is expected to have lasting outcomes on creating decent jobs and incomes for the communities, thereby improving livelihoods for citizens.

54. In addition, Government approved the Strategy on Private Sector Participation in Land Servicing in April 2015. Among the areas already identified

for piloting the initiative include: Gerald Estate Block 1 and Central Business District in Francistown, Kasane, Ramotswa, and Morwa/Bokaa area in Kgatleng District. Under this strategy, the private sector is expected to participate in land servicing. Meanwhile, Government will continue to undertake servicing of land in some districts by providing waterlines, storm water drainage, and de-bushing, in order to facilitate plot development.

SOCIAL WELFARE PROGRAMMES

55. Madam Speaker, in an effort to enhance the living standards of the most vulnerable members of our society, Government continues to provide social welfare programmes. These programmes are intended for the vulnerable groups such as the elderly, orphans and people living with disabilities, and should not be confused with short term relief programmes such as *Ipelegeng*. This Government is committed to ensuring that, through the social welfare programmes, people who fall under the vulnerable group category live in dignity. On the other hand, those people engaged under short term relief measures such as *Ipelegeng* are expected to graduate into sustainable employment opportunities, which is a necessary condition for reducing poverty. Nonetheless, Government is committed to ensure the sustainability of these programmes through continuous evaluation of their effectiveness, and better targeting of their beneficiaries.

56. Over the years, the social welfare programmes have combined both cash transfers and income generating micro projects, mainly under the Poverty Eradication Programme. As at August 2015, a total of 207,385 beneficiaries were registered under temporary relief programmes. In addition, cash allowances were increased effective April 2015 as follows: old age pensions allowance increased from P300 to P330; world war veterans' allowance increased from P420 to P450; while destitute persons' allowance was increased from P120 to P150. The disability cash transfer of P300, targeting people with severe and profound disabilities, was also introduced in April, 2015.

IV. 2014/2015 BUDGET OUTTURN

57. Madam Speaker, total revenues and grants for the 2014/2015 financial year amounted to P55.90 billion, an increase of P4.36 billion or 8.46 percent over the revised budget of P51.54 billion. This performance was underpinned by the increase in mineral and Bank of Botswana revenues. Mineral revenues increased due to more than expected dividend receipts, while an extra amount of P1.7 billion was received from Bank of Botswana as additional dividends and residual income. Total expenditure and net lending, on the other hand, declined from the revised budget of P51.26 billion to P50.56 billion, mainly due to under-expenditure in the development budget.

58. As a result, the overall budget outturn for the 2014/2015 financial year was a surplus of P5.34 billion or 3.7 percent of GDP, which is significantly higher compared to a marginal surplus of P280.83 million projected in the revised budget for the same year.

V. 2015/2016 REVISED BUDGET ESTIMATES

59. Madam Speaker, for 2015/2016 revised budget, total revenues and grants of P51.76 billion, represents a decrease of P3.62 billion or 6.5 percent, from the original budget of P55.38 billion. The decline in total revenue is due to the fall in Mineral revenue, which is expected to decrease by P1.85 billion. In addition, Customs and Excise revenue and Value Added Tax (VAT) are also estimated to decline from their original budget by P885.41 million and P1.17 billion, respectively. The decline in the Customs and Excise revenue emanates from the appreciation of the Pula against the Rand. VAT revenue, on the other hand, declined due to unexpected substantial refund claims, especially from mining companies.

60. On the other hand, the revised total expenditure and net lending for 2015/2016 is estimated at P55.96 billion, an increase of P1.81 billion or 3.3 percent from the original budget estimate of P54.15 billion. This increase is due to supplementary funding of P423.36 million under recurrent and P1.39 billion for the development budget. As a result, the revised 2015/2016 budget shows a deficit of P4.20 billion or minus 2.8 percent of GDP compared to the original projected surplus of P1.23 billion.

VI. 2016/2017 BUDGET PROPOSALS

61. Madam Speaker, at this juncture, I would like to present the budget proposals for the 2016/2017 financial year. I must emphasise that the proposed budget allocations were informed by the need to stimulate economic growth and create job opportunities in line with the ESP objectives. The implementation of the ESP will be done prudently to ensure continued fiscal sustainability. Special emphasis will be placed on the phased implementation of Government programmes and projects, taking into account constrained fiscal space and available implementation capacity. This calls for strict discipline in utilising available public funds by Ministries and Departments. Furthermore, it means that implementation capacity and expenditure quality must improve significantly to yield the desired outcome, otherwise, less resources would be available for future economic activities.

Revenues and Grants

62. Madam Speaker, total revenues and grants for 2016/2017 are estimated at P48.40 billion, a decrease of P3.36 billion compared to the revised budget of P51.76 billion for 2015/2016; with Mineral revenue contributing 35.2 percent of

the total revenues, followed by Customs and Excise at 24.3 percent. Non-Mineral Income Tax and Value Added Tax come third and fourth at 21.2 percent and 12.4 percent, respectively. The reduction in the 2016/2017 revenues compared to 2015/2016 is a result of the projected fall of 6.9 percent in mineral revenues and 23.8 percent in customs and excise receipts.

Recurrent Budget

63. Madam Speaker, the proposed Ministerial Recurrent Budget for 2016/2017 financial year amounts to P36.99 billion, an increase of P0.29 billion or 0.8 percent compared to the current year's original budget of P36.70 billion.

64. The largest share of the Ministerial Recurrent Budget is proposed for allocation to the Ministry of Education and Skills Development, with a budget of P10.64 billion or 28.8 percent of the total. Through the implementation of the Education and Training Sector Strategic Plan, Government is committed to ensure that issues of quality of education and skills mismatch are addressed. This substantial budget caters for, among others, teaching services' wage bill, post-secondary bursaries, and subventions to University of Botswana and other Government funded tertiary institutions, increased enrolment for the Botswana International University of Science and Technology, provision for examination costs, maintenance of institutional facilities, food for secondary school students, and utility costs for the various education facilities.

65. The second largest share of the proposed Ministerial Recurrent Budget of P5.75 billion or 15.5 percent is proposed for allocation to the Ministry of Health. This budget will cover the cost of drugs, dressings and vaccines, service charges, anti-retroviral therapy, replacement of obsolete medical equipment, medical specialists' fees, running costs for the new Teaching Hospital, and the establishment of the Medicine Regulatory Authority, among others.

66. An amount of P4.99 billion or 13.5 percent of the total, being the third largest share, is proposed for allocation to the Ministry of Local Government and Rural Development. The bulk of this amount is mainly to cater for: revenue support grants to Councils, social protection programmes including the Old Age Pension scheme, Orphan Care programme, and the Destitute programme, which includes the special Okavango Destitute initiative.

67. The fourth largest share is proposed for allocation to the Ministry of Defence Justice and Security at P4.95 billion or 13.4 percent to cater for among others operational costs for; the BDF, Botswana Police, and Botswana Prison Services.

68. An amount of P2.02 billion or 5.5 percent is recommended for the Ministry of Transport and Communications which is the fifth largest share. This will cover maintenance of roads, replacement of vehicles, upgrading of the Government Data Network, subvention to the Civil Aviation Authority of Botswana and Botswana Post's Universal Service Obligation costs.

69. The sixth largest share of P1.11 billion or 3.0 percent of the total, is proposed for allocation to the Ministry of State President to cover, among others; service charges, programme development costs of the Department of Broadcasting Services, printing costs, office rent, Vision 2016 Council winding up expenses, and additional budget provision arising from the transfer of District Administration and Public Enterprise Evaluation and Privatization Agency to the Ministry.

70. Madam Speaker, the balance of P7.53 billion or 20.4 percent of the total is proposed for allocation to the remaining Ministries and Departments. Among these, the largest share of the balance is proposed for the Ministry of Agriculture at P1.09 billion, to cater for operating charges including service charges, purchase of material, foot and mouth disease, and animal identification devices. The second largest share of the balance amounting to P908.53 million is recommended for the Ministry of Trade and Industry to cover subventions for its parastatals, especially Selebi-Phikwe Economic Diversification Unit (SPEDU) and its transformation into a company limited by guarantee.

STATUTORY EXPENDITURE

71. Madam Speaker, the proposed Statutory Expenditure for 2016/2017 financial year amounts to P6.91 billion, a decrease of 12.9 percent compared to P7.93 billion allocated for the 2015/2016 financial year. The reduction in this provision is due to the P1.64 billion payment of Government Bond BW003, in the 2015/2016 financial year.

DEVELOPMENT BUDGET

72. Madam Speaker, a total development budget of P14.82 billion is proposed for the financial year 2016/2017. The Ministry of Defence, Justice and Security, with a proposed allocation of P3.59 billion or 24.2 percent, takes the largest share of the proposed budget, mainly to cater for provision of defence equipment, communication equipment, and infrastructure, in order to improve BDF's defence capabilities. In addition, the allocation caters for construction of police stations at Mmathubudukwane, Maitengwe and Semolale, as well as staff houses in different locations in order to improve safety and security.

73. The second largest share of P3.43 billion or 23.1 percent is proposed for the Ministry of Minerals, Energy and Water Resources. The budget caters for

energy and water infrastructure in order to address the current supply shortages which have affected the welfare of Batswana. The major energy infrastructure projects include; Morupule A Power Station rehabilitation at P135 million, North-West Electricity Transmission Grid at P225 million and Rakola sub-station at P257 million. In addition, the Botswana Power Corporation requires cash injection of P1.35 billion to cater for emergency power supply and P257 million under ESP for rural electrification. The water infrastructure projects include: the North South Carrier (NSC) II from Palapye to Mmamashia; Mahalapye and Palapye network extensions; connection of Kanye and Molepolole to NSC; Maun Water Supply and Sanitation and Kanye Sanitation; country-wide ground water investigation; as well as various water supply interconnections.

74. The Ministry of Transport and Communications, with a proposed budget of P1.41 billion or 9.5 percent, takes the third largest share to cater for construction of secondary roads, bridges, bitumen and trunk roads. The major projects under this Ministry are: Kazungula and Mohembo bridges; Output Performance Road Contract for Mankgodi-Jwaneng and Rakhuna-Mabule roads; as well as the Traffic signals improvements and centralised traffic control in Gaborone, an initiative which is aimed at improving the flow of traffic. The proposed budget includes an estimated amount of P250 million for road projects under the ESP.

75. The fourth largest share is proposed for the Ministry of Local Government and Rural Development at P1.22 billion or 8.3 percent. The budget mainly caters for *Ipelegeng* and Destitute Housing programmes. Part of the Ministry's budget is for ESP projects at P315.04 million for backlog eradication for primary school facilities, village infrastructure and construction of customary courts. The Ministry of Education and Skills Development with a proposed budget of P1.09 billion or 7.4 percent gets the fifth largest share; out of which a sum of P440.35 million is for the construction of teachers' houses, classrooms and laboratories under ESP.

76. Madam Speaker, the other Ministries and Departments share the remaining balance of the proposed Development Budget of P4.17 billion. The largest share of the balance is proposed for the Ministry of Lands and Housing at P910.37 million. The budget mainly caters for: Land Servicing at P338.38 million; Land Administration and Processes, Capacity and System (LAPCAS) at P354 million. The proposed budget also includes an amount of P272.9 million under ESP aimed at accelerating ongoing programmes. The second largest share of the balance at P813.04 million is proposed for the Ministry of Agriculture, of which, P35 million is for ESP, to cater for; grey water re-use, Lotsane irrigation project, Glenn Valley infrastructure rehabilitation, grading of roads, and Agricultural Service Centres. The third largest share of the balance amounting to P741.81

million is proposed for the Ministry Health to cater for upgrading of health facilities and construction of staff houses throughout the country. A total of P600.08 million inclusive of ESP amounting to P50 million is proposed for the Ministry of State President. This caters for additional poverty eradication packages.

OVERALL BALANCE

77. Madam Speaker, with an estimated total revenues and grants of P48.40 billion for 2016/2017 financial year, and proposed total expenditure and net lending of P54.44 billion, the net result is an estimated budget deficit of P6.05 billion or 3.8 percent of GDP. In line with the principles of our Medium Term Debt Management Strategy, this budget deficit will be financed through a combination of drawing down on Government savings, domestic borrowing and foreign borrowing, subject to the analysis of the opportunity cost of each of these financing instruments, and within the provisions of the relevant legislation such as *Public Finance Management Act of 2011 and the Stock, Bonds and Treasury Bills Act of 2005.* In any event, this deficit, and any other future budget deficits, will be restricted to a ratio up to 4 percent of GDP to avoid the country sliding into an unstainable fiscal path.

VII. PUBLIC SERVICE SALARIES

78. Madam Speaker, negotiations on public service salaries are the prerogative of the Bargaining Council, which comprises the Government and Trade Unions. It is important, however, to consider the prevailing global and domestic economic outlook, in particular, the constrained fiscal space for 2016/2017, arising from the depressed global demand for, and prices of diamonds. We all need to take into account these unfavourable economic fundamentals to ensure the country's future fiscal sustainability.

VIII. CONCLUSION

79. Madam Speaker, as I conclude, I wish to point out that, the medium term fiscal outlook is a cause for concern, given the modest growth prospects for the domestic economy. I therefore, call upon Ministries to exercise restraint in requesting for additional funding through supplementary budgets during the course of the financial year, as this would simply worsen the fiscal situation.

80. I must also hasten to add that, the development of this country is a matter of mutual social responsibility, and not that of Government alone. While the Government has shown, and continues to show visionary leadership by adopting policies and programmes aimed at inclusive growth, it is the responsibility of both the public service and the private sector to deliver on these programmes and associated projects. I therefore, call upon those charged with project implementation in Government to avoid deficiencies in project designs; provide

accurate initial estimates of the costs of projects; reengineer the tendering and adjudication processes to ensure speedy delivery of projects; and ensure adequate supervision of contractors to avoid cost overruns and unnecessary delays in project delivery. Most importantly, such projects should deliver on intended impact anchored on sustainable inclusive growth and economic diversification.

81. The private sector plays a key role in the delivery of development programmes, in particular, through contractors who will be undertaking various projects and activities planned for the financial year. Private contractors are critical in ensuring timely delivery of planned projects and the quality of the final products. I therefore, implore upon all contractors, to demonstrate their social responsibility and ensure that projects are delivered on time; according to specifications; within budgets; and are of good quality. Furthermore, it is my hope that, given the importance of the recently introduced Economic Stimulus Programme to *economic growth and job creation,* private contractors will cooperate with Government in the delivery of the budget, rather than stalling project implementation, resulting in cost over-runs. Since most projects envisaged for 2016/2017 and beyond are in the construction area; which requires land, I would also appeal to the land authorities throughout the country to expedite the process of land allocation and servicing, as part of their social responsibility in the delivery of our development programmes and projects.

82. Madam Speaker, let me take this opportunity to thank our bilateral and multilateral development partners, as well as private foundations for their contribution to our development agenda through their technical and financial support.

83. Madam Speaker, I now move that the Appropriation (2016/2017) Bill, No. 1 of 2016 be read for the second time.

ECONOMIC ENVIRONMENT

MAIN FEATURES

Botswana's economic performance relies heavily on its main driver of growth, diamonds. Such exports depend in turn on global economic prospects, especially in the major gem markets, e.g. the United States, which imports more than 50% of Botswana's diamonds. In the current global financial and economic crisis, the short-term economic outlook is bleak; the IMF expects Botswana's real GDP to contract by 10.4% in 2009 but to rebound by 14.3% in 2010. [16] Large investments in electricity generation are expected to lead to an increase in the growth rate of non-mineral GDP over the medium term. [17]

The economy's longer term will outlook be influenced by economic strategies used to accelerate economic diversification, in anticipation of a decline of diamond output expected after 2015. Diversification is likely to remain the central theme of the new NDP 10, which is to cover the period until March 2016. [18] The Government intends to further shift its focus from growth of government spending, to private-sector development as a stimulus to growth. Its priorities remain investment in infrastructure, and in education and training, as well as improvements of the business environment. The Government also plans to support (electronic) services exports, to overcome some of the transport cost disadvantage linked to Botswana's land-locked position.

Botswana ranks 56th in the global competitiveness rankings of the World Economic Forum, second only to South Africa in sub-Saharan Africa. [1] Botswana owes its competitiveness, *inter alia*, to sound macroeconomic policies; it is also rated as the country with the lowest rate of corruption in Africa. [2] Development has been driven mainly by revenue from diamonds. Mineral taxation has also enabled the Government to improve basic infrastructure, such as transportation, and social services, such as health and education. Impressive economic performance since independence has raised average GDP per head to over US$7,000, higher than most other sub-Saharan African countries (Table I.1); however, income distribution is highly skewed. [3]

Under the National HIV/AIDS Strategic Framework 2003-09 considerable progress has been made in the prevention, treatment, and care of AIDS. [4] According to the authorities, the national prevalence rate (old and new infections) has been reduced to 17.6% in 2008 and the rate of new infections to 2.9%. [5] It is estimated that 90% of the infected needing treatment receive anti-retroviral drugs free of charge, which has contributed to reducing mortality to 10%. The Government's goal is for an "AIDS-free generation" by 2016. Combating HIV/AIDS has long-term repercussions in terms of productivity losses, and budgetary expenditures. Government spending for health, food, and social welfare increased by 17.3% on average in 2001-06, far exceeding annual growth of overall spending (8.7%), reflecting mainly increased expenditures for various programmes to address HIV/AIDS. [6]

RECENT ECONOMIC DEVELOPMENTS

Real GDP increased by an average of 4.4% per annum in 2003-08, ranging from 1.6% in 2005 to 6.3% in 2003 (Table I.1) . [7] The volatility of national output was mainly due to the cyclical nature of the diamond industry, which contributes about 30% to GDP. [8] Non-mining activities (accounting for about 60% of GDP) maintained strong growth, averaging almost 6% annually in 2003-08. Unemployment remains high, though it declined from over 19.5% in 2001 to 17.5% in

2005/06. [9] Formal employment increased by only 1.5% per year in 2003/04-2005/06, in part due to insufficient (labour-intensive) investment to generate significant employment growth.

Following three successive budget deficits from 2001/02 to 2003/04, the government posted budget surpluses until 2007/08, which have been the norm in Botswana since independence (Table I.1) . However, as the result of the current global financial crisis, a budget deficit of 14% of GDP is forecast for 2009/10. A continuing concern is the principal reliance on tax receipts from Botswana's diamonds. Diversification of its revenue base is therefore one of the Government's priorities. A growing proportion of revenues has come from the SACU Common Revenue Pool, reflecting the increase of imports in the SACU region, and a more favourable revenue-sharing formula introduced in 2004/05. These receipts increased from P 2.2 billion in 2003/04 to P 7.8 billion in 2007/08, representing over one quarter of total government revenues in 2007/08. The Government has also diversified away from mineral income tax revenues through the introduction of value-added tax in 2002, and improved tax collection.

Grants from external sources account for less than 2% of total government revenues. Government expenditures are controlled over the medium term by the National Development Plan 9 (NDP 9) aimed at balancing the budget over the duration of the six-year plan (2003/04 to 2008/09) . To stimulate growth, the budget has been rebalanced towards capital investment (development expenditures), with an increase of development spending from 24% of the overall budget in 2004/05 to 30% in the 2008/09 budget.

Monetary policy focuses on achieving a low, sustainable, and predictable level of inflation over the medium-term, currently set at 3-6% per year. Primary monetary policy instruments are the Central Bank's discount rate (bank rate) and open market operations, mainly through issues of Bank of Botswana Certificates (BoBCs), to influence interest rates and absorb excess liquidity in the banking subsector. As a result of relatively tight monetary policy, annual inflation was brought down from a peak of 14.2% in April 2006 to below 7% in mid-2007. However, annual inflation increased to 12.6% in 2008 due to a sharp increase in prices, notably for food and fuel.

4. The exchange rate policy is implemented by the Central Bank on behalf of the Government with the objective of achieving stability of the real effective exchange rate (REER) . This policy is part of the economic diversification strategy to maintain the competitiveness of non-traditional exports, as well as other tradeable goods and services. [10] To reverse an increase in the REER, the pula was devaluated by 7.5% in February 2004, and 12% in May 2005. [11] Also in May 2005, Botswana switched from pegging the pula to the South African rand and the SDR, to a crawling band exchange rate mechanism based on a basket of currencies (comprising the South African rand and the SDR) . This change was made to ensure stability of the REER, while avoiding large discrete adjustments of the nominal exchange rates. The REER appreciated by 4.5% in 2008, in particular against the South African rand, weakening Botswana's competitiveness (Table I.1) .

Structural reforms to improve the economy's productivity and competitiveness have been limited in recent years. Botswana still has no competition law to regulate anti-competitive conduct (Chapter III(4)(iii)) . The Government adopted a Privatization Master Plan in June 2005 but privatizations of poorly performing parastatals, such as Air Botswana, have been deferred (Chapter III(4)(ii)) . A number of goods and services remain subject to price controls, undermining an efficient functioning of Botswana's market economy (Chapter III(4)(iii)) . [12]

Botswana has achieved substantial current account surpluses since 2003, with a peak of 17.2% of GDP in 2006. The underlying factors have been a burgeoning merchandise trade surplus driven by large diamond export earnings, favourable international base metal prices (until mid-2008), as well as rising net transfers from the SACU. Overall, the balance of payments remains healthy with official foreign exchange reserves at US$9.1 billion at the end of 2008, equivalent to about 23 months of import cover (goods and non-factor services) . Botswana has a relatively modest level of external debt, at 1.9% of GDP (end of 2008), equivalent to about 4% of total exports.

TRADE PERFORMANCE

(i) Trade in goods

Botswana remains heavily dependent on exports of diamonds (including industrial diamonds), which accounted for 63.7% of total merchandise exports in 2007, down from 78.3% in 2003 (Table AI.1 and Chart I.1) . The value of other traditional exports – copper-nickel, beef, and soda ash – has increased considerably in recent years, mainly as the result of favourable world market prices. [13] The main change in export patterns is the substantial increase of apparel exports (non-traditional exports), largely due to preferential access to the U.S. market; and the declining share of automotive products exports due to the relocation of car manufacturers to South Africa (Chapter IV(5)(ii)) .

Botswana's merchandise exports remain concentrated in Europe, especially the United Kingdom [14], and SACU members, notably South Africa. Exports have become marginally more diversified geographically, with an increasing share of exports destined for America and Asia (Table AI.2 and Chart I.2) .

Merchandise imports consist mainly of machinery and transport equipment, fuels, and food and beverages, mainly from South Africa (Tables AI.3 and AI.4, and Chart I.1) . The import bill increased sharply in 2007 to a level last experienced in 2003, reflecting not only the surge in international commodity and fuel prices, but also investment in capital imports for major infrastructure and mining projects.

(ii) Trade in services

1. Botswana is a net importer of services, especially of transportation services (Table I.2) . The growing trade deficit in services is also due to an increase in imports of "other services", linked mainly to services for prospecting and mine development; tourism receipts have stagnated in recent years.

(4) INVESTMENT PATTERNS

1. The stock of foreign direct investment (FDI) was US$1.3 billion at the end of 2007 (Table I.3) . Preliminary balance of payments data for 2008 show that the flow of FDI declined significantly in 2008 as a result of the global financial crisis (Table I.2) . There has been little foreign investment outside the mining and the finance sectors. Botswana has been successful in attracting foreign investment in financial services, which can be linked to, *inter alia*, the establishment of the offshore International Financial Services Centre (Chapter IV(6)(i)) . Most FDI is from Europe, especially Luxembourg, which is the seat of De Beers, the diamond company; and from South Africa. Botswana's stock of FDI abroad amounted to US$809 million at the end of 2007.

In the FDI world rankings, Botswana fell from 46th place in 2003-05 to 66th place in 2005-07, although with an Inward FDI Performance Index of 1.5 (2005-07) it has attracted more FDI than would be expected by the size of its economy. Overall, Botswana's appears to have slipped from being a "front-runner FDI performer with high FDI potential" in 2003-05 to "performing below its high FDI potential" in 2004-06. [15]

TRADE AND INVESTMENT REGIMES

Botswana has been a member of SACU[2] from its inception, and thus for a long time most of its trade policy instruments (especially customs matters) have been determined at the regional level There has been little change in this position since the last Trade Policy Review (TPR) of SACU in 2003.

Nevertheless, Botswana has its own national policy initiatives in areas not yet harmonized at the regional level or not covered by the SACU Agreement. Within this context, the formulation and implementation of trade policy reside with the Ministry of Trade and Industry. The detailed structure of the Ministry of Trade and Industry was described in the 2003 TPR report, and remains largely unchanged. [19] In essence, the Ministry comprises the Trade Section, which is made up of the International Trade and Internal Trade Directorates; and the section for Industry and Cooperative Affairs, which is made up of the Registrar of Companies; Directorate of Industrial Affairs, and Cooperative Development Commissioner.

Other institutions that also have important input into trade-related policies include the ministries responsible for finance; mineral resources; transport and communications; and agriculture; as well as the Bank of Botswana.

The 2002 SACU Agreement provides for the establishment of a national body in each member country to be responsible for all SACU issues (including tariff changes) at the national level, and for making recommendations to the Customs Union Commission (Main Report, Chapter II(2)(ii)) . Botswana is currently drafting legislation establishing the national body; the draft is expected to be finalized before the end of 2009.

Botswana has a well-established consultative process for formulating trade policies. [20] The highest level of this process is the High Level Consultative Council, chaired by the President, and comprising the Vice-President, Ministers, and private-sector representatives. The Government of Botswana also established a National Committee on Trade Policy and Negotiations in 2003, whose mandate is to provide a forum for stakeholders to discuss and identify positions for Botswana's trade negotiations, and to coordinate the formulation and implementation of trade policy for the implementation of the WTO obligations and regional trade negotiations.

Private-sector input in trade and industrial policy (including from small and medium-sized businesses) is channelled through the Botswana Confederation of Commerce, Industry and Manpower (BOCCIM) . The BOCCIM reviews implementation of policies at the national level every three years. The Botswana Exporters and Manufacturers Association safeguards the interests of exporters; it also provides specialized export services, including assistance in identifying foreign markets. The workers are represented in the consultative process with business and government through the Botswana Federation of Trade Unions. There is also an independent Botswana Institute for Development Policy Analysis (BIDPA), created in 1995, to conduct public policy research for the Government and other clients, including monitoring of economic performance.[21] This process finally leads to the adoption/implementation of trade-related legal instruments at the national level (Table II.1) .

[2] Southern African Customs Union SACU)

MAIN TRADE-RELATED LEGISLATION

Area	Legislation
Imports and exports	Customs and Excise Act, and 2001 amendments and regulations; Customs and Excise Act, Amendment, Act 31, 2004; Customs and Excise Duty Regulations S.I. 127, 2004; S.I 88, 2005; and S.I. 49, 2006 Botswana Unified Revenue Act, 2004; Trade Act, 2003; Trade Regulations, 2008; Liquor Act, 2003; Export and Import of Rough Diamonds Regulations, 2004
Registration procedures	Companies Act, 2003 (Act No. 32 of 2004); Cooperative Societies Act, 1989
Intellectual property	Industrial Property Act CAP 68:03; Copyright and Neighbouring Rights Act (CAP 68:02)
Government procurement	Public Procurement and Asset Disposal Act, 2001; Public Procurement and Asset Disposal Regulation, 2006
Price controls	Control of Goods, Prices, and Other Charges Act (CAP 63:08)
Standards	Standards Act, 1995; Standards (Import Inspection) Regulations, 2008; Weights and Measures Act and Regulations, 2006 (CAP 46:06)
Agriculture	Botswana Agricultural Marketing Board Act, 1974 (CAP 74:06); Branding of Cattle Act (CAP 36:02), Branding (Amendment) Regulations, 2004; Livestock and Meat Industries Act (CAP 36:03), Grading of carcasses (Amendment) Regulations, 2004; Hides and Skins Export Act (CAP 49:01), Hides and Skins (Amendment), Regulations, 2004; Disease of Animal Act CAP 37:01
Mining	Mines and Minerals Act, 1999
Electricity	Botswana Power Corporations Act, 1971
Services	Banking Act, 1995; Insurance Industry Act, 1987; International Insurance Act, 2005; Telecommunications (Amendment) Bill, 2004; Tourism Act, 1992; Tourism Regulations, 1996
Foreign investment	Botswana Export Development and Investment Authority Act, 1997

Source: WTO Secretariat; and information provided by the Botswana authorities.

Trade liberalization and investment promotion remain key elements of Botswana's trade policy framework and its development strategy. The overall goal of broadening Botswana's manufacturing base for further diversification purposes remains a key objective of the Government. Developing small and medium-sized enterprises is also a high priority. The Government remains committed to creating a more enabling business environment to facilitate private sector growth, which it sees as essential to the economy's sustained and balanced development. Botswana's overall trade policy will, therefore, lay the framework for diversifying the production of goods and services for the local, regional, and international markets. Trade policy, as supported by other national policies and strategies, is to ensure that supply-side constraints are addressed, propelling the private sector to diversify and expand its production and become more competitive.

Botswana's four development planning objectives are: economic growth, social justice, economic independence, and sustainable development. Botswana's 9th National Development Plan (NDP) aims to have Botswana as a developed economy by 2016, built upon a sustainable, diversified, and competitive export-based economy. The NDP recognizes the private sector as the engine of growth and the driver of the export-led growth that Botswana envisages. The 10th NDP takes up most of the themes in the 9th NDP, and is due to commence before the end of 2009 [22]. The Government aims to play a major role in creating a conducive environment for private-sector development by building institutional capacity, as well as ensuring infrastructural development.

TRADE AGREEMENTS

Botswana is an original member of the WTO, and is committed to a fair trade regime based on multilaterally agreed principles. Jointly with the other SACU members, Botswana notified the 2002 SACU Agreement to the WTO in 2007 (Table II.2) .

Botswana is a member of the Southern African Development Community (SADC) and is currently implementing the SADC Protocol on Trade. [23] Botswana is also a member of the African Union (Main Report, Chapter II(3)(ii)) .

Botswana has very few bilateral trade agreements. One of these is an agreement with Zimbabwe, signed in 1988, which provides for reciprocal duty-free entry of goods and is currently under review with a view to improving its rules of origin and thereby facilitating more trade. Botswana also has a trade agreement with Malawi dating back to 1956: it has occasionally imported sugar from Malawi under this agreement, but much of this trade is now conducted under the SADC trade protocol.

Botswana is eligible for GSP treatment from Australia, Canada, EC, Japan, New Zealand, Norway, Switzerland, and the United States. This treatment provides preferential access to these markets (at zero or reduced tariffs) for eligible Botswanan products, subject to rules of origin. Product coverage and rules of origin vary between countries.

Botswana has been a beneficiary of the U.S. African Growth and Opportunity Act (AGOA) from inception (Main Report, Chapter II(3)(v)), but became eligible for enhanced access afforded to "lesser developed beneficiary sub-Saharan African countries" from 6 August 2002. Botswana's exports under AGOA are mainly textiles, apparel, and a small amount of furniture. The Government of Botswana has recognized the need to address the current inability to effectively capitalize on the preferential market access and the need to increase the competitiveness of its products in the U.S. market.

Botswana is currently negotiating an Economic Partnership Agreement (EPA) with the European Communities under the SADC Group, which comprises the SACU members plus Angola and Mozambique. This would be a reciprocal agreement that would allow duty-free and quota-free access for Botswana products into the EC market. [24]

INVESTMENT FRAMEWORK

1. Botswana generally maintains an open foreign investment regime. However, under its policy of citizen empowerment, a few manufacturing activities and services are reserved for Botswana citizens or companies owned by citizens of Botswana (Table II.3) . The mining subsector is open to foreign investment, with the exception of small-scale projects.

Activities reserved for Botswana citizens or citizen-owned companies

Legislation	Reserved activities
Industrial Development (Amendment) Regulations, 2008[a]	Manufacture of school uniforms; manufacture of school furniture; manufacture of burglar bars; manufacture of protective clothing; milling of sorghum; manufacture of cement bricks and baked earth (mud) bricks; baking of bread and confectionery; manufacture of peanut butter; bottling of water; production of traditional sour milk; packaging; manufacture of floor polish; manufacture of traditional leather products; manufacture of traditional crafts; signage, including electronic signage; fencing materials, excluding gum poles; manufacture of candles; ice making; and meat processing
Trade Act, 2003[b]	Auctioneers; bookshops; boutiques; car washes; cleaning services; curio shops; department stores; distributors; dry cleaning; fresh produce; funeral parlours; furniture shops; general clothing; general dealers; hair dressers; hardware; hire services; laundromats; motor dealers; petrol filling stations; restaurants; supermarkets/chain stores; take-away restaurants; wholesale; and workshops
Liquor Act, 2003[b]	Liquor bars/clubs (other than bars linked to hotel establishments); bottle stores; liquor depots; discotheques/night clubs; and liquor distribution/wholesaling
Mines and Minerals Act, 1999	Small-scale mining[c]

a Small-scale manufacturing reserved for Botswana citizens or companies wholly owned by Botswana citizens.
b Reserved for Botswana citizens or companies wholly owned by Botswana citizens. Joint ventures in the reserved activities are permitted with up to 49% foreign participation (or otherwise subject to approval by the Minister of Industry and Trade) in "medium business enterprises" with less than 100 employees and annual sales between P 1.5 million and P 5 million.
c Small-scale mining means the intentional mining of minerals other than diamonds in operations involving the mining and processing of less than 50,000 tonnes of raw ore per annum and in which the overall investment in fixed assets does not exceed P 1 million.
Source: WTO Secretariat.

Botswana does not have a stand-alone foreign investment law, but relies on sectoral laws to implement its investment policy. Because of the size of the domestic market, the Government is targeting investment in export-oriented industries, including textiles and garments, leather goods, information technology, minerals, diamond cutting and polishing, glass products, automobiles, electrical goods, and printing and publishing. [25]FDI is also encouraged in the energy subsector, financial services, tourism, and healthcare.

Botswana's model Bilateral Investment Treaty (BIT) provides for non-discriminatory treatment of foreign investors. The Citizen Entrepreneurial Development Agency (CEDA) was set up to provide financial assistance schemes to build citizens' enterprises, and operates a Venture Capital Fund for joint ventures between citizens and foreigners. Foreign investors are encouraged, but not compelled, to establish joint ventures. The Export Credit and Guarantee Insurance Company (BECI) offers export credit to Botswana companies, regardless of whether citizen owned or foreign owned. There is no minimum required investment level, including from foreigners. However financial institutions, such as the Botswana Development Corporation or the National Development Bank, require a minimum contribution from the investor of 25% of the total project cost.

Investment is promoted and facilitated by the Botswana Export Development and Investment Authority (BEDIA) . BEDIA operates a "one-stop-shop" designed to assist investors with pre-investment services, such as obtaining land, buildings, work and residency permits, licences, and grants, and satisfying other regulatory requirements. Investment projects are subject to a Preliminary Environmental Impact Assessment to be submitted to the Department of Environmental Affairs. Investments in offshore financial services are promoted by the Botswana International Financial Services Centre (Chapter IV(6)(i)) .

The new Companies Act, which entered into force in July 2007, *inter alia*, introduced simplified procedures for company registration; this has reduced registration time from twelve weeks to five working days. [26] Business licences for manufacturing are issued by the Industrial Licensing Authority, under the authority of the Ministry of Trade and Industry, which considers applications on a weekly basis; decisions are communicated to applicants within a week. The licences must be renewed every year. The Registrar of Companies and Intellectual Property, within the Ministry of Trade and Industry, maintains a register of registered entities.

Freehold land can be purchased by both citizens and non-citizens. A transfer duty applies to property sales: for citizens, no duty is charged on freehold land valued at P 200,000 or less; a 5% duty is charged on any amount in excess of this threshold. Non-citizens, including companies with less than majority local ownership, pay 5% duty on the total value of freehold land. State-owned land can be leased, for 50 years for business purposes and 99 years for residential use, subject to renewable options. Tribal (communal) land can be leased for 50 years for commercial, agricultural, and industrial use. A shortage of serviced industrial land has been identified as a major investment constraint in Botswana.

Work permits for foreign personnel are subject to a local labour availability market test (i.e. that there are no suitable national candidates) and submission of a satisfactory training programme for "localizing" each position. The fees for work permits were increased in 2005 to P 600 for employees, and P 1,000 for self-employed applicants.

8. The corporate tax rate, at 15% for registered manufacturing companies and 25% for other companies, is one of the lowest in the region. The Minister of Finance and Development Planning may also grant tax relief for certain businesses under Development Approval Orders (Chapter III(4)(i)) . Profits, dividends, and capital can be readily repatriated. There are no restrictions on portfolio investment, and the Botswana Stock Exchange allows dual company listings.

Botswana's Constitution prohibits nationalization of private property. Domestic law assures the right to establish, acquire, and dispose of business interests, and guarantees the right to private ownership.

Botswana is currently ranked 8th in sub-Saharan Africa and 38th globally (out of 141 countries) in terms of ease of starting a business; a major improvement on its 52nd position world-wide in 2008. [27]

Botswana is a member of the International Centre for the Settlement of Investment Disputes and the World Bank's Multilateral Investment Guarantee Agency. Botswana also signed a bilateral investment treaty in 1997 with the Overseas Private Investment Corporation (OPIC), which provides guarantees for U.S. private investors. Botswana has investment promotion and protection treaties with Belgium and Luxembourg, China, Germany, Ghana, Malaysia, Mauritius, and Switzerland. It has double taxation agreements with France, India, Mauritius, Namibia, Russia, South Africa, Sweden, the United Kingdom, and Zimbabwe.

TRADE-RELATED TECHNICAL ASSISTANCE

Trade-related technical assistance (TRTA) has a critical role in enabling Botswana to derive benefits from open trade policies, as well as in its participation in the multilateral trading system. Botswana needs technical assistance in the following areas: (i) implementation of WTO agreements (and in deriving benefits from such implementation); (ii) building of human and institutional capacity, including for trade negotiations; (iii) supply-side constraints; and (iv) the integration of trade into overall development strategies.

Botswana's submission of TRTA needs to the WTO for 2008-09 outlined the following areas: (i) agriculture and notifications relating thereto; (ii) non-agricultural market access (NAMA) issues; (iii) rules of origin; (iv) scheduling of commitments in services; and (v) development of skills in trade negotiation techniques.

The delivery of technical assistance, including for capacity building, to Botswana and other SACU countries has the potential, if properly coordinated, to strengthen the integration of SACU countries into the multilateral trading system, as well as their evolution into common trade policy formulation at the regional level.

Implementation of WTO Agreements

Botswana intends to implement legislation on anti-dumping, safeguards, and countervailing measures, although in view of the 2002 SACU Agreement this must, ultimately, be coordinated at the SACU level. Enhancing Botswana's capacity to develop such rules-based trade measures may contribute to stable and predictable trade policies.

The last SACU TPR noted that as other trade barriers are progressively reduced, standards, technical regulations, and sanitary and phytosanitary (SPS) measures are likely to emerge as constraints on exports. Given the relative importance to Botswana of agricultural exports – notably of bovine meat and products – compliance with SPS requirements is a particular challenge. The Government has underlined the need for training in relation to equivalence, transparency, and pest-risk analysis. The shortage of trained personnel and "hard infrastructure" in relation to SPS remains a challenge.

Botswana benefited from the establishment of an SPS Enquiry Point under the Joint Integrated Technical Assistance Programme (JITAP) . [28]

Capacity building is also needed for the development of enforcement capacity on intellectual property rights.

On customs-related matters, in addition to regular WTO technical assistance, Botswana has also benefited from technical assistance from the World Customs Organisation (WCO) . However, the Government still needs much more capacity-building assistance in customs reforms and trade facilitation. In this regard, Botswana would like to use its relatively well developed road linkages and central position in the SACU region to become a regional transit hub.

Trade negotiations

Botswana is involved in trade negotiations at a number of levels, including with the EC in the context of the EPAs (as part of the SADC) (Main Report, Chapter II(3)(iv)), SADC, SACU, and the Doha Development Agenda (DDA) negotiations. This multifaceted, and sometimes overlapping, negotiating agenda entails an urgent need to develop and coordinate negotiating positions on various fronts.

Since negotiations can be used as a means of strengthening and "locking-in" domestic reforms, capacity building should focus on formulating negotiating positions and strategies that are based on the domestic reform process. [29] In relation to the DDA negotiations, the Government has continuously highlighted trade in services as being a key area for technical assistance, including for institutional capacity building. This is in view of the fact that trade in services has been identified as having a key role in Botswana's economic diversification.

Botswana, like many other small developing countries, faces considerable challenges in dealing with the volume of work involved in the WTO work programme, especially in light of the DDA negotiations.

Supply-side constraints and integration of trade into development strategies

Botswana suffers from a range of supply-side constraints. Its main challenge with respect to trade is its landlocked position. In addition, since the country is fairly large (though sparsely populated), its main port access is a considerable distance from the production/consumption centres. Nevertheless, it has a relatively good internal road network, which guarantees quick transit for goods to and from the ports.

Botswana still faces the challenge of diversifying away from heavy dependence on diamonds. This is particularly relevant in view of the significantly reduced demand as a result of the global financial crisis. [30]Botswana, therefore, needs assistance in identifying measures to diversify the economy, but without introducing inefficiency.

Botswana's participation in international trade and its trade reforms have been significant factors in promoting economic growth and alleviating poverty. It is also assisted by its periodic national development plans in which policy priorities are set out, although some trade-related policy issues are considered on a sectoral basis. While inter-ministerial coordination exists in relation to the formulation of trade policy, greater collaboration between ministries and departments on integrating trade into the overall architecture of development policy would be beneficial. Botswana would also benefit from a more systematic analysis of trade policy options geared towards poverty reduction.

The Botswana Trade and Poverty Programme with the UK Department for International Development (DFID) has been finalized, and Botswana has benefited through DFID funding for capacity building in trade and development policy, and supported poverty programmes. The programme has benefited both the public and private sectors.

Challenges identified at the national level may be addressed through priority areas for AFT intervention to improve the country's capacity to benefit from trade expansion. These priorities fall within six broad thematic areas: infrastructure and institutional development; capacity building for the private sector and government officials; export diversification; regional integration; trade facilitation; and trade policy analysis and negotiations.

Botswana, like most other countries in the sub-region, is currently faced with many challenges such as HIV/AIDS, lack of capacity, and an undiversified economy, and as such is still in need of aid dedicated to trade to, *inter alia*, build infrastructure for trade facilitation purposes. This will help Botswana to achieve greater integration into the global economy. Botswana has benefited from a range of trade-related technical assistance activities; the commitment of development partners has materialised in various activities in support of trade development, including capacity-building activities in various trade disciplines, and trade facilitation initiatives. Nonetheless, the volume of aid available to it is not commensurate with its needs.

INTERNATIONAL TRADE RELATIONS

WTO

Botswana is a founding Member of the WTO.[21] Botswana provides MFN treatment to all Members and other trading partners.

Botswana is not an observer to the Committee on Government Procurement, nor is it a signatory to the Information Technology Agreement.

In the last Ministerial Conference, Botswana recognized the importance of the conclusion of the Doha Round especially for small economies and restated its commitment to the work programme of the WTO.[22]

Botswana has not participated in any trade disputes.

During the period under review, Botswana submitted a number of notifications (Table A2.1) . However, some remain outstanding, particularly those related to import licensing.

Regional trade agreements

During the period under review, Botswana renegotiated a bilateral trade agreement with Zimbabwe and together with other African countries finalized the negotiations of an EPA with the EU. Botswana is also participating in the negotiations of the different regional integration processes with the Southern African Customs Union (SACU), SADC and SADC-EAC-COMESA (Main Report) . Botswana is currently implementing the SADC Trade Protocol.[23] The negotiations on the SADC Protocol on Services have been concluded and the protocol was adopted in August 2012 but has not yet been implemented (Main Report) .

As a member of SACU, Botswana is a signatory to the SACU-MERCOSUR Preferential Trade Agreement of 2004, the SACU-USA Trade, Investment and Development Cooperation Agreement (TIDCA) of 2007[24], and the SACU-EFTA FTA, which entered into force in 2008 (Main Report) .[25]

The EPA negotiations between the EU and the SADC EPA Group concluded in mid-July 2014. This agreement will replace the interim EPA, signed by the EU and by Botswana, Lesotho,

Mozambique and Swaziland in 2009, which was never ratified. The recently concluded agreement has not yet been signed.[26]

Botswana, together with the other SACU members, is negotiating a Preferential Trade Agreement (PTA) with India.[27]

Botswana has bilateral agreements with Zimbabwe and Malawi. The trade agreement with Zimbabwe was initially signed in 1956 and amended in 1988 and 2010.[28] The agreement provides for duty-free access to goods that are either wholly originated in either country or meet a local content requirement of 25%. Manufacturers are required to produce for a period of three months before starting to export to enable customs to confirm local content requirements. The amended agreement allows accumulation to confer origin, recognizes waste and scrap as inputs in the manufacturing processes, and grants an exemption to the three-month "production requirement".[29] The Botswana-Malawi Customs Agreement was signed in 1956; it has not since been renegotiated but is at present being evaluated. The agreement allows duty-free access to goods grown, produced and manufactured in Botswana and Malawi. Although Botswana has not signed a large number of bilateral and regional trade agreements, the overlap in concessions becomes evident as preferences under these two agreements and the SADC Protocol on Trade are very similar. Hence, trade between Botswana and Malawi is currently mainly undertaken through the SADC Protocol on Trade, except in cases where the rules of origin under the agreement between Botswana and Malawi are easier to comply with.

Botswana is a beneficiary of the African Growth and Opportunity Act (AGOA) . Botswana exports mainly textiles and apparel under AGOA.[30] According to the authorities, exports under this preferential system have fluctuated over the years mainly due to supply-side constraints. Botswana still benefits from Generalized System of Preferences schemes from, *inter alia*, Norway.[31]

INVESTMENT REGIME

Botswana does not have a specific foreign investment law; foreign investment is regulated by an array of laws. General investment restrictions, reservations, licensing requirements and incentives are all regulated by different legal instruments and policies.[32] These include: the Industrial Development Act, the Trade Act, the Companies Act, the Companies Amendment Act, the Companies Regulations, the Co-operative Societies Act, the Companies and Intellectual Property Authority Act and the Registration of Business Names Act.[33] Sectoral laws also stipulate the requirements and restrictions regarding investment in specific sectors (Section 4) .[34] In addition, Botswana imposes a series of reservations on foreign investment which are outlined in several documents. The citizen reservation requirements affect foreign investors' decisions, as they are perceived to be discriminatory and non-transparent especially if reservations are not well-defined and/or change often.

According to the authorities, Botswana is committed to having transparent investment policies that accord the same treatment to all investors. However, the myriad of laws and regulations that regulate FDI, together with the administrative and bureaucratic bottlenecks that exist to obtain licences and permits, considerably compromise the country's competitiveness to attract FDI. The consolidation of all regulations and policies related to FDI would clarify Botswana's FDI regime. It would also help to make foreign investment rules more understandable and predictable, thus creating a more favourable environment for domestic and foreign investment, which would in turn allow the Government to attain the objectives outlined in its Investment and Private Sector

Development Strategies. The NDP10 also deems that foreign and domestic investment need to increase to attain higher sustainable rates of growth (Section 1).[35]

A number of activities are reserved for citizens of Botswana or are restricted for foreign investors. Under the Industrial Development (Amendment) Regulations (2008), small-scale manufacturing is reserved for citizens of Botswana or companies wholly owned by citizens of Botswana, as is small-scale mining (Section 4).[36] Establishments that sell liquor, other than bars linked to hotels, are also reserved for citizens of Botswana or companies wholly owned by citizens of Botswana.[37] Similarly, the Trade Act (2003) lists several activities that are reserved for citizens of Botswana or for companies wholly owned by citizens of Botswana. However, despite these restrictions, medium and large enterprises[38] operating as joint ventures between citizens and foreigners are allowed to engage in these reserved activities, provided that 51% of the company is held by citizens (or otherwise subject to approval by the Minister of Industry and Trade).[39]

A foreign investor is required to either register its company under the Registration of Business Names Act or incorporate it under the Companies Act, and obtain the required licences to operate in Botswana.[40] Licences are required to manufacture or sell manufactured products; these are issued by the relevant licensing committee or the Industrial Licensing Authority for an indefinite period. A licensee would require a new licence to manufacture (sell) a new product or to change the location of its enterprise. Permission is also required to transfer the licence. The Minister of Trade and Industry may decide that licences, for a particular activity (or in a prescribed area of the country), will only be issued to nationals or to companies wholly owned by citizens of Botswana.[41] In contrast, the Minister may prescribe that licences to undertake activities reserved for citizens, carried out by medium or large enterprises may be issued to joint-ventures between citizens and foreigners, provided that 51% of the company is held by citizens.[42]

Botswana registered companies providing specific financial services may seek IFSC certification to obtain fiscal incentives (Box 2.1). The Minister may grant IFSC certification for other operations on a case-by-case basis.[43] There are no requirements to have resident shareholders in an IFSC accredited company, but the Companies Act (2004) requires that at least one director resides in Botswana IFSCs are allowed to hire experts from outside Botswana but are required to employ qualified nationals.

Land in Botswana is divided into three categories (freehold, state and tribal). Land, no matter its category, can be put to any use. Freehold land, which amounts to 3% of Botswana's land area, is the only type of land that can be purchased by (or transferred to) foreign nationals, without government approval, except if it is agricultural land. State-owned land accounts for 27% of Botswana's total land. Foreign-owned companies registered in Botswana can lease this type of land. This land is allocated through an application process or on a first-come-first-served basis by the Ministry of Lands and Housing. Leases are renewable and are granted for 50 years for commercial purposes and 99 years for residential use. The Government has set aside land for investors, which is managed by the Botswana Investment Trade Centre (BITC). Tribal (communal) land can be leased for 50 years for commercial, agricultural, and industrial use and it accounts for 70% of the country.[44] The use of tribal land may be granted to a foreigner subject to the Minister of Lands and Housing's approval.

The BITC was established in 2011 to, *inter alia*, attract FDI.[45] In addition to promoting Botswana as an investment destination, the BITC functions as a "one-stop shop" to facilitate investment procedures, such as the acquisition of licences and permits, and access to industrial and commercial land.[46] To attract FDI, Botswana has established a number of "hubs" and is in the process of establishing Special Economic Zones.[47]

Botswana also provides fiscal incentives and grants to attract FDI (Box 2.1) . Some incentives are granted only to companies that have IFSC certification[48], others are sector-specific or provided on a case-by-case basis. The Minister of Finance and Development Planning may grant tax relief under Development Approval Orders. Tax incentives provided under these orders may include tax holidays for income tax for up to 5 years; they are granted on a case-by-case-basis depending on the projects' prospects of benefiting the economy or contributing to the economic advancement of Botswana's nationals (Section 3) . According to the authorities, Development Approval Orders are rarely used; at present only two projects are beneficiaries under these orders. The tax regime for diamond projects may also be negotiated on a case-by-case basis (Section 4) .[49] Foreign investors also have access to grants, through the Citizen Entrepreneurial Development Agency (CEDA), provided that they partner with nationals.[50]

Botswana investment incentives, 2014

Specific fiscal incentive
IFSC certified companies are entitled to: A corporate tax rate of 15% until 2020 Exemption from withholding taxes on interest, dividends and management fees Exemption from VAT and capital gains tax A tax rebate of 200% on income tax on training costs Tax exemption on income derived from the disposal of shares in IFSCs Credits for withholding taxes in other jurisdictions Collective investment undertakings (CIUs) (a pass-through fund management mechanism) managed by IFSC are taxed exempt.
Companies accredited to an Innovation Hub are entitled to: a corporate tax rate of 15%
Manufacturing companies are entitled to: A corporate tax rate of 15% Import machinery and equipment duty-free Manufacturing companies registered under Schedule 470.03 are entitled to import raw materials duty-free, provided that 100% of output is exported outside the CCA. Companies that sell some of their produce within the CCA pay duty only on those raw materials used to manufacture those goods sold within the CCA (Section 3) .

Source: SADC online information. Viewed at: www.sadc.int/files/8813/9323/6319/Botswana.doc; andhttp://www.bitc.co.bw/incentives-investors.

Botswana has signed several bilateral investment treaties; however, there are only two in force (with Germany and Switzerland) .[51] It has also signed double taxation agreements with Barbados, France, India, Mauritius, Mozambique, Namibia, Seychelles, South Africa, Sweden, United Kingdom, the Russian Federation and Zimbabwe.[52] Similar agreements have been signed with China, Ireland, Swaziland and Zambia but are awaiting ratification; while others with Belgium, Lesotho, Luxembourg and Malawi have been concluded but have not yet been signed.[53] Botswana is a member of the Multilateral Investment Guarantee Agency and of the International Centre for the Settlement of Investment Disputes.[54]

TRADE POLICIES AND PRACTICES

Botswana applies SACU common external tariffs and excise duties, related exemptions and rebates, as well as any contingency trade remedies. Under SACU's provisions for infant industry protection, Botswana imposes additional duties on imports of ultra-heat-treated milk from all sources, it also levies additional duties on flour imports deemed to constitute unfair competition.

Botswana's Customs is using UNCTAD's Automated System for Customs Data (ASYCUDA) with a risk-based inspection system. It has also introduced a post-clearance audit system as a trade facilitation measure. Internal taxes on imports and domestic goods and services consist mainly of value-added tax, fuel and alcohol levies, and a copyright levy introduced in 2009.

Botswana has applied seasonal or temporary quantitative restrictions on imports of dairy products, poultry products, grains and some vegetables, to protect domestic producers. Technical regulations and standards are based on international norms, including those of Botswana's major trading partners, especially South Africa. Exports of cattle are taxed, and the Botswana Meat Commission has a statutory monopoly on beef exports. The textiles and automotive industries have access to import duty credit schemes that are linked to export performance; the schemes are designed to promote exports to non-SACU markets.

4. Botswana applies price preference and reservation schemes in public procurement. The privatization process has slowed in recent years. A competition law is pending, while price controls are maintained on certain goods (petroleum products, water, electricity) and services. Botswana has taken steps to strengthen its intellectual property regime, notably in the area of copyright.

MEASURES DIRECTLY AFFECTING IMPORTS

Under the SACU Agreement, Botswana, Lesotho, Namibia, and Swaziland apply import duties and related measures set by South Africa in consultation with BLNS countries. In practice, ordinary customs duties, excise duties, tariff exemptions and concessions, valuation methods, non-preferential rules of origin, and contingency trade remedies are, so far, the only trade policy measures harmonized throughout SACU (Main Report, Chapter III) .

Registration

Trading licences are issued by the Ministry of Trade and Industry for non-liquor products under the Trade Act, 2003 and for liquor products under the Liquor Act, 2003. Under both acts, a number of activities are reserved for citizens of Botswana or companies wholly owned by citizens of Botswana (Table II.3) .[31]According to the authorities, importer/exporter licences and "specialized dealer's" licences were phased out in May 2008, since such licences were abused by traders for business in the reserved activities, due to lack of appropriate definition of licences. Importers and exporters have since been required to obtain distributor licences, on condition of holding a valid contract with the supplier. The Trade Act and the Liquor Act are under review to improve procedures for obtaining business licences.

Customs procedures

The Botswana United Revenue Service (BURS) is, *inter alia*, responsible for assessing and collecting customs and excise duties, value-added tax, and fuel levies. It also collects flour levies, alcohol levies, road-user charges, and road-safety levies on behalf of other government authorities. All importers (and exporters) with an annual turnover of at least P 20,000 are required to register with the Customs and Excise Division of BURS, and are given a Trader Identification Number (TIN) . Clearing agents are mandatory for commercial imports.[32]

The principal documents required for customs clearance are the customs declaration, commercial invoice, bill of lading (or air waybill), certificate of origin (for goods covered by preferential trade agreements), and packing list. Depending on the nature of the product, a technical conformity/health/veterinary certificate and/or an import permit (licence) may be required.

Customs procedures have been computerized using UNCTAD's ASYCUDA, enabling traders to submit customs declarations electronically (Direct Trader Input) using the single administrative document (SAD) . Imported goods may be subject to inspection using a risk-based system, based on the importer's profile and profile of imports; the selectivity parameters are reviewed from time to time. This system has helped Customs to increase interception of illegal consignments.[33] Customs performs inspections on behalf of, *inter alia*, the Departments for Animal Health and Protection; Water Affairs; Wildlife and National Parks; and the Botswana Police Service. BURS is planning to undertake a time-release study in 2009/10 to assess clearance procedures at port of entry and the average time between arrival of goods and their release.

Botswana does not apply pre-shipment inspection. To facilitate trade, BURS has implemented a post-clearance audit system to verify import and export declarations: 9% of total processed declarations (656,478) were audited in 2006/07. Botswana and Namibia are planning to establish a one-stop border post at the Mamuno-Trans Kalahari border post to reduce transit times (Chapter IV(6)(iii)(a)) .

The customs legislation (the Customs and Excise Duty Act (CAP 50:01) of 1970) was last amended in 2003, to update and align it with the South African Customs and Excise Act. Goods infringing intellectual property rights may be placed under embargo, destroyed or otherwise disposed of. Administrative decisions by Customs can be appealed in Court within three months of the decision.

According to World Bank analyses, Botswana does not perform well on a global scale, in terms of the ease of trading across borders: it is currently ranked 148th among 181 economies (Lesotho 141st; South Africa 147th; Namibia 149th; and Swaziland 154th) .[34] This analysis compares the costs and procedures involved in importing and exporting a standardized cargo of goods by ocean transport.

Other duties, levies, and charges

Botswana exercises its right under the SACU Agreement to levy additional duties in specific cases to protect infant industries; temporary protection may be provided for a maximum of eight years. Since 2007, the dairy industry has received protection through additional duties imposed on imports of ultra-heat-treated (UHT) milk; Botswana imports over half of its fresh milk requirements.[35] Since April 2008, the additional duty has been levied at a rate of 40%; the revenues are deposited in the Common Revenue Pool.

A 15% flour levy is collected on imports of bread flour from all sources with the objective of protecting the domestic milling industry from unfair competition; Botswana does not have an institutional framework to address unfair competition. The flour levy is not shared in the SACU Common Revenue Pool.[36]

Road-user charges and road-safety levies are imposed at the border on foreign-registered vehicles for the purpose of providing revenue for the maintenance of roads, and for road safety campaigns (Chapter IV(6)(iii)(a)) . Receipts from road-user charges amounted to P 48.8 million in 2006/07.

Botswana has notified the WTO Committee on Agriculture that it did not apply the special agricultural safeguard in the period 1997/98 to 2007/08. [37]

(b) Tariff and tax exemptions

Botswana provides tariff exemptions and concessions on imported inputs used for manufacturing (or exporting) goods. All schemes applied by Botswana are harmonized within SACU (Main Report, Chapter III) . Goods imported under such schemes must be taken directly from the port of entry to a customs bonded warehouse. Commercial importers (and exporters) may apply to Botswana United Revenue Service for a licence to operate a bonded warehouse.

(c) Internal taxes

Botswana applies VAT on domestic and imported goods and services, including from SACU members. The standard rate is 10%. Zero-rated items include staple foods (millet grain and meal, wheat, maize cobs, flour, sugar, maize meal, sorghum meal, and Setswana beans); fuel (petrol, diesel, paraffin); and fertilizers, pesticides, farming tractors, and transport services. Goods and services exported from Botswana are also zero-rated. The main VAT-exempt items are financial, educational, and medical services; long-term residential letting (including provision of hostel accommodation on a non-profit basis); leasing or renting of land for erecting a dwelling; and prescription drugs.

The business threshold for VAT registration is an annual turnover above P250,000. The base for levying VAT on imports differs slightly between SACU and non-SACU countries. For non-SACU countries, VAT is levied on the import's landed duty-paid price, i.e. f.o.b. price and import duties, plus the value of any services relating to the good, such as commission, packaging, transportation, and insurance. Imports from SACU members are levied on the greater of their f.o.b. price plus freight and insurance costs (i.e. landed duty-free price), and their transaction value. Botswana has a bond guarantee system for the deferred payment of VAT and customs duties. [38] Goods held in bonded warehouses are not subject to VAT until they are cleared for use.

Imports and domestic sales of petroleum products are subject to a levy (fuel levy) at the rate of P 0.04 per litre.

In 2008, an alcohol levy was introduced at the rate of 30% on imported and locally manufactured liquor. The levy is remitted by BURS to a special fund designed to promote activities to combat alcohol abuse and its effects.

5. On 1 April 2009, Botswana introduced a copyright levy on imported and locally manufactured carrier media (section (4)(iv)) .

(v) Import prohibitions and licensing

There have been few changes to Botswana's import licensing regime since 2003. Import permits are generally required for imports of industrial products from outside SACU, except from Malawi and Zimbabwe. Permits are issued by the Ministry of Trade and Industry (Department of International Trade) .

Prior to obtaining an import permit, imports of agricultural products, plants, livestock, and soil from all sources require approval from the Ministry of Agriculture for sanitary and phytosanitary reasons. Imports of vegetables, dairy products, meat and meat products, and poultry require an import permit on food security grounds. Poultry imports are permitted only when there is a shortfall of poultry products in the domestic market. Import restrictions have also been imposed on grains from time to time to protect local producers. Imports of some vegetables and dairy products are seasonally banned when it is determined that domestic supplies are adequate. Milk imports, including from SACU, are subject to import quotas established on a quarterly basis by a Milk Importation Committee comprising producers and processors.

Imports of firearms and ammunition require a permit for security reasons. Import licences are also required for boats (issued by the Department of Water Affairs), and for imports of second-hand goods, such as motor vehicles and clothing. The Ministry of Environment, Wildlife, and Tourism licenses imports of endangered species covered by the Convention on International Trade in Endangered Species of Wild Fauna and Flora (CITES) .

4. Import prohibitions apply to goods such as narcotic drugs, obscene material, and environmentally hazardous products, such as toxic or radio-active waste, mainly to protect health, safety, and morality.

(vi) Standards and other technical requirements

(a) Technical barriers to trade

The Botswana Bureau of Standards (BOBS), established in 1997 (Standards Act No. 16, 1995), is responsible for preparing and promoting technical regulations and standards on goods, services, and processes. The Bureau, headed by a 12-member Standards Council, is a member of the International Organization for Standardization (ISO) and participates in regional standardization initiatives, including SADC Cooperation in Standardization (SADCSTAN) . It also functions as the national notification authority and national enquiry point under the WTO TBT Agreement. [39]

Botswana has accepted the Code of Good Practice for the Preparation, Adoption and Application of Standards contained in Annex 3 of the WTO TBT Agreement. Standards are based on international norms (e.g. ISO or International Electrotechnical Commission) and those of Botswana's major trading partners, especially South Africa. They are developed in six stages: proposal, drafting, technical committee review, public comment, approval, and publication. Standardization projects are initiated through requests from interested parties (including technical committee members, government departments, consumers, manufacturers, BOBS, individuals) . The Bureau of Standards evaluates the requests and makes recommendations to the Standards Council for priority areas, on the basis of which the Council approves annual work programmes. Draft standards are reviewed by technical committees and circulated for public comment. Accepted comments are incorporated and draft standards are sent to the Standards Council for approval. The public has a two-month period to comment on draft standards. In the case of a technical regulation, the public notice must contain full details of the "mandatory standard"; it does not become effective until the date specified in the notice, which must not be less than two months after the date of publication (Section 19 of the Standards Act) . In principle, all product standards that affect health, safety, and the environment are mandatory, such as on dairy products, animal feeds, and electrical appliances. Botswana has seven technical regulations (mandatory standards), which are revised periodically. Violations of mandatory standards are liable to a fine of P 5,000 and imprisonment of three years (Section 14 of the Standards Act) .

The Standards (Import Inspection) Regulations of 2008, implemented since 1 April 2009, require a pre-arrival compliance certificate from the Bureau of Standards for imports of designated products. [40] The certificate is issued by the Bureau of Standards or a recognized certifying body to attest compliance with a Botswana or foreign technical regulation recognized by the Bureau of Standards (Article 6) . Imports that are not covered by a certificate issued by the relevant authority in the exporting country are sampled at the border to determine compliance; non-compliant imports are re-exported at the expense of the importers, or otherwise disposed of. [41]

Botswana's conformity testing infrastructure is limited: there are three accredited laboratories in Botswana. The Bureau of Standards is in the process of equipping its laboratories with adequate testing facilities; it relies on private laboratories to test products. Botswana recognizes foreign test results from accredited testing laboratories.

Botswana has not signed any mutual recognition agreements, but is collaborating with SADC countries to develop a regional body for accreditation of conformity assessment facilities (SADCAS), which would allow mutual recognition among all members. The Botswana National Accreditation Focal Point (BNAFP) was launched in August 2007 as a link to SADCAS, to facilitate the elimination of technical barriers to trade among SADC members, in the region and with other regional blocs. [42] Under Article 28 of 2002 SACU Agreement, Botswana and other members have agreed to strive to harmonize product standards and technical regulations (Main Report, Chapter II(2)(v)) .

(b) Sanitary and phytosanitary (SPS) measures

The Ministry of Health is responsible for food safety, and is advised by the National Food Control Board. The Board, established under the Food Control Act of 1993, comprises government officials from a number of ministries, including the Ministries of Health, and Agriculture.

The Ministry of Agriculture (through the Departments of Crop Production and Veterinary Services) is responsible for the implementation of veterinary and phytosanitary measures. The Ministry is also the national enquiry point, and notification authority on SPS matters. However, the last notification submitted by Botswana under the SPS Agreement dates back to 1997. [43]

3. Foot-and-mouth disease (FMD) is endemic in northern Botswana. The virus is carried by wild buffalos roaming freely in the northern game reserves and national parks; for this reason, it is considered that complete freedom from FMD is practically impossible in Botswana. [44] Outbreaks of FMD are considered a national disaster. There were no outbreaks between 1980 and 2001 but since 2002 outbreaks have occurred every year, except in 2004. The last outbreak occurred in the district of Ghanzi on 23 October 2008, leading to the temporary suspension of meat exports.

Disease prevention and control is based on the Diseases of Animals Act of 1977 (as amended), under which FMD is a notifiable disease requiring any person who suspects or has reason to suspect the disease to report it immediately. Botswana has moved from a control policy of destruction of the affected herds (applied until 2002) to a policy based on strict border controls, quarantine, vaccination in high-risk areas, and regionalization. The policy has been shaped by OIE recommendations and standards. About two thirds of the country is FMD-free without vaccination; elsewhere, bovine animals are vaccinated against FMD. As part of the disease control strategy, the country is divided into fenced-off control zones. The Government also maintains quarantine points for animal movements (Chapter IV(2)(iii)) .

The use of hormonal growth promoters in livestock and of animal protein in livestock feed are prohibited. Residues of antibiotics, heavy metals, and pesticides in meat and milk are monitored to ensure they do not exceed maximum allowable levels.

Measures to prevent the introduction and spread of pests and plant diseases are governed by the Plant Diseases and Pests Act of 1959 (as amended) . A permit is required for imports of plants. Imported plants and plant products are subject to inspection at approved ports of entry and may be destroyed if necessary, and premises may be quarantined. [46]

The Plant Diseases and Pest Act has been superseded by the Plant Protection Act of 2007, which entered into force on 1 April 2009. Under the new Act, a National Plant Protection Organisation (NPPO) is to be established whose main functions include implementing the International Plant Protection Convention and international phytosanitary standards; issuing phytosanitary and import certificates; inspecting and certifying consignments for export; establishing auditing and traceability procedures; and notifying phytosanitary measures in accordance with international obligations. While Botswana is not yet a signatory to the International Plant Protection Convention, instruments of adherence were submitted to the FAO in April 2009.

Botswana is also in the process of adopting a regulatory framework for biotechnology products, including genetically modified organisms. Overall, Botswana's SPS regime has insufficient capacity to provide adequate plant protection services. [47]

GOVERNMENT PROCUREMENT

Botswana's procurement policy is driven by the objective of ensuring competition, fairness, value for money, efficiency, transparency, and accountability in the management of tenders. At the same time, the policy seeks to assist the economic empowerment of Botswana citizens through reservation and preference schemes. Botswana is not a member nor observer of the WTO Plurilateral Agreement on Government Procurement.

Public procurement by central government entities is governed by the Public Procurement and Asset Disposal Act of 2001, and the Public Procurement and Asset Disposal Regulations of 2006. The law applies to the procurement of works, services, and supplies.[48] As part of efforts to curb corruption in public procurement, the Local Authorities Procurement and Asset and Disposal Bill was passed in July 2008; this authorizes the Ministry of Local Government to monitor the procurement by local authorities.[49]

Since 2003, public procurement at central government level has been managed by the Public Procurement and Asset Disposal Board (PPADB), an independent seven-member body appointed by the Minister of Finance and Development Planning.[50] PPADP has a pre-eminent role in Botswana: its Board awards tenders for infrastructure projects and services that are financed by the Government's development budget; the development budget totalled P 7.2 billion in 2007/08. The PPADP also has a role in the privatization of state-owned enterprises (see section (4)(ii)) .

The procuring entities under the supervision of PPADB are the District Administrative Tender Committees (DATCs), Ministerial Tender Committees (MTCs), and a Special Procurement and Asset Disposal Committee; ad hoc committees may also be established. As of 1 April 2008, the tendering thresholds were P 500,000 for DATCs and P 5 million for MTCs. The PPADB is required to examine, at least once a year, the business practices and compliance of each procuring entity. The PPADB is audited by the Auditor General, and its performance is reviewed by an independent advisory body appointed by the Minister. A first version of an operations manual was published in July 2008 to assist procurement staff and to establish a standardized national approach to public procurement activities.[51] The specification of brands in government tenders is not permitted.

The following procurement methods are used at central government level: (i) open domestic bidding; (ii) open international bidding; (iii) restricted domestic bidding; (iv) restricted international domestic bidding; (v) quotation proposal procurement; (vi) micro procurement; and (vii) direct procurement. The appropriate tender method in each case is selected by PPADB.

Under open domestic tenders, participation of foreign companies registered in Botswana is permitted but reservation/preferences schemes may apply. Open international bidding must be used for contracts above P 50 million. Tenders exceeding a value of P 100,000 are published in the *Botswana Government Gazette*, in local newspapers and on the Government's central website. [52] Pre-qualification is used under open bidding procedures to obtain a short-list of bidders with proven capability and the resources to perform the contract satisfactorily. The pre-qualification period is advertised and open to all bidders for at least 14 days. The PPADB publishes pre-qualification lists and newly registered contractors. The minimum bidding periods are: six weeks for open international bidding, four weeks for open domestic bidding, and two weeks for a selective tendering. Standardized bidding packages are available for works, supplies, and services.

Under restricted domestic tenders, bids are solicited from a limited number of potential suppliers. Restricted domestic bidding is used where the supplies, works or services are available only from a limited number of providers; or where there is insufficient time for an open bidding procedure due to an emergency situation or other exceptional circumstances. The quotation proposal method requires that bids are sought from at least five suppliers; this is used when there is insufficient time for an open or restricted bidding procedure due to an emergency situation, or other exceptional circumstances. In micro procurement (up to a threshold of P 20,000), the supplier is selected without competition; under this procedure, there is no bidding documentation, written bid, or signed contract. In direct procurement, the supplier is selected without competition, e.g. where there is insufficient time for other procurement methods due to an emergency situation; the supplies, works or services are available from only one provider; an existing procurement contract is extended; additional supplies, works or services are required to be compatible with existing ones; or it is advantageous or necessary to purchase from the original supplier to ensure continuity. [53]

Bid evaluation, which is the responsibility of the procuring entities, is based on one of the following methods: (i) quality- and cost-based selection; (ii) quality-based selection; (iii) fixed-budget selection; (iv) least-cost selection; and (v) qualification selection. For works, the quality and cost method, or the least-cost method are used; for supplies, the least-cost method, and for services, any of the above methods may be used. Following the bid evaluation, procuring entity makes a recommendation to PPADB for adjudication and approval based on an assessment of cost and technical merit, and citizen participation considerations (reservation and preference schemes) . Award decisions by PPADB are published in the *Government Daily News* and on the PPADB website, and distributed to District Commissioners' offices country-wide.

The Independent Complaints Review Committee, established in November 2004, deals with complaints against tender awards and other grievances by bidders. Administrative decisions may subsequently be challenged before the High Court. Numerous PPADB decisions have been challenged in court. [54]

Botswana has reservation and price preference schemes in place that have the effect of discriminating between domestic and foreign-owned goods, services or suppliers. [55] Botswana-citizen-owned companies benefit from a price preference margin over foreign companies in the range of 2-5%. [56] Price preferences may also be capped to meet the dual objectives of citizen empowerment and of value-for-money in government procurement (for example, for information technology and consulting services, the maximum preference allowed is P 100,000) . [57] No reservation or preference is permitted in open international bidding for contracts over P 50 million.

The Local Procurement Programme (LPP) was renewed in August 2004 and expanded by a Presidential Directive on the Use of Locally Manufactured Goods and Services. [58] The Directive instructs the central government, local authorities, and parastatals to procure 30% of annual public purchases of goods and services from locally registered manufacturers and service providers. [59] The programme applies to tenders of up to P 300,000. Eligible firms, local or foreign, must register annually with the Ministry of Trade and Industry (Department of Industrial Affairs): the registration list is used by procuring entities as a source of information on the availability of locally produced goods and services. The firms must be properly licensed, and their products must meet the Botswana Bureau of Standards and other requirements.

Issues of concern with regard to the LPP are the lack of quality certification of many goods and services, and the limited availability or high price of locally manufactured goods and services; some local suppliers may end up importing finished goods, while service providers may subcontract to foreign service providers. [60]

Reservation and price preference schemes are also implemented by the Ministry of Works and Transport for locally manufactured building and construction products; by the Ministry of Finance and Development Planning for citizen-owned consultancy companies and information technology providers; and by the Ministry of Health for citizen-owned companies manufacturing and/or supplying medicines, laboratory reagents, medical equipment, and related medical supplies. [61]

LOCAL-CONTENT REQUIREMENTS

1. Local-content requirements are an important element of Botswana's government procurement policy. As part of a "Buy Botswana" campaign, a task force (comprising the Government, the Botswana Confederation of Commerce, Industry, and Manpower (BOCCIM), and the private sector) has been established with the aim of opening outlets for local suppliers.

(ix) Other measures

1. Botswana has no official countertrade or offset arrangements, or agreements designed to influence the quantity or value of goods and services exported to Botswana. Botswana has no trade sanctions in force.

2. Botswana maintains strategic reserve stocks in grains and petroleum products. The Botswana Agricultural Marketing Board holds grain reserves, which are estimated to cover 240 days of domestic consumption of sorghum, and 75 days of maize (Chapter IV(2)(ii)) . Under the Government's Oil Storage Development Programme, strategic fuel storage facilities, constructed at Gaborone and Francistown, maintain stocks equivalent to 90 days of national consumption.

MEASURES DIRECTLY AFFECTING EXPORTS

(i) Registration and taxes

1. The same registration procedures apply to importers and exporters (section (2)(ii) above) . An export declaration is required for all commercial exports.

2. The Cattle Export and Slaughter Levy Act 10 of 2005 provides for the imposition of a levy per head of cattle exported from Botswana or slaughtered at the Botswana Meat Corporation, municipal abattoirs, private abattoirs, and butchers. The levy rate is currently P 10 per animal; a fine of P 300 per head, a term of two months imprisonment or both are imposed for exporting or attempting to export cattle without paying the levy (Chapter IV(2)(iii)) .

(ii) Export prohibitions, restrictions, and licensing

Licences are required for all exports, including to other SACU members, for food security, sanitary and phytosanitary, and statistical reasons, and under international conventions to which Botswana is a signatory. Under the Control of Livestock Industry Act of 1941 (as amended), exports of livestock and animal products are subject to a permit issued by the Director of the Veterinary Service. In addition, exports of wild animals or their products (trophy or meat) require a permit from the Department of Wildlife and National Parks.

Exports of rough diamonds have been affected by the terms of commercial agreements governing the sale of diamonds by Debswana (currently Botswana's only diamond producer, in which the Government holds a 50% stake with De Beers) to the London-based Diamond Trading Company (DTC), an international cartel operated by De Beers, through which virtually Debswana's entire output is distributed (Chapter IV(3)(i)) .

Botswana is a founding member of the United Nations' Kimberley Process Certification Scheme (KPCS), launched on 1 January 2003. [62] This requires, *inter alia*, all rough diamonds exported from Botswana to have a valid Kimberley Process Certificate issued by the competent authority (all imports must also have a valid certificate issued by the exporting country) . [63] Under a peer review conducted in 2004, Botswana was judged a "role model" in implementing the Kimberley Process. [64] Kimberley Process Certificates are issued by the Ministry of Minerals, Energy, and Water Resources (Mineral Affairs Division) .

Exports of unprocessed (uncut) semi-precious stones are prohibited to ensure processing in Botswana.

(iii) Export subsidies, finance, and assistance

Under the 1969 and 2002 SACU agreements, SACU members agreed to harmonize their duty and tax concessions on imports (Main Report, Chapter III(3)(v)), but competition among governments in the region to provide incentives for investment and exports remains fierce. The Government of Botswana is in the process of developing special economic zones.

Furthermore, Botswana operates two industry-specific import duty credit schemes linked to export performance, which are designed to promote exports to non-SACU markets (the Duty Credit Certificate scheme for textiles and clothing, and the Motor Industry Development Programme (MIDP) for the automobile industry (Main Report, Chapter III) .

Duty drawback is available on capital equipment and manufactured inputs used for exports outside of SACU. Claims must be made within six months of the date of export and are settled within three months.

Unlike South Africa and other SADC countries, Botswana does not provide concessional trade finance or credit, but it offers export credit insurance. [65] The parastatal Botswana Export Credit Insurance and Guarantee Company (BECI) provides export credit insurance for exporters of local or foreign ownership. The company was established in 1996 as a wholly owned subsidiary of the Botswana Development Corporation, and is a member of the Prague Club of the Berne Union. [66] BECI offers insurance against non-payment by foreign buyers resulting from commercial risk (default and insolvency) and political risk (transfer delays, strikes, war or import restrictions that prevent entry in the buying country) . [67] It covers up to 85% of commercial risks and up to 90% of political risks. Goods and services are eligible. Exports covered in 2007-08 included mainly steel, paper bags, tobacco, construction material, leather, textiles, agricultural products, and motor parts. The Government has reinsured political risks since 1997 (Political Risk Reinsurance Act 1997), while commercial risks are reinsured by the private reinsurance market.

Export promotion is mainly the responsibility of the Botswana Export Development and Investment Authority (BEDIA), established in 1998. It arranges participation of manufacturing enterprises in regional and international exhibitions, and facilitates buyer-seller contacts. It also conducts overseas market research aimed at finding export markets for Botswana-made products. In 2007, BEDIA launched an export development programme aimed at improving exporters' marketing and promotion skills, targeted, in particular, at the apparel, handicraft, leather and products, and agricultural products (mainly beef) subsectors. [68]

Botswana notified the WTO Committee on Agriculture that it did not provide any agricultural export subsidies during the financial years 1997/98 to 2007/08. [69]

MEASURES AFFECTING PRODUCTION AND TRADE

(i) Incentives

Botswana has one of lowest corporate tax rates in the region. [70] The standard company tax rate is 25%; manufacturing companies registered in Botswana approved by the Minister of Finance and Development Planning, and offshore financial services companies are subject to a reduced rate of 15%. The taxation regimes for large diamond projects may be negotiated on a case-by-case basis and the tax agreements are subject to ratification by Parliament (Chapter IV(3)(i))) . Botswana does not provide special tax incentives for companies that export, except offshore financial services companies.

The Minister of Finance and Development Planning may also authorize Development Approval Orders granting tax relief, such as tax holidays for 5-10 years, and/or education training grants for specific projects. Such projects must benefit the economy or contribute to the economic advancement of citizens. Applications are assessed on a case-by-case basis according to the applicants' job-creation prospects, training plans for citizens, plans to localize non-citizen positions, citizen participation in management, citizens' equity, investment location, effects on other economic activities, and effects on reducing consumer prices. The instrument to attract investment through Development Approval Orders has been used sparingly.

The Government funds a number of assistance schemes to promote the economic empowerment of Botswana's citizens. The Citizen Entrepreneurial Development Agency

(CEDA), established in 2001, provides, *inter alia*, training, mentoring, and concessional loans to citizen-owned businesses. The CEDA was allocated P 15.6 million in the 2007/08 Budget.

The CEDA Credit Guarantee Scheme was established to address the difficulties of small, micro, and medium enterprises (SMMEs) with limited securities in obtaining bank loans. Participating loans institutions are guaranteed 75% of the net loss on loans provided to SMMEs; the loan threshold is P 4 million. CEDA provides concessional loans at 5% interest rate for loans up to P 500,000 and at 7.5% for loans up to P 4 million (with repayment periods up to 15 years) .

In 2003, CEDA established a Venture Capital Fund to provide equity to citizen-owned enterprises and joint ventures between citizens and foreign investors. [71] In 2007, CEDA started operating the Young Farmers' Fund, which provides subsidized loans and training to young agricultural producers (Chapter IV(2)(ii)) .

(ii) State-trading, state-owned enterprises, and privatization

Botswana notified the WTO in 1997 that it had no state-trading enterprises within the meaning of Article XVII:4(a) of the GATT 1994. [72] However, the Botswana Meat Commission has a statutory monopoly on beef exports (Chapter IV(2)(iii)) . [73] The monopoly of the Botswana Agricultural Marketing Board over imports and exports of staple food products (designated grains, oilseeds, and pulses) was eliminated in 1991 and trade was opened to competition from the private sector (Chapter IV(2)(ii)) . Debwana, the diamond mining company, holds a *de facto* monopoly over exports of rough diamonds (Chapter IV(3)(i)) .

Botswana has a number of state-owned enterprises (parastatals) (Table III.1), including *de facto* or *de jure*monopolies that provide public utilities, e.g. electricity, certain telecommunications, and other services, such as air and rail transport. [74] Many private firms have indirect state ownership through equity investments by the commercially run Botswana Development Corporation. [75]

State participation in parastatals and commercial enterprises, 2008

	State equity participation, 2008[a]		Main activities	Privatization scenario
	(P million)	(%)		
Non-financial enterprises				
Air Botswana	35.0	100	Air transport services	Planned management contract, then divestiture
Banyana Pty Ltd.		100	Commercial cattle ranch	Planned divestiture
BCL	5,027.7	..	Copper/nickel mining (commercial joint	n.a.

			venture)	
Botswana Agricultural Marketing Board	30.5	100	Import/export, marketing, and storage of selected agricultural products; and sale of agricultural services and inputs	Planned divestiture
Botswana Housing Corporation	250.2	100	Property development	None
Botswana Meat Commission	0.2	100	Cattle abattoir; canning and tanning; beef export; and transport	Planned outsourcing of non-core services
Botswana Postal Services	38.4	100	Postal services	Planned restructuring
Botswana Power Corporation	145.6	100	Electricity generation, transmission, and distribution	Planned restructuring
Botswana Railways	696.5	100	Rail transport services	Planned restructuring
Botswana Telecommunications Corporation	21.0	100	Telecommunications services	Planned divestiture
Botswana Vaccine Institute	8.3	100	Production and marketing of vaccines	Completed corporatization and partial divestiture
Debswana	542.1	50	Diamond mining (commercial joint venture)	n.a.
DTC Botswana	..	50	Diamond sorting, valuation, cutting, and polishing (commercial joint venture)	n.a.
Soda Ash Botswana Ltd.	65.8	..	Commercial mining company	n.a.

Tati Nickel Mining Co.	..	15	Copper/nickel mining (commercial joint venture)	n.a.
Water Utilities Corporation	752.7	100	Provision of water to urban centres	Planned restructuring
Financial services				
Botswana Building Society	..	100	Property finance	Planned divestiture
Botswana Development Corporation	535.2	100	Development finance	Planned restructuring
Botswana Motor Vehicles Accidents Fund	..	100	Insurance services	None
Botswana Savings Bank	19.7	100	Banking services	Planned restructuring
Government Employees Motor Vehicle and Residential Property Advance Scheme	..	100	Loan guarantee fund	Planned management contract
Guaranteed Loans Insurance Fund	..	100	Insurance fund	Completed management contract
National Development Bank	77.7	100	Development finance	Planned divestiture

Source: Bank of Botswana (2009), *Annual Report 2008*; and information provided by the Botswana authorities.

The government announced a privatization policy in 2000, with the aim of, *inter alia*, promoting competition, improving efficiency and productivity of enterprises, and relieving the financial and administrative burden of the State in providing services and investments in infrastructure.[76] A key element of the policy is the promotion of citizen participation in the ownership of national assets. Foreign participation in privatization is encouraged and any restrictions on foreign ownership are to be decided on a case-by-case basis. Where ownership of privatized companies is limited to Botswana citizens, foreign participation would be through management contracts and franchising. Concessions such as build-operate-transfer (BOT) or build-own-operate-transfer (BOOT) would be considered in cases where foreign expertise and technology are needed. The

Government would also consider retaining a "golden share" to counter any perceived risk of foreign control of privatized enterprises.

4. Botswana Privatisation Asset Holdings, a state-owned company, was established to hold portions of the assets of privatized entities that are reserved for later sale to Botswana citizens and citizen-owned companies. The autonomous Public Enterprises Evaluation and Privatization Agency (PEEPA) was established to oversee privatization and monitor the performance of public enterprises. It reports to the Minister of Finance and Development Planning and has prepared a master plan and identified priorities for privatization. [77]Privatization methods include commercialization, corporatization, management contracts, franchising, leases, concessions, joint ventures, and stock market flotation. The bidding process would be managed by the Public Procurement and Asset Disposal Board (PPADB) (section (2)(vi)) .

5. There has been little privatization in Botswana. Priority candidates for privatization through divestiture include Air Botswana, the Botswana Telecommunications Corporation, the National Development Bank and the Botswana Vaccine Institute (Table III.1) . The privatization of Air Botswana has been suspended and the Government has decided to recapitalize the company, to create a viable national carrier (Chapter IV(6)(iii)(c)); privatization of Botswana Telecommunications Corporation is ongoing; and privatization of National Development Bank is at the planning stage. The Government has partially divested the State's stake in the Botswana Vaccine Institute, through the sale of preference shares, but intends to maintain a majority stake because it considers the production of vaccines for the livestock industry to be of a strategic nature.

(iii) Competition policy and price controls

Under the SACU Agreement of 2002 (Article 40 and 41), members are encouraged to develop competition policies. The need for competition rules has long been recognized in Botswana, especially in a post-privatization environment where a public utility is transferred to the private sector. In 2005, Parliament approved a competition policy framework as a basis for a competition law. [79] The Competition Bill was approved by Cabinet, in April 2009, to be submitted for approval by Parliament. The act would prohibit, *inter alia*, anti-competitive practices, unless warranted by public interest (when welfare gains to society outweigh the costs of anti-competitive behaviour) . A Competition Authority would be established to oversee implementation of the law. All sector-specific regulatory bodies, such as the Botswana Telecommunications Authority or professional associations, would be covered by the new competition law but not infrastructural facilities of public utilities, nor intellectual property matters. Sector-specific competition rules exist, for example in the telecommunications subsector (Chapter IV(6)(ii)) .

In the absence of a general competition law, the Ministry of Trade and Industry (Department of Trade and Consumer Affairs) is mandated to protect consumers against unfair business practices on the basis of the Consumer Protection Act of 1998. [80] The Department's role is confined to education, investigation, mediation, and negotiation on behalf of consumers; consumer matters that are related, for example, to the Food Control Act, Public Health Act, Hire Purchase Act, Standards Act, or Trade Act, are the responsibility of specialized regulatory agencies.

Price controls are currently applied by the Government at the retail level and on profit margins for petroleum products (Control of Goods, Prices, and Other Charges Act) . All petroleum products are imported, mainly from South Africa, and the Government believes that price controls are necessary due to the limited number of suppliers. The Petroleum Management Unit, responsible for the price controls, has been transferred from the Ministry of Trade and Industry to the Ministry of Minerals, Energy, and Water Resources. Other goods and services subject to administered prices (as of 8 January 2007) include water; electricity; train, certain bus, and taxi fares; certain mail and parcel delivery; and telephone installation and certain telephone tariffs.

(iv) Protection of intellectual property rights

1. Botswana has taken steps to strengthen its intellectual property regime, notably in the area of copyright. Since its last TPR in 2003, it has become a party to a number of WIPO-administered intellectual property conventions (Table III.2) . Botswana is a member of the World Intellectual Property Organization (WIPO), and a founding member of the African Regional Intellectual Property Organization. The Office of the Registrar of Companies and Intellectual Property (a Department within the Ministry of Trade and Industry) is responsible for administering intellectual property laws. The Office of the Registrar houses the national IPR enquiry point, which was established in September 2006. However, Botswana has not yet notified to the WTO any contact point under the TRIPS Agreement. [81]

Botswana's participation in intellectual property agreements, 2009

	Date of membership
Intellectual property protection agreements[a]	
Paris Convention for the Protection of Industrial Property in the 1967 Act of Stockholm (Paris Union)	15 April 1998
Berne Convention for the Protection of Literary and Artistic Works in the Act of Paris of 24 July 1971	15 April 1998
WIPO Copyright Treaty (Geneva, 1996)	27 January 2005
WIPO Performances and Phonograms Treaty (Geneva, 1996)	27 January 2005
Global protection agreements[b]	
Patent Cooperation Treaty (Washington 1970, as amended in 1979 and modified in 1984)	30 October 2003
Hague Agreement for the International Registration of Industrial Designs (1999)	5 December 2006
Madrid Agreement concerning the International Registration of Marks in the 1969 Act of Stockholm (Madrid Union)	5 December 2006

a Treaties that define internationally agreed basic standards of intellectual property protection in each country.
b Treaties that ensure that one international registration or filing will have effect in any of the signatory states.
Source: WIPO online information. Viewed at: http://www.wipo.int .

(b) Copyright

1. The Copyright and Neighbouring Rights Act (CAP 68:02), implemented since 2007, protects literary, artistic and musical works embodied in films, sound recordings, broadcasts and published editions, by providing exclusive rights to the owner as required by the Berne

Convention. Computer programs, databases or compilations of data are protected as literary works. Performers also have exclusive rights to broadcast or communicate to the public, to make fixations and reproductions. Copyright is protected for the life of the author plus 50 years. Performers and producers of sound recordings receive the same protection. Rental rights are recognized, and specified according to the type of work, such as for phonograms, computer programs, databases, and cinematographic works. Exemptions or limitations to exclusive rights include reproduction and importation for personal purposes.

2. The Copyright Society of Botswana (a non-profit organization) was established in June 2008 to develop rules and regulations to ensure protection of right-holders and to set royalties in accordance with international standards. Royalties will be payable at a rate of 15% for non-residents for the use of, or rights to, copyrights, patents, trademarks, and secret formulas.

3. A copyright levy was introduced on 1 April 2009 on imported and locally manufactured blank sound and audiovisual carriers, compact discs, and equipment capable of being used to copy protected materials. [82] The levy of 1-2% of the sales price is designated to compensate right-holders for unauthorized copying of their works, as well as for training and public awareness campaigns. Furthermore, all sound and audiovisual recordings on sale in Botswana must have an anti-piracy device (i.e. a tamper-proof sticker or hologram) affixed to it, to enable consumers to distinguish between genuine and fake products. It is sold to the owner of the copyright or persons authorized by the owner of the copyright work to sell, rent, lend or otherwise distribute the work. [83]

4. The right holder (including the licensee) may seek civil remedies and criminal sanctions against infringements in Botswana's courts. Relief may take the form of injunctions restraining illegal activity and impounding or destruction of illegal works. Imports of unauthorized reproductions of any works relating to copyright are unlawful under the copyright legislation, which requires customs officials to use their powers under the Customs and Excise Duty Act to prohibit or destroy illegal imports. [84] Copyright infringements are prescribed as criminal offences subject to penalties of imprisonment and/or fines, of up to ten years and P 20,000 for first offence, and of up to ten years and from P 30,000 to P 5 million for subsequent convictions.

(c) Industrial property rights

1. Industrial Property Law No. 14 of 1996, last amended in 1997 (Industrial property (Amendment) Act No. 19) [85], provides protection for patents, trade marks, industrial designs, and utility models. Any decision of the intellectual property Registrar or the Minister can be appealed to the High Court.

Patents

1. Patents cover inventions, whether products or processes, provided they are new, involve an inventive step, and have an industrial application. Patent protection is for 20 years from the filing date. [86] The legislation provides for exclusions from patentability, including discoveries; scientific theories and mathematical methods; literary, dramatic, musical or artistic work; schemes or methods of doing business; computer programs; and surgical or diagnostic methods for treatment of humans or animals. Patent holders have exclusive rights over making, selling and importing products, which are enforceable in the courts. There are specific limited exceptions to exclusive rights, such as experimental acts relating to a patented invention and right of prior use done in good faith. Patent applications are received by the Registrar; foreign applicants are required to submit applications through a local agent. Applications are examined by the African Regional Intellectual Property Organization and granted by the intellectual property Registrar in

Botswana. The cost of international application through the Patent Corporation Treaty is estimated at about US$1,600-1,800. [87]

2. The Government may authorize compulsory non-exclusive licences (without the holder's consent), predominantly for domestic supply, when deemed to be in the public interest or to remedy anti-competitive behaviour by the right holder, subject to payment of "equitable remuneration". Public interest covers national security, nutrition, health or the development of other vital sectors. Compulsory licences may also be issued if the patent has been insufficiently used in Botswana, or is not being "supplied on reasonable terms", as determined by the High Court. Legal action is only possible where the applicant has taken "all reasonable steps" and failed to acquire the licence "on reasonable terms", and after four years from the date of filing of the patent application or three years from when the patent was granted, whichever expired last. Imports are considered as "working a patent"; compulsory licences cannot be granted where the product is being imported, since the legislation allows a licence to be granted only where the market is not being supplied on reasonable terms. To date, no compulsory licences have been issued by Botswana.

3. The proposed Industrial Property (Amendment) Bill, 2009 is to cover the matter of parallel importation; it will also cover importation of patented products by the Government or third parties in relation to generic pharmaceutical products.

4. Remedies available to the right holder include damages or profits derived from the infringement, injunctions restraining the illegal activity, and destruction of illegal works. Criminal penalties comprise fines of between P 2 million and P 5 million and/or imprisonment of six months to two years.

Trade marks

1. Botswana's industrial property legislation (CAP 68:03) protects trade marks and services marks. A mark is defined as covering any visible sign capable of distinguishing goods and services of an enterprise. The law also protects well known marks by preventing registration of identical or confusingly similar marks. The determination whether a mark is well known depends on the extent of advertisement featuring of the mark, and the degree of popular awareness of the mark among consumers through submission of surveys and statements by customers.

2. Foreign applicants are required to submit applications to the Registrar through a local agent. Applications are published for a three-month opposition period; it takes five months to register a trade mark in Botswana. Once granted, trade marks are protected for ten years, and are renewable indefinitely every ten years, provided the mark has been used for a minimum of three years from the time of registration. Botswana applies (but has not signed) the Nice Agreement concerning the International Classification of Goods and Services for the purposes of the Registration of Marks (Geneva 1977/1979) .

3. The registered owner of a trade mark may take court action against unauthorized use. Civil remedies include damages or profits derived from the infringement, injunctions against illegal use, and destruction of infringing products. Criminal penalties also apply to illegal use of trade marks in accordance with Section 76(6) of the Industrial Property Act.

Industrial designs

1. The legislation extends protection of industrial designs in line with the Locarno Agreement Establishing an International Classification for Industrial Designs, although Botswana has not signed the convention. Textile designs are covered. International registration of an industrial

design may be requested at WIPO or the Registrar in Botswana. The registered owner of a design has exclusive rights of use, including importation. There are no provisions for issuing compulsory licences. Registered industrial designs are protected for 15 years (5 years initially, renewable twice) . The owner of a registered design may seek civil remedies for illegal use by way of damages, or profits derived from infringements, injunctions against illegal activity, and destruction of infringing products.

Other industrial property rights

1. Botswana has not yet developed legislation on geographical indications, layout designs (topographies) of integrated circuits or protection of undisclosed information, including trade secrets.

2. The current Industrial Property Act provides no specific protection for micro-organisms, non-essentially-biological or microbiological processes. However, the proposed amendment bill excludes plants, animals, and essentially biological processes from patentability. A sui generis system of protection for new plant varieties is being developed by the Ministry of Agriculture.

(d) Enforcement of intellectual property rights

1. Imports of illegal products are regulated by the customs legislation; those infringing trade marks or patents may be suspended pending legal action. Such legal action takes place in Botswana's ordinary civil courts, and may involve criminal prosecution and damages, injunctions, and destruction of illegal works. Courts may order interlocutory or temporary injunctions pending final judgement. In order to obtain evidence, the High Court may also instruct its legal officer to enter the premises of the alleged infringer to seize the offending material and equipment (the "Anton Piller Order") . Only the police have ex officio powers under the copyright and industrial property legislation.

BOTSWANA TAXATION SYSTEM - STRATEGIC INFORMATION AND DEVELOPMENTS

BASIC INFORMATION

Botswana - a former British colony in South Africa. Now it is one of the most prominent countries on the black continent: a strong economy, one of the most developed banking systems, as well as a stable representative democracy. Botswana is the 4th highest GDP among African countries. The government encourages the development of the economy, creating favorable conditions for investment and setting a low tax rate.

Businesses in Botswana are taxed only on the income which is received within the country. The Botswana companies are subject to 4 main taxes: corporate tax, VAT, customs and excise duties.The basic rate of corporation tax for resident and non-resident companies is 25%. Reduced rate of 15% and a rate of 0% applicable to companies BITC (Botswana Investment and Trade Centre).Moreover, investors are creating a company in Botswana, which promotes social and economic development of the country can use preferential treatment under the name Development Approval Order, which establishes the tax rate of 0% for a period of 5 to 10 years.

MINING COMPANIES TAXATION

Profits form mining activities, excluding profits from diamond mining, are taxed by applying the following formula:

Annual tax rate = 70 minus (1,500/x)

'x' in the above formula represents the taxable income as a percentage of gross income. Please note that the tax rate cannot be less than 22% (the CIT rate) and is normally a rate between 22% and 55%. Diamond mining is generally taxed in accordance with the terms of a specific agreement agreed with the Botswana government

Other tax rates that apply to certain profits or income are as follows:

• The corporate income tax rate applying to non-resident companies is 30%

• Foreign dividends are taxed at 15%

• Other taxable income is taxed at a rate of 22%

• Taxable income of an Accredited Innovation Hub (AIH) business is taxed at 15%

CAPITAL GAINS TAX

Capital gains tax applies to companies and individuals.

• The capital gains tax rate for companies is 22%, the same rate as the CIT rate.

• Individuals are subject to a progressive capital tax rate up to a maximum rate applying to capital gains over BWP 144,000.

From (BWP)	To (BWP)	Tax liability
0	18,000	0%
18,001	72,000	BWP 0 + 5% of excess over BWP 18,000
72,001	108,000	BWP 2,700 + 12.50% of excess over BWP 72,000
108,001	144,000	BWP 7,200 + 18.75% of excess over BWP 108,000
144,001	---	BWP 13,950 + 25% of excess over 144,000

Capital gains on moveable properties are arrived at by taking the gross sales price less indexed acquisition costs, improvement costs, and transaction costs. If an individual or company disposes of shares only 75% of the gain is taxable i.e. a 25% reduction applies.

CAPITAL ALLOWANCES

The rates of straight line annual capital allowances on plant or machinery range between 10% and 25%.

Rate Asset Detail

10% - Furniture and fittings including soft furnishings

15% - Other plant or machinery including farming equipment

25% - Heavy plant or machinery used in construction

25% - Motor vehicles and aircraft (limited to BWP 175,000 for passenger motor vehicles)

25% - Plant or machinery used directly in manufacturing or production

25% - Computer hardware

100% - Computer software - off the shelf

Statutory straight line allowances are as follows:

Rate Asset Detail

25.0% - Industrial buildings - initial allowance

2.5% - Industrial buildings - annual allowances

2.5% - Commercial buildings - annual allowances

100% - Farm buildings, improvements, water supplies and other farm capital works

BUSINESS AND EMPLOYMENT INCOME RATES:

Earnings (BWP) Tax

0 – 36,000 BWP 0

36,001 – 72,000 BWP 0 + 5% over BWP 36,000

72,001 – 108,000 BWP 1,800 + 12.5% over BWP 72,000

108,001 – 144,000 BWP 6,300 + 18.75% over BWP 108,000

144,001 and over BWP 13,050 + 25% over BWP 144,000

WITHHOLDING TAX

Withholding tax must be deducted from certain payments made to a resident or non-resident, subject to any relieving provisions of an applicable tax treaty.

Generally, payments made to a resident which are:

1) Due under certain construction contracts, - to 3% withholding tax;

2) Interest, - to 10% withholding tax;

3) Dividends, - to 7.5% withholding tax;

Generally, payments made to a non-resident which are:

1) Due under certain construction contracts, - to 3% withholding tax;

2) Interest, - to 15% withholding tax;

3) Dividends, - to 7.5% withholding tax;

4) Royalties, management or consultancy fees, - to 15% withholding tax;

5) Entertainment fees, - to 10% withholding tax.

TAX RATES AND PROCEDURES[3]

Tax or mandatory contribution	Payments (number)	Notes on Payments	Time (hours)	Statutory tax rate	Tax base	Total tax rate (% of profit)	Notes on TTR
Training tax	0	jointly		0.2%	turnover	3.54	
Corporate income tax	5		40	22%	taxable profit	20.41	
Capital gains tax	1			22%	capital gains	1.11	

[3] The World Bank materials

Tax or mandatory contribution	Payments (number)	Notes on Payments	Time (hours)	Statutory tax rate	Tax base	Total tax rate (% of profit)	Notes on TTR
Vehicle license fee	1			various rates	Unladen weight	0.04	
Land tax	1			P0.8 per sq. meter of land	Land plot size	0.01	
Fuel tax	1				included into fuel price	0.00	small amount
Personal income tax	13		40			0.00	withheld
Value added tax (VAT)	12		72	12%	value added	0.00	not included
Totals:	34.0		152.0			25.1	

Taxes by type	Answer
Profit tax (% of profit)	21.5
Labor tax and contributions (% of profit)	0.0
Other taxes (% of profit)	3.6

	Answer	Score
Postfiling index (0-100)		89.9
VAT refunds		
Does VAT/GST exist?	Yes	
Frequency of VAT/GST refund submission	monthly	
Does a VAT/GST refund process exist per the case study?	Yes	
Restrictions on VAT refund process	None	
Likelihood of VAT audit	Likely	
Time to comply with VAT refund (hours)	10.0	80.0
Time to obtain a VAT refund (weeks)	10.5	86.0
Corporate income tax audits		
Does corporate income tax exist?	Yes	
Likelihood of corporate income tax audit	Unlikely	
Time to comply with a corporate income tax audit (hours)	5.0	93.6
Time to complete a corporate income tax audit (weeks)	0.0	100.0
Administrative appeal process		
First level administrative appeal authority	Commissioner General of the Botswana Unified Revenue Service	
Is the appeal authority independent?	Independent department within tax office	
Are appeal guidelines accessible to the public?	Yes	

	Answer	Score
Source of appeal guidelines	Online/in printed publication/in person at the tax office	
Is there a legal time limit for the appeal authority to issue a decision on the tax appeal?	No	

According to Botswana Income Tax Act, an amount, which accrues to person, is deemed to have accrued –

(a) in case of employment, at the time it is:

(i) received by that person;

(ii) due and payable, even though not actually paid to him; or

Credited in account, reinvested, accumulated, capitalized, carried to reserve or otherwise disposed

(b) in case of business, in relation to which the Commissioner is satisfied that a commercially recognized system of accounting is regularly followed, at the time it is credited in the books of account of such person; or

(c) In any other case, at the time it becomes due and payable to the person.

An amount accrued to any person is deemed to have accrued from a source situated in Botswana where it has accrued to such person in respect of:

(a) any contract made by such person in Botswana for sale of goods, whether such goods have been or are to be delivered in or out of Botswana;

(b) any service rendered or work done by such person in Botswana, whether the payment thereof is made by a resident or a non-resident and wherever payment is made.

(c) any service rendered or work done out of Botswana:

(i) by such person under a contract of employment with the Government,

(ii) by such person, being a resident, for or on behalf of his employer in Botswana during that person's temporary absence from Botswana, whether the payment for such service rendered or work done is made by a resident or a non resident and wherever the payment is made;

(d) any pension, bonus, gratuity or compensation granted to such person in respect of past services-

i) by the Government; or

ii) where such past services were performed in Botswana by any other persons, and wherever payment is made or the funds from which payment is made are situate.

Where any pension, bonus, gratuity or compensation is payable in respect of

(e) any business carried on by such person, being a resident, as the owner or character on any aircraft, whether such aircraft may be operated;

(f) Any service rendered or work done out of Botswana by such person, being a resident, as an officer or a member of the crew of any aircraft referred to in paragraph above statement whenever payment is made;

The disposal by such person of any interest in mineral rights over land situate in Botswana or the disposal of any share or interest in the capita) any business carried on by such person, being a resident, as the owner or character on any aircraft, whether such aircraft may be operated;

(g) The disposal by such person of any interest in mineral rights over land situate in Botswana or the disposal of any share or interest in the capital or l or

(h) The disposal by such person of mining or prospecting information or mining or prospecting rights over land situate in Botswana or any investment made outside Botswana or any business carried on outside Botswana by a resident of Botswana

BOTSWANA INCOME TAX RATES

Botswana personal income tax rates are progressive, up to 25%.

Botswana personal tax regime is based on taxable income brackets. Botswana tax rates for individuals have been amended so that the non-taxable threshold for resident individuals is increased from BWP 25,000 to BWP 30,000 per year and the top marginal tax rate of 25% will now apply to income over BWP 120,000 per year. Nonresident individual tax rates and rates for net aggregate gains of the individuals have also been amended. The new tax rates and the new tax bands are are in the following tables:

Botswana Income Tax Rates for Resident Individuals

Taxable Income (BWP) / Tax Rate %

BWP 0 – 30,000 Exempt

BWP 30,000 – 60,000 BWP 0 + 5% of the excess over BWP 30,000

BWP 60,000 – 90,000 BWP 1,500 + 12.5 % of excess over BWP 60,000

BWP 90,000 – 120,000 BWP 5,250 + 18.75% of excess over BWP 90,000

Above BWP 120,000 BWP 10,875 + 25% of excess over BWP 120,000

Botswana Income Tax Rates for Nonresident Individuals, Trusts Falling under Botswana Tax Law Section 14 (2) and Estates of Deceased Persons, 2009

Taxable Income (BWP) / Tax Rate %

BWP 0 – 60,000 5% of every Pula

BWP 60,000 – 90,000 BWP 3,000 + 12.5% of excess over BWP 60,000

BWP 90,000 – 120,000 BWP 6,750 + 18.75% of excess over BWP 90,000

Over BWP 120,000 BWP 12,375 + 25% of excess over BWP 120,000

– The definition of 'employment income' has been modified while that of 'retrenchment package' no longer makes reference to the Employment Act.

– Non-corporate taxpayers that are obliged to file income tax returns have the option to self assess their tax liabilities for a tax year and to pay the taxes in one lump sum when they file their returns for the tax year.

– The exemption limit of interest income for resident individuals has been increased from BWP 2,500 per year to BWP 6,000 per year.

Tax Table for Net Aggregate Gains of Individuals in Botswana

Taxable Income (BWP) / Tax Rate %

BWP 0 – 15 000 Exempt

BWP 15,000 – 60,000 BWP 0 + 5% of the excess over BWP 15,000

BWP 60,000 – 90,000 BWP 2,250 + 12.5% of the excess over BWP 30,000

BWP 90,000 – 120,000 BWP 6, 000 + 18.75% of excess over BWP 60,000

Over BWP 120,000 BWP 11,625 + 25% of excess over BWP 120,000

Basis – Resident and nonresident individuals are liable for tax only on Botswana-source income. Residence status is nevertheless important because nonresidents - to tax at different rates.

Residence – A resident is an individual who has resided in Botswana for 183 days or more in any tax year.

Filing status – Spouses are taxed separately on income.

Taxable income – Taxable income comprises employment, business income, passive income (e.g. dividends, interest, royalties, etc.) and capital gains.

Capital gains – Capital gains are treated as taxable income subject to the normal personal income tax rate.

Tax Deductions and allowances – Few deductions are allowed. Contributions to a pension or superannuation fund are deductible. Taxpayers with business income are allowed the same deductions as for companies.

Tax Rates – Tax Rates are progressive to 25%.

Other taxes on individuals:

Capital duty – No

Stamp duty – No

Capital acquisitions tax – No

Real property tax – See under "Other taxes on corporations".

Inheritance/estate tax – Donations, other gratuitous disposals (such as inter vivos gifts) and estates of deceased individuals - to capital transfer tax. The rate is graduated up to 5% for individuals.

Net wealth/net worth tax – No

Social security – No

Administration and compliance:

Tax year – The tax year runs from 1 July to 30 June.

Filing and payment – Only individuals earning non-employment income are required to file a return. Tax on employment income is deducted at source. The income tax return must be filed within 3 months of the end of the tax year, although reasonable extensions may be granted. Any balance of tax due when the tax authorities issue an assessment is payable within 30 days of receipt of the assessment. Unincorporated businesses pay tax on the same basis as individuals.

Tax Penalties – Failure to pay tax or late filing may give rise to interest or penalties. Late payment interest is 1.5% per month and currently there are no penalties for late filing of returns by individuals.

BOTSWANA CORPORATE TAX RATES

Botswana has a very well developped tax incentives. The manufacturing and the International Financial Services Centre are taxed at a reduced rate of 15% (compared to the current corporate tax rate of 25%)

Promotions for companies are covered under Development Approval Order.
Under this order, depending on the scale and the magnitude of the project companies can apply for tax holidays. Normally it is granted to companies, which are carrying out big projects. The tax holidays are restricted to five or ten years depending the scale and the magnitude of the project.

Botswana corporate tax rate is 15% or 25%.

The corporate income tax rate in Botswana is split into 2 tiers:

1) A basic company tax of 15%, or

A special tax rate of 5% for manufacturing, and for companies in Botswana International Financial Services Centre (IFSC)

2) An Additional Company Tax (ACT) of 10%, which applies to both tax rates above.

Botswana corporate income tax rate for basic companies is:

Basic Company Tax:	15%
Additional Company Tax (ACT):	10%

TOTAL TAX RATE: 25%

Botswana corporate income tax rate for for Manufacturing and IFSC Companies is:

Tax for Manufacturing and IFSC Companies: 5%

Additional Company Tax (ACT): 10%

CAPITAL TRANSFER TAX

Capital Transfer Tax (CTT) is levied under the Capital Transfer Tax Act, 1985.(Chapter 53:02)

It is tax on transfer of property (tangible, intangible movable or immovable), by way of

- Gift or
- Inheritance.

Taxable Persons

The person liable is the donee or beneficiary of a chargeable disposal including a trustee to whom such property has been disposed for the benefit of any beneficiary.

Charge to Tax

CTT is charged on the aggregate taxable value of all chargeable disposals made by a donor to a donee in any tax year at the rates specified.

*Value means the market value

Exemptions

CTT is not chargeable in respect of

A. The value of property which is disposed off

- By way of inheritance to a spouse on the death of another spouse
- To a person on his marriage if the value is less than P5000
- Household goods of a deceased person if the value is less than P15000
- Livestock or produce which has been included in the income of the donor.

B. Disposal of property outside Botswana if the beneficiary lives outside Botswana

C. Disposal of any property for maintenance , education or training of a child until the age of 21.

D. The value of any debt which is included in the gross income of the debtor under section 28(2)(h) of the Income Tax Act.

E. Aggregate value of all casual gifts of not more than P5000 donated to a person in any tax year.

Allowable deductions

In ascertaining the aggregate taxable value of any chargeable disposal, the following deductions are made;

a. The first P100 000 of distributable value of the estate of a deceased person

b. Any expenditure wholly, exclusively and necessarily incurred by the donee in effecting the disposal or obtaining possession of the property.

c. All debts due by the donor to persons resident in Botswana in respect of the property disposed off.

Liability of certain property to CTT

Any property that has been disposed off for a consideration which in the opinion of the Commissioner General is not adequate, will be chargeable to Capital Transfer Tax. Taxable value will be the difference between the actual consideration and the market value.

BUSINESS TAX REGISTRATION

Company Tax and VAT

All taxes have to be registered by using the same tax forms. For corporate tax, the applicant is required to declare whether any taxes will be withheld, in which case withholding tax registration included. Registration for VAT is possible once corporate tax registration has been completed. Application forms can be collected from any BURS office or downloaded from the BURS website, www.burs.org.bw.

The following documents must be submitted with the registration application forms:

Copy of Certificate of Incorporation and Registration.

Memorandum and articles of association/partnership deed/constitution (for companies registered before July 2007).

Copies of forms 2, 2A, 2B, 2C, 2D, 8, 13, 14, and 15 (for companies registered on or after 1 July 2007). The requirements for constitution in section b) and forms in section c) are unnecessary.

Copies of Omang/passports for the public officer and directors.

List of assets owned by the company.

Bank account details. Tax registration is conditional on having a registered bank account.

If projected annual turnover is less than P500,000, a company applying for VAT is required to write a letter requesting to be registered voluntarily. No additional supporting explanation is required.

Registration usually takes five days, following which the company will be issued with a Tax Identification Number (TIN).

Individual Tax Registration

The following documents and details are required for registration as a taxpayer. Once registered, the individual will be provided with a TIN. The threshold for personal income tax is P2,499.00 per month:

Certified copy of Omang (citizens), or certified copy of passport (non-citizens)

Residence and work permits (non-citizens)

Postal address

Residential/physical address

Registered office address

Contact details

Source of income

INCENTIVES OF INVESTORS

Investors are entitled to Low general tax rate: resident companies pay company tax at 22% of the taxable income and the general rate of withholding tax is 7.5% on all dividends distributed.

Manufacturing companies pay tax at 15% of taxable income – subject to approval.

Development Approval Order – tax holiday (zero corporate tax) can be made available to investors for a period of 5 to 10 years.

There are no foreign exchange controls in Botswana – hence free repatriation of profits, dividends and capital.

Operational double taxation avoidance agreements with South Africa, United Kingdom, Sweden, France, Mauritius, Namibia, Zimbabwe and Russia.

International Financial Services Centre (IFSC) accredited companies pay tax at 15% on profits from approved operations.

Companies accredited by the Innovation Hub pay tax at 15% of profit.

IFSC Company Certification

The Botswana IFSC offers a range of tax incentives to approved companies. These include, but are not limited to:

Flat Corporate Tax rate at 15%

No withholding tax on dividends, interest, royalties, management fees

Unilateral credit for withholding tax suffered in other jurisdictions whether or not a Double Tax Avoidance Agreement exists

Specified Collective Investment Undertakings (CIUs) managed by IFSC companies are tax exempt

Requirements to Become an IFSC Company

To register as an IFSC company, the company must be registered in Botswana must make a formal application to the International Financial Services Centre Certification Committee through BITC. If the company meets criteria for IFSC certification, BITC will forward a recommendation to the Minister of Finance and Development Planning who will issue a certificate stipulating approved activities

Activities Eligible for IFSC Certification

he following activities are approved financial operations, broadly defined in the Income Tax Act, provided they are carried out by non-residents or IFSC companies:

Banking and finance operations transacted in foreign currency

Broking and trading of securities denominated in foreign currency

Investment advice

Management and custodial functions related to CIUs

Insurance and related activities

Registrars and transfer agency services

Exploitation of intellectual property

Development and supply of computer software for use in provision of the aforementioned services

Accounting and financial administration

Holding and administration of group companies

Business process outsourcing and call centres

Shared financial services

Mutual funds

Other operations that the Minister may declare by order to be approved financial operations on a case by case basis.

Development Approval Order (DAO)

The DAO provides special tax relief and/or education and training grants and is subject to the authority of the Minister of Finance and Development Planning. Zero-rate tax holidays for between 5 and 10 years can be obtained through the DAO.

Requirements for Development Approval Order

The Minister must be satisfied that the proposed project will be beneficial to Botswana's economy. Any firm, local or foreign, may apply to the Permanent Secretary for Finance and Development Planning for a DAO.

Applications are evaluated against the following criteria:

Job creation for Botswana citizens

The company's training plans for Botswana citizens

The company's plans to localise non-citizen positions

Botswana citizen participation in company management

Amount of equity held by Botswana citizens in the company

The location of the proposed investment

The project's effect on stimulation of other economic activities

The project's effect on reducing local consumer prices

Botswana investment incentives, 2014

Specific fiscal incentive
IFSC certified companies are entitled to: A corporate tax rate of 15% until 2020 Exemption from withholding taxes on interest, dividends and management fees Exemption from VAT and capital gains tax A tax rebate of 200% on income tax on training costs Tax exemption on income derived from the disposal of shares in IFSCs Credits for withholding taxes in other jurisdictions Collective investment undertakings (CIUs) (a pass-through fund management mechanism) managed by IFSC are taxed exempt.
Companies accredited to an Innovation Hub are entitled to: a corporate tax rate of 15%
Manufacturing companies are entitled to: A corporate tax rate of 15% Import machinery and equipment duty-free Manufacturing companies registered under Schedule 470.03 are entitled to import raw materials duty-free, provided that 100% of output is exported outside the CCA. Companies that sell some of their produce within the CCA pay duty only on those raw materials used to manufacture those goods sold within the CCA (Section 3) .

Botswana has signed several bilateral investment treaties; however, there are only two in force (with Germany and Switzerland) . It has also signed double taxation agreements with Barbados, France, India, Mauritius, Mozambique, Namibia, Seychelles, South Africa, Sweden, United Kingdom, the Russian Federation and Zimbabwe. Similar agreements have been signed with China, Ireland, Swaziland and Zambia but are awaiting ratification; while others with Belgium, Lesotho, Luxembourg and Malawi have been concluded but have not yet been signed.[53] Botswana is a member of the Multilateral Investment Guarantee Agency and of the International Centre for the Settlement of Investment Disputes

CUSTOMS PROCEDURES AND REQUIREMENTS

3.1. Customs procedures in Botswana continue to be regulated by the Customs and Excise Duty Act (as amended) and by the Customs and Excise Duty Regulations (as amended) .[55] The Customs and Excise Duty Act is currently under review to develop new regulations.

The documents required for customs clearance are the same as those specified in the previous Review. These are: the customs declaration, commercial invoice, bill of lading, certificate of origin (for goods covered by preferential trade agreements), and packing list. Depending on the nature of the product, a technical conformity/health/veterinary certificate and/or an import licence or permit may also be required. Declarations of origin are required for goods subject to preferences or to anti-dumping and countervailing duties or to safeguard measures.

Importers need to register as a business or a company, under the Companies Act, and obtain a trading licence under the Trade Act. If an individual, rather than a registered company, seeks to import, they require a hawker's/street vendor licence. In addition to the trading licence, all importers are required to register with the Customs and Excise Division of the Botswana Unified Revenue Service (BURS) and importers with an annual turnover of at least P 30,000 (in 2015) are required to obtain a Trader Identification Number (TIN) from Customs in order to facilitate the payment of taxes and the import procedures.[56] The use of clearing agents is not compulsory in Botswana.[57] There are no nationality restrictions to become a clearing agent; however, as to perform any other business clearing agents need to be licensed.

Botswana continues to use UNCTAD's Automated System for Customs Data (ASYCUDA), a risk-based inspection system, to clear customs. The customs declaration form is processed electronically but the supporting documents must be submitted in paper format.

Botswana operates a post-clearance audit system to verify import (and export) declarations. Nevertheless, imported goods, including those originating in any of the SACU countries, may be subject to inspection using a risk-based system, based on the importer's profile and profile of imports; the selectivity parameters are reviewed from time to time. Products are checked to ensure compliance with sanitary and technical requirements, and to enforce intellectual property rights (IPRs) . Customs has the authority to stop any goods from entering Botswana if they do not comply with the country's SPS and TBT regulations or if they infringe IPRs. Goods infringing any of these requirements or IPRs may be placed under embargo, destroyed or otherwise disposed of. If after an investigation it is determined that there was no infringement, goods are returned to the importer. Customs performs inspections on behalf of, *inter alia*, the Departments for Animal Health and Protection, Water Affairs, Wildlife and National Parks and the Botswana Police Service.

Administrative decisions by Customs can be appealed in Court within three months of the decision. According to the authorities, there have not been many cases of such appeals. Since 2009 there have been three appeals to decisions taken by Customs mainly related to the searching of warehouses and the seizure of smuggled cigarettes.[58]

3.7. Schedule 8 of Botswana's Customs and Excise Duty Regulations stipulate the ports of entry and exit into the national territory. In general these entry (and exit) points can be used for any type of goods, with the exception of the airfields located in Orapa and Jwaneng, which can only be used for the importation (and exportation) of goods consigned (to) by the Orapa and Jwaneng mines from (or to) any place within or outside the Common Customs Area.[59]

3.8. Imported goods may be kept in licensed bonded warehouses for a period of up to five years. Such warehouses may be licensed either for the storage of goods (known as customs and excise storage warehouses) or for the manufacture of goods (known as customs and excise manufacturing warehouses); a warehouse may be licensed both as a storage and a manufacturing warehouse provided that both activities are separated.[60] Sorting, packing and/or repacking in a customs and excise storage warehouse may be allowed if such activities are required to preserve the goods, sell them locally or export them. Duties and the VAT will only become due and payable when goods are entered for home consumption. An appropriate bill of entry filled out in the prescribed manner must be used to clear goods from a bonded warehouse. Customs duties and sales tax could also be charged if, during any of the Customs' routine inspections, the stocks stored in a warehouse are found to be less or greater than the quantity allowed in such warehouses. Botswana does not apply pre-shipment inspection.

CUSTOMS VALUATION

The Customs and Excise Duty Act and its Regulations, as amended, set the customs valuation procedures in Botswana. According to these Regulations, the value of imported goods at the time of entry for home consumption should be the transaction value. If the transaction value cannot be ascertained at the time of entry, the customs value will be assessed according to the

WTO Agreement on Implementation of Article VII of the General Agreement on Tariffs and Trade 1994 and any of its Interpretative Notes.

DUTIES AND CHARGES

Imports into Botswana - to the excise duties and levies that are imposed as a result of being party to the Customs Union. These include: specific excise duties on locally manufactured or imported goods; *ad valorem* excise duties on locally manufactured or imported goods; environmental levies; fuel levy; road accident fund levy and ordinary levy (please refer to the Main Report) .[66]

3.19. Article 26 of the SACU Agreement allows members to provide temporary protection to infant industries for a maximum of 8 years, through the imposition of additional duties. Revenues from these additional duties must be deposited in the Common Revenue Pool. Under this provision, Botswana has levied an additional duty of 40% on imports of UHT milk since 2008, which will be eliminated by 2016.[67]

Botswana also charges a flour levy at a rate of 15% on imports of wheat flour to protect the milling industry in order to promote its development.[68] The levy will be gradually phased-out over a period of ten years starting in 2015.[69]

The internal taxes levied by Botswana on imports and domestic goods and services remain mostly unchanged since the last Review in 2009. These are: the value-added tax, fuel levy, alcohol levy, and a copyright levy. In 2013, Botswana introduced a tobacco levy.

VAT is applied both on domestic and imported goods and services, including from other SACU members. The major changes regarding the application of VAT since the last Review were: an increase in the standard rate from 10% to 12% in 2010, and the removal of some food items from the list of items that were zero-rated and their inclusion in the list of goods that are exempt.[70] Up to 2014, zero-rate VAT goods included: staple foods (brown bread, rice, milk, sorghum or maize meal, millet grain and meal, wheat grain, maize cobs, flour, sugar, Setswana beans, and some vegetables and fruits); fuel (petrol, unleaded petrol, diesel oil and illuminating paraffin); fertilizers, pesticides, and farming tractors; and international transport services.[71] Domestic passenger transport services; financial, educational and medical services; long-term residential letting; and the supply of prescription drugs are amongst the services that are exempt from VAT.[72] In addition, since 2015: staple foods and farming equipment, have been exempt from VAT.[73]

Imports and domestic sales of petroleum products (i.e. petrol and diesel) - to a fuel levy of P 0.12 per litre of petrol and P 0.07 per litre of diesel.[74] The levy is collected at point of entry and finances the National Petroleum Fund (NPF) that is used to stabilize the price of oil products in the domestic market.

Domestically produced and imported liquor are subject to a levy of 30% which was increased to 50% in 2013 and to 55% in 2014.[75] The value used to assess the intoxicating liquor levy for locally produced items is the price paid or payable for the alcoholic beverages when sold for home consumption to any buyer, inclusive of the import duty but exclusive of VAT; and for imported items, it is the value used to assess customs duties plus the duty paid or payable on the goods transport and insurance costs, exclusive of VAT. Revenue from this levy is credited to the Levy on Alcoholic Beverages Fund to promote activities aimed at combating alcohol abuse. The levy is not charged on products that are exported directly by the manufacturer or from a bonded warehouse.

The Ministry of Health introduced a tobacco levy of 30% in 2014. The base to calculate the levy on domestically produced tobacco products is the purchase/invoice price and for imported products it is the landed cost plus the applied import duty. The revenue collected is used to finance anti-tobacco initiatives and other related activities.Botswana charges a copyright levy on imported and locally manufactured carrier media.

TARIFF AND TAX EXEMPTIONS

3.27. The 2002 SACU Agreement stipulates that all members need to apply the same rebates[77], refunds[78] or drawbacks[79] of customs duties on imported goods. There are, however, some country-specific rebates. In general, Botswana applies the tariff exemptions and other concessions that are stipulated in the Schedules to the Customs and Excise Act of 1964, which are: the Industrial Rebate of Customs Duty; the General Rebate of Custom Duties; the Specific Drawbacks and Refunds of Custom Duties; Fuel levy and Environmental Levy; and Refunds and Rebates of Excise Duties, Fuel Levy and Environmental Levy[80] (Main Report) . Other country-specific rebates are those for wheat (HS1011) (excluding durum wheat) and dairy products (HS 04), which are used only by Botswana, Lesotho, Namibia, and Swaziland (BLNS) . However, the use of these rebates has to be allowed by the agricultural authorities of the four BLNS countries.

Concessions applied by SACU countries (including Botswana) include rebates that affect specific industries and those that are more general and apply to imports by diplomats (based on reciprocal treatment), special events such as international exhibitions, relief in cases of natural disasters and famines, and to goods being re-imported into Botswana or goods sent abroad for processing or repair that are re-imported.[81] Industrial rebates (Schedule 3) are available to stimulate selected industries such as: food and beverages; textile and clothing; pharmaceuticals; pulp and paper; wood and articles of wood; and vehicles. These rebates allow for imported raw materials, usually not available locally, to enter the SACU territory, at a reduced rate of duty, if they are to be used in one of the specific scheduled industries. The rate of the rebate varies according to product; however, in many instances it is as high as 100%. Rebated inputs can be used either to manufacture products to be sold in the SACU market, upon payment of duties, or for export outside the SACU region. According to the authorities, during the period under review only two firms in the textile industry benefited from industrial rebates. All duly registered and licensed businesses may benefit from the existing rebates.[82]

Goods imported for a specific purpose or under different customs regimes may also be exempt from VAT. As a result, goods imported, *inter alia*, (1) for the relief of distress of persons in cases of famine or other natural disaster; (2) under any technical assistance agreement; (3) to fulfil obligations under any multilateral international agreement to which Botswana is a party; or (4) for welfare or charitable purposes, are exempt from VAT.[83] In addition, imported or locally manufactured articles sent abroad for processing or repair, provided they retain their essential character, and are returned to the same exporter, are exempt from VAT. Goods that are temporarily exported for outward processing are also exempt from VAT when re-imported and so are goods temporarily admitted for processing, repair, cleaning or reconditioning or to be exported in the same state at a later stage.

BASIC REGULATIONS FOR TAXATION

IMPORTANT PRACTICAL REGULATIONS[4]

ON TAX DEDUCTIBLE FROM PAYMENTS OF MANAGEMENT OR CONSULTANCY FEES TO NON-RESIDENTS

(Section 58* and Seventh Schedule to the Income Tax Act, 1995)

1. INTRODUCTION:

1.1. Purpose of this DGN:

This Departmental Guidance Note is issued to explain the provisions and procedure relating to tax treatment of management or consultancy fees paid to non-residents. The purpose of this Note is to enumerate and explain the respective obligations of the persons making payment for management or consultancy fees and the procedure to be followed to comply with those obligations under the Income Tax Act 1995 as amended with effect from 1 July 2006.

This Note has no force in Law. It does not bind the Commissioner nor does it restrict the rights of Objection and Appeal as provided by the Income Tax Act 1995.

1.2. Relevant provisions of law:

The law relating to tax treatment of management or consultancy fees payable to a non-resident person is enshrined in Section 58 and the Seventh Schedule of the Income Tax Act 1995. Section 58 which lays down the substantive law in this regard, reads as under:

58*. "(1) Every person who –

(a) being a resident company, makes any payment of dividend to a resident or a non-resident;

(b) makes any payment of interest to a resident or a non-resident;

(c) makes any payment of commercial royalty, entertainment fee, or management or consultancy fee to a non-resident,

shall deduct tax from such payment in accordance with and in the manner specified in the Seven Schedule and shall carry out such other obligations as are imposed by that Schedule.

(2) For the purposes of this section a person, including a partnership, to whom any payment is made to which this section applies shall be presumed, unless the contrary is proved, to be a non-resident if such payment is made to an address outside Botswana.

(3) The Commissioner may direct that this section shall not apply to any payment of interest to a non-resident, if he is satisfied that, by reason of the small amount of the payment or any other special circumstances, it is reasonable to so direct.

---

[4] All references to the provisions of the Income Tax Act are based on the latest edition of Laws of Botswana published in 2002.

4) This section shall not apply to –

(a) any payment of interest, commercial royalty or management or consultancy fee; and

(b) the payment of a dividend to a non resident, an international financial services center company or a collective investment undertaking,

where the payment is made by an international financial service centre company or a collective investment undertaking which is exempt from tax under paragraph (xvi) of Part I of the Second Schedule.

(c) any payment of interest to a resident where the recipient of such interest is a person exempt from taxation; and

(d) an IFSC company, a banking company or a financial institution receiving such interest in its ordinary course of business."

The amount of tax to be deducted and the relevant procedure is laid down in the Seventh Schedule as amended by the Income Tax (Amendment)Act 2006. The amount of tax to be deducted is @15 % of the gross payment of management or consultancy fees to a non-resident.

1.3. Persons covered :

The persons covered under the provisions referred to in 1.2 above are

a. Every person who makes any payment of management or consultancy fees to a non-resident.

b. Every non-resident person who receives any payment of management or consultancy fees.

1.4. Registration requirements

Every person responsible for making payments of management or consultancy fees must register with the Commissioner of Taxes for the purposes of withholding tax.

The relevant form is ITRG 1, which can be obtained from the Taxpayer Assistance Centre (TAC) of the Botswana Unified Revenue Service(BURS) (Phone: 3614600) and should be submitted after completing the same to the TAC / Registration Section of BURS.

2. RELEVANT PAYMENTS

2.1. Payments covered:

The payments covered under this DGN are "management or consultancy fees".

2.2. Management or consultancy fees:

'Management or consultancy fee' has been defined under section 2 of the Income Tax Act as under:

"Management or consultancy fee means any amount payable for administrative, managerial, technical or consultative services or any similar services, whether such services are of a professional nature or not."

It is to be noted that the definition embraces amounts payable for all types of services whether of a professional nature or not.

The source of any management or consultancy fees is deemed to be in Botswana if the payer is resident in Botswana or has a permanent establishment in Botswana.

2.3. Exempted Payments:

The provisions of section 58 and the Seventh Schedule are not applicable in the following cases :

(i) If the amount is exempt under a Double Taxation Avoidance Agreement with another country (paragraph (xxiv), Part II of Second Schedule).Currently, Botswana has effective Double Taxation

Avoidance Agreements with the UK, South Africa, Sweden, Mauritius, France, Namibia, Seychelles and Barbados

(ii) If exemption is granted by virtue of an agreement entered into with the Minister and approved by a resolution of the National Assembly(Section 54 and paragraph (xxiv) Part II of Second Schedule).

(iii) Where business is carried on or services are rendered under an agreement for provision of technical assistance with the Government (Paragraph (xix) Part II of Second Schedule). The exemption must be approved by the Minister under a notice in writing to the Commissioner General of BURS. This exemption will apply only to the contracts between the Government of Botswana and the Government or government agency of another country.

(iv) If the payer of such management or consultancy fees is either an IFSC company or a Collective Investment Undertaking exempt under paragraph (xvi) of Part I of the Second Schedule to the Income Tax Act 1995.

Wherever exemption is claimed by the non-resident receiving the management or consultancy fees, the person responsible for payment shall allow exemption only when a ruling to that effect is issued by the Commissioner General. The payer must verify the claim of exemption with the Commissioner General's Office if the person receiving the management or consultancy fees fails to produce the ruling from the Commissioner General.

3. WITHHOLDING REQUIREMENTS

3.1. Amount to be withheld

Every person making any payment of management or consultancy fees to a non-resident shall deduct tax @ of 15% from all payments made .

3.2. Payment to the Commissioner General , BURS

The tax withheld is to be paid over to the Commissioner General by the 15th of the month following the month in which the tax was withheld. Delay in paying over the tax creates a liability to charge of interest @ 2% per month or part of a month besides penalty under section 118 (7) at the rate of P100 per day or 1 percent of the tax due, whichever is greater , for each month or part of the month during which the violation continues. Such a person will also be liable for prosecution under section 127 of the Income Tax Act which may result in a fine of Pula 4000 and to imprisonment for two years.

3.3. Certificate of Deduction

Every person who deducts any tax @ 15% from payments of management or consultancy fees must within 15 days issue a tax deduction certificate to the person to whom payment was made , in the prescribed Form ITW 9 after getting it duly approved by the office of the Commissioner General.

Form ITW 9s are available with the Taxpayer Assistance Centre / Withholding Taxes Division of BURS (Phone No 3614600), which may be obtained by the payer in advance to facilitate handing over of tax deduction certificates to the payee within the prescribed time of 15 days.

3.4. Final withholding

The tax withheld from payments made as management or consultancy fees to a non-resident is a final withholding tax.

4. TAX TREATMENT OF THE PAYER

4.1. Allowable as deduction

Although expenditure on management or consultancy fees can be claimed under the general deductions provisions under Part VI section 39 (2).,specific provision is made in section 41 (2) (b) to deal with such fees, thus casting a greater burden on the claimant to prove to the satisfaction of the Commissioner General that the amount paid was wholly , exclusively and necessarily incurred by the payer in the production of his assessable income.

4.2. Powers of the Commissioner General to disregard a transaction between connected parties

In the anti-avoidance provisions of the Act (Section 36), an agreement or contract between connected parties for providing such services is deemed not to be an arm's length transaction. This gives the Commissioner General the power to disregard such contracts and deal with the transaction in a manner, which he deems appropriate.

4.3. Strict Proof required for allowance of deduction to the payer

In order to give effect to these provisions, the Commissioner will be looking for strict proof (among other matters) before allowing a claim. He will look

i) For proper documentation of the contract giving full details of services to be rendered and payments to be made.

ii) At the ability and capacity of the person providing the services to provide the services.

iii) For the necessity of such services, in regard to extent and cost for the Botswana business.

iv) At the reasonableness of the payment.

5. TAX TREATMENT OF PAYEE

5.1. Two Categories of payees

Management or consultancy services can be rendered either by enterprises (companies, partnership and similar organisations) or individuals. The tax treatment will depend on the category which the payee falls in.

5.2 Enterprises:

i) With a fixed base:-Where an enterprise renders services from a fixed base in Botswana regularly available to it to render such services then liability to tax on Botswana income will be by assessment or through self assessment in the case of companies.

It would not be necessary to deduct withholding tax in such cases.

ii) Without a fixed base:-Where there is no fixed base, the withholding tax @ 15% would be the final tax.

5.3 Individuals:

Where a non-resident individual renders such services to a Botswana entity , any payment for such services shall be subject to the 15 % final withholding tax by the payer. This applies to all non-resident individuals, who practice their profession, like engineers, architects, doctors, surveyors etc.

6. Effect of Double Taxation Avoidance Agreements:

Botswana at present, has double taxation avoidance agreements (DTAAs) with the United Kingdom (UK) , the Republic of South Africa (RSA), Sweden , Mauritius , France , Namibia , Seychelles and Barbados. These DTAAs modify the law so that

i) Where a U.K. enterprise renders management or consultancy service without having a permanent establishment in Botswana, then income from such services does not attract tax in Botswana. However, under the new renegotiated DTAA with the UK , with effect from 1 July 2007, a 7.5% withholding tax will apply in all such cases.

If the services are rendered by a permanent establishment, then income from such services is liable to tax in Botswana by assessment or self assessment in the case of companies.

ii) Where a U.K. individual renders services without a fixed base in Botswana, his income from such services does not attract tax in Botswana. However, under the new renegotiated DTAA with the UK, with effect from 1 July 2007, a 7.5% withholding tax will apply in all such cases.

iii) Where an individual or enterprise of RSA renders management or consultancy services in Botswana, without a fixed base or permanent establishment in Botswana , such management or consultancy fees would be taxable in Botswana @10% as per the Technical Fees article of the renegotiated Botswana – RSA DTAA effective 20th May 2004.If the services are rendered through a permanent establishment or a fixed base, then the taxation will be in accordance with the article relevant to business profits.

iv) Where an individual or enterprise of Sweden or Mauritius or Namibia renders management or consultancy services in Botswana, without a fixed base or permanent establishment in Botswana , such management or consultancy fees would be taxable in Botswana @15% as per the relevant articles of the respective DTAAs .If the services are rendered through a permanent establishment or a fixed base, then the taxation

will be in accordance with the article relevant to business profits or independent personal services as the case may be.

v) Where an individual or enterprise of France renders management or consultancy services in Botswana, without a fixed base or a permanent establishment in Botswana , such management or consultancy fees would be taxable in Botswana @7.5% as per the relevant article of the Botswana-France DTAA effective from 1 July 2004 . If the services are rendered through a permanent establishment or a fixed base, then the taxation will be in accordance with the article relevant to business profits or independent personal services as the case may be.

vi) Where an individual or enterprise of Seychelles renders management or consultancy services in Botswana, without a fixed base or a permanent establishment in Botswana , such management or consultancy fees would be taxable in Botswana @10% as per the relevant article of the Botswana-Seychelles DTAA. If the services are rendered through a permanent establishment or a fixed base, then the taxation will be in accordance with the article relevant to business profits or independent personal services as the case may be.

vii) Where an individual or enterprise of Barbados renders management or consultancy services in Botswana, without a fixed base or a permanent establishment in Botswana , such management or consultancy fees would be taxable in Botswana @10% as per the relevant article of the Botswana-Barbados DTAA. If the services are rendered through a permanent establishment or a fixed base, then the taxation will be in accordance with the article relevant to business profits or independent personal services as the case may be.

7. LIABILITY IN THE EVENT OF NON-DEDUCTION AND /OR NONPAYMENT

7.1 Personal liability of the payer:

The person making payments to which Section 58 applies shall be personally liable for the tax to be withheld and in case of his failure to deduct tax, the tax will be recoverable from him.

7.2 Non-deduction and/or non-payment are punishable:

Failure to deduct tax and pay the same and maintain record for inspection by the Commissioner General shall, besides inviting interest under Section 101 of the Income Tax Act, also attract penalty under sections 118(6) and 118(7) of the Income Tax Act. Where the failure to deduct is willful with the intent to evade tax, the person responsible for deducting may also be prosecuted under Section 127 and 128 of the Income Tax Act.

8.CONCLUSION

8.1. Payer's Responsibilities

It is the responsibility of the person making the payments of management or consultancy fees to a non-resident individual or enterprise to deduct tax @ 15% in terms of section 58 and in accordance with the provisions of the Seventh Schedule to the Income Tax Act. The person withholding tax on such payment of management or consultancy fees shall do the following:

(i) Deduct tax and pay the same within 15 days of such deduction to the Commissioner General. Taxes withheld and paid by him will be recorded in ITW.7, the statement of monthly tax deduction and payments.

(ii) Any variation in the rate of withholding tax should be applied only if variation is approved by the Commissioner General by virtue of the payee being covered under the relevant article of the relevant Double Taxation Avoidance Agreement as enumerated in paragraph 6 above.

(iii) Furnish to the payee certificate of such deduction in ITW.9 with the stamp of the Commissioner General within 15 days of the deduction. The white copy of ITW.9 shall be furnished to the payee, the green copy will be filed with the Commissioner General and the pink will be retained by the payer.

(iv) Furnish annual return of withholding taxes in Form ITW.10 to the Commissioner General within 31 days of the end of the relevant tax year.

(v) Maintain record of all payments and produce the same for inspection by the Commissioner General whenever required by him to do so.

8.2. Assistance available

In need of any clarification, please contact the offices of the Botswana Unified Revenue Service at the addresses and phone numbers given below:

Department of Taxes	Department of Taxes	Department of Taxes
Private Bag 0013	Collection Division	Collection Division
Gaborone	Private Bag 38	Private Bag 13
Phone: 3614600	Francistown	Selebi-Phikwe
Fax: 3953101	Phone: 212734	Phone: 810795
	Fax: 214267	Fax: 814862

ON TAX DEDUCTIBLE FROM PAYMENTS UNDER CONTRACTS RELATING TO CONSTRUCTION OPERATIONS

Section 56 and Sixth Schedule to the Income Tax Act, 1995)

1. INTRODUCTION

1.1. Purpose of this DGN:

This Departmental Guidance Note is issued to explain the provisions and procedure relating to deduction of tax from contracts relating to construction operations. The purpose of this Note is to enumerate and explain the respective obligations of the persons entering into a contract relating to construction operation and the procedure to be followed to comply with those obligations under the Income Tax Act 1995.

1.2. Relevant provisions of law:

The law relating to deduction of tax in the case of contracts relating to construction operations is enshrined in Section 56 and the Sixth Schedule of the Income Tax Act 1995. Section 56 which lays down the substantive law in this regard, reads as under:

"(1) Every person who makes any payment to any person under a contract relating to construction operations shall deduct tax from such payment, in accordance with and in the manner specified in the Sixth Schedule and shall carry out such other obligations as are imposed by that Schedule.

Provided that this section shall not apply to contracts with a value less than P2,000,000 being executed by construction companies which fall under categories OC, A and B of the Central Tender Board.[1]

The amount of tax to be deducted and the relevant procedure is laid down in the Sixth Schedule as amended by the Income Tax (Amendment)Act 2001.

[1] New sub section 1 inserted by Income Tax Amendment Act 2001

1.3. Registration requirements of persons covered :

The persons covered under the provisions referred to in 1.2 above are

a. Every person who makes any payment to any person under a contract relating to construction operations; and

b. Every person who receives any payment under a contract relating to construction operations.

Every person responsible for making payments under contracts relating to construction operations must register with the Commissioner of Taxes for the purposes of withholding tax.

Every person receiving payment under a contract relating to construction operations must register with the Commissioner of Taxes if he or the company is not already registered as a taxpayer.

The relevant form is ITRG 1 which can be obtained from the Central Processing Unit of the Commissioner of Taxes. (Phone: 300723/375988).

2. RELEVANT CONTRACTS

2.1 Contracts covered:

The contracts covered under the provisions of section 56 and the Sixth Schedule of the Income Tax Act are "contracts relating to construction operations".

2.2 Contracts relating to Construction operations:

Though contracts relating to construction operations have not been defined under the Income Tax Act, they include in particular, any contracts or subcontracts where either the entire or part of the work includes activities such as erection, demolition, installation or assembly, site preparation, drilling, road works and any services such as architectural and engineering services related to such activities. A contract where supply of services is incidental to construction operations will be deemed to be a construction contract.

2.3 Exempted contracts:

Provisions of Section 56 and the Sixth Schedule are not applicable in the following situations:

(i)

If the person executing the contract is classified as OC , A or B by the Central Tender Board, **and** the value of such a contract is less than P 2 Million. For exemption, both the conditions must be fulfilled simultaneously.

(ii)

If the person executing the contract is exempt under a Double Taxation Avoidance Agreement with another country (paragraph (xxiv), Part II of Second Schedule).Currently, Botswana has Double Taxation Avoidance Agreements with the UK, South Africa, Sweden, Mauritius and France.

(iii) If exemption is granted by virtue of an agreement entered into with the Minister and approved by a resolution of the National Assembly(Section 53 and paragraph (xxiv) Part II of Second Schedule).

(iv) Where business is carried on or services are rendered under an agreement for provision of technical assistance with the Government (Paragraph (xix) Part II of Second Schedule). The exemption must be approved by the Minister under a notice in writing to the Commissioner of Taxes. This exemption will apply only to the contracts between the Government of Botswana and the Government or government agency of another country.

(v) Where exemption is granted under a tax certificate issued by the Commissioner of Taxes under paragraph 3(3) of the Sixth Schedule of the Income Tax Act.

In cases of claim of exemption under (i) above, the person responsible for payment should ensure that the person executing the contract is actually registered under categories A , B or OC with the Central Tender Board with reference to the certificate issued by the Central Tender Board.

Wherever exemption is claimed by the person executing the contract , the person responsible for payment shall allow exemption only when a ruling to that effect is issued by the Commissioner of Taxes. The payer must verify the claim of exemption with the Commissioner of Taxes if the person executing the contract fails to produce the ruling from the Commissioner of Taxes.

3. NOTIFICATION REQUIREMENTS :

Every person entering into contracts relating to construction operations where the total amount of payments expected to be made under a contract or series of contracts exceeds P5 000.00., shall notify in writing to the Commissioner of Taxes, Private Bag 0013, Gaborone of

(**a**) the nature of the work;

(b) the likely duration of the contract;

(c) name and address of the contractor and Taxpayer identification number and

(d) the total amount payable under the contract.

This notification is to be given in writing within 30 days of the date of entering into the contract and failure to notify is subject to penalty. ***The Commissioner of Taxes has prescribed Form ITW 1A for use by persons entering into relevant contracts.***

4. WITHHOLDING REQUIREMENTS

4.1. Amount to be withheld

From 1 July 2001, any person making any payment under a contract relating to construction operations shall deduct tax @ of 3% from all payments made under such a contract, irrespective of whether the person receiving payment is a resident or a nonresident.

4.2. Payment to the Commissioner

The tax withheld is to be paid over to the Commissioner by the 15th of the month following the month in which the tax was withheld. Delay in paying over the tax creates a liability to charge of interest besides penalty under section 117 (7) and prosecution under section 125 of the Income Tax Act.

4.3. Certificate of Deduction

Every person who deducts any tax @ 3% from payments to be made under contracts relating to construction operations must within 15 days issue a tax deduction certificate to the person whom payment was made , in the prescribed Form ITW 9 after getting it duly approved by the office of the Commissioner of Taxes.

Form ITW 9s are available with the Withholding Taxes Division of the Department (Phone No 3914859), which may be obtained by the payer in advance to facilitate handing over of tax deduction certificates to the payee within the prescribed time of 15 days.

4.4. **Credit for the tax withheld**

The tax withheld from payments made under a contract relating to construction operations is not a final tax. The amount of tax withheld and paid over to the Commissioner will be available as a credit against the self assessment tax liability in the case of companies. Other taxpayers not covered under the self assessment system can claim the amount of tax withheld as a credit against their tax liability by submitting a tax return for the relevant tax year. Such credit can be claimed by enclosing with the tax return, the tax deduction certificate in duly approved Form ITW9 (i.e. duly stamped by the Commissioner of Taxes).

5. EXCLUSION/EXEMPTION FROM WITHHOLDING IN CERTAIN CASES:

5.1. Exclusion of amounts to be paid to sub-contractors

The Income Tax (Amendment) Act 2001 has amended the provisions of the Sixth Schedule. Under the amended provisions, when a person who is in receipt of payments which are subject to tax deduction at 3% under sixth schedule, engages sub contractors for executing part of the contract work, he may apply (in form ITW 22) to the Commissioner to issue a directive to his principal to exclude that portion of the payments received by him which he has applied or intends to apply for payments to specified sub contractors from deduction of tax at 3%. The Commissioner on being satisfied with his application, may issue the directive to his principal to deduct tax on only so much of the payments under the contract remaining after deduction of payments to subcontractors as given in the application furnished by the contractor.

The following **illustration** will explain this provision contained in sub-paragraph (2) of paragraph 3 of the Sixth Schedule.

Total payments receivable by the Contractor – P10 million

Payments to be made by the contractor to sub contractors as per application furnished by him in Form ITW.22 -P2 million

Commissioner may issue directive that tax be deducted from only P8 million i.e. total payments as reduced by payments to be made to sub contractors (P10 million less P2 million = P8 million) instead of total payment of P10 million. The contractor, in turn will deduct tax at 3% on payments to be made by him to sub-contractors. In a case where the sub-contract is exempt under proviso to section 56 (category OC, A or B contract and the value of contract is less than P 2 Million), no tax will be deducted.

5.2. Variation / Exemption from withholding on the basis of compliance history

Under paragraph 3(3) of the Sixth Schedule, a person due to receive any payment under a contract relating to construction operations may also apply in Form ITW.22 for a tax certificate. This tax certificate is issued only after the Commissioner has scrutinized the tax compliance history of the taxpayer. If the Commissioner is satisfied that the taxpayer is registered with the Commissioner of Taxes and has a very good history of compliance with various tax obligations, including his obligations relating to self-assessment tax and withholding taxes, he may issue a tax certificate. The tax certificate may either exempt the payments made to such contractor from withholding taxes under Sixth schedule or may vary the amount of tax to be withheld from the payments to be made to him.

5.3. Exclusion and Exemption are not mutually exclusive

The provisions discussed at 5.1 and 5.2 above are not mutually exclusive. A person may apply both for exclusion, for the purpose of tax deduction, from payments received by him of payments in turn made by him to sub contractors and for a tax certificate based on compliance history. However, for the purpose of administrative convenience, the contractor is advised to make a single application in respect of a contract. This application (Form ITW.22) combines the provisions of sub paragraphs (2) and (3) of paragraph 3 of the Sixth Schedule.

5.4. Application for exclusion /exemption is to be made for each tax year

Since the tax withheld under the provision of section 56 is to be set off against the final tax liability of the respective tax year , the application for exclusion or variation is to be made for each tax year separately.

6. LIABILITY IN THE EVENT OF NON-DEDUCTION AND /OR NON-PAYMENT

6.1 Personal liability of the payer:

The person making payments under a contract to which section 56 applies shall be personally liable for the tax to be withheld and in case of his failure to deduct tax, the tax will be recoverable from him.

6.2. Non-deduction and/or non-payment are punishable:

Failure to deduct tax and pay the same and maintain record for inspection by the Commissioner shall, besides inviting interest under Section 100 of the Income Tax Act, also attract penalty under sections 117(6) and 117(7) of the Income Tax Act. Where the failure to deduct is willful with the intent to evade tax, the person responsible for deducting may also be prosecuted under Section 125 and 127 of the Income Tax Act.

7. CONCLUSION

7.1. Payer's Responsibilities

It is the responsibility of the person making the payments under a contract relating to construction operations to deduct tax @ 3% in terms of section 56 and in accordance with the provisions of the Sixth Schedule of the Income Tax Act. The person withholding tax on payment for such a contract relating to construction operations shall do the following:

(i) Furnish information on such payments in terms of paragraph 1 of the Sixth Schedule.

(ii) Deduct tax and pay the same within 15 days of such deduction to the Commissioner of Taxes. Taxes withheld and paid by him will be recorded in ITW.7, the statement of monthly tax deduction and payments.

(iii) Exempt from deduction of tax only if satisfied that the payee falls within categories OC, A and B of the Central Tender Board and the value of contract executed by the payee is less than P2 million.

(iv) Insist on furnishing a exclusion or exemption certificate from the Commissioner of Taxes, where the payee claims such exclusion or exemption from withholding tax.

(v) Furnish to the payee certificate of such deduction in ITW.9 with the stamp of the Commissioner of Taxes within 15 days of the deduction. The white copy of ITC9 shall be furnished to the payee, the green copy will be filed with the Commissioner and the pink will be retained by the payer.

(vi)

Furnish annual return of withholding taxes in Form ITW.10 to the Commissioner within 31 days of the end of the relevant tax year.

(vii) Maintain record of all payments and produce the same for inspection by the Commissioner whenever required by him to do so.

7.2. Payee's responsibilities:

The person receiving payment under a contract relating to construction operation shall do the following:

(a)

Furnish evidence to the payer for supporting the claim that the relevant contract is exempt from withholding due to classification as OC, A or B by the Central Tender Board.

(b) Apply to the Commissioner of Taxes in Form ITW22 for claiming exclusion or exemption from withholding and once received the ruling / tax certificate , furnish the same to the payer. The exclusion /exemption will be granted tax year wise and therefore application for the same is to be made for each tax year separately.

(c) Ask the payer to hand over a tax deduction certificate in Form ITW9, duly approved by the Commissioner of Taxes . Do not accept the certificates unless they are approved by the Commissioner of Taxes.

(d) Enclose the tax deduction certificate in Form ITW 9 with the tax return for the relevant tax year for claiming credit for the tax withheld .

7.3. Assistance available

In need of any clarification, please contact the offices of the Commissioner of Taxes at the addresses and phone numbers given below:

Department of Taxes	**Department of Taxes**	**Department of Taxes**
Withholding Division	Collection Division	Collection Division
Private Bag 00207	Private Bag 38	Private Bag 13
Gaborone	Francistown	Selebi-Phikwe
Phone: 3914859	Phone: 2412734	Phone: 810795
Fax: 581729	Fax: 2414267	Fax: 814862

Central Processing Unit Commissioner of Taxes 3rd Floor, BSB Building Private Bag 0013 Opp: BBS Mall Gaborone Private Bag 00171 Gaborone. **Phone: 3952444**

Fax: 3953101 Phone: 3900723 Fax: 3900778

8. **WITHDRAWAL OF EARLIER DGNs**

All earlier Departmental Guidance Notes on the subject covered by this DGN are hereby withdrawn.

12 November 2002

Private Bag 0013, Gaborone

TERMINAL EXPENSES PAYABLE UNDER EMPLOYMENT CONTRACTS.

Part VI (Ascertainment of Chargeable Income) of the Income Tax Act 1995*.

1. Introduction

The purpose of this Note is to advise practices which will be followed with regard to deductions which will be allowed in respect of various contractual terminal payments to employees in determining business chargeable income of the employer. To the extent that such payments are made to expatriate employees the guidelines which follow do no more than confirm what has been Departmental practice for very many years. Over recent years however regard has been had to similar payments made to citizen employees, in particular, Approved Service Gratuities (Section 32* of the Income Tax Act) and Severance Benefits (Section 28 of the Employment Act). The various amendments to the Income Tax Act have made provision for the income tax treatment of such payments in the hands of the employee but as far as employers are concerned the deductions allowable in respect of all terminal expenses, relating to employees, must be considered within Part VI (Ascertainment of Chargeable Income) of the Income Tax Act. This Note attempts to cover acceptable bases for deductions of all such payments whether made to citizen or expatriate employees.

The terms of the Note have no force in law and do not restrict any taxpayer's rights under the Income Tax Act, in particular, the rights of objection or appeal.

2. General

Payments covered under the terms of this Note are those which are to be met by an employer, out of his own funds, in terms of a contract or general conditions of service, when an employee's engagement terminates. In this regard termination of a fixed period contract is seen as termination of an agreement. The particular payments, which are covered here, are:

(a) To expatriate employees – gratuities, leave pay, passages and related costs;

(b) To citizen employees -service gratuities, whether or not approved Under section 32 (8) of the Act; and

(c) Severance benefits payable in terms of the Employment Act.

Due to the differing methods of calculation of the various terminal payments, it is necessary to set out slightly varying guidelines for each of the above categories of payments. Also some qualifications will be needed in the case of employees who are participators in close companies (i.e. terminal payments which are treated as dividends under section 133).

3. **Bases for deduction**

Two alternative bases for deduction are provided either of which, if consistently used by an employer, will be accepted. But the same basis must be used for all employees who may receive terminal payments.

The two bases are:

(a) year of payment of the expense; and
(b) annual provision during contract period, calculated by reference to the expenditure incurred in respect of each specific employee during the accounting period.

No other basis of deduction will be permitted for tax purposes.

No general or arbitrary provisions will be allowed.

A change from basis (a) to basis (b) or vice-versa will be permitted but one change only will be accepted. A subsequent reversion to the previous basis will not be accepted.

4. Year of Payment basis

Where an employer chooses to claim a deduction for the year in which the amounts become due and payable, the deduction, if related to specific employees and otherwise in order, will be allowed. This will apply to all such payments mentioned in paragraph 2.

If an annual provision has been claimed and allowed for an earlier year it will be assumed that the employer has changed from basis (b) to basis (a) and the Commissioner will retain the right to either, as he sees fit :

(i) re-open earlier years to disallow the provisions previously allowed or,
(ii) restrict the deduction in the year of claim to the excess over the provisions previously allowed.

No further annual provisions will be allowed.

5. Annual provision basis

5.1. Expatriates employees

Where an employer chooses to claim a deduction annually, by provision in his accounts or otherwise, this will be allowed subject to the amounts claimed being related to specific employees and for each:

(a)

a gratuity deduction being the contractual percentage of salary on base remuneration for the year;

(b) a leave pay deduction being the amount due for leave accrued to the accounting date at the latest known leave pay rate less any amount deducted in an earlier year; and
(c) a deduction for passages and related costs

being the estimated future cost apportioned to the expired period of the employment less any amount deducted in earlier years.

5.2. Service Gratuities – Citizen employees

Where an employer has a scheme which provides for or the written conditions of employment provide for payments of gratuities to citizen employees either on termination of employment after a minimum period of employment or at periodic intervals during the course of employment the annual provision method of deduction will be permitted. It is not necessary that the gratuity be an "Approved Service Gratuity" within the provisions of section 32(8) of the Act – the subsection only sets out conditions that must be met if an employee **is to be exempted wholly or partially. It is expected that the calculation of the provision for the gratuity will be calculated by reference to the employee's basic rate of pay at the time he becomes entitled to payment of the gratuity.**

The provision method is thus acceptable provided it is applied consistently and subject to the following:

(a) provision must be made for all relevant employees;
(b) the provision must be specific to each of those employees;

(c) the provision is no more than the gratuity accrued to each employee during the accounting period;
(d) the provision is calculated by reference to each employee's basic pay at the end of the accounting period;
(e) the provision made for any particular accounting period does not contain any under-provision for an earlier accounting period except where a recalculation of the provision becomes necessary by reason of an increase in the basic pay of any employee;
(f) provisions made in earlier accounting periods in respect of employees who by reason of termination of their employment, or for any other reason, have lost their entitlement to any gratuity are brought back into credit against other provisions; and
(g) no provision is made in respect of any other terminal benefit in respect of any particular employee.

5.3. Severance Benefits

A severance Benefit is a payment, which an employer may have a statutory obligation to make to an employee under section 28 of the Employment Act. By virtue of section 2(3) of that Act an employee for this purpose does not include "an employee who falls into a category of persons commonly known as managers, administrators or executives or as professional staff or into some other category of persons of the same or a similar status".

The provision basis of deduction will be permitted for eligible employees who may become entitled to such a benefit and the guidelines, as set out in the previous paragraph, in respect of Service Gratuities should be followed. In particular, attention is drawn to the following :

(a) an employee may cease to be entitled to a Severance Benefit because he moves into one of the non-eligible categories, and
(b) no provisions in respect of any other terminal benefit will be permitted as section 28 of the Employment Act relieves the employer of the obligation to make any other terminal benefits if an employee requires payment of a Severance Benefit.

6. Participatory Payments

6.1.Year of payment basis

If this basis is adopted and a payment is made to an employee which falls to be treated as a dividend in the hands of a participator, deduction will not be allowed from assessable income but from chargeable income in ascertaining taxable income in terms of section 50.

6.2. Annual provision basis

If this basis is adopted and a payment is made to an employee which falls to be treated as a dividend in the hands of a participator, the related provisions for years prior to the year of payment will be allowed as a deduction from assessable income in ascertaining chargeable income. In the year of payment, the provisions for the prior years will be added back to chargeable income as "provisions no longer required". There will also be added back in the year of payment, any balances of the payments made which have been deducted in ascertaining chargeable income. The total payments will then be deducted from chargeable income, in terms of section 50, in ascertaining taxable income.

IF however a taxpayer requires adjustments made in the tax years in which the provisions were made this will be permitted. The Commissioner will also make similar adjustments, if he is required to do so to avoid loss of tax.

7. Conclusion

As indicated earlier the contents of this Note are without prejudice to the rights of objection and appeal of any aggrieved taxpayer.

It is also recognised that, as always with income Tax, there are exceptions to the rule and cases may arise which will have to be considered on their own merits. It is hoped however that little need will arise to depart from the guidelines set out in this Note.

8. Assistance available

In need of any clarification, please contact the offices of the Commissioner of Taxes at the addresses and phone numbers given below:

Department of Taxes Department of Taxes Department of Taxes

Private Bag 0013 Collection Division Collection Division Gaborone Private Bag 38 Private Bag 13 Phone: 3614600 Francistown Selebi-Phikwe
Fax: 3953101 Phone: 212734 Phone: 810795
Fax: 214267 Fax: 814862

TAXABLE INCOME REGULATIONS[5]

TAXABLE INCOME, GENERAL

(1) Subject to the provisions of this Part, the taxable income of any person for any tax year shall be the aggregate of his or her chargeable income from all sources, other than chargeable income under section 40, and the amount of his or her net aggregate gains ascertained under the Tenth Schedule for the tax year, less any deductions he or she may be entitled to under subsections (2) and (3) .

(2) Where a person makes a donation to

(*a*) any educational institution recommended by the Ministry of Education; or

(*b*) any sports clubs or sports associations recommended by the Ministry responsible for sports, and approved by the Commissioner General, the taxable income ascertained in respect of that person under subsection (1) shall be subject to the deduction of not less than P1,000 of the aggregate value in money's worth of donations made by him or her:

Provided that such deduction does not exceed 20 per cent of the person's aggregate chargeable income for that tax year.

(3) In the case of a resident individual, the taxable income as ascertained in respect of any other person under subsection (1) shall be subject to the deduction of 15 per cent of his or her chargeable income, other than his or her investment income in respect of contributions made by him or her to an approved superannuation fund for that tax year:

Provided that

[5] Source: Botswana Income Tax Law.

(i) this subsection shall not apply to an employee who, not being a citizen of Botswana, commenced a contract of employment before the 1st July, 1999, and is entitled on the termination of that contract to a bonus or gratuity which is exempt from tax under paragraph (xviii) of II of the Second Schedule.

(ii) a Minister or Member of Parliament who is entitled to pension and gratuity which is exempt from tax under paragraph (xxxiv) of II of the Second Schedule;

(iii) an employee who is entitled on termination of his or her contract to a gratuity which is exempt from tax under paragraph (xxxv) of II of the Second Schedule;

(iv) the contributions made and which are claimed as deductions, were made wholly out of income accrued from a source situated in or deemed to be situated in Botswana.

(4) ....

(5) No person shall be entitled to any deduction under this except upon due claim and subject to the production of such evidence as the Commissioner General may require.

ORDERS AND AGREEMENTS

DEVELOPMENT APPROVAL ORDERS AND ADDITIONAL TAX RELIEF

(1) The Minister may make an Order, to be known as a development approval order, prescribing

(*a*) any business which proposes to carry out a project which would be beneficial to the economy of Botswana or to the economic advancement of the citizens of Botswana as a business which may be granted additional tax relief;

(*b*) any business activity which would be beneficial to the economy of Botswana or to the economic advancement of the citizens of Botswana as an activity which, if carried out by any business, will entitle that business to the grant of additional tax relief;

(*c*) the type of development project or activity in respect of which additional tax relief may be granted;

(*d*) the area in which any such development project or activity is to be carried out; or

(*e*) the types and rates of additional tax relief which may be granted in respect of any development project or activity.

(2) Notwithstanding any other provision of this Act, the Minister may, in any development approval order, prescribe that such additional amount as he or she may determine shall be deducted in ascertaining the chargeable income of the business insofar as it is derived from the development project or activity and such deduction may relate to any expenditure incurred by the business in relation to the development project or activity, including any expenditure to which VI applies.

(3) A business which wishes to be granted additional tax relief in respect of a development project or in respect of any activity under this section shall apply on such form as may be prescribed or approved by the Minister, and shall submit such application to the Permanent Secretary of the Ministry responsible for finance.

(4) In considering any application made under subsection (3) , the Minister shall have regard to

(*a*) the number of Botswana citizens who will be employed in relation to the project or activity and the capacities in which they will be employed;

(*b*) any facilities proposed for the training and imparting of skills to Botswana citizens;

(*c*) any provisions made for the eventual replacement of non-resident employees by Botswana citizens;

(*d*) any provision made for participation by Botswana citizens in the management of the business;

(*e*) the degree of investment in the business of capital owned by Botswana citizens;

(*f*) the area in which the proposed development project or activity will be carried on; and

(*g*) any effect which the proposed project or activity might be expected to have

(i) on stimulating the development of other economic, industrial or commercial activities in Botswana, whether of the business or otherwise; or

(ii) in reducing the price in Botswana of consumer goods or services.

(5) Where the Minister is satisfied that the proposed project or activity would be beneficial to the development of the economy of Botswana or to the economic advancement of its citizens, he or she may issue a development approval order in respect of such business or business activity.

(6) A development approval order may be issued subject to such conditions and for such period of time as the Minister deems fit.

(7) The Minister may, at any time, by a further order, amend or revoke a development approval order if he or she is satisfied that

(*a*) a business has failed substantially to carry out the development project or activity specified in the order; or

(*b*) there has been a substantial breach of any conditions specified in the order, but no such order of amendment or revocation shall be made until the business has, by notice in writing, been given the opportunity to rectify that failure or breach, or to show cause within such time as may be specified, not being less than 30 days from the date of such notice, why the development approval order should not be amended or revoked.

(8) Any person who is aggrieved by the proposed amendment or revocation of a development approval order may appeal to a magistrate's court presided over by a Magistrate Grade I or above, on the grounds that it has carried out the development or activity specified in the order, or that it is not in breach of any condition of the order; and if such appeal is upheld the proposed amendment or revocation of the development approval order shall not proceed.

(9) A business to which a development approval order relates shall be entitled to the relief specified in the order where the Commissioner General is satisfied that the development project or activity to which the order relates has been carried out.

(10) Where, under subsection (7) , the Minister has, by further order, amended or revoked a development approval order relating to a development project or activity carried on by any business, such adjustment shall be made in respect of the liability to the tax of such business for any tax year as is necessary to give effect to that further order.

(11) A development approval order or further order made under this section shall be laid before the National Assembly as soon as possible after it is made, and shall not take effect until one month thereafter, provided that it is not sooner disapproved by resolution of the National Assembly, but upon taking effect, it shall come into operation or be deemed to have come into operation from the date specified in the order or further order.

(12) Where a development approval order made in respect of any business activity has been approved by the National Assembly and has come into operation in accordance with the provisions of subsection (11) , then any subsequent development approval order made by the Minister in respect of a business activity which carries on such business activity as that approved by the National Assembly shall not be laid before the National Assembly.

INTERNATIONAL AGREEMENTS FOR THE AVOIDANCE OF DOUBLE TAXATION

(1) The Minister may, on behalf of the Government, enter into an agreement with the government of any other country with a view to the prevention, mitigation or discontinuance of double taxation, the levying of tax under this Act and the income tax laws of that other country, or to the rendering of reciprocal assistance in the administration of and in the collection of tax under this Act and such income tax laws.

(2) Any agreement entered into under this subsection (1) shall, by order, be laid before the National Assembly as soon as possible after the agreement is entered into but shall not take effect unless or until it is approved by resolution of the National Assembly, when it shall come into operation or be deemed to have come into operation on the date specified in the agreement.

(3) The Minister may at any time by order, which shall be laid before the National Assembly as soon as may be after it is issued, amend or cancel any agreement entered into under subsection (1) , and if such order of amendment or cancellation is approved by resolution of the National Assembly such agreement shall, as the case may be, from the date specified in such order

(*a*) stand amended, and operate in its amended form; or

(*b*) cease to operate.

TAX AGREEMENTS

(1) The Minister may, on behalf of the Government, enter into a tax agreement with any person who is or may become liable to tax under this Act.

(2) (*a*) Any agreement entered into under this section shall, by order, be laid before the National Assembly as soon as possible after it is entered into, and shall not take effect unless or until it is approved by resolution of the National Assembly, when it shall come into operation, or be deemed to have come into operation on the date specified in the agreement.

(*b*) Any agreement entered into under this section may be amended or cancelled in like manner as is provided in paragraph (*a*) .

(3) Any agreement entered into under this section may, in respect of the person with whom it is made, vary the provisions of this Act insofar as such provisions either impose liability to tax, or regulate the imposition of such liability, and may provide for

(*a*) the exemption of any dividend, interest, commercial royalty, entertainment fee or management or consultancy fee paid by that person to a non-resident;

(*b*) the exemption or limitation of liability in respect of any amount accrued or deemed to have accrued, or any benefits derived from employment carried on by a person or any class of persons who are not citizens of Botswana, in terms of a contract of employment entered into by the person with whom the tax agreement under this section is made; or

(*c*) the relief of that person from any duty, responsibility and liability under any provision of this Act.

(4) If any agreement entered into under this section imposes any liability to tax such liability shall be deemed to be a liability imposed under this Act and all the provisions of this Act including any variations thereto which may have been made under subsection (3) shall apply thereto.

TAXATION O OF COMPANIES AND BUSINESS

Notwithstanding anything contained in this Act-

(*a*) the taxable income of the Botswana Meat Commission shall be ascertained in accordance with the provisions of I of the Fourth Schedule;

(*b*) the chargeable income of any company which is a member of the Botswana Development Corporation Limited group of companies shall be ascertained in accordance with the provisions of sections 36 to 49 inclusive and II of the Fourth Schedule;

(*c*) the chargeable income derived from the carrying on of insurance business by any person shall be ascertained in accordance with the provisions of III of the Fourth Schedule; and

(*d*) the chargeable income of mining operations shall be ascertained in accordance with the provisions of the Twelfth Schedule.

WITHHOLDING AND DEDUCTED TAXES

DEDUCTION OF TAX BY EMPLOYERS

(1) Every employer shall deduct tax from the remuneration paid to his or her employees in accordance with and in the manner specified in the Fifth Schedule and shall carry out such other obligations as are imposed by that Schedule.

(2) In this section the word "employer" has the meaning given to it in the Fifth Schedule.

DEDUCTION OF TAX UNDER CERTAIN CONTRACTS

Every person who makes any payment to any person under a contract relating to construction operations shall deduct tax from such payment in accordance with and in the manner specified in the Sixth Schedule and shall carry out such other obligations as are imposed by that Schedule:

Provided that this section shall not apply to

(*a*) contracts with a value of less than P2 000 000 being executed by construction companies which have been classified as falling under categories OC, A and B by the Public Procurement and Asset Disposal Board in terms of section 121 of the Public Procurement and Asset Disposal Act; and

(*b*) contracts exclusively for design, engineering, surveying work, and other related professional services.

DEDUCTION OF TAX FROM PAYMENTS OF DIVIDENDS, INTEREST AND CERTAIN ROYALTIES AND FEES

(1) Every person who

(*a*) being a resident company, makes any payment of dividend to a resident or a non-resident; or

(*b*) makes any payment of interest to a resident or a non-resident;

(*c*) makes any payment of commercial royalty, entertainment fee, or management or consultancy fee to a non-resident,

shall deduct tax from such payment in accordance with and in the manner specified in the Seventh Schedule and shall carry out such other obligations as are imposed by that Schedule.

(2) For the purposes of this section a person, including a partnership, to whom any payment is made to which this section applies shall be presumed, unless the contrary is proved, to be a non-resident if such payment is made to an address outside Botswana.

(3) The Commissioner General may direct that this section shall not apply to any payment of interest to a non-resident, if he or she is satisfied that, by reason of the small amount of the payment or any other special circumstances, it is reasonable to so direct.

(4) This section shall not apply to

(*a*) any payment of interest, commercial royalty or management consultancy fee;

(*b*) the payment of a dividend to a non resident, an international financial services centre company or a collective investment undertaking,

(*c*) any payment of interest to a resident where the recipient of such interest is a person exempt from taxation; and

(*d*) an IFSC company, a banking company or a financial institution receiving such interest in its ordinary course of business, where the payment is made by an international financial services centre company or a collective investment undertaking which is exempt from tax under paragraph (xvi) of I of the Second Schedule.

RATES OF TAX

RATE OF TAX, GENERAL

(1) Subject to this Part, tax shall be charged on the taxable income for each tax year at the relevant rates specified in the Eighth Schedule:

Provided that in the case of an individual, the tax payable on the amount of his or her net aggregate gains shall be calculated in accordance with Table IV of the Eighth Schedule.

(2) Where any interest, commercial royalty, entertainment fee, or management or consultancy fee accrues from Botswana to a non-resident, tax shall be charged for each tax year at the rates specified in paragraph 2 of the Seventh Schedule.

(3) Where a resident company pays withholding tax under paragraph 2 of the Seventh Schedule, at the rate specified therein, on dividends distributed to a shareholder, this shall be a final charge to tax, and the dividends shall not form of the assessable income of the shareholder.

(4) Where an international financial services centre company pays a dividend which is exempt from withholding tax under section 58(4) , such dividend shall not form of the assessable income of the shareholder.

(5) The tax rate specified in Table III paragraph 7 of the Eighth Schedule or such lesser rate as Parliament may from time to time specify, shall apply for each tax year until the tax year 2019/2020.

SET-OFF AGAINST ADDITIONAL COMPANY TAX

(1) Subject to subsections (2) and (3) , where in any tax year a resident company is liable to deduct tax from dividends in accordance with section 58(1) and the Seventh Schedule, hereinafter referred to as "witholding tax", and has paid such tax to the Commissioner General, and such company is also liable for additional company tax as provided in Table III of the Eighth Schedule, the amount of witholding tax shall be set off, in whole or in part, against the additional company tax due for that tax year:

Provided that the witholding tax shall be set-off in chronological order of withholding, and no amount of such deducted tax shall be set-off more than once.

(2) Where additional company tax due for any tax year exceeds the amount of witholding tax, paid or payable, which can be set-off against such additional company tax under subsection (1) , the excess is payable upon assessment for that tax year.

(3) Where additional company tax has been paid for a tax year under subsection (2) , the amount paid shall be carried over to the next tax year as a set-off against the witholding tax in that tax year; and the remaining amount of witholding tax shall be set-off against any additional company tax due for that tax year.

(3A) No additional company tax shall be carried forward for set-off against withholding tax for more than five years following the tax year in which it was paid.

(4) Notwithstanding the provisions of subsections (1) , (2) and (3) and any other provision of this Act, the liability to tax of any company carrying on business under an agreement with the Government in terms of section 54 of this Act, or any other agreement, or the liability to tax of any other person which is determined by such agreement, shall be in terms of the law in force at the time such agreement was signed, and such law shall be applicable for the duration of the agreement, unless the Government and the parties thereto agree otherwise.

CREDIT FOR TAX PAID

CREDIT FOR TAX DEDUCTED AT SOURCE

Where under Division III of VIII any tax has been deducted from any amount accrued to any person, the tax so deducted shall be set off against the tax charged under section 59 for the tax year in which such amounts accrued or are deemed to have accrued:

Provided that any tax deducted from

(*a*) dividends payable to a resident or non-resident; or

(*b*) interest, commercial royalty, entertainment fee or management or consultancy fee, payable to a non-resident which is a final charge under this Act shall not be deducted from any tax charged under section 59.

CREDIT FOR TAX PAID

Where any tax has been paid by a person under subsection (2) , (3) or (4) of section 95 or section 114, the tax so paid shall be set off against the tax charged under section 59, for the tax year in respect of which such payment was made.

CREDIT FOR TAX PAID OUTSIDE BOTSWANA

(1) Where an agreement which has effect under section 53 provides that tax payable under the laws of the country with which such agreement has been made shall be allowed as a credit against tax charged in Botswana, credit for such tax shall be calculated in the manner provided in section 64, and shall be set off against the tax charged under this Act.

(2) Subject to subsection (1) , where employment income, interest or dividends accrued to a resident from a source outside Botswana are charged to tax under this Act, credit for any tax payable under the laws of the country from which such employment income, interest or dividends accrued shall be calculated in the manner provided in section 64, and shall be set off against the tax charged under this Act.

(3) Subject to subsection (1) , where an amount accrued to any person from a source outside Botswana is charged to tax under section 11 or section 31, credit for any tax payable under the laws of the country from which such amount accrued shall be given to such extent as in the opinion of the Commissioner General is reasonable.

(4) Notwithstanding the provisions of subsection (3) , where an amount accrued to a resident of Botswana from a source outside Botswana is charged to tax under section 11, credit for any tax payable under the laws of the country from which such amount accrued shall be allowed as a credit against tax charged in Botswana, and credit for such tax shall be calculated in the manner provided under section 64.

(5) Where an international financial services centre company has gross income accrued from a source outside Botswana which is charged to tax under this Act, credit for any tax payable under the laws of the country from which such gross income accrued shall be calculated in accordance with section 64 and shall be set off against the tax charged under this Act and the credit shall apply whether or not an agreement referred to in section 53 is in place with that country.

CALCULATION OF TAX CREDIT

(1) The credit to be set off in respect of tax payable in another country on the amount referred to in section 63, shall be the lesser of the following

(*a*) the tax payable in the other country; or

(*b*) the tax charged under this Act, on such amount.

(2) In this section

"the tax payable in the other country" means the amount of tax payable, either directly or by deduction, for which the taxpayer was personally liable and ultimately bears in that other country; and

"the tax charged under this Act", in relation to any tax year, means that proportion of such tax which the amount accrued from a source outside Botswana referred to in section 63 bears to the chargeable income of that tax year.

(3) In the case of an international financial services centre company, the tax charged under this Act in relation to any tax year, means that proportion of such tax which is equal to the proportion that gross income which is accrued from a source outside Botswana bears to the gross income of that tax year as defined in section 139 and the credit available for foreign tax shall be restricted in accordance with the following formula:

Tax payable X Gross income from foreign source in Botswana Gross income

Provided that the foreign tax credit will be restricted to the tax payable in the foreign country if less than the amount determined by the above formula.

RETURNS AND NOTICES

TAX RETURNS, GENERAL

(1) Subject to section 77, every person shall furnish a return in the prescribed form of his or her gross income (hereinafter referred to as a "tax return") in respect of any tax year, either personally or in a representative capacity, within three months after the end of that tax year, and such form shall be signed by him or her or by an agent authorized by him or her on his her behalf.

(2) Subject to section 77, every person shall furnish a return of the gross income and such other particulars as may be required in the return, computation of taxable income and tax payable as well as payments made thereof, in the prescribed form, in respect of any tax year in accordance with the provisions of this Act, either personally or in a representative capacity within four months of the end of that tax year, or in the case of a person whose accounting period is different from that of the tax year, within four months from the end of such accounting period, and such form and other documents shall be signed by the person or by an agent authorized by such person:

Provided that the provisions of this subsection shall become applicable to taxpayers or to categories of taxpayer's from such dates as the Minister, by order, may determine:

Provided further that upon the application of this subsection to a taxpayer, the provisions of subsection (1) shall cease to apply to such taxpayer.

(3) The Commissioner General shall give general notice in the *Gazette* and in such other manner and at such other places as he or she deems fit of the obligations imposed by this section, but failure to give any such notice shall in no way relieve any person liable to furnish a tax return from his or her obligation to comply with subsection (1) .

(4) Tax return forms may be obtained from the Commissioner General or from any income tax office or from any other place specified in the notice under subsection (3) , and it shall be the duty of all persons liable to furnish a tax return to obtain such forms.

(5) Notwithstanding subsection (4) the Commissioner General may, if he or she deems it so advisable, cause forms to be delivered by hand or post to any person.

(6) Notwithstanding the provisions of subsection (1) , the following persons shall not, unless specifically requested by the Commissioner General, be required to furnish a return

(*a*) any person who has been informed in writing or by any general notification that a return is not required for the tax year;

(*b*) any resident individual in respect of whose taxable income for any tax year there is no liability to tax;

(*c*) any individual the whole of whose income is remuneration subject to the provisions of the Fifth Schedule;

(*d*) a person whose gross income accrued or is deemed to have accrued from sources situated or deemed to be situated in Botswana to a non-resident for any tax year, and consists only of amounts to which section 33(1) relates, and tax is deducted from the payment of all such amounts under section 58 and in accordance with the Seventh Schedule.

PROVISIONAL TAX RETURN

Where under section 77 the Commissioner General has extended the period in which a tax return for any tax year is to be furnished by any person other than a person to whom section 65(2) applies, he or she may by notice in writing require such person, within such time as may be specified in the notice, not being less than seven days from the date of service of that notice, to furnish a provisional return containing an estimate by such person of his or her taxable income for such tax year.

TAX RETURNS: CESSATION OF INCOME DURING A TAX YEAR

Where it appears to the Commissioner General that

(*a*) a person may leave Botswana during the current tax year or shortly after its expiry, and that the absence from Botswana of such person is unlikely to be temporary only;

(*b*) a person has ceased to carry on business in any tax year; or

(*c*) in the case of any other person it is expedient to do so, the Commissioner General may at any time serve upon such person a notice in writing requiring him or her to furnish within such time as may be specified in the notice, not being less than seven days from the date of service of such notice, a tax return for any tax year.

TAX RETURNS: WHERE NO RETURN IS FURNISHED

(1) Where it appears to the Commissioner General that any person is or may be liable to furnish a tax return for any tax year and has not done so, he or she may, by notice in writing, require such person to furnish a tax return within such time as may be specified in the notice, not being less than seven days from the date of service of such notice.

(2) Nothing in this section shall be construed as extending the time limits provided by section 65 for the furnishing of any tax return.

FURTHER RETURNS OR INFORMATION, PRODUCTION OF BOOKS AND GIVING OF EVIDENCE TO COMMISSIONER

(1) For the purpose of obtaining full information in respect of the chargeable income of any person, the Commissioner General may, by notice in writing, require any person

(*a*) to furnish to the Commissioner General such further tax return, statement of assets and liabilities or other information as may be required by the Commissioner General;

(*b*) to produce at such time and place as may be specified in such notice, for examination by the Commissioner General or for retention by him or her for such period as may be reasonable for their examination, any accounts, books of account, statement of assets and liabilities or other documents which the Commissioner General may consider necessary for such purpose and, if any such information is not available in the English or Setswana language, to produce at the taxpayer's expense a translation in English prepared and certified by an approved translator; or

(*c*) to attend at such time and place as may be specified in such notice, for the purpose of being examined by the Commissioner General respecting his or her chargeable income or the chargeable income of any other person or any transactions or matters appearing to be relevant thereto.

(2) Where any person is required to attend and give information under subsection (1) in relation to any other person, he or she may be allowed such expenses of attending as may be prescribed.

(3) Notwithstanding the provisions of subsection (1) , the Commissioner General may, by notice in writing, require any person to furnish annually, or at such intervals as the Commissioner

General may determine, any information that the Commissioner General considers necessary to enable him or her to fulfil his or her duties under this Act.

Powers of entry, inspection and removal of documents

(1) The Commissioner General, or any officer authorized by him or her, may, for the purposes of obtaining information which he or she considers necessary in relation to the liability of any person to tax, enter any premises at any time during the day, without previous notice, and search for any moneys or documents; and in carrying out any search he or she may

(*a*) open, or cause to be removed and opened, any article in which he or she considers any moneys or documents may be contained;

(*b*) seize any documents which he or she considers may afford material evidence of the liability of any person to tax;

(*c*) retain any such documents for such period as may be reasonable for their examination or for the purposes of a prosecution; or

(*d*) make copies of any such documents.

(2) Any officer exercising any power under subsection (1) shall, upon demand, produce the authority furnished to him or her by the Commissioner General.

(3) Where any documents are seized and retained under subsection (1) , the person to whom such documents belong shall be entitled to examine and make copies of or extracts from them at such time and place and under such supervision as the Commissioner General may determine.

(4) In this section "documents" includes any books, records or accounts.

SUBMISSION OF ACCOUNTS WITH TAX RETURN AND CERTIFICATE RELATING TO PREPARATION OF ACCOUNTS

(1) Where any person carries on business in any tax year, his or her tax return for such year shall be accompanied by a copy of the accounts of the business together with a reconciliation of the accounts with the chargeable income disclosed in that return in relation to the business.

(2) Where the accounts referred to in subsection (1) have been prepared by the person carrying on the business, he or she shall furnish together with the accounts a certificate signed by him or her stating

(*a*) the nature of the books of account and documents from which such accounts were prepared; and

(*b*) whether such accounts present a true and fair view of the profits from his or her business for the accounting period.

(3) Where the accounts referred to in subsection (1) have been prepared by a person other than the person carrying on the business, such other person shall provide on the face of such accounts a certificate giving his or her name, address and occupation and stating

(*a*) the extent of the examination made of the books of account and of the documents from which such books of account were prepared; and (*b*) whether or not, as far as he or she was able to ascertain from such examination, the entries in those documents and books of account disclosed the true nature of every transaction, receipt, accrual, payment and debit.

(4) The manager or trustee of any charitable, religious or educational institution or a trust or an association referred to in the proviso to paragraph (xxxix) or in paragraph (xl) of II of the Second Schedule shall, in accordance with the provisions of section 65, furnish a tax return of the gross income of such institution, trust or association, for the tax year including statements of accounts, certificates and other relevant documents in relation to the return, signed by such manager or trustee, as the case may be, and shall also furnish such evidence as may be required by the Commissioner General as to the application of such income during the tax year.

. ANNUAL RETURNS BY COMPANIES OF INTEREST AND DIVIDENDS PAID

Every resident company shall, on or before 31st August next following each tax year, furnish to the Commissioner General a return showing the name and address of each person

(*a*) to whom interest was paid in such tax year in respect of any debentures, debenture stock, loans or advances and the amount of interest paid; or

(*b*) to whom dividends were paid or any bonus shares, debentures or securities were awarded in such tax year and the amount or value of such payment or award, and, for the purposes of this section, where any interest or dividend is not paid but is reinvested, accumulated, capitalized, carried to any reserve or otherwise dealt with on his or her behalf or as he or her directs, it shall be deemed to have been paid.

ANNUAL RETURN BY PRIVATE COMPANIES OF SHAREHOLDERS

Every resident private company shall, on or before 31st August next following each tax year, furnish to the Commissioner General a return showing the name and address of, and number of shares held by, each shareholder on the last day of that tax year.

COMPANIES: DOCUMENTS OF INCORPORATION, AMENDMENTS AND PROSPECTUS

(1) Every company shall furnish to the Commissioner General, within the time specified in this section

(*a*) a copy of the memorandum and articles of association constituting the company, or any other documents setting out the powers, aims and objects of and the rules or regulations governing the company;

(*b*) a copy of any amendment made to such documents; and

(*c*) a copy of any prospectus proposed to be issued by the company.

(2) In the case of a company incorporated or formed in Botswana, the documents referred to in subsection (1) shall be furnished within 60 days of the date of incorporation or formation, amendment thereof or, in the case of a prospectus, registration thereof.

(3) In the case of a company incorporated or formed outside Botswana but carrying on business in Botswana, the documents referred to in subsection (1) shall be furnished within 60 days of the

date of commencing to carry on business in Botswana, amendment of the documents constituting or governing the company or, in the case of a prospectus, registration thereof.

RETURNS DEEMED TO BE FURNISHED BY DUE AUTHORITY

Every return, statement or form purporting to be furnished under this Act by or on behalf of any person shall for all purposes of this Act be deemed to have been furnished by that person or with his or her authority, as the case may be, unless the contrary is proved; and any person signing such return, statement or form shall be deemed to be cognizant of all matters contained therein.

RETURNS: METHOD OF FURNISHING

Any return required to be furnished shall be delivered by hand or post to the address specified in the prescribed form.

EXTENSION OF TIME

Where under this Act any return is required to be furnished by any person within a specified period, such person may, on just cause, request for an extension of the period in which such return is to be furnished, and the Commissioner General may, by notice in writing served on that person, extend the period in which the return is to be furnished.

BOTSWANA TAX TREATIES

Botswana has a number double taxation agreements - with

Barbados,
Mozambique,
India,
Namibia,
South Africa,
the United Kingdom,
Sweden,
Mauritius,
Zimbabwe,
France,
Lesotho,
Swaziland and
the Seychelles.

Double tax agreements with

Russia,
Belgium,
Malawi,
Tanzania,
Zambia,
China and
Luxembourg

are awaiting ratification.

Discussions towards possible tax agreements are taking place with the following countries:
Kenya,

Angola,

Nigeria,

Uganda and

Japan.

When the agreement with South Africa was signed in 2003, the IFSC's CEO Alan Boshwaen hailed it, saying SA was a key trading partner and the gesture would see an improvement in the profile of Botswana in the international financial services sector. "This is a welcome development as it gives certainty and predictability on tax treatment, both to SA companies seeking to domicile themselves in Botswana and to Botswana companies operating in SA. Our intention through the center initiative is to enable South African companies to have access to the relatively low tax and a stable environment on their doorstep as they expand north of the Limpopo", Boshwaen said.

In April, 2004, Botswana concluded and signed a double taxation treaty with Russia. "As Botswana continues to attract investors to help diversify the economy and develop international financial services capacity, a double taxation agreement will help to improve our international competitiveness and enhance our image with foreign investors," observed Finance and Development Planning Minister, Baledzi Gaolathe, of the agreement.

The deal between Botswana and Russia will lower the rates of taxation on dividends, interest, royalties and management fees in a bid to boost inward investment, Gaolathe explained.

Urging parliament to adopt the Botswana/Seychelles Double Taxation Avoidance Agreement in July, 2005, Botswanian Minister of Finance and Development Planning Baledzi Gaolathe, stated that such agreements will help support and encourage foreign investment.

Gaolathe told Parliament that the agreement covers taxes on income and provides for co-operation on avoidance of double taxation and prevention of tax evasion on income and capital gains.

The minister went on stress the importance of such agreements in the development of Botswana as an international financial services centre where firms will be conducting much of their business with foreign-based businesses.

Gaolathe explained that the Botswana/Seychelles agreement would also open up possibilities for mutual co-operation in the prevention of tax evasion, avoidance and fraud by providing for the exchange of information on taxpayers.

The DTA was due to enter into force in July, 2006, following the ratification of the agreement by lawmakers in both countries.

The Double Taxation Avoidance Agreement between Botswana and the United Kingdom was approved by lawmakers in the African state in January, 2006. The agreement was signed in Gaborone on 9 September 2005 and entered into force on 4 September 2006.

Gaolathe told Parliament that the agreement also facilitates close co-operation and exchange of information between the tax authorities and addresses the problem of international tax evasion and avoidance.

"Further, double taxation avoidance agreements are of great significance as part of efforts to attract direct foreign investment," said Gaolathe.

"In establishing their business, multinational companies worldwide consider the existence of double taxation avoidance agreements as a distinct advantage as it eliminates uncertainty about how their incomes will be taxed in the contracting countries," Gaolathe added.

The double taxation avoidance agreement is a re-negotiation of the 1977 agreement between the two countries and it seeks to replace the older one.

Gaolathe explained that the salient provisions of the new Botswana/United Kingdom Double Taxation Avoidance Agreement are: "An enterprise of the contracting state will be taxed in the other state in its business income, only if it carries on business in the other state through permanent establishment".

The scope of a permanent establishment has been extended, in the new agreement to cover construction, assembly and/or installations as well as services rendered through employees.

Also income derived from, as well as gains from sale of, immovable property will be taxed only in the country where the property is situated.

The same principle applies to gains from the sale of shares in a company whose assets consist substantially of immovable property located in one of the countries.

Dividends will be subjected to 5% withholding tax, if the company receiving such dividends holds at least 25% of the shareholding of the company paying the dividend, and 12% withholding tax on gross amounts where the share holding is below 25%.

UK/BOTSWANA DOUBLE TAXATION CONVENTION

SIGNED 9 SEPTEMBER 2005

Entered into force 4 September 2006

Effective in United Kingdom from 1 April 2007 for corporation tax and from 6 April 2007 for income tax and capital gains tax.

Effective in Botswana from 1 July 2007

CONVENTION BETWEEN THE GOVERNMENT OF THE UNITED KINGDOM OF GREAT BRITAIN AND NORTHERN IRELAND AND THE GOVERNMENT OF THE REPUBLIC OF BOTSWANA FOR THE AVOIDANCE OF DOUBLE TAXATION AND THE PREVENTION OF FISCAL EVASION WITH RESPECT TO TAXES ON INCOME AND CAPITAL GAINS

The Government of the United Kingdom of Great Britain and Northern Ireland and the Government of the Republic of Botswana;

Desiring to conclude a Convention for the avoidance of double taxation and the prevention of fiscal evasion with respect to taxes on income and capital gains;

Have agreed as follows:

ARTICLE 1 PERSONS COVERED

This Convention shall apply to persons who are residents of one or both of the Contracting States.

ARTICLE 2 TAXES COVERED

(1) This Convention shall apply to taxes on income and on capital gains imposed on behalf of a Contracting State, irrespective of the manner in which they are levied.

(2) There shall be regarded as taxes on income and on capital gains all taxes imposed on total income, or on elements of income, including taxes on gains from the alienation of movable or immovable property.

(3) The existing taxes to which this Convention shall apply are in particular:

(a) in the case of the Republic of Botswana:

(i) the income tax; and

(ii) the capital gains tax; (hereinafter referred to as "Botswana tax");

(b) in the case of the United Kingdom:

(i) the income tax;

(ii) the corporation tax; and

(iii) the capital gains tax; (hereinafter referred to as "United Kingdom tax").

(4) Nothing in this Convention shall limit the right of either Contracting State to charge tax on the profits of a mineral enterprise at an effective rate different from that charged on the profits of any other enterprise. The term 'a mineral enterprise' means an enterprise carrying on the business of mining.

(5) This Convention shall also apply to any identical or substantially similar taxes which are imposed by either Contracting State after the date of signature of this Convention in addition to, or in place of, the existing taxes. The competent authorities of the Contracting States shall notify each other of any significant changes which have been made in their respective taxation laws.

ARTICLE 3 GENERAL DEFINITIONS

(**1**) For the purposes of this Convention, unless the context otherwise requires:

(a) the term "Botswana" means the Republic of Botswana;

(b) the term "United Kingdom" means Great Britain and Northern Ireland, including any area outside the territorial sea of the United Kingdom which in accordance with international law has been or may hereafter be designated, under the laws of the United Kingdom concerning the Continental Shelf, as an area within which the rights of the United Kingdom with respect to the sea bed and sub-soil and their natural resources may be exercised;

(c) the terms "a Contracting State" and "the other Contracting State" mean Botswana or the United Kingdom, as the context requires;

(d) the term "person" includes an individual, a company, a trust, an estate and any other body of persons, and does not include a partnership;

(e) the term "company" means any body corporate or any entity that is treated as a body corporate for tax purposes;

(f) the terms "enterprise of a Contracting State" and "enterprise of the other Contracting State" mean respectively an enterprise carried on by a resident of a Contracting State and an enterprise carried on by a resident of the other Contracting State;

(g) the term "international traffic" means any transport by a ship or aircraft operated by an enterprise of a Contracting State, except when the ship or aircraft is operated solely between places in the other Contracting State;

(h) the term "competent authority" means:

(i) in the case of Botswana, the Minister of Finance and Development Planning, represented by the Commissioner General of the Botswana Unified Revenue Service;

(ii) in the case of the United Kingdom, the Commissioners for Her Majesty's Revenue and Customs or their authorised representative; and

(i) the term "national" means:

(i) in relation to Botswana, any individual possessing the nationality of Botswana and any legal person, partnership or association deriving its status as such from the laws in force in Botswana;

(ii) in relation to the United Kingdom, any British citizen, or any British subject not possessing the citizenship of any other Commonwealth country or territory, provided he has the right of abode in the United Kingdom; and any legal person, partnership, association or other entity deriving its status as such from the law in force in the United Kingdom.

(2) As regards the application of this Convention at any time by a Contracting State, any term not defined therein shall, unless the context otherwise requires, have the meaning that it has at that time under the laws of that State for the purposes of the taxes to which this Convention applies, any meaning under the applicable tax laws of that State prevailing over a meaning given to the term under other laws of that State.

ARTICLE 4 RESIDENT

(1) For the purposes of this Convention, the term "resident of a Contracting State" means any person who, under the laws of that State, is liable to tax therein by reason of his domicile, residence, place of management, place of incorporation or any other criterion of a similar nature, and also includes that State and any political subdivision or local authority thereof. This term, however, does not include any person who is liable to tax in that State in respect only of income or capital gains from sources in that State.

(2)

Where by reason of the provisions of paragraph (1) of this Article an individual is a resident of both Contracting States, then his status shall be determined in accordance with the following rules:

(a) he shall be deemed to be a resident only of the Contracting State in which he has a permanent home available to him; if he has a permanent home available to him in both States, he shall be deemed to be a resident only of the State with which his personal and economic relations are closer (centre of vital interests);

(b) if the Contracting State in which he has his centre of vital interests cannot be determined, or if he does not have a permanent home available to him in either State, he shall be deemed to be a resident only of the State in which he has an habitual abode;

(c) if he has an habitual abode in both Contracting States or in neither of them, he shall be deemed to be a resident only of the State of which he is a national;

(d) if he is a national of both Contracting States or of neither of them, the competent authorities of the Contracting States shall settle the question by mutual agreement.

(3) Where by reason of the provisions of paragraph (1) of this Article a person other than an individual is a resident of both Contracting States, then it shall be deemed to be a resident only of the State in which its place of effective management is situated.

ARTICLE 5 PERMANENT ESTABLISHMENT

(1) For the purposes of this Convention, the term "permanent establishment" means a fixed place of business through which the business of an enterprise is wholly or partly carried on.

(2) The term "permanent establishment" includes especially:

(a) a place of management;
(b) a branch;
(c) an office;
(d) a factory;
(e) a workshop;
(f) an installation or structure for the exploration of natural resources;

(g) a mine, an oil or gas well, a quarry or any other place of extraction of or exploration for natural resources.

(3) The term “permanent establishment” likewise encompasses:

(a) a building site, a construction, assembly or installation project or supervisory activities in connection therewith, but only if such site, project or activities last more than six months;

(b) the furnishing of services, including consultancy services, by an enterprise through employees or other personnel engaged by the enterprise for such purpose, but only where activities of that nature continue (for the same or connected project) within the Contracting State for a period or periods aggregating more than 183 days in any twelve-month period commencing or ending in the fiscal year concerned.

(4) Notwithstanding the preceding provisions of this Article, the term "permanent establishment" shall be deemed not to include:

(a) the use of facilities solely for the purpose of storage or display of goods or merchandise belonging to the enterprise;

(b) the maintenance of a stock of goods or merchandise belonging to the enterprise solely for the purpose of storage or display;

(c) the maintenance of a stock of goods or merchandise belonging to the enterprise solely for the purpose of processing by another enterprise;

(d) the maintenance of a fixed place of business solely for the purpose of purchasing goods or merchandise, or of collecting information, for the enterprise;

(e) the maintenance of a fixed place of business solely for the purpose of carrying on, for the enterprise, any othe- activity of a preparatory or auxiliary character;

(f) the maintenance of a fixed place of business solely for any combination of activities mentioned in sub-paragraphs (a) to (e) of this paragraph, provided that the overall activity of the fixed place of business resulting from this combination is of a preparatory or auxiliary character.

(5) Notwithstanding the provisions of paragraphs (1) and (2) of this Article, where a person - other than an agent of an independent status to whom paragraph (6) of this Article applies - is acting on behalf of an enterprise and has, and habitually exercises, in a Contracting State an authority to conclude contracts on behalf of the enterprise, that enterprise shall be deemed to have a permanent establishment in that State in respect of any activities which that person undertakes for the enterprise, unless the activities of such person are limited to those mentioned in paragraph (4) of this Article which, if exercised through a fixed place of business, would not make this fixed place of business a permanent establishment under the provisions of that paragraph.

(6) An enterprise shall not be deemed to have a permanent establishment in a Contracting State merely because it carries on business in that State through a broker, general commission agent or any other agent of an independent status, provided that such persons are acting in the ordinary course of their business.

(6) The fact that a company which is a resident of a Contracting State controls or is controlled by a company which is a resident of the other Contracting State, or which carries on business in that other State (whether through a permanent establishment or otherwise), shall not of itself constitute either company a permanent establishment of the other.

ARTICLE 6 INCOME FROM IMMOVABLE PROPERTY

(1) Income derived by a resident of a Contracting State from immovable property (including income from agriculture or forestry) situated in the other Contracting State may be taxed in that other State.

(2) The term "immovable property" shall have the meaning which it has under the law of the Contracting State in which the property in question is situated. The term shall in any case include property accessory to immovable property, livestock and equipment used in agriculture and forestry, rights to which the provisions of general law respecting landed property apply, usufruct of immovable property and rights to variable or fixed payments as consideration for the working of, or the right to work, mineral deposits, sources and other natural resources; ships and aircraft shall not be regarded as immovable property.

(3) The provisions of paragraph (1) of this Article shall apply to income derived from the direct use, letting, or use in any other form of immovable property.

(4) The provisions of paragraphs (1) and (3) of this Article shall also apply to the income from immovable property of an enterprise and to income from immovable property used for the performance of independent personal services.

ARTICLE 7 BUSINESS PROFITS

(1) The profits of an enterprise of a Contracting State shall be taxable only in that State unless the enterprise carries on business in the other Contracting State through a permanent establishment situated therein. If the enterprise carries on business as aforesaid, the profits of the enterprise may be taxed in the other State but only so much of them as is attributable to that permanent establishment.

(2) Subject to the provisions of paragraph (3) of this Article, where an enterprise of a Contracting State carries on business in the other Contracting State through a permanent establishment

situated therein, there shall in each Contracting State be attributed to that permanent establishment the profits which it might be expected to make if it were a distinct and separate enterprise engaged in the same or similar activities under the same or similar conditions and dealing wholly independently with the enterprise of which it is a permanent establishment.

(3) In determining the profits of a permanent establishment, there shall be allowed as deductions expenses which are incurred for the purposes of the permanent establishment, including executive and general administrative expenses so incurred, whether in the Contracting State in which the permanent establishment is situated or elsewhere. However, no such deduction shall be allowed in respect of amounts, if any, paid (otherwise than towards reimbursement of actual expenses) by the permanent establishment to the head office of the enterprise or any of its other offices, by way of royalties, fees or other similar payments in return for the use of patents or other rights, or by way of commission, for specific services performed or for management, or, except in the case of a banking enterprise, by way of interest on moneys lent to the permanent establishment. Likewise, no account shall be taken, in the determination of the profits of a permanent establishment, for amounts charged (otherwise than towards reimbursement of actual expenses), by the permanent establishment to the head office of the enterprise or any of its other offices, by way of royalties, fees or other similar payments in return for the use of patents or other rights, or by way of commission for specific services performed or for management, or, except in the case of a banking enterprise by way of interest on moneys lent to the head office of the enterprise or any of its other offices.

(4) No profits shall be attributed to a permanent establishment by reason of the mere purchase by that permanent establishment of goods or merchandise for the enterprise.

(5) For the purposes of the preceding paragraphs, the profits to be attributed to the permanent establishment shall be determined by the same method year by year unless there is good and sufficient reason to the contrary.

(6) Where profits include items of income or capital gains which are dealt with separately in other Articles of this Convention, then the provisions of those Articles shall not be affected by the provisions of this Article.

ARTICLE 8 SHIPPING AND AIR TRANSPORT

(1) Profits of an enterprise of a Contracting State from the operation of ships or aircraft in international traffic shall be taxable only in that State.

(2) For the purposes of this Article, profits from the operation of ships or aircraft in international traffic include:

(a) profits from the rental on a bareboat basis of ships or aircraft; and

(b) profits from the use, maintenance or rental of containers (including trailers and related equipment for the transport of containers) used for the transport of goods or merchandise; where such rental or such use, maintenance or rental, as the case may be, is incidental to the operation of ships or aircraft in international traffic.

(3) The provisions of paragraph (1) of this Article shall also apply to profits from the participation in a pool, a joint business or an international operating agency, but only to so much of the profits so derived as is attributable to the participant in proportion to its share in the joint operation.

ARTICLE 9 ASSOCIATED ENTERPRISES

(1) Where:

(a) an enterprise of a Contracting State participates directly or indirectly in the management, control or capital of an enterprise of the other Contracting State; or

(b) the same persons participate directly or indirectly in the management, control or capital of an enterprise of a Contracting State and an enterprise of the other Contracting State;

and in either case conditions are made or imposed between the two enterprises in their commercial or financial relations which differ from those which would be made between independent enterprises, then any profits which would, but for those conditions, have accrued to one of the enterprises, but, by reason of those conditions, have not so accrued, may be included by a Contracting State in the profits of that enterprise and taxed accordingly.

(2) Where a Contracting State includes in the profits of an enterprise of that State

- and taxes accordingly - profits on which an enterprise of the other Contracting State has been charged to tax in that other State and the profits so included are profits which would have accrued to the enterprise of the first-mentioned State if the conditions made between the two enterprises had been those which would have been made between independent enterprises, then that other State shall make an appropriate adjustment to the amount of the tax charged therein on those profits. In determining such adjustment, due regard shall be had to the other provisions of this Convention and the competent authorities of the Contracting States shall if necessary consult each other.

ARTICLE 10 DIVIDENDS

(1) Dividends paid by a company which is a resident of a Contracting State to a resident of the other Contracting State may be taxed in that other State.

(2) However, such dividends may also be taxed in the Contracting State of which the company paying the dividends is a resident and according to the laws of that State, but if the beneficial owner of the dividends is a resident of the other Contracting State, the tax so charged shall not exceed:

(a) 5 per cent of the gross amount of the dividends if the beneficial owner is a company which controls, directly or indirectly, at least 25 per cent of the voting power in the company paying the dividends;

(b) 12 per cent of the gross amount of the dividends in all other cases.

(3) The term "dividends" as used in this Article means income from shares, or other rights, not being debt-claims, participating in profits, as well as income from other corporate rights which is subjected to the same taxation treatment as income from shares by the laws of the State of which the company making the distribution is a resident and also includes any other item which, under the laws of the Contracting State of which the company paying the dividend is a resident, is treated as a dividend or distribution of a company.

(4) The provisions of paragraphs (1) and (2) of this Article shall not apply if the beneficial owner of the dividends, being a resident of a Contracting State, carries on business in the other

Contracting State of which the company paying the dividends is a resident, through a permanent establishment situated therein, or performs in that other State independent personal services from a fixed base situated therein, and the holding in respect of which the dividends are paid is effectively connected with such permanent establishment or fixed base. In such case the provisions of Article 7 or Article 15 of this Convention, as the case may be, shall apply.

(5) Where a company which is a resident of a Contracting State derives profits or income from the other Contracting State, that other State may not impose any tax on the dividends paid by the company, except insofar as such dividends are paid to a resident of that other State or insofar as the holding in respect of which the dividends are paid is effectively connected with a permanent establishment or a fixed base situated in that other State, nor subject the company's undistributed profits to a tax on undistributed profits, even if the dividends paid or the undistributed profits consist wholly or partly of profits or income arising in that other State.

(6) The provisions of this Article shall not apply if it was the main purpose or one of the main purposes of any person concerned with the creation or assignment of the shares or other rights in respect of which the dividend is paid to take advantage of this Article by means of that creation or assignment.

ARTICLE 11 INTEREST

(1) Interest arising in a Contracting State and paid to a resident of the other Contracting State may be taxed in that other State.

(2) However, such interest may also be taxed in the Contracting State in which it arises and according to the laws of that State, but if the beneficial owner of the interest is a resident of the other Contracting State, the tax so charged shall not exceed 10 per cent of the gross amount of the interest.

(3) The term "interest" as used in this Article means income from debt-claims of every kind, whether or not secured by mortgage and whether or not carrying a right to participate in the debtor's profits, and in particular, income from government securities and income from bonds or debentures including premiums and prizes attaching to such securities, bonds or debentures. The term interest shall not include any item which is treated as a dividend under the provisions of Article 10 of this Convention.

(4) The provisions of paragraphs (1) and (2) of this Article shall not apply if the beneficial owner of the interest, being a resident of a Contracting State, carries on business in the other Contracting State in which the interest arises, through a permanent establishment situated therein, or performs in that other State independent personal services from a fixed base situated therein, and the debt-claim in respect of which the interest is paid is effectively connected with such permanent establishment or fixed base. In such case the provisions of Article 7 or Article 15 of this Convention, as the case may be, shall apply.

(5) Interest shall be deemed to arise in a Contracting State when the payer is a resident of that State. Where, however, the person paying the interest, whether he is a resident of a Contracting State or not, has in a Contracting State a permanent establishment or a fixed base in connection with which the indebtedness on which the interest is paid was incurred, and such interest is borne by such permanent establishment or fixed base, then such interest shall be deemed to arise in the State in which the permanent establishment or fixed base is situated.

(6) Where, by reason of a special relationship between the payer and the beneficial owner or between both of them and some other person, the amount of the interest paid exceeds, for whatever reason, the amount which would have been agreed upon by the payer and the beneficial owner in the absence of such relationship, the provisions of this Article shall apply only to the last-mentioned amount of interest. In

such case, the excess part of the payments shall remain taxable according to the laws of each Contracting State, due regard being had to the other provisions of this Convention.

(7) The provisions of this Article shall not apply if it was the main purpose or one of the main purposes of any person concerned with the creation or assignment of the debt-claim in respect of which the interest is paid to take advantage of this Article by means of that creation or assignment.

(8) Notwithstanding the provisions of paragraph (2) of this Article, interest arising in a Contracting State shall be exempt from tax in that State if it is paid to and beneficially owned by the Government of the other Contracting State, a local authority thereof, any agency or instrumentality wholly owned by that Government or local authority, or the Commonwealth Development Corporation or the Botswana Development Corporation.

(9) Notwithstanding the provisions of Article 7 of this Convention and paragraph

(2)of this Article interest arising in a Contracting State and paid to a resident of the other Contracting State shall be taxable only in that other State if such a resident is the beneficial owner of the interest and the interest is paid in respect of a loan made, guaranteed or insured by the United Kingdom Exports Credit Guarantee Department or the Botswana Development Corporation or the Botswana Export Credit Insurance.

ARTICLE 12 ROYALTIES

(1) Royalties arising in a Contracting State and paid to a resident of the other Contracting State may be taxed in that other State.

(2) However, such royalties may also be taxed in the Contracting State in which they arise and according to the laws of that State, but if the beneficial owner of the royalties is a resident of the other Contracting State, the tax so charged shall not exceed 10 per cent of the gross amount of the royalties.

(3) The term "royalties" as used in this Article means payments of any kind received as a consideration for the use of, or the right to use, any copyright of literary, artistic or scientific work (including cinematograph films, and films, tapes or discs for radio or television broadcasting), any patent, trade mark, design or model, plan, secret formula or process, or for the use of or the right to use industrial, commercial or scientific equipment or for information (know-how) concerning industrial, commercial or scientific experience.

(4) The provisions of paragraphs (1) and (2) of this Article shall not apply if the beneficial owner of the royalties, being a resident of a Contracting State, carries on business in the other Contracting State in which the royalties arise, through a permanent establishment situated therein, or performs in that other State independent personal services from a fixed base situated therein, and the right or property in respect of which the royalties are paid is effectively connected with such permanent establishment or fixed base. In such case the provisions of Article 7 or Article 15 of this Convention, as the case may be, shall apply.

(5) Royalties shall be deemed to arise in a Contracting State when the payer is a resident of that State. Where, however, the person paying the royalties, whether he is a resident of a Contracting State or not, has in a Contracting State a permanent establishment or fixed base in connection with which the liability to pay the royalties was incurred and such royalties are borne by such permanent establishment or fixed base, then such royalties shall be deemed to arise in the Contracting State in which the permanent establishment or fixed base is situated.

(6) Where, by reason of a special relationship between the payer and the beneficial owner or between both of them and some other person, the amount of the royalties paid exceeds, for whatever reason, the amount which would have been agreed upon by the payer and the beneficial owner in the absence of such relationship, the provisions of this Article shall apply only to the last-mentioned amount. In such case, the excess part of the payments shall remain taxable according to the laws of each Contracting State, due regard being had to the other provisions of this Convention.

(7) The provisions of this Article shall not apply if it was the main purpose or one of the main purposes of any person concerned with the creation or assignment of the rights in respect of which the royalties are paid to take advantage of this Article by means of that creation or assignment.

ARTICLE 13 TECHNICAL FEES

(1) Technical fees arising in a Contracting State and paid to a resident of the other Contracting State may be taxed in that other State.

(2) However, such technical fees may also be taxed in the Contracting State in which they arise and according to the law of that State, but if the beneficial owner of the technical fees is a resident of, and is subject to tax in respect of the technical fees in, the other Contracting State, the tax so charged shall not exceed 7.5 per cent of the gross amount of the technical fees.

(3) The term "technical fees" as used in this Article means payments of any kind to any person, other than to an employee of the person making the payments, in consideration for any services of an administrative, technical, managerial or consultancy nature.

(4) The provisions of paragraphs (1) and (2) of this Article shall not apply if the beneficial owner of the technical fees, being a resident of a Contracting State, carries on business in the other Contracting State in which the technical fees arise, through a permanent establishment situated therein, or performs in that other State independent personal services from a fixed base situated therein, and the technical fees are effectively connected with such permanent establishment or fixed base. In such case the provisions of Article 7 or Article 15 of this Convention, as the case may be, shall apply.

(5) Technical fees shall be deemed to arise in a Contracting State when the payer is a resident of that State. Where, however, the person paying the technical fees, whether he is a resident of a Contracting State or not, has in a Contracting State a permanent establishment or a fixed base in connection with which the obligation to pay the technical fees was incurred, and such technical fees are borne by that permanent establishment or fixed base, then such technical fees shall be deemed to arise in the Contracting State in which the permanent establishment or fixed base is situated.

(6) Where, by reason of a special relationship between the payer and the beneficial owner or between both of them and some other person, the amount of the technical fees paid exceeds, for

whatever reason, the amount which would have been agreed upon by the payer and the beneficial owner in the absence of such relationship, the provisions of this Article shall apply only to the last-mentioned amount. In such case, the excess part of the payments shall remain taxable according to the laws of each Contracting State, due regard being had to the other provisions of this Convention.

(7) The provisions of this Article shall not apply if it was the main purpose or one of the main purposes of any person concerned with the creation or assignment of the rights in respect of which the technical fees are paid to take advantage of this Article by means of that creation or assignment.

ARTICLE 14 CAPITAL GAINS

(1) Gains derived by a resident of a Contracting State from the alienation of immovable property referred to in Article 6 of this Convention and situated in the other Contracting State may be taxed in that other State.

(2) Gains derived by a resident of a Contracting State from the alienation of:

(a)

shares, other than shares in which there is substantial and regular trading on a Stock Exchange, deriving their value or the greater part of their value directly or indirectly from immovable property situated in the other Contracting State, or

(b) an interest in a partnership or trust the assets of which consist principally of immovable property situated in the other Contracting State, or of shares referred to in sub-paragraph (a) of this paragraph,

(3) Gains from the alienation of movable property forming part of the business property of a permanent establishment which an enterprise of a Contracting State has in the other Contracting State or of movable property pertaining to a fixed base available to a resident of a Contracting State in the other Contracting State for the purpose of performing independent personal services, including such gains from the alienation of such a permanent establishment (alone or with the whole enterprise) or of such fixed base, may be taxed in that other State.

(4) Gains derived by a resident of a Contracting State from the alienation of ships or aircraft operated in international traffic by an enterprise of that Contracting State or movable property pertaining to the operation of such ships or aircraft, shall be taxable only in that Contracting State.

(5) Gains from the alienation of any property other than that referred to in paragraphs (1), (2), (3) and (4) of this Article shall be taxable only in the Contracting State of which the alienator is a resident.

(6) The provisions of this Article shall not affect the right of a Contracting State to levy according to its law a tax chargeable in respect of gains from the alienation of any property on a person who is a resident of that State at any time during the fiscal year in which the property is alienated, or has been so resident at any time during the six fiscal years immediately preceding that year.

May be taxed in that other State.

ARTICLE 15 INDEPENDENT PERSONAL SERVICES

(1) Subject to the provisions of Article 13 of this Convention, income derived by a resident of a Contracting State in respect of professional services or other activities of an independent character shall be taxable only in that State unless he has a fixed base regularly available to him in the other Contracting State for the purpose of performing his activities. If he has such a fixed base, the income may be taxed in the other State but only so much of it as is attributable to that fixed base. For the purposes of this Convention, where an individual who is a resident of a Contracting State is present in the other Contracting State for a period or periods exceeding in the aggregate 183 days in any twelve-month period commencing or ending in the fiscal year concerned, he shall be deemed to have a fixed base regularly available to him in that other State and the income that is derived from his activities that are performed in that other State shall be attributable to that fixed base.

(2) The term "professional services" includes especially independent scientific, literary, artistic, educational or teaching activities as well as the independent activities of physicians, lawyers, engineers, architects, dentists and accountants.

ARTICLE 16 DEPENDENT PERSONAL SERVICES

(1) Subject to the provisions of Articles 17, 19, 20 and 21 of this Convention, salaries, wages and other similar remuneration derived by a resident of a Contracting State in respect of an employment shall be taxable only in that State unless the employment is exercised in the other Contracting State. If the employment is so exercised, such remuneration as is derived therefrom may be taxed in that other State.

(2) Notwithstanding the provisions of paragraph (1) of this Article, remuneration derived by a resident of a Contracting State in respect of an employment exercised in the other Contracting State shall be taxable only in the first-mentioned State if:

(a) the recipient is present in the other State for a period or periods not exceeding in the aggregate 183 days in any twelve month period commencing or ending in the fiscal year concerned; and

(b) the remuneration is paid by, or on behalf of, an employer who is not a resident of the other State; and

(c) the remuneration is not borne by a permanent establishment or a fixed base which the employer has in the other State.

(4) Notwithstanding the preceding provisions of this Article, remuneration derived in respect of an employment exercised aboard a ship or aircraft operated in international traffic may be taxed in the Contracting State of which the enterprise operating the ship or aircraft is a resident.

ARTICLE 17 DIRECTORS' FEES

Directors' fees and other similar payments derived by a resident of a Contracting State in his capacity as a member of the board of directors of a company which is a resident of the other Contracting State may be taxed in that other State.

ARTICLE 18 ENTERTAINERS AND SPORTSPERSONS

(1) Notwithstanding the provisions of Articles 15 and 16 of this Convention, income derived by a resident of a Contracting State as an entertainer, such as a theatre, motion picture, radio or television artiste, or a musician, or as a sportsperson, from his personal activities as such exercised in the other Contracting State, may be taxed in that other State.

(2) Where income in respect of personal activities exercised by an entertainer or a sportsperson in his capacity as such accrues not to the entertainer or sportsperson himself but to another person, that income may, notwithstanding the provisions of Articles 7, 15 and 16 of this Convention, be taxed in the Contracting State in which the activities of the entertainer or sportsperson are exercised.

(3) The provisions of paragraphs (1) and (2) of this Article shall not apply to income derived from activities performed in a Contracting State by entertainers or sportspersons if the visit to that State is wholly or substantially supported by public funds. In such a case, the income shall be taxable only in the Contracting State of which the entertainer or sportsperson is a resident.

ARTICLE 19 PENSIONS

(1) Subject to the provisions of paragraph (2) of Article 20 of this Convention:

(a) pensions and other similar remuneration paid in consideration of past employment, and

(b) any annuity paid,

to an individual who is a resident of a Contracting State, and is subject to tax in respect thereof in that State, shall be taxable only in that State.

(2) The term "annuity" means a stated sum payable to an individual periodically at stated times during his life or during a specified or ascertainable period of time under an obligation to make the payments in return for adequate and full consideration in money or money's worth.

ARTICLE 20 GOVERNMENT SERVICE

(1) (a) Salaries, wages and other similar remuneration, other than a pension, paid by a Contracting State or a political subdivision or a local authority thereof to an individual in respect of services rendered to that State or subdivision or authority shall be taxable only in that State.

(b) Notwithstanding the provisions of sub-paragraph (a) of this paragraph, such salaries, wages and other similar remuneration shall be taxable only in the other Contracting State if the services are rendered in that State and the individual is a resident of that State who:

(i) is a national of that State; or

(ii) did not become a resident of that State solely for the purpose of rendering the services.

(2) (a) Any pension paid by, or out of funds created by, a Contracting State or a political subdivision or a local authority thereof to an individual in respect of services rendered to that State or subdivision or authority shall be taxable only in that State.

(b) Notwithstanding the provisions of sub-paragraph (a) of this paragraph, such pension shall be taxable only in the other Contracting State if the individual is a resident of, and a national of, that State.

(3) The provisions of Articles 16, 17, 18 and 19 of this Convention shall apply to salaries, wages and other similar remuneration, and to pensions, in respect of services rendered in connection with a business carried on by a Contracting State or a political subdivision or a local authority thereof.

ARTICLE 21 STUDENTS

Payments which a student or business apprentice who is or was immediately before visiting a Contracting State a resident of the other Contracting State and who is present in the first-mentioned State solely for the purpose of his education or training receives for the purpose of his maintenance, education or training shall not be taxed in that first-mentioned State, provided that such payments arise from sources outside that State.

ARTICLE 22 OTHER INCOME

(1) Items of income of a resident of a Contracting State wherever arising not dealt with in the foregoing Articles of this Convention shall be taxable only in that State.

(2) The provisions of paragraph (1) of this Article shall not apply to income, other than income from immovable property as defined in paragraph (2) of Article 6 of this Convention, if the recipient of such income, being a resident of a Contracting State, carries on business in the other Contracting State through a permanent establishment situated therein, or performs in that other State independent personal services from a fixed base situated therein, and the right or property in respect of which the income is paid is effectively connected with such permanent establishment or fixed base. In such case the provisions of Article 7 or Article 15 of this Convention, as the case may be, shall apply.

(3) Notwithstanding the provisions of paragraphs (1) and (2), items of income of a resident of a Contracting State not dealt with in the foregoing Articles of the Convention and arising in the other Contracting State may also be taxed in that other State.

(4) Where, by reason of a special relationship between the person referred to in paragraph (1) of this Article and some other person, or between both of them and some third person, the amount of the income referred to in that paragraph exceeds the amount (if any) which would have been agreed upon between them in the absence of such a relationship, the provisions of this Article shall apply only to the last-mentioned amount. In such a case, the excess part of the income shall remain taxable according to the laws of each Contracting State, due regard being had to the other applicable provisions of this Convention.

(4) The provisions of this Article shall not apply if it was the main purpose or one of the main purposes of any person concerned with the creation or assignment of the rights in respect of which the income is paid to take advantage of this Article by means of that creation or assignment.

ARTICLE 23 ELIMINATION OF DOUBLE TAXATION

(1) In the case of Botswana, double taxation shall be avoided as follows: subject to the provisions of the law of Botswana regarding the allowance of a credit against Botswana tax of tax payable under the laws of a country outside Botswana, United Kingdom tax payable under the laws of the United Kingdom and in accordance with this Convention, whether directly or by deduction, on profits, income or chargeable gains liable to tax in the United Kingdom shall be allowed as a credit against any Botswana tax payable in respect of the same profits, income or chargeable gains by reference to which the United Kingdom tax is computed. However, the amount of such credit shall not exceed the amount of the Botswana tax payable on that profits, income or chargeable gains in accordance with the laws of Botswana.

(2) Subject to the provisions of the law of the United Kingdom regarding the allowance as a credit against United Kingdom tax of tax payable in a territory outside the United Kingdom (which shall not affect the general principle hereof):

(a) Botswana tax payable under the laws of Botswana and in accordance with this Convention, whether directly or by deduction, on profits, income or chargeable gains from sources within Botswana (excluding in the case of a dividend, tax payable in respect of the profits out of which the dividend is paid) shall be allowed as a credit against any United Kingdom tax computed by reference to the same profits, income or chargeable gains by reference to which the Botswana tax is computed;

(b) in the case of a dividend paid by a company which is a resident of Botswana to a company which is a resident of the United Kingdom and which controls directly or indirectly at least 10 per cent of the voting power in the company paying the dividend, the credit shall take into account (in addition to any Botswana tax for which credit may be allowed under the provisions of sub-paragraph (a) of this paragraph) the Botswana tax payable by the company in respect of the profits out of which such dividend is paid.

(3) For the purposes of paragraph (1) of this Article, where a development approval order is made under Section 52 or a tax agreement is entered into under Section 54 of the provisions of the Income Tax Act of Botswana, the term "Botswana tax payable" shall, subject to the mutual agreement of the competent authorities in

each such case, be deemed to include the whole or part of any amount which would have been payable as Botswana tax for any year but for an exemption or reduction of tax granted for that year or any part thereof under the order or tax agreement in question.

(4) Relief from United Kingdom tax by virtue of paragraph (3) of this Article shall not be given where the profits, income or chargeable gains in respect of which tax would have been payable but for the exemption or reduction of tax granted under the provisions referred to in that paragraph arise or accrue more than twelve years after the date on which this Convention enters into force.

(5) The period referred to in paragraph (4) of this Article may be extended by agreement between the Contracting States.

(6) For the purposes of paragraphs (1) and (2) of this Article, profits, income and capital gains owned by a resident of a Contracting State which may be taxed in the other Contracting State in accordance with this Convention shall be deemed to arise from sources in that other Contracting State.

ARTICLE 24 LIMITATION OF RELIEF

Where under any provision of this Convention any income or gains are relieved from tax in a Contracting State and, under the law in force in the other Contracting State a person, in respect of that income or those gains, is subject to tax by reference to the amount thereof which is remitted to or received in that other Contracting State and not by reference to the full amount thereof, then the relief to be allowed under this Convention in the first-mentioned Contracting State shall apply only to so much of the income or gains as is taxed in the other Contracting State.

ARTICLE 25 NON-DISCRIMINATION

(1) Nationals of a Contracting State shall not be subjected in the other Contracting State to any taxation or any requirement connected therewith, which is other or more burdensome than the taxation and connected requirements to which nationals of that other State in the same circumstances, in particular with respect to residence, are or may be subjected.

(2) The taxation on a permanent establishment which an enterprise of a Contracting State has in the other Contracting State shall not be less favourably levied in that other State than the taxation levied on enterprises of that other State carrying on the same activities.

(3) Except where the provisions of paragraph (1) of Article 9, paragraph (6) of Article 10, paragraph (6) or (7) of Article 11, paragraph (6) or (7) of Article 12, paragraph (6) or (7) of Article 13 or paragraph (4) or (5) of Article 22 of this Convention apply, interest, royalties, technical fees and other disbursements paid by an enterprise of a Contracting State to a resident of the other Contracting State shall, for the purpose of determining the taxable profits of such enterprise, be deductible under the same conditions as if they had been paid to a resident of the first-mentioned State.

(4) Enterprises of a Contracting State, the capital of which is wholly or partly owned or controlled, directly or indirectly, by one or more residents of the other Contracting State, shall not be subjected in the first-mentioned State to any taxation or any requirement connected therewith which is other or more burdensome than the taxation and connected requirements to which other similar enterprises of the first-mentioned State are or may be subjected.

(5) Nothing contained in this Article shall be construed as obliging either Contracting State to grant to individuals not resident in that State any of the personal allowances, reliefs and reductions for tax purposes which are granted to individuals so resident.

(6) The provisions of this Article shall apply to the taxes which are the subject of this Convention.

ARTICLE 26 MUTUAL AGREEMENT PROCEDURE

(1) Where a resident of a Contracting State considers that the actions of one or both of the Contracting States result or will result for him in taxation not in accordance with the provisions of this Convention, he may, irrespective of the remedies provided by the domestic law of those States, present his case to the competent authority of the Contracting State of which he is a resident or, if his case comes under paragraph (1) of Article 25 of this Convention, to that of the Contracting State of which he is a national.

(2) The competent authority shall endeavour, if the objection appears to it to be justified and if it is not itself able to arrive at a satisfactory solution, to resolve the case by mutual agreement with the competent authority of the other Contracting State, with a view to the avoidance of taxation which is not in accordance with this Convention.

(3) The competent authorities of the Contracting States shall endeavour to resolve by mutual agreement any difficulties or doubts arising as to the interpretation or application of this Convention.

(4) The competent authorities of the Contracting States may communicate with each other directly for the purpose of reaching an agreement in the sense of the preceding paragraphs.

ARTICLE 27 EXCHANGE OF INFORMATION

(1) The competent authorities of the Contracting States shall exchange such information as is foreseeably relevant for carrying out the provisions of this Convention or to the administration or enforcement of the domestic laws of the Contracting States concerning taxes covered by this Convention insofar as the taxation thereunder is not contrary to this Convention, in particular, to prevent fraud and to facilitate the administration of statutory provisions against legal avoidance. The exchange of information is not restricted by Article 1 of this Convention.

(2) Any information received under paragraph (1) of this Article by a Contracting State shall be treated as secret in the same manner as information obtained under the domestic laws of that State and shall be disclosed only to persons or authorities (including courts and administrative bodies) concerned with the assessment or collection of, the enforcement or prosecution in respect of, the determination of appeals in relation to the taxes covered by this Convention, or the oversight of the above. Such persons or authorities shall use the information only for such purposes. They may disclose the information in public court proceedings or in judicial decisions.

(3) In no case shall the provisions of paragraphs (1) and (2) of this Article be construed so as to impose on a Contracting State the obligation:

(a) to carry out administrative measures at variance with the laws and administrative practice of that or of the other Contracting State;

(b) to supply information which is not obtainable under the laws or in the normal course of the administration of that or of the other Contracting State;

(c) to supply information which would disclose any trade, business, industrial, commercial or professional secret or trade process, or information the disclosure of which would be contrary to public policy.

(4) If information is requested by a Contracting State in accordance with this Article, the other Contracting State shall use its information gathering measures to obtain the requested information, even though that other State may not need such information for its own tax purposes. The obligation contained in the preceding sentence is subject to the limitations of paragraph (3) of this Article but in no case shall such limitations be construed to permit a Contracting State to decline to supply information solely because it has no domestic interest in such information.

(5) In no case shall the provisions of paragraph (3) of this Article be construed to permit a Contracting State to decline to supply information solely because the information is held by a

bank, other financial institution, nominee or person acting in an agency or a fiduciary capacity or because it relates to ownership interests in a person.

(5) The competent authorities shall, through consultation, develop appropriate conditions, methods and techniques concerning the matters respecting which such exchange of information shall be made.

ARTICLE 28 MEMBERS OF DIPLOMATIC OR PERMANENT MISSIONS AND CONSULAR POSTS

Nothing in this Convention shall affect the fiscal privileges of members of diplomatic or permanent missions or consular posts under the general rules of international law or under the provisions of special agreements.

ARTICLE 29 ENTRY INTO FORCE

(1) Each of the Contracting States shall notify to the other, through diplomatic channels, the completion of the procedures required by its law for the bringing into force of this Convention. This Convention shall enter into force on the date of the later of these notifications and shall thereupon have effect:

(a) in Botswana:

in respect of income tax and capital gains tax, on taxable income and gains derived on or after 1st July of the year next following that of the entry into force of this Convention;

(b) in the United Kingdom:

(i) in respect of income tax and capital gains tax, for any year of assessment beginning on or after 6th April in the calendar year next following that in which this Convention enters into force;

(ii) in respect of corporation tax, for any financial year beginning on or after 1st April in the calendar year next following that in which this Convention enters into force.

(2) The Convention between the United Kingdom and Botswana signed at London on 5th October 1977 shall terminate and cease to be effective from the date upon which this Convention has effect in respect of the taxes to which this Convention applies in accordance with the provisions of paragraph (1) of this Article.

ARTICLE 30 TERMINATION

This Convention shall remain in force until terminated by one of the Contracting States. Either Contracting State may terminate this Convention, through diplomatic channels, by giving notice of termination at least six months before the end of any calendar year beginning after the expiry of five years from the date of entry into force of this Convention. In such event, this Convention shall cease to have effect:

(a) in Botswana:

in respect of income tax and capital gains tax, on taxable income and gains derived on or after 1st July of the year next following that in which the notice of termination is given;

(b) in the United Kingdom:

(i) in respect of income tax and capital gains tax, for any year of assessment beginning on or after 6th April in the calendar year next following that in which the notice is given;

(ii) in respect of corporation tax, for any financial year beginning on or after 1st April in the calendar year next following that in which the notice is given.

In witness whereof, the undersigned, duly authorised thereto by their respective Governments, have signed this Convention.

Done in duplicate at Gaborone this 9th day of September 2005

SOUTHERN AFRICAN CUSTOMS UNION (SACU) AGREEMENT

The Governments of the Republic of South Africa, the Republic of Botswana, the Kingdom of Lesotho and the Kingdom of Swaziland -

Being desirous of maintaining the free interchange of goods between their countries and of applying the same tariffs and trade regulations to goods imported from outside the common customs area as hereinafter defined;

Recognizing that the Customs Agreement concluded on 29 June 1910, as amended from time to time, requires modification to provide for the continuance of the customs union arrangements in the changed circumstances on a basis designed to ensure the continued economic development of the customs union area as a whole, and to ensure in particular that these arrangements encourage the development of the less advanced members of the customs union and the diversification of their economies, and afford to all parties equitable benefits arising from trade among themselves and with other countries;

Have agreed as follows:

PART 1

ARTICLE 1
DEFINITIONS

In this Agreement, unless inconsistent with the context -

"additional duties" - means duties imposed in terms of Article 6 of this Agreement;
"Botswana" - means the area of the Republic of Botswana;
"common customs area" - means the combined areas of Botswana, Lesotho, South Africa and Swaziland;
"customs duties", "excise duties" and "sales duties" - mean customs duties, excise duties and sales duties as defined in the customs and excise legislation in force in the countries of the contracting parties;
"financial year" - means the period of twelve months commencing on the first of April;
"Lesotho" - means the area of the Kingdom of Lesotho;
"South Africa" - means the area in respect of which the Government of the Republic of South Africa is a contracting party to the General Agreement on Tariffs and Trade;

"Swaziland" - means the area of the Kingdom of Swaziland;
and cognate expressions shall be construed accordingly.

ARTICLE 2
INTERCHANGE OF DOMESTIC PRODUCTS

Except as elsewhere provided herein, a contracting party shall not apply quantitative restrictions or impose any duties on goods grown, produced or manufactured in the common customs area on importation of such goods from the area of any other contracting party.

ARTICLE 3
INTERCHANGE OF GOODS IMPORTED FROM OUTSIDE THE COMMON CUSTOMS AREA

Except as elsewhere provided herein a contracting party shall not impose any duties on goods which were imported from outside the common customs area on importation of such goods from the area of any other contracting party.

PART 2

ARTICLE 4
CUSTOMS AND SALES DUTIES ON IMPORTED GOODS

(1) Except as elsewhere provided herein, the customs tariff and duties and the sales duties as in force in South Africa from time to time shall be applied to goods imported into the common customs area from outside such area.
(2) Any rebates, refunds or drawbacks of customs duty or sales duty on imported goods granted by the Government of Botswana, Lesotho or Swaziland in respect of such goods for use in or used in any industry shall be identical to any such rebates, refunds or drawbacks in force in South Africa in respect of such goods for use in or used in a corresponding industry in South Africa.
(3) Subject to paragraph (2) and (4), all other rebates, refunds or drawbacks of customs duty or sales duty on imported goods granted by the Government of Botswana, Lesotho or Swaziland in respect of such goods shall be similar to any such rebates, refunds or drawbacks in force in South Africa.
(4) (a) A Contracting party may grant a full rebate of the customs and sales duties in respect of goods imported into its area:
(i) for the relief of distress of persons in cases of famine and other national disaster;
(ii) under any technical assistance agreement; and
(iii) in terms of an obligation under any multilateral international agreement to which such contracting party is or becomes a party.
(b) A contracting party may, with the prior approval of the other contracting parties, grant full rebate of the customs and sales duties in respect of goods imported into its area for such other purposes as may be agreed upon by the parties to this Agreement from time to time.

ARTICLE 5
IMPOSITION AND AMENDMENT OF CUSTOMS DUTIES

(1) Subject to the provisions of paragraph (2) of this Article, the Government of South Africa shall give the other contracting parties adequate opportunity for consultations before imposing, amending or abrogating any customs duty with respect to goods imported into the common customs area from outside such area.
(2) Paragraph (1) of this Article shall not apply if the imposition of, or the removal of, or an

amendment to any customs duty either forms part of the measures of the Government of South Africa designed primarily for fiscal purposes, or is resorted to as interim measure designed to assist a local industry in the common customs area pending the completion of an investigation by the appropriate South African authorities.

ARTICLE 6
IMPOSITION OF ADDITIONAL DUTIES FOR PROTECTIVE PURPOSES BY BOTSWANA, LESOTHO OR SWAZILAND

(1) The Government of Botswana, Lesotho or Swaziland may levy additional duties on goods imported into its area to enable new industries in its area to meet competition from other producers or manufacturers in the common customs area, provided that such duties are levied equally on goods grown, produced or manufactured in other parts of the common customs area and like products imported from outside that area, irrespective of whether the latter goods are imported directly or from the area of any other party to this Agreement and subject to payment of the customs duties applicable to such goods on importation into the common customs area.
(2) Before any such duties are imposed or amended the Government concerned shall consult the other contracting parties in terms of Article 20, and such parties may make recommendations thereon. If the recommendations of any such parties are not acted upon, the Government concerned shall inform the other contracting parties of the reason for its decision.
(3) Protection which is afforded to a new industry in terms of this Article shall not be given for a period exceeding eight years without the prior consent of the contracting parties.
(4) In this Article, "new industry" in relation to any contracting party means an industry which has been established in the area of that party for not more than eight years.

PART 3

ARTICLE 7
SPECIFICATION OF INDUSTRIES OF MAJOR IMPORTANCE TO BOTSWANA, LESOTHO OF SWAZILAND

(1) The Government of Botswana, Lesotho or Swaziland may with the concurrence of the other contracting parties -
(a) specify industries which are or are likely to be of major importance to its economy; and
(b) specify period in relation to such industries for the purposes of paragraph (2) of this Article.
(2) The customs duties applicable to goods, imported from outside the common customs area and competing with those of any industry specified in terms of this Article, shall not for the period specified in terms of paragraph (1) (b) above in relation to that industry be decreased or abrogated without the consent of the Government specifying the industry; and during such period of the Government of South Africa shall with due regard to the interests of the other contracting parties and to the criteria usually applied by it in the consideration of representations for tariff assistance and relief, give sympathetic consideration to proposals by any other contracting party to increase any customs duty applicable to such goods or to afford relief of customs duty applicable to any material, used directly in the production or manufacture thereof and to requirements for such industries, where the Government concerned regards such increase or relief necessary to assist the establishment of such industry or to prevent its contraction.

ARTICLE 8
EXCISE AND SALES DUTIES ON GOODS PRODUCED IN THE COMMON CUSTOMS AREA

(1) The excise duties and the sales duties as in force in South Africa from time to time shall be applied to goods grown, produced or manufactured in the common customs area.
(2) Any rebates, refunds or drawbacks of excise duty or sales duty granted by the Government of Botswana, Lesotho or Swaziland in respect of goods grown, produced or manufactured in the common customs area, for use in or used in any industry shall be identical to any such rebates, refunds or drawbacks in force in South Africa in respect of such goods for use in or used in a corresponding industry in South Africa.
(3) All other rebates, refunds or draw-backs of excise duty or sales duty granted by the Government of Botswana, Lesotho or Swaziland in respect of goods grown, produced or manufactured in the common customs area shall be similar to any such rebates, refunds or drawbacks in force in South Africa.

ARTICLE 9
DUTIES ON GOODS PRODUCED BY SPECIFIED INDUSTRIES

(1) If goods grown, produced or manufactured in Botswana, Lesotho or Swaziland, by an industry specified in pursuance of Article 7 of this Agreement, are subject to excise duties, the margin of protection afforded by the customs duty applicable to such goods shall be maintained for the period specified under that Article and may be changed only with the agreement of the Government specifying the industry.
(2) During the specified period the Government of South Africa shall with due regard to the interests of the other contracting parties and to the criteria usually applied by it in the consideration of representations for tariff assistance and relief, give sympathetic consideration to proposals by such a Government to reduce or abrogate any excise duty applicable to such goods where such a Government regards such duty as injurious to that industry.

PART 5

ARTICLE 10
LAWS RELATING TO CUSTOMS, EXCISE AND SALES DUTIES

Subject to the provisions of Articles 4 and 8, the Governments of Botswana, Lesotho and Swaziland shall apply laws relating to customs, excise and sales duty similar to such laws in force in South Africa from time to time.

ARTICLE 11
IMPORT AND EXPORT PROHIBITIONS AND RESTRICTIONS

(1) The contracting parties recognise the right of each party to prohibit or restrict the importation into or exportation from its area of any goods for economic, social, cultural or other reasons.
(2) Except in so far as may be agreed upon between the parties from time to time the provisions of this Agreement shall not be deemed to suspend or supersede the provisions of any law within any part of the common customs area which prohibits or restricts the importation or exportation of goods.
(3) The provisions of paragraphs (1) and (2) shall not be so construed as to permit the prohibition or restriction of the importation by any contracting party into its area of goods grown, produced or manufactured in other areas of the common customs area for the purpose of protecting its own industries producing such goods.
(4) A contracting party shall upon request by any other contracting party take such steps as may be agreed upon between the parties concerned (including action to make such steps legally enforceable within its area) to prevent the exportation or unrestricted exportation from its area to the area of such other contracting party of such prohibited or restricted goods imported from

outside the common customs area or grown, produced or manufactured in its area or to prevent the exportation or unrestricted exportation from its area to a country outside the common customs area of such prohibited or restricted goods imported from the area of such other contracting party.
(5) The contracting parties shall co-operate in the application of import restrictions with a view to ensuring that the economic objectives of any import control legislation in any country in the common customs area are attained.

ARTICLE 12
ARRANGEMENTS FOR REGULATING THE MARKETING OF AGRICULTURAL PRODUCTS

(1) Whenever an arrangement for regulating the marketing of an agricultural commodity is in operation in any area of the common customs area, such arrangement shall be applied on an equitable basis to similar commodities produced in any other area of the common customs area and marketed in the area where the marketing arrangement is in operation, and the contracting parties concerned, cognisant of the advantages deriving from the effective operation of these arrangements, shall co-operate in such arrangements on a basis to be mutually agreed upon.
(2) The contracting parties agree to consult from time to time on matters affecting production and consumption of agricultural commodities and the improvement and extension of marketing arrangements, for such commodities.

PART 5

ARTICLE 13
POOL OF CUSTOMS, EXCISE, SALES AND ADDITIONAL DUTIES

Any customs, excise, sales and additional duties collected in the common customs area shall be paid quarterly into the Consolidated Revenue Fund of South Africa.

ARTICLE 14
THE POOL OF CUSTOMS, EXCISE, SALES AND ADDITIONAL DUTIES

(1) The common revenue pool of the common customs area shall consist of the gross amounts of customs, excise, sales and additional duties leviable and collected on goods imported into or produced in the common customs area, and any other duties collected in terms of Article 19 (3), but shall not include any duties rebated or refunded under the provisions of any law relating to customs, excise and sales duty (including any rebate or refund specifically provided for in any such law but which is paid from voted funds and not deducted from customs, excise and sales duty revenue).
(2) The contracting parties agree that in determining the share of Botswana, Lesotho or Swaziland of the common revenue pool in respect of any financial year the following formula shall be used:
The cost-insurance-freight value at border of goods from all sources imported during the financial year into the area of each party, plus the value of excisable and sales duty goods produced and consumed in such area during such year, plus the excise and sales duties paid thereon during such year shall be expressed as a percentage of the cost-insurance-freight value of the goods imported during the financial year into the common customs area, plus the customs and sales duties paid thereon during such year, plus the value of excisable and sales duty goods, produced and consumed during such year in the common customs area, plus the excise and sales duties paid thereon during such year. The amount calculated by the application to the common revenue pool of the percentage so obtained, enhanced by a multiplying factor of 1-42, shall represent the share of each of the three countries in respect of that financial year.

(3) There shall be paid from the Consolidated Revenue Fund of South Africa to the Governments of Botswana, Lesotho and Swaziland, in respect of their share of the common revenue pool, amounts calculated on the following basis:

(a) in respect of the financial year 1972/73 and each financial year thereafter:
(i) an amount resulting from the application to the formula referred to in paragraph (2) above, of the relevant data for the financial year two years before the financial year in question; plus or minus
(ii) a first adjustment in respect of the financial year in question equal to the difference between the total amount actually received by each country in respect of that year and the amount due to each country in terms of the formula referred to in paragraph (2) above, recalculated on the basis of the latest available data for that particular financial year; plus or minus
(iii) a final adjustment in respect of the financial year three years before the financial year in question equal to the difference between the total amount actually received by each country in respect of that year and the amount due to each country in terms of the formula referred to in paragraph (2) above, recalculated on the basis of the final data for that particular financial year;

(b) in respect of the financial year 1971/72:
(i) an amount resulting from the application to the formula referred to in paragraph (2) above of the relevant data for the financial year 1969/70; plus or minus
(ii) an amount in respect of the financial year 1969/70 equal to the difference between the total amount actually received by each country in respect of that year and the amount due to each country in terms of the formula referred to in paragraph (2) above, recalculated on the basis of the latest available data for the financial year 1969/70; (

(c) in respect of the financial year 1970/71; an amount resulting from the application to the formula referred to in paragraph (2) above, of the relevant data for the financial year 1968/69 except that in the case of import values 1968 data shall be used and that agreed estimates of the values of sales duty goods produced and consumed in the financial year 1969/70 and the sales duties collected thereon shall be included;

(d) in respect of the financial year 1969/0; an amount equal to the difference between the total amount actually received by each country in respect of that year and the amount due to each country in terms of the formula referred to in paragraph (2) above, calculated on the basis of the relevant data for the financial year 1968/69, except that in the case of import values 1968 data shall be used, and that no imputed allowances for the values of sales duty goods produced and consumed and the sales duties thereon shall be included.
(4) The amounts referred to in subparagraphs (a) and (b) of paragraph (3) above shall be determined and agreed upon between the contracting parties approximately six months before the beginning of the financial year in question.
(5) The amounts referred to in subparagraph (a), (b) and (c) of paragraph (3) above shall be remitted in equal quarterly installments during the financial year in question.
(6) The payment referred to in subparagraph (d) of paragraph (3) above shall be made before the end of the financial year 1969/70.
(7) The Government of South Africa undertakes to consult the Governments of Botswana, Lesotho and Swaziland prior to the introduction of changes in the fiscal structure of South Africa where these are expected to have a substantial effect on the structure of taxation measures relating to the common revenue pool.
(8) This Article shall be deemed to have come into operation on the first day of April, 1969, and to have been substituted from that date for the corresponding provisions of the Customs Agreement concluded on 29 June 1910.

ARTICLE 15
RAIL AND ROAD TRAFFIC

(1) The contracting parties undertake that the transit through their areas of goods imported from outside the common customs area to or exported to a country outside the common customs area from the areas of the other contracting parties shall not be subject to transport rate discrimination.
(2) Each contracting party shall ensure that the tariffs applicable within its area to the conveyance of goods by publicly-owned transport to and from the other areas of the common customs area shall be no less favourable than the tariffs applicable to the carriage of similar goods within its area.
(3) Each contracting party undertakes to extend to the motor transport operators registered in the areas of the other contracting parties treatment no less favourable than that accorded to motor transport operators registered within its own area for the conveyance of goods or passengers for reward or in the course of any trade or business.

PART 6

ARTICLE 16
FREEDOM OF TRANSIT

A contracting party shall afford freedom of transit without discrimination to goods consigned to and from the areas of the other contracting parties: Provided, however, that a contracting party may impose such conditions upon such transit as it deems necessary to protect its legitimate interests in respect of goods of a kind of which the importation into its area is prohibited on grounds of public morals, public health or security, or as a precaution against animal or plant diseases, parasites and insects, or in pursuance of the provisions of a multilateral international convention to which it is a party: And provided, further, that a contracting party shall not be precluded from refusing transit, or from taking any measures deemed necessary by it in connection with such transit, for the purpose of protecting its security interests.

ARTICLE 17
BILATERAL CONSULTATIONS

Notwithstanding the provisions of Article 2, if, as a result of unforeseen developments, any product is being introduced into the area of one of the contracting parties from the area of another contracting party in such increased quantities and under in such increased quantities and under such conditions as to cause or threaten serious injury to producers or manufacturers of like or directly competitive products in the area into which such goods are so introduced, the Government of the latter area shall have the right to require the other party to consult at the earliest possible opportunity and to co-operate with it in finding as soon as possible a mutually acceptable solution.

ARTICLE 18
CONSULTATIONS ON ZOO - SANITARY AND PHYTO-SANITARY MATTERS

Subject to the provisions of Article 11, the contracting parties recognise the importance of measures prescribing zoo-sanitary and phyto-sanitary requirements aimed at the prevention of the spread of animal and plant diseases, parasites and insects and agree to consult from time to time to achieve such aim in the common customs area with due regard to the need to facilitate the flow of trade in products affected by such measures.

PART 7

ARTICLE 19
TRADE AGREEMENTS WITH COUNTRIES OUTSIDE THE COMMON CUSTOMS AREA

(1) A contracting party shall not, without the prior concurrence of the other contracting parties and subject to such conditions as my be agreed upon by the contracting parties, enter separately into or amend a trade agreement with a country outside the common customs area in terms of which concessions on the duties in force in the common customs area are granted to that country.
(2) A contracting party may enter separately into or amend a trade agreement, other than a trade agreement mentioned in paragraph (1), with a country outside the common customs area, provided the terms of such an agreement or amendment do not conflict in any way with the provisions of this Agreement. Such contracting party shall, as soon as possible after the conclusion of the agreement or amendment, supply each of the other contracting parties with a copy of the agreement or amendment.
(3) (a) A contracting party, having an agreement with a country outside the common customs area which provides for the importation into its area from such country of goods at lower rates of duty than those applicable to like goods in the common customs area, shall collect the duties payable on importation into its area.
(b) Unless the contracting parties have otherwise agreed in respect of any such agreement, where such goods are to be removed from the area of such contracting party to the area of any of the other contracting parties the duties applicable in the common customs area shall become due and payable and the contracting party from whose area such goods are to be removed shall, prior to such removal, collect the differences between the lower duties paid and the duties applicable. If proof of payment of the differences in duty cannot be furnished in the area to which the goods are subsequently removed, the goods shall be liable to forfeiture.
(c) Any duties and differences in duties thus collected shall be paid into the Consolidated Revenue Fund of South Africa. Any payments due by that contracting party under such agreement with a country outside the common customs area, shall be paid on its behalf from the Consolidated Revenue Fund.

ARTICLE 20
GENERAL CONSULTATIONS

(1) A Customs Union Commission shall be established, comprising representatives of all the contracting parties, for the purpose of discussing any matter arising out of this Agreement.
(2) The Commission shall meet once a year. A contracting party may, however, at any time request a meeting of the Commission for the purpose of discussing a matter connected with this Agreement and the Commission shall meet as soon as possible thereafter.
(3) Where contracting parties have consulted on a matter which may affect the rights of the other parties under this Agreement and arising under Article 12, 17 of 18 or on a matter arising under paragraph (5) of this Article, a report on the results of these consultations shall be furnished to the Commission before its next meeting.
(4) Where a matter has been referred to the Commission for discussion, the Commission shall use its best endeavours to find a mutually agreeable solution to the particular problem or difficulty and the representatives shall report to their respective Governments for consideration of any remedial measures.
(5) Any difficulty or problem arising out of this Agreement which does not directly affect the interests of all the contracting parties may, with the concurrence of all the contracting parties, form the subject of direct consultation between the parties affected with a view to seeking a solution thereof.

ARTICLE 21
TERMINATION OF 1910 AGREEMENT

The Customs Agreement concluded on 29 June 1910, as amended from time to time, shall terminate on the entry into force of this Agreement.

ARTICLE 22
ENTRY INTO FORCE OF, AND WITH-DRAWAL FROM AGREEMENT

This Agreement shall, subject to the provisions of Article 14 (8) enter into force on 1 March 1970.
If a contracting party wishes to withdraw from this Agreement that party shall give notice thereof to all the other contracting parties.
If after consultation the contracting parties fail to agree on the date and conditions of the withdrawal this Agreement shall remain in force until twelve months from the date of such notice and shall then cease to apply to the withdrawing party.
In witness whereof the undersigned, being duly authorised thereto by their respective Governments, have signed this agreement.
Done at Pretoria, in quadruplicate, in Afrikaans and English texts, each of which texts shall be of equal authenticity, this eleventh day of December, 1969.
For the Government of the Republic of South Africa: J.F.W. HAAK.
For the Government of the Republic of Botswana: J.G. HASKINS.
For the Government of the Kingdom of Lesotho: P.N. PEETE.
For the Government of the Kingdom of Swaziland: L. LOVELL.

PART 8

MEMORANDUM OF UNDERSTANDING

With reference to the Customs Union Agreement dated 11 December 1969, between the Governments of South Africa, Botswana, Lesotho and Swaziland, it is desired to place on record the following additional understandings on which agreement has been reached among the four Governments and which shall be read with, and shall form part of the Agreement:

AD ARTICLES 3, 4, 8 AND 10
ADMINISTRATION OF CUSTOMS, EXCISE AND SALES DUTY PROVISIONS

(1) The Governments of Botswana, Lesotho and Swaziland undertake to establish customs and excise administrations capable of administering the terms of the Agreement and any arrangements thereunder, customs and excise storage and manufacturing warehouse provisions, excise provisions and the collection of excise duties and sales duty provisions and the collection of sales duties.
(2) The Contracting parties agree that: (a) goods (including goods for warehousing) destined for Botswana, Lesotho or Swaziland and imported through any place of entry in South Africa (including Lourenco Marques and Jan Smuts Airport) shall be entered for customs, excise or sales duty purposes through South African customs and for that purpose the laws relating to customs, excise and sales duty of Sough Africa will apply to such goods as if such goods were destined for South Africa: Provided that if the laws relating to customs, excise and sales duty of Botswana, Lesotho or Swaziland as the case may be, should, in relation to such goods, differ in respect of any restriction, prohibition, tariff of rebate under the Agreement, the relative law of the country of destination of such goods shall in that respect be deemed to be the law relating to customs, excise or sales duty, as the case may be, of South Africa in relation to such goods;
(b) goods destined for South Africa and imported other than by road through any place in

Botswana, Lesotho or Swaziland shall be entered for customs, excise or sales duty purposes at the place of entry in South Africa. Goods so destined and imported by road shall be so entered at the place of entry into the common customs area;
(c) goods destined for Botswana, Lesotho or Swaziland and imported directly into the country in question shall, subject to the provisions of subparagraph (a), be entered for customs, excise of sales duty purposes in that country;
(d) goods for warehousing in any customs and excise storage warehouse established in the area of Botswana, Lesotho or Swaziland shall be cleared for warehousing at places of entry in South Africa for removal to such warehouse without further entry, but any clearance ex such warehouse of such goods and collection of any customs, excise or sales duty thereon shall be the responsibility of the country in whose area the warehouse is situated;
(e) the administration of any customs and excise manufacturing warehouse (including the collection of any customs, excise or sales duty on any goods manufactured in such warehouse) in Botswana, Lesotho and Swaziland shall be the responsibility of the country in whose area the warehouse is situated; and
(f) provisions relating to drawbacks of duty on goods used in the manufacture of exported goods shall be administered by the Government in whose area the exporter is situated, but the Government of South Africa shall accept responsibility for the processing of claims for drawback of any duty emanating from exporters in Botswana, Lesotho or Swaziland in respect of goods exported from the common customs area and payment of such claims shall be effected from the Consolidated Revenue Fund of South Africa.
Done at Pretoria, in quadruplicate, in Afrikaans and English texts, each of which texts shall be of equal authenticity, this eleventh day of December, 1969.
For the Government of the Republic of South Africa: J.F.W. HAAK.
For the Government of the Republic of Botswana: J.G. HASKINS.
For the Government of the Kingdom of Lesotho: P.N. PEETE.
For the Government of the Kingdom of Swaziland: L. LOVELL

AMENDMENTS
MEMORANDUM OF UNDERSTANDING

With reference to the Memorandum of Understanding which is to be read with and forms part of the Customs Union Agreement dated 11 December 1969, between the Government of Botswana, Lesotho, South Africa and Swaziland, it is desired to place on record that agreement has been reached among the four Governments to amend the aforementioned Memorandum of Understanding by the addition to paragraph (2) thereof of the following new subparagraph (g):
"(g) Notwithstanding the provisions of subparagraph (a) goods destined for Botswana, Lesotho or Swaziland imported by air may be removed in bond for entry at any place of entry in Botswana, Lesotho or Swaziland."
Done in quadruplicate in the Afrikaans and English languages, both texts being of equal authenticity.
For the Government of the Kingdom of Swaziland: Mbabane, 19 November 1973.
For the Government of the Kingdom of Botswana: Gaborone, 23 October 1973.
For the Government of the Kingdom of Lesotho: Maseru, 31 October 1973.
For the Government of the Republic of South Africa: Pretoria, 19 September 1973.

AGREEMENT AMENDING THE CUSTOMS UNION AGREEMENT OF 11 DECEMBER 1969 BETWEEN THE GOVERNMENTS OF SOUTH AFRICA, SWAZILAND, BOTSWANA AND LESOTHO

With reference to the Customs Union Agreement dated 11 December 1969, between the Governments of South Africa, Swaziland, Botswana and Lesotho, it is desired to place on record that agreement has been reached among the four Governments to amend the aforementioned Agreement as follows:

ARTICLE 4
Heading: CUSTOMS AND SALES DUTIES ON IMPORTED GOODS AND EXCISE AND SALES DUTIES ON MOTOR VEHICLES MANUFACTURED IN THE COMMON CUSTOMS AREA.

Paragraph 4 (a) A contracting party may grant a full rebate of the customs and sales duties in respect of goods imported into its area and a full rebate of the excise and sales duties on motor vehicles manufactured in the common customs area, required: -
(i) for the relief of distress of persons in cases of famine and other national disaster;
(ii) under any technical assistance agreement; and
(iii) in terms of an obligation under any multilateral international agreement to which such contracting party is or becomes a party.
DONE in quadruplicate, in English and Afrikaans texts, each of which shall be of equal authenticity.
For the Government of the Republic of South Africa: Pretoria, 27 October 1975.
For the Government of the Kingdom of Swaziland: Mbabane, 27 November 1975.
For the Government of the Republic of Botswana: Gaborone, 10 November 1975.
For the Government of the Kingdom of Lesotho: Maseru, 18 December 1975.

AGREEMENT AMENDING THE CUSTOMS UNION AGREEMENT OF 11 DECEMBER 1969

With reference to the Customs Union Agreement of 11 December 1969 between the Governments of South Africa, Botswana, Lesotho and Swaziland, it is desired to place on record that agreement has been reached among the four Governments to amend Article 14 of the said Agreement by inserting after Article 14 (3) the following:
(3) (a) Should in respect of the financial year 1976/77 and for subsequent years, the shares of Botswana, Lesotho and Swaziland of the common revenue pool calculated in terms of paragraph (3) (a) (i) above in respect of the relevant data for the financial year two years before (that is, for 1974/75 and subsequent years) expressed as a percentage of the cost, insurance, freight value at border of goods from all sources including all duties paid or payable thereon imported during the financial year into the area of each party (A), plus the value of excisable and sales duty goods produced and consumed in such area during such year (B), plus the excise and sales duties paid thereon during such year (C), be less that 20% then an additional amount to be termed the stabilization factor, equal to 50% of the difference between the amount calculated in terms of the formula referred to in paragraph (5) (a) (i) on the relevant data for the financial year two years before and 20% of the factors A - B - C referred to in this paragraph shall be paid to Botswana, Lesotho and Swaziland from the common revenue pool in addition to the amount calculated under paragraph (3) (a) (i) above, on the understanding that the amount calculated under paragraph (3) (a) (i) together with the stabilization factor in respect of the relevant data two years before shall not be less that 17% of the factors A - B - C referred to in this paragraph.
(b) Should in respect of the financial year 1976/77 and for subsequent years, the shares of Botswana, Lesotho and Swaziland of the common revenue pool calculated in terms of paragraph (3) (a) (i) above in respect of the relevant data for the financial year two years before (that is, for 1974/75 and subsequent years) expressed as a percentage of the cost, insurance, freight value at border of goods from all sources including all duties paid or payable thereon imported during the financial year into the area of each party (A), plus the value of excisable and sales duty goods produces and consumed in such area during such year (B), plus the excise and sales duties paid thereon during such year (C) be more than 20% then an amount equal to 50% of the difference between the amount calculated in terms of the formula referred to in paragraph (3) (a)

(i) on the relevant data for the financial year two years before and 20% of the factors A - B - C referred to in this paragraph shall be deducted from the amount calculated under paragraph (3) (a) (i) above, on the understanding that the amount calculated under paragraph (3) (a) (i) together with the stabilization factor in respect of the relevant data two years before shall not be more than 23% of the factors A - B - C referred to in this paragraph.
(c) In respect of the financial year 1977/78 and for subsequent years the stabilization factor calculated on the basis of subparagraphs (a) and (b) shall be adjusted in respect of the final revised data for the financial year three years before the financial year in question and the relevant difference shall, as the case may be, be added to or subtracted from the payment due in respect of the financial year in question.
Done in quadruplicate, in the English and Afrikaans languages, both texts being of equal authenticity.
For the government of the Republic of South Africa PRETORIA, 3 July 1978.
For the government of the Republic of Botswana GABORONE, 2 February 1978.
For the government of the Kingdom of Lesotho MASERU, 30 March 1978
For the government of the Kingdom of Swaziland MBABANE 11 May 1978

MEMORANDUM OF UNDERSTANDING

With reference to the Memorandum of Understanding which is to be read with and forms part of the Customs Union Agreement dated 11 December 1969, between the Governments of South Africa, Swaziland, Botswana and Lesotho, it is desired to place on record that agreement has been reached among the four Governments to amend the aforementioned Memorandum of Understanding by the addition to paragraph (2) thereof of the following new subparagraph (h):
"(h) Notwithstanding the provisions of subparagraph (a), goods consisting of imported parcel post destined for Botswana, Lesotho or Swaziland may be entered for customs, excise or sales duty purposes at any place of entry in those countries provided such goods have remained at all times under the control of the postal authorities concerned."
DONE in quadruplicate in the Afrikaans and English languages, both texts being of equal authenticity.
For the Government of the Republic of South Africa: Pretoria, 25 November1983.
For the Government of the Kingdom of Swaziland: Mbabane, 29 July 1983.
For the Government of the Republic of Botswana: Gaborone, 18 April 1983.
For the Government of the Kingdom of Lesotho: Maseru, 18 September 1983.

MEMORANDUM OF UNDERSTANDING AMENDING THE MEMORANDUM OF UNDERSTANDING, DATED 11 DECEMBER 1969, THAT MUST BE READ WITH THE CUSTOMS UNION AGREEMENT DATED 11 DECEMBER 1969.

With reference to the Memorandum of Understanding dated 11 December 1969 which is to be read with and forms part of the Customs Union Agreement dated 11 December 1969, between the Governments of Botswana, Lesotho, South Africa and Swaziland, it is desired to place on record that agreement has been reached among the four Governments to amend the aforementioned Memorandum of Understanding by the addition to paragraph (2) thereof of the following new subparagraph (i):
"(i) Notwithstanding the provisions of paragraph (a), should any goods -
(i) which are destined for Botswana, Lesotho, South Africa and Swaziland; and
(ii) which, for a period exceeding the period specified in the applicable laws relating to customs, remain unentered in any one of the said countries, excluding the country for which such goods are destined, be received in the State warehouse of such country, the customs authorities of the country for which such goods are destined shall be notified of such receipt and shall be requested to arrange for the removal in bond of such goods for entry at any place of entry in

Botswana, Lesotho, South Africa or Swaziland. If at the expiration of a period of 14 days as from the date of such notification a written advice to the effect that the goods in question will be removed in bond has not been received from the country for which the goods are destined, the country in which the goods are destined, the country in which the goods so remain unentered shall dispose thereof and the proceeds shall be dealt with in accordance with the provisions of the applicable laws relating to customs and of Article 13 of the Agreement. It is also agreed and accepted that the authorities of the country for which such goods are destined will assume full and unconditional liability in respect of all claims emanating from the subsequent sale of unentered goods so removed in bond."

DONE in quadruplicate, in English and Afrikaans texts, each of which texts shall be of equal authenticity.

MEMORANDUM OF UNDERSTANDING

With reference to the Memorandum of Understanding which is to be read with and forms part of the Customs Union Agreement dated 11 December 1969, between the Governments of Botswana, Lesotho, South Africa and Swaziland, it is desired to place on record that agreement has been reached among the four Governments to amend the aforementioned Memorandum of Understanding by the addition to paragraph (2) thereof of the following subparagraph:

"(j) Notwithstanding the provisions of subparagraph (a), goods imported in containers manifested for Botswana, Lesotho or Swaziland and destined for importers in those countries or other countries outside the common customs area, may be removed at places of landing in South Africa to container terminals or depots appointed or designated in those countries in accordance with applicable laws relating to customs and excise, and shall be entered for customs, excise and sales duty purposes."

The said amendment shall enter into force on such date as this Memorandum of Understanding shall have been signed on behalf of all four Governments.

DONE in quadruplicate in the English and Afrikaans languages, both texts being of equal authenticity.

For the Government of the Republic of Botswana: Gaborone 9 October 1989.
For the Government of the Kingdom of Lesotho: Maseru, 16 October 1988.
For the Government of the Republic of South Africa: Pretoria, 9 April 1990.
For the Government of the Kingdom of Swaziland: Mbabane, 5 December 1989.

AGREEMENT AMENDING THE CUSTOMS UNION AGREEMENT BETWEEN THE GOVERNMENT OF THE REPUBLIC OF BOTSWANA, THE GOVERNMENT OF THE KINGDOM OF LESOTHO, THE GOVERNMENT OF THE REPUBLIC OF SOUTH AFRICA AND THE GOVERNMENT OF THE KINGDOM OF SWAZILAND OF 11 DEVEMBER 1969.

With reference to the Customs Union Agreement between the Government of the Republic of Botswana, the Government of the Kingdom of Lesotho, the Government of the Republic of South Africa and the Government of the Kingdom of Swaziland dated 11 December 1969, as amended from time to time, it is desired to place on record that agreement has been reached among the four Governments to amend the aforementioned Agreement as follows:

ARTICLE 1

The following new Article is inserted immediately after Article 22 of the Customs Union Agreement:

ARTICLE 23
ADMISSION OF NEW CONTRACTING PARTIES

(1) The contracting parties may, on application by a State not a party to this Agreement, by unanimous decision admit such State as a contracting party to this Agreement.
(2) An application as contemplated in paragraph (1) of this Article shall be in the form of a diplomatic note addressed to each of the contracting parties.
(3) Accession to this Agreement shall be effected by the deposit of an instrument of accession with each of the contracting parties.
(4) On accession, the common customs area shall be extended to include the area of such acceding State, and the rights and obligations applicable to such acceding State under this Agreement shall not be more or less favourable than those applicable to the Governments of Botswana, Lesotho and Swaziland."

ARTICLE 2

This agreement shall enter into force on the date of its signature and shall be read with and form part of the Customs Union Agreement.
IN WITNESS WHEREOF, the undersigned, being duly authorized by their respective Governments, have signed this Agreement.
DONE at Gaborone in quadruplicate, in the English Language, on 30 March 1990.
DONE at Maseru in quadruplicate, in the English Language, on 2 April 1990.
DONE at Pretoria in quadruplicate, in the English Language, on 9 April 1990.
DONE at Mbabane in quadruplicate, in the English Language, on 29 March 1990

PRACTICAL INFORMATION FOR CONDUCTING BUSINESS

INVESTMENT AND BUSINESS CLIMATE - STRATEGIC INFORMATION AND CONTACTS FOR STARTING BUSINESS

Botswana is a land-connected country located in Southern Africa. Botswana has historically enjoyed among the highest economic growth rates in the world and its export-driven economy is highly correlated with global economic trends. Development has been driven mainly by revenue from the diamond industry, which has enabled Botswana to provide infrastructure such as transportation and social services. During the 12 months prior to September 2014, Botswana's economy grew by 4.2 percent and inflation remained at the bottom end of the central bank's 3 percent to 6 percent spectrum. According to Government of Botswana (GOB), investments within Botswana totaled USD 4 billion in 2012. In accordance to the World Bank's rating scale, Botswana's per capita income of USD 7,730 makes it higher than most other sub-Sahara countries. As of December 2014, Moody's and S&P rate Botswana's sovereign debt as A2 and A-, respectively.

Botswana is a stable, democratic country with an independent judiciary system. It maintains a stable macroeconomic environment, fiscal discipline, a well-capitalized banking system, and a sensible crawling peg exchange rate system. Corruption in Botswana remains less pervasive than in other parts of Africa; nevertheless, foreign and national companies have commented an increasing tender-related corruption where colluding officials manipulate the process. The GOB has launched initiatives to promote foreign investment in key sectors in order to diversify its economy beyond diamond industry and it created the Botswana Investment and Trade Centre to assist local and foreign investors in this endeavor. Botswana is a member state to both the ICSID convention and the 1958 New York convention.

Despite a commitment towards attracting investment, GOB policies do not always facilitate foreign business operations in Botswana. Currently they do not have a consolidated legal framework that clarifies the protections and incentives afforded to investors and there are limitations on foreign participation in the market. At least twenty different service sector businesses are reserved for nationals. Complimentary to this are the institutionalized preferences of procuring goods and services from citizen-owned sources. Managers cite local skills deficits, low labor productivity, and challenges obtaining work permits for foreign workers as key business constraints in Botswana. Bureaucratic hurdles and shortages of water and electricity also hamper economic activity in Botswana and the government's increasing number of state-owned enterprises (SOEs) and market holdings crowd out the private sector. The GOB is seeking to improve its customs and procurement processes with assistance from USAID, and the U.S. Trade and Development Agency.

The World Bank ranked Botswana 74 out of 189 economies in the category of Ease of Doing Business. Key investment opportunities include large water, electricity, transportation, and telecommunications infrastructure projects that the GOB has plans to implement. The lion's share of economic activities outside the diamond sector are driven by government procurement and the GOB has an approximate USD 5 billion budget for the 2015 fiscal year. Economic experts have noted that Botswana has considerable potential in areas such as; mining beneficiation, electricity, meat industry, tourism, and financial services sectors.

1. OPENNESS TO, AND RESTRICTIONS UPON, FOREIGN INVESTMENT

Attitude toward Foreign Direct Investment

The GOB publicly emphasizes the importance of attracting foreign direct investment (FDI). The GOB has launched initiatives to promote economic activity and foreign investment in specific areas, including the establishment of hubs to promote economic growth in the agriculture, diamond, education, health and transportation sectors. Additional investment opportunities in Botswana include large water, electricity, transportation, and telecommunication infrastructure. Botswana imports the majority of its products for consumption; food, clothing, appliances, mining equipment, and raw materials.

In 2012, the Ministry of Trade and Industry (MTI) drafted a position paper for a proposed Investment Facilitation Law and requested an OECD Investment Policy Review in order to inform its discussions of consolidating a legal regime for investment. It has abolished all foreign exchange controls, instituted low corporate tax rates, and the Botswana Investment and Trade Centre provides assistance to foreign investors (reference Investment Incentives section). Despite the desire to attract foreign investment, certain GOB's policies do not make it easy for foreign firms to do business.

Other Investment Policy Reviews

In December of 2014, the Organization for Economic Cooperation and Development (OECD) released an Investment Policy Review on Botswana. (**http://www.oecd-ilibrary.org/finance-and-investment/oecd-investment-policy-reviews-botswana-2014_9789264203365-en**).

Botswana has been a World Trade Organization (WTO) since 1995. As a member of the Southern African Customs Union (SACU) the WTO last conducted a trade policy review in 2009. (**https://www.wto.org/english/tratop_e/tpr_e/tp322_e.htm**)

Laws/Regulations of Foreign Direct Investment

Under Botswana's Company Act, foreigners who wish to operate a business are required to register as well as obtain the relevant licenses and permits as prescribed by the Trade Act of 2008.

Licenses are required for a wide spectrum of businesses, including banking, non-bank financial services, transportation, medical services, mining, energy provision, and alcohol sales. Although recent amendments to the Trade Act have eliminated the catch-all miscellaneous business license category, investors have reported on local authorities insisting that a business apply for a license even when it does not fall within the established categories. In addition, some businesses have observed that the enforcement of licenses, as well as the time taken for inspections to comply with licensing requirements, varies widely across local government authorities. Botswana's processes to obtain a construction permit are lengthy (an average of 110 days) in addition to needing to complete twenty separate steps. The U.S Embassy continues to engage with the GOB to highlight these and other licensing challenges.

The Botswana Investment and Trade Centre serves as a useful resource when registering a company and obtaining licenses and permits. The MTI also provides guidance on the process of registering a company on its website (http://www.mti.gov.bw/businessregistration).

Industrial Promotion

The GOB's National Export Strategy identifies eight priority sectors targeted for growth: (1) arts and crafts; (2) garments; (3) textiles; (4) jewelry; (5) mineral processing (including diamonds); (6) glass and glass products; (7) leather and leather products; and, (8) beef. The Economic Diversification Drive, a government program used to implement a strategy to diversify the economy beyond diamond industry, added five additional areas: (9) renewable energy; (10) recycled material products; (11) auxiliary support services; (12) banking, finance and insurance; and, (13) construction/building.

Limits on Foreign Control

Botswana reserves some licenses solely for citizens, including butcheries, general trading establishments, gas stations, liquor stores, supermarkets (excludes chain stores), bars (other than those associated with hotels), certain types of restaurants, boutiques, auctioneers, car washes, domestic cleaning services, curio shops, fresh produce vendors, funeral homes, hairdressers, various types of rental/hire services, laundromats, specific types of government construction projects under a certain dollar amount, certain activities related to road and railway construction and maintenance, and certain types of manufacturing activities including the production of furniture for schools, welding, and bricklaying.

The MTI reported to the National Doing Business Committee (NDBC) in 2015 that it would allow foreigners to begin operating an undetermined number of business sectors currently limited to Batswana citizens.

The MTI, which administers the citizen participation initiative, has taken an expansive interpretation of the term chain stores, so that it encompasses any store with more than one outlet. This broad interpretation has resulted in the need to apply exemptions to certain supermarkets, simple specialty operations, and general trading stores. Consequently, many large general merchandise markets, restaurants, and grocery networks are owned by foreigners.

Privatization Program

The GOB has represented itself a deeply committed towards privatization, even putting a task force together in 1997. This task force approved regulations back in 2000 to privatize all of its state-owned companies; and formed a Public Enterprises Evaluation and Privatization Agency (PEEPA) to oversee this process. In practice, none of the state-owned entities (SOE), known as parastatals, have been privatized and the GOB has expanded its SOEs in recent years. In 2012, the GOB created the Okavango Diamond Company and the Mineral Development Company Botswana in order to oversee their mineral industry holdings. In 2014, the GOB acquired operations to form a mining hub under a grand economic diversification strategy dubbed Polaris II and launched Botswana Oil Limited to manage the country's fuel supply.

After more than 12 years of effort and multiple attempts to reach a privatization agreement regarding the state-owned airline, Air Botswana, to this day the airline still remains part of the GOB. The privatizations of six other state organizations, including the Botswana Telecommunications Corporation (BTC) and the National Development Bank, are also behind schedule. In September 2014, the GOB announced that it would hold an initial public offering to sell 49 percent of its current BTC holdings only to nationals as well a citizen-owned companies, while retaining a 51 percent., Since making this announcement in 2014, GOB has deferred this initial public offering on three separate occasions. No new date has been announced.

The ability of PEEPA to manage the privatization of state-owned enterprises is hampered by the lack of corresponding legislation to enforce the process. As a result, the decision to privatize, and the speed with which it is done, remains at the discretion of the ministry or department.

Screening of FDI

The Botswana Investment and Trade Center screens foreign direct investment (FDI) in Botswana when evaluating whether to assist investors.

Competition Law

Botswana has developed anti-trust legislation and policies to ensure appropriate competition in the business environment. Under the Competition Act, the newly-established Competition Authority is now monitoring mergers and acquisitions. Between April 2013 and March of 2014, the Competition Authority investigated 61 cases of alleged monopoly practices. The Competition Authority is empowered to reject mergers when they are deemed not to be in the public best interest. The Competition Authority has interpreted this ability to mean that it can prohibit mergers when the end result is the concentration of a majority of shares in the hands of foreign investors.

Investment Trends

The GOB has stated its desire to attract additional foreign investment, nevertheless its existing policies do not always make it easy for foreign firms to do business. There is no consolidated legal framework to clarify the protections and incentives afforded to investors and the limitations on foreign participation in the market. The 2014 Botswana Investor's Handbook (**http://botswana.usembassy.gov/economic_information_reports.html**) published by the Investment and Trade Centre (BITC) does shed some light onto aspects of the investment framework. Botswana's political parties emphasize the importance of citizen empowerment, an interchangeable term that refers to either social safety or the creation of economic policies that create new opportunities for its citizens. Over twenty businesses in the service sector are reserved exclusively for citizens. The 2012 Citizen Economic Empowerment Policy has emphasized the preference for local companies. In October 2014 the GOB and the Chamber of Mines created a committee to oversee the purchasing of mining supplies with a preference towards those produced locally.

Botswana dropped eight places in the 2015 World Bank, Doing Business Report to 74 out of 189 due to the deterioration of procedures such as paying taxes, starting a business, registering property, and it's continued low ranking in cross-border trade. Burdensome bureaucratic procedures in addition to water rationing, power outages and weak infrastructure hamper economic activity. The Ministry of Labor and Home Affairs, has denied permits to a large number of skilled foreign workers without providing any explanation, prompting foreign chambers of commerce, to express concern over their ability to establish or maintain commercial operations within the country. In 2014 the GOB increased its market share by acquiring private mining operations and launching the new state-owned Botswana Oil Limited to manage the country's fuel supply. Botswana's leading chamber of commerce spoke out in response against the government's increasing number of state-owned enterprises, noting that it crowds out the private sector.

Over the last year, the GOB has taken steps to improve the investment climate. If implemented, these reforms would facilitate investment in Botswana; however, the GoB's implementation of planned reforms has historically lagged. In May 2014, parliament approved an E-

Communications and Transactions Bill designed to streamline procedures by creating a centralized online system for storing and approving documents. The GOB also began granting license waivers for businesses in 2014, and has stated that it will remove in 2015 requirements for licenses that are not related to health or safety. In January 2015, the GOB Cabinet approved the establishment of Botswana's National Single Window which enables international traders to submit regulatory documents at a single location in order to facilitate trade. As of March 2015, the Botswana Unified Revenue Services is consulting with the private sector on a draft to amend the Customs and Excise Duty Act with the view of streamlining procedures and lowering importing and exporting costs. USAID's Southern African Trade Hub provided technical assistance to the GOB during the drafting process.

The MTI reported to the National Doing Business Committee (NDBC) in March 2015 that it approved an unprecedented set of business reforms in December 2014. Key changes it presented include creating a corps of commercial specialized judges within the civil court system, streamlining property registration, and allowing foreigners to operate in an undetermined number of business sectors currently limited to Batswana citizens. The MTI reported to the NDBC that the GOB would implement administrative reforms included in the packet by the end of 2015 and legal reforms by the end of 2016. The GOB is also considering implementing a procurement reform roadmap with the U.S. Trade and Development Agency's Global Procurement Initiative: Understanding Best Value technical assistance program.

Table 1

Measure	Year	Index or Rank	Website Address
TI Corruption Perceptions index	2014	31 of 175	transparency.org/cpi2014/results
World Bank's Doing Business Report "Ease of Doing Business"	2015	74 of 189	doingbusiness.org/rankings
Global Innovation Index	2014	92 of 143	globalinnovationindex.org/content.aspx?page=data-analysis
World Bank GNI per capita	2013	USD 7,770	data.worldbank.org/indicator/NY.GNP.PCAP.CD

2. CONVERSION AND TRANSFER POLICIES

Foreign Exchange

There are no foreign exchange controls in Botswana or restrictions on capital outflows through financial institutions. Commercial banks are required to ensure customers complete basic forms indicating name, address, purpose and other details prior to processing funds transfer requests or loan applications. The Ministry of Finance monitors data collected on the forms for statistical information on capital flows, but the form does not require government approval prior to the processing of a transaction and does not delay capital transfers.

To encourage portfolio investment, develop domestic capital markets, and diversify investment instruments, non-residents are able to trade in and issue Botswana Pula-denominated bonds with maturity periods of more than one year, provided such instruments are listed on the Botswana Stock Exchange (BSE). Botswana's Letlole Saving Certificate (equivalent to a U.S. Treasury bond) can be purchased only by Botswana citizens. Foreigners can only hold shares in BSE-listed Botswana companies.

Travelers are not restricted to the amount of currency they may carry, but they are required to declare to customs at the port of departure any cash amount in excess of BWP 10,000 (USD 1,200). There are no quantitative limits on foreign currency access for current account transactions.

Bank accounts denominated in foreign currency are allowed in Botswana. Commercial banks offer accounts denominated in U.S. Dollars, British Pounds, Euros and South African Rand. Businesses and other bodies incorporated or registered domestically may open accounts without prior approval from the Bank of Botswana. The government also permits the issuance of foreign currency denominated loans.

Upon disinvestment by a non-resident, the non-resident is allowed immediate repatriation of all proceeds including profits, rents, fees, etc.

The Botswana Pula (BWP) has a crawling peg exchange rate and is tied to a basket of currencies comprised of the South African rand, weighted at 50 percent, with the IMF's Special Drawing Rights (consisting of the U.S. dollar, the Euro, British pound, and Japanese yen) comprising the other 50 percent. The Bank of Botswana reduced the weighting of the South African rand from 55 percent to 50 percent in January 2015. The BWP continues to be heavily influenced by movements of the South African rand against the U.S. dollar. There is no difficulty in obtaining foreign exchange. Shortages of foreign exchange that would lead banks to block transactions are highly unlikely.

In 2014, the Ministry of Finance's Financial Intelligence Agency (FIA) began processing suspicious transaction reports. The FIA is set to assist the Botswana Police Service, Directorate on Corruption and Economic Crime, and Department of Public Prosecution to identify and investigate money laundering offenses. Under the FIA's oversight, Batswana banks have begun improving anti-money laundering practices by introducing AML compliance systems. In addition, in 2014 the parliament passed the Counter-Terrorism Act and Proceeds and Instruments of Crime Act, meeting the Eastern and Southern Africa Anti-Money Laundering Group's (ESAAMLG) requirements. Botswana was previously under enhanced monitoring by ESAAMLG before they introduced these reforms.

3. EXPROPRIATION AND COMPENSATION

Section 8 of the country's Constitution prohibits the nationalization of private property. The GOB has never pursued a policy of forced nationalization and is highly unlikely to adopt one. The Acquisition of Property Act provides a process for any expropriation, including parameters to determine market value and receive compensation. The 2007 Amendment to the Electricity Supply Act allows the GOB to revoke an Independent Power Producer's license and confiscate the operations with compensation for public interest purposes.

4. DISPUTE SETTLEMENT

Legal System, Specialized Courts, Judicial Independence, Judgments of Foreign Courts

The local Constitution provides for an independent judiciary system. The legal system of Botswana is based on Roman-Dutch law as influenced by English common law. This type of system cohabits with legislation, judicial decisions and local customary law. The courts enforce properly enforce commercial contracts, and the judicial system is widely regarded as being fair. Both foreign and domestic investors have equal access to the judicial system. Botswana does not have a dedicated commercial court. The Industrial Court set up by the Trade Dispute Act of 2004 primarily addresses labor matters.

As part of the December 2014, reforms packet that the MTI presented to the National Doing Business Committee, the GOB is planning to create a corps of commercial specialized judges within the civil court system. Under the new system, commercial cases will be overseen by commercial judges in order to expedite the handling and ensure relevant expertise. The GoB plans to implement these changes by the end of 2016; however implementation of GoB-planned reforms has historically lagged.

U.S. litigants have complained that the time taken to obtain and enforce a judgment in a commercial dispute is unreasonably long. The turnaround time for civil cases is approximately two years. In an effort to create more efficient adjudications, the government has established land tribunal, industrial, small claims and corruption courts. During the past several years, some dockets have improved but progress has been uneven.

Local laws are accessible through the Botswana Attorney General's Office web site (www.laws.gov.bw). It can take up to 24 months for a law, once passed, to appear on the web site.

Bankruptcy

Botswana's commercial and bankruptcy laws are comprehensive. Secured and unsecured creditors enjoy similar rights under bankruptcy proceedings as they would in the United States.

Investment Disputes

There are no known investment disputes involving U.S. persons.

International Arbitration

Botswana accepts international arbitration to settle investment disputes.

ICSID Convention and New York Convention

Botswana has ratified the convention on the Recognition and Enforcement of Foreign Arbitral Awards (1958 New York Convention). They are also a member state to the International Centre for the Settlement of Investment Disputes (ICSID convention), and the Multilateral Investment Guarantee Agency (MIGA).

Duration of Dispute Resolution

The duration in reaching a resolution involving an investment dispute depends on a number of factors. When local courts are involved they will usually call the aggrieved parties and recommend that they try to settle their differences out-of-court. If negotiations fail, the matter will be assigned to a judge whom will place the case on his docket. There is also an option to label the matter as urgent in order to speed up the process but this too requires a subsequent judicial assessment to determine if the matter is urgent.

Performance Requirements and Investment Incentives

WTO/TRIMS

Botswana is a World Trade Organization (WTO) member since 1995. Botswana does not keep any policies that are inconsistent with WTO TRIMS requirements.

Investment Incentives

Botswana has several mechanisms in place to attract foreign direct investment (FDI). The BITC provides assistance to local and foreign investors. BITC is responsible for promoting foreign direct investment, investor aftercare, and the promotion of locally-manufactured goods in export markets. It assists investors with company registration, land acquisition, factory shells, utility connections, and work and residence permits for essential staff. Requests by investors for investor support from BITC and other agencies are evaluated based on the extent to which the proposed project assists in the government's diversification efforts, contributes to the growth of priority sectors, and provides employment and training to Botswana citizens. The government also makes grants available to investors who partner with citizens and will extend credit to investors presenting proposals that have undergone appropriate due diligence and which have completed a feasibility study. Foreign investors are encouraged to transfer technology to Botswana and skills to Botswana citizens with a view to preparing them for promotion into management positions.

Botswana offers a relatively low tax rate of 22 percent of the corporate taxable income and 7.5 percent withholding tax on all dividends distributed. The MTI can grant manufacturing companies the reduced level of 15 percent taxable income. Companies can pay the reduced rate of 15 percent of profit with accreditation from the Innovation Hub or the International Financial Services Centre on approved operations.

The Minister of Finance and Development Planning has the authority to issue development approval orders which are used for specific projects, which include providing tax holiday and education and training grants. The Minister must be satisfied that the proposed project will be beneficial to Botswana's economy. Any firm, local or foreign, may apply for a Development Approval Order through the Permanent Secretary for Finance and Development Planning. Applications will be evaluated against the following criteria: job creation for Botswana citizens; the company's training plans for Botswana citizens; the company's plans to localize non-citizen positions; Botswana citizen participation in company management; amount of equity held by Botswana citizens in the company; the location of the proposed investment; the project's effect on the stimulation of other economic activities; and the project's effect on reducing local consumer prices. The MTI also offers rebates on imported materials for manufactures that produce products for export.

Performance Requirements

Performance requirements are not imposed as a condition for establishing, maintaining, or expanding an investment in Botswana, or for access to tax and investment incentives. Foreign investors are encouraged, but not compelled, to establish joint ventures with citizens or citizen-owned companies.

Foreign investors wishing to invest in Botswana are required to register the company in accordance with the Companies Act and comply with other applicable legislation. Investors are encouraged, but not required, to purchase from local sources. The Government does not require investors to locate in specific geographical areas, use a specific percentage of local content, permit local equity in projects, manufacture substitutes for imports, meet export requirements or targets, or use national sources of financing for private-sector investments.

As a matter of policy, the GOB encourages foreign firms to hire qualified Botswana nationals rather than expatriates. The granting of work permits foreign workers may be made contingent upon establishment of demonstrable localization efforts. The government may additionally require evidence that a local is being trained to assume duties currently being fulfilled by foreign worker, specially focused at the middle-management level. The GOB offers incentives to companies that train local employees, including the deduction of 200 percent of training expenses when training is carried out by an accredited institution. The government has introduced a range of policy initiatives intended to mitigate the impending loss of diamond revenue and decrease government spending, including an Economic Diversification Drive, which employs government purchases to stimulate local production and consumption, as well as a wage freeze to reduce the size of the public sector wage bill.

Investors who rely on expatriate managerial and technical expertise see these limitations on immigration as a major regulatory constraint. In 2012, Botswana implemented a Points Based System (PBS) to evaluate work permits, in response to complaints that immigration authorities lacked the necessary expertise to properly evaluate applications for individuals with certain skill sets. This resulted in immediate and widespread complaints that the PBS was too stringent. The government then announced that it would review the policy; however, there is no indication that restrictions have not relaxed. The Ministry of Labor and Home Affairs has recently denied work permits to a large number of skilled foreign workers.. Even recent amendments to the Immigration Law do not appear to address the problem. Firms that retain BITC's investment services are afforded priority in the permitting process and may avoid some of the delays that have been reported in finalizing immigration documents.

Grants are available to foreign investors who partner with Botswana citizens. The Citizen Entrepreneurial Development Agency has established a venture capital fund to provide equity to citizens and ventures between citizens and foreign investors. Foreign investors do not have access to Botswana government loans and grants designed specifically for citizen-owned contracting firms or for small enterprises.

The government, the largest procuring entity in the country, has directed central government, local authorities and state-owned enterprises to purchase all products and services from locally-based manufacturers and service providers if the goods and services are locally available, competitively priced, and meet tender specifications in terms of quality standards as certified or recognized by the Botswana Bureau of Standards. The Department of Industrial Affairs under the MTI administers this program.

In order for a foreign firm to qualify with the Department of Industrial Affairs as a locally-based manufacturer or service provider to sell goods or services to the government of Botswana, the firm first must be registered with the Registrar of Companies and possess a relevant license or waiver letter. Few of these procedures can be completed online. Therefore, in practice companies see the need to hire an agent on the ground to handle registrations.

For Companies Act registration purposes, enterprises are classified as follows: Micro Enterprises —less than 6 employees including owner and annual turnover of up to BWP 60,000; Small Enterprises — less than 25 employees and annual revenue between BWP 60,000 and 1,500,000; Medium Enterprises — less than 100 employees and an annual revenue between BWP 1,500,000 and 5,000,000; Large Enterprises —more than 100 employees and an annual revenue between BWP 5,000,000 or more.

Data Storage

There are no requirements to store data within the country.

6. RIGHT TO PRIVATE OWNERSHIP AND ESTABLISHMENT

The GOB reserves some business sectors for citizen ownership, has instituted local procurement preferences, and limits the land permitted to be sold to foreigners (see Sections 1, 7, and 8). Botswana has no other known restrictions on investment ownership, the sources of financing for investments, the marketing of products, the sources of technology used by companies, or the methods of training used by companies; however the absence of a consolidated investment framework has resulted in a lack of clarity regarding limitations on foreign investment.

6. PROTECTION OF PROPERTY RIGHTS

Real Property

As part of the December 2014 reforms packet that the MTI presented to the National Doing Business Committee, the GOB plans to streamline and standardize property registration procedures by the end of 2016; however implementation of GOB-planned reforms has historically lagged. There are three main categories of land in Botswana: freehold, state land, and tribal land. Tribal and state land cannot be sold to foreigners. There are no restrictions on the sale of freehold land, but only about 5 percent of land in Botswana is freehold. In the capital city of Gaborone, the number of freehold plots is limited.

State land represents about 25 percent of land in Botswana. On application to the Department of Lands, both foreign-owned and local enterprises registered in Botswana may lease state land for industrial or residential use. Commercial use leases are for 50 years and residential leases are for 99 years. Waiting periods tend to be long for leasehold applications, but subleases from current leaseholders are available. In 2014, the GOB changed its implementing regulation to allow companies with less than five employees to operate in residential areas if their operations do not pose a health or safety risk to residents.

Tribal land represents 70 percent of land in Botswana. To obtain a lease for tribal land, the investor must approach the relevant local Land Board. Processes are unlikely to be streamlined or consistent across Land Boards.

Since independence, the trend in Botswana has been to increase the area of tribal land at the expense of both state and freehold land. Landlord-tenant law in Botswana tends to be moderately pro-landlord.

In addition to helping investors who meet its criteria obtain appropriate land leaseholds, the Botswana Investment and Trade Centre has also built factory units for lease to industrialists with the option to purchase at market value.

Intellectual Property Rights

Intellectual property rights are protected under the Industrial Property Act of 2010, the Registration of Business Names Act of 1975 and the Copyright & Neighboring Rights Act of 2000. Other IP-related Laws include the Competition Act, the Value Added Tax Act, the

Botswana Penal Code, the Customs and Excise Duty Act, the Monuments and Relics Act, the Broadcasting Act, and the Societies Act.

Botswana is a signatory to the Beijing Treaty on Audiovisual Performances, the Hague Agreement Concerning the International Deposit of Industrial Designs, the Protocol Relating to the Madrid Agreement Concerning the International Registration of Marks, the Convention Establishing the World Intellectual Property Organization (WIPO), the WIPO Copyright Treaty, the WIPO Performances and Phonograms Treaty, the Patent Cooperation Treaty, the Berne Convention for the Protection of Literary and Artistic Works and the Paris Convention for the Protection of Industrial Property.

In June 2014 GOB authorities worked with Namibian authorities and Interpol to seize 644,000 counterfeit items valued over USD 3 million in Botswana and Namibia.

For additional information about treaty obligations and points of contact at local IP offices, please see WIPO's country profiles at **http://www.wipo.int/directory/en/**.

Resources for Rights Holders

Embassy point of contact: Goitseone Montsho: **MontshoG@state.gov**

8. TRANSPARENCY OF THE REGULATORY SYSTEM

Bureaucratic procedures necessary to start and maintain a business tend to be open, though slow. Foreign investors' complaints generally focus on the inefficiency and/or unresponsiveness of mid-level and low-level bureaucrats in government. The government has introduced a Performance Management System to improve the service and accountability of government employees, but its effectiveness has not yet been evaluated.

The Public Procurement and Asset Disposal Board (PPADB) oversee all government tenders. Prospective government contractors are required to register with the PPADB. The PPADB maintains a process by which tender decisions can be challenged, and a bidder can also challenge a tender procedure in the courts. The PPADB publishes its decisions concerning awarded tenders, prequalification lists, and newly registered contractors.

The PPADB Act calls for preferential procurement of citizen-owned contractors for works, service and supplies, as well as specific, disadvantaged women's communities, though it states that such preferences must be time-bound, phased in and out as necessary, and consistent with the country's external obligations and its "market-oriented, macroeconomic framework." When a procuring entity wishes to reserve a tender for citizen-only participation, it is required to publish a notice to that effect either in the bid document or the pre-qualification notice.

Health and safety laws, embodied in the Factories Act of 1973, provide basic protection for workers from unsafe working conditions. Minimum working conditions required on work premises include cleanliness of the premises, adequate ventilation and sanitation, sufficient lighting and the provision of safety precautions. Health inspectors and the Botswana Bureau of Standards carry out periodic checks at both new and operating factories.

9. EFFICIENT CAPITAL MARKETS AND PORTFOLIO INVESTMENT

The government encourages the establishment of new and diverse financial institutions to support increased foreign and domestic investment and to fill existing gaps where finance is not commercially available. There are eight commercial banks, one merchant bank and one offshore bank, one statutory deposit-taking institution and one credit union operating in Botswana. All have corresponding relationships with U.S. banks. Additional financial institutions include various pension funds, insurance companies, microfinance institutions, stock brokerage companies, asset management companies, statutory finance institutions, collective investment undertakings, and statutory funds. Historically, commercial banks have accounted for 92 percent of total deposits and 98 percent of total loans in Botswana. A large portion of the population does not participate in the formal banking sector.

Money and Banking System, Hostile Takeovers

The Non-Bank Financial Institutions Regulatory Authority (NBFIRA) was established in 2008 and provides regulatory oversight for the non-banking sector. It extends know-your-customer practices to non-banking financial institutions and is intended to help deter money laundering and terrorist financing. NBFIRA is also responsible for regulating the International Financial Services Centre, a hub charged with promoting the financial services industry in Botswana.

The central bank, the Bank of Botswana (BOB), acts as banker and financial advisor to the government and is responsible for the management of the country's foreign exchange reserves, the administration of monetary and exchange rate policies, and the regulation and supervision of financial institutions in the country. Monetary policy in Botswana is widely regarded as prudent and the government has successfully managed to maintain sensible exchange rate and stable inflation rate, generally within the target of 3 to 6 percent.

Banks may lend to non-resident controlled companies without seeking approval from the Bank of Botswana. Foreign investors usually enjoy better access to credit than local firms due. In July 2014 USAID's Development Credit Authority, in collaboration with the Barclays Bank of Botswana, implemented a program to allow Small and Medium Enterprises (SME) to access up to USD 15 million in loans in an effort to diversify the current economy.

The local Stock Exchange (BSE) has 36 publicly traded companies. As of 2015, 22 companies on the Domestic Board and 12 companies on the Foreign Equities Board. In addition, three exchange traded funds are listed on the exchange. The total market capitalization for listed companies, as of March 2015 was USD 41.95 billion though most of that is taken up by one company, Anglo-American Plc, which has a market capitalization of some USD 35 billion. The BSE is still highly illiquid compared to larger African markets and is dominated by mining companies which adds to index volatility. Laws prohibiting insider trading and securities fraud are still under development.

The government has legitimized offshore capital investments and allows foreign investors, individuals and corporate bodies, and companies incorporated in Botswana to open foreign currency accounts in specified currencies. The designated currencies are U.S. Dollar, Pound Sterling, Euro and the South African Rand. There are no known practices by private firms to restrict foreign investment participation or control in domestic enterprises. Private firms are not permitted to adopt articles of incorporation or association which limit or prohibit foreign investment, participation or control.

In general, Botswana exercises careful control over credit expansion, the Pula exchange rate, interest rates, and foreign and domestic borrowing. Banking legislation is largely in line with industry norms for regulation, supervision, and payments, and its anti-money laundering and combating the financing of terrorism regime is improving (see section two).

10. COMPETITION FROM STATE-OWNED ENTERPRISES

State-owned enterprises (SOEs), known as "parastatals," are majority or one hundred percent owned by the Government. There is a published list of SOEs at the GoB portal (www.gov.bw) with profiles of financial and development SOEs. Some SOEs are state-sanctioned monopolies, including the Botswana Telecommunications Corporation, Botswana Meat Commission, the Water Utilities Corporation, Botswana Railways, and the Botswana Power Corporation.

Private and government-owned enterprises are governed by the same business registration and licensing laws. No law or regulation prohibits or restricts private enterprises from competing with SOEs. Botswana law requires SOEs to publish annual reports and, depending on how they are constituted, SOEs are audited by private sector accountants or the Auditor General. In 2011, Parliament also began overseeing SOEs, compelling Presidents and Chairmen to appear before Parliamentary committees to provide reports and answer questions regarding their performance. Many SOEs are not performing well and several, including the Botswana Meat Commission, the Botswana Telecommunications Corporation (BTC) and the Botswana Power Corporation, have been embroiled in scandals involving alleged fraud and mismanagement. One former CEO and several employees of the BTC were indicted on corruption charges in 2012. In 2013, the Parliamentary Committee investigated allegations of corruption and mismanagement at Botswana Meat Commission.

OECD Guidelines on Corporate Governance of SOEs

SOEs appoint a CEO, who reports to a Board of Directors, which reports to the relevant government Ministry. Board members are appointed by line ministers and are drawn from both the government and the private sector. Corporate governance is still a very new phenomenon in Botswana, but most SOEs are moving towards implementing it. CEOs of some SOEs, i.e. Bank of Botswana, Public Procurement & Asset Disposable Board, are still holding the Chairman positions of their boards while the OECD guidelines good practice calls for separation of duties. Appointment of Board members and CEO is very much politically motivated. Nominated candidates for these positions are submitted to the parliament for approval and they can either accept or reject a candidate.

Sovereign Wealth Funds

The Bank of Botswana maintains a long-term sovereign wealth fund, known as the Pula Fund, in addition to a regular foreign reserve account providing basic import cover. The Pula Fund, with an estimated value of some USD 7 billion, was established under the Bank of Botswana Act and forms part of the country's foreign exchange reserves, which are primarily funded by diamond revenues. The Pula Fund is wholly invested in foreign currency-denominated assets and is managed by the Bank of Botswana Board with input from recognized international financial management and investment firms. All realized market and currency gains or losses are reported in the Bank of Botswana's income statement.

11. CORPORATE SOCIAL RESPONSIBILITY

Corporate Social Responsibility (CSR) is recognized and embraced by government, some foreign and local firms, and customers. Major banks such as Standard Chartered and cell phone providers such as Mascom have established CSR programs, sponsor projects and support local nonprofit concerns. However, the CSR ethos has not taken hold in many smaller firms. The U.S. Embassy worked with the Botswana Confederation of Commerce, Industry and Manpower (BOCCIM) on the issue of CSR and ethical compliance to help enlist companies to sign onto a

Corporate Code of Conduct that covers, among other things, conflicts of interest, bribery, political interference, political party funding, procurement and bidding and issues surrounding residence and work permits. While the Code of Conduct is voluntary, it envisions amending Botswana's Procurement Act to allow only firms that have signed on to participate in tenders. It also envisages procedures whereby firms may be de-listed as signatories. To date, more than 70 firms have signed the Code of Conduct.

OECD Guidelines for Multinational Enterprises

The GoB actively encourages companies to embrace corporate social responsibility. The President of Botswana has publicly commended companies that exercise corporate social responsibility and challenged others to do the same.

12. Political Violence

The threat of political violence is considered low in Botswana. Public demonstrations are rare and seldom turn violent. The most recent protest involved public sector employees and occurred in April to June 2011. There were reports of police deployments and clashes with protestors. With the exception of a few minor instances demonstrations were largely peaceful.

13. CORRUPTION

UN Anticorruption Convention, OECD Convention on Combatting Bribery

Botswana has a reputation for a relative lack of corruption and a willingness to prosecute corrupt officials. Transparency International ranks Botswana as the least corrupt country in Africa (31st overall), and a 2014 report by the World Justice Project ranked Botswana number one on its regional rule of law index. Investors with experience in other developing nations describe the relative lack of obstruction or interference by law enforcement or other government agents as among the country's most important assets. Nevertheless, private sector representatives now note rising corruption levels in government tender procurements.

The major corruption investigation body is the Directorate on Corruption and Economic Crimes (DCEC). Overall, the DCEC is regarded as an active and independent organization. The DCEC has embarked on an education campaign to raise public awareness about the cost of corruption and is also working with Government departments to reform their accountability procedures.

Corruption is punishable by a prison term of up to 10 years, a fine of USD 50,000, or both. The DCEC received 1,471 reports of corruption in 2013, an 18 percent decrease from the 2011 statistics. The DCEC investigated 520 allegations in 2013, and the government typically obtains 16-20 convictions per year for corruption-related crimes. High level officials have been prosecuted. Allegations that the Director of Intelligence and Security Services escaped corruption charges because of his personal connections circulated widely in Batswana media in 2014. The Directorate of Public Prosecutions applied for a withdrawal of corruption charges against MTI Vincent Seretse in March 2015 citing the grounds that key witnesses were unavailable. The charges stemmed from alleged tender manipulation in 2008 when he was CEO of SOE Botswana Telecommunication Company.

The 2000 Proceeds of Serious Crime Act expanded the DCEC's mandate to include money laundering. The 2009 Financial Intelligence Act provides a comprehensive legal framework to address money laundering and establishes a financial intelligence agency (FIA). The FIA, which operates under the Ministry of Finance and Development Planning, cooperates with various institutions, such as Directorate of Public Prosecutions (DPP), Botswana Police Service, Bank of Botswana, the Non-Banking Financial Institutions Regulatory Authority (NBFIRA), the DCEC, and foreign FIAs to uncover and investigate suspicious financial transactions. Botswana is a member of the Eastern and Southern Anti-Money Laundering Group (ESAAMLG), a regional standards-setting body for ensuring appropriate laws, policies and practices to fight money laundering and the financing of terrorism.

Botswana is not a party to the OECD Anti-bribery Convention but is a party to the 2005 UN Anticorruption Convention.

Resources to Report Corruption

Contacts for agencies responsible for combating corruption:

Name: Ms. Rose Seretse
Tittle: Director
Organization: Directorate on Corruption and Economic Crime
Address: Madirelo Extension 6, Gaborone, Botswana
Telephone Number: +267 3914002/+267 3604200
Email: **dcec@gov.bw**

Name: Ms. Bridget John
Tittle: Executive Director
Organization: Public Procurement & Asset Disposal Board
Address: Private Bag 0058, Gaborone, Botswana
Telephone Number: +267 3602000
Email: **webmaster@ppadb.co.bw**

Name: Mr. Abraham Sethibe
Tittle: Director
Organization: Financial Intelligence Agency
Address: Private Bag 0190, Gaborone, Botswana
Telephone Number: +267 3998400
Email: **asethibe@gov.bw**

One can also reach out to the Minister of the relevant Ministry for a particular tender and provide a copy of the complaint to the Public Procurement & Asset Disposal Board Executive Director.

14. BILATERAL INVESTMENT AGREEMENTS

The U.S. and the Southern Africa Customs Union (SACU), which includes Botswana, signed a Trade, Investment, and Development Cooperative Agreement (TIDCA) in 2008. The TIDCA establishes a forum for consultative discussions, cooperative work, and possible agreements on a wide range of trade issues, with a special focus on customs and trade facilitation, technical barriers to trade, sanitary and phytosanitary (SPS) measures, and trade and investment promotion.

SACU has Free Trade Agreements with Iceland, Liechtenstein, Norway, Switzerland, and the European Free Trade Association. The preferential trade agreement between SACU countries and MERCOSUR (Argentina, Brazil, Paraguay and Uruguay) was signed by MERCOSUR and SACU States in December 2008 and April 2009 respectively. The PTA establishes fixed preference margins as a first step towards the creation of a free trade area between SACU and

MERCOSUR. Botswana has ratified the Agreement and is awaiting remaining Member States to complete ratification for the agreement to be implemented.

For more information on SACU's tariff regime see the World Trade Organization (WTO) document:**http://www.wto.org/english/tratop_e/tpr_e/s222-00_e.doc**.

Botswana is also a member of the Southern African Development Community (SADC), is currently implementing the SADC Protocol on Trade. For more information about SADC, visit: **www.sadc.int**.

In 2014, Botswana concluded an Economic Partnership Agreement (EPA) with the European Union as part of SADC EPA Group. The EPA guarantees access to the EU market without any duties or quotas for Botswana, and gives asymmetric access to the SADC EPA Group.

Botswana has a trade agreement with Zimbabwe which provides duty-free access for goods that meet the 25 percent local content requirement.

Botswana's trade regime is more open than that of an average sub-Saharan Africa country. According to the 2012 World Trade Indicators published by the World Bank, Botswana's MFN Tariff Trade Restrictiveness Index (TTRI) was 5.2 percent, as compared to 7.4 percent in 2011 for sub-Saharan Africa (the lower percentage indicates fewer trade restrictions). Nevertheless customs procedures remain a challenge for businesses in Botswana. Botswana ranked 157 out of 189 in trade in the World Bank's, 2015 Doing Business Report because it takes USD 3,145 and 27 days to export a container and USD 3,710 and 35 days for import procedures.

In 2015, the GOB Cabinet approved the establishment of Botswana's National Single Window which enables international traders to submit regulatory documents at a single location in order to facilitate trade. The Botswana Unified Revenue Services is consulting with the private sector on a draft to amend the Customs and Excise Duty Act with the view of streamlining procedures and lowering importing and exporting costs.

Botswana has erected some non-tariff barriers to trade, including import permit requirements for a variety of food products, seasonal trade bans on selected agricultural goods, and a state monopoly on beef exports.

Bilateral Taxation Treaties

Botswana has not signed a double taxation treaty with the United States.

15. OPIC AND OTHER INVESTMENT INSURANCE PROGRAMS

The Overseas Private Investment Corporation (OPIC) makes insurance available for projects in Botswana. In October 2008, OPIC approved a USD 250 million guarantee facility for the diamond industry. The purpose of the guarantee was to develop a robust lending market to Botswana's emerging cutting and polishing industry.

Botswana is a member of the Multilateral Investment Guarantee Agency (MIGA). MIGA offers investors protection against inconvertibility or transfer of currency, expropriation, breach of contract, and war and civil disturbance.

The Botswana Export Credit Insurance and Guarantee Ltd. allows investors to purchase coverage against certain events and losses such as the insolvency and inability of buyers to pay for purchases, unanticipated import restrictions, or the blockage by the buyer's country of foreign exchange transfer.

16. LABOR

Botswana has high unemployment (estimated to be 20 percent) and a severely constricted worker skills base. Employers can expect to engage in significant training efforts, depending on the industry. Retention of workers and absenteeism can pose problems. In addition, managers often cite workforce productivity as a point of frustration. The lack of trained local citizen professionals is generally resolved by the use of expatriates if they can secure work permits.

The Employment Act of 1992 provides basic guidelines for employment in Botswana. The legislation sets requirements for a minimum wage, length of the workweek, annual and maternity leave, hiring and termination. Standards set by the Act are consistent with international best practice as described by ILO model legislation and guidelines.

Employment-related litigation occurs and is both an example of trust in the court system and a cost to doing business in Botswana. Considerable expense and frustration can be avoided if an employer observes the provisions of the Employment Act, relevant labor regulations and prudence in advance of potential litigation. Before a potential litigant goes to one of eleven labor courts, the parties must attempt mediation through the Department of Labor.

All Botswana citizens, except those working in the Botswana Defense Force, police, and prisons are permitted to participate in trade unions. The largest unions are comprised of public sector workers. Although workers have a right to strike, those engaged in certain categories of "essential" services, including air traffic control, electricity services, fire services, the Bank of Botswana, health services, and sewage services are not permitted to strike. When the GoB tried to add diamond workers, veterinarians, and teachers to this list in the wake of a public sector strike in 2011, the public sector union sued the government to be taken off the list. The union won the case in April 2014. However, certain law provisions are found inconsistent with the ILO Conventions on Freedom of Association and Collective Bargaining Rights, including section 35(1)(b) of the Trade Disputes Act, which permits an employer or employers' organization to apply to the commissioner to withdraw the recognition granted to a trade union on the grounds that the trade union refuses to negotiate in good faith with the employer; section 20(3) of the Trade Disputes Act which imposes compulsory arbitration of disputes of interest in non-essential service sectors. According to the ILO Committee of Experts, there is a lack of provisions of law which provide for adequate protection against acts of interference by employers.

17. FOREIGN TRADE ZONES/FREE PORTS/TRADE FACILITATION

Botswana currently has no domestic free trade zones or free ports. Botswana approved a Special Economic Zone (SEZ) policy in 2009 and the government is currently drafting legislation to establish a SEZ authority. The government has allocated 426.6 hectares for SEZs to be overseen by the MTI.

18. FOREIGN DIRECT INVESTMENT AND FOREIGN PORTFOLIO INVESTMENT STATISTICS

Table 2: Key Macroeconomic Data, U.S. FDI in Host Country/Economy

	Host Country Statistical source*		USG or international statistical source		USG or International Source of Data: BEA; IMF; Eurostat; UNCTAD, Other
Economic Data	Year	Amount	Year	Amount	
Host Country Gross Domestic Product (GDP) ($B USD)	2014	13.8	2013	14.7	www.worldbank.org/en/country
Foreign Direct Investment	Host Country Statistical source*		USG or international statistical source		USG or international Source of data: BEA; IMF; Eurostat; UNCTAD, Other
U.S. FDI in partner country ($M USD, stock positions)	2012	0	N/A	N/A	
Host country's FDI in the United States ($M USD, stock positions)	N/A	N/A	N/A	N/A	
Total inbound stock of FDI as % host GDP	2012	16%	2013	22.7%	

*Bank of Botswana

According to the Bank of Botswana, investment in Botswana totaled USD 4 billion in 2012. Foreign direct investment statistics trends show that FDI forms slightly over half of capital flows into Botswana, followed by portfolio and other types of investments. Portfolio investments, though small, have increased since the founding of the Botswana Stock Exchange. The mining sector continues to dominate Botswana's investments, accounting for 72 percent of FDI and 42 percent of other investment inflows in 2012. The financing sector followed, comprising 22 percent of FDI and 10 percent of other investments. Europe was the primary source of FDI (75 percent), followed by Africa (22 percent). According to Bank of Botswana statistics the dominant countries contributing FDI in Botswana are Luxembourg (69 percent) and South Africa (14 percent). Non-FDI investments are dominated by an unspecified category of "other" countries (63 percent) and the bulk (77 percent) of non-FDI investments were provided to the public administration sector as external debt. The United States' non-FDI investments totaled approximately USD 5.3 million. The Bank of Botswana announced that there were substantive changes to the 2012 data following revisions to align it with balance of payment flows.

IMPORTANT AND LEGAL CONTACTS

Contact for More Information

Goitseone Montsho
Commercial Specialist
MontshoG@state.gov
+267 373-2431

Chansonette Yun
Economic/Commercial Officer
YunCR@state.gov
+267 373-2354

LAW SOCIETY

The Law Society of Botswana is a non-profit making organization, which aims to regulate the behavior and uphold the standards of legal professions in Botswana. **The Law Society of Botswana,** P.O. Box 50889, Gaborone, Plot 69921, Chobe Way Village, Telephone # 390 0200, 390 0777, Fax # 390 0660 www.lawsociety.org.bw ATT: Ms. Tebo Faith More Administration Officer

GABORONE AND SURROUNDING AREAS
ARMSTRONGS ATTORNEYS Attorneys,
Notaries and Conveyancers Prime Plaza Plot 74358
Acacia House, Corner Khama Crescent Ext. & PG
Matante Road, New CBD,
Second Floor, Gaborone
P.O. Box 1368 Gaborone, Botswana
Tel: 395 3481-5
Fax: 395 2757
Email: commercial@armstrongs.bw
Web: http://www.armstrongs.bw

BRISCOE ATTORNEYS
Plot 222 Ext: 9 Independence Avenue
P.O. Box 402492
Gaborone
Tel: 395 3377
Fax: 390 4809
Email: Admin@briscoe.co.bw

COLLINS NEWMAN & CO
Dinatla Court, Plot 4863
P.O. Box 882
Gaborone
Tel: 395 2702-4
Fax: 391 4230
E-mail: partners@collinsnewman.bw
Web: www.collinsnewman.bw
LYONS, RICHARD ATTORNEYS
Ext. 9 Plot 2662 Kgori Close
P.O. Box 160
Gaborone
Tel: 395 2364
Fax: 395 2061

Email: ral@botsnet.bw

MODIMO & ASSOCIATES
2nd floor BBS Bldg
Private Bag B077
Gaborone
Tel: 390 5645
Fax: 391 2347
Email: mtm@botsnet.bw ; awmodimo@modimos.co.bw

TAFA & COMPANY
Plot 51 – Unit 3, Crystal Plaza
Gaborone International Commerce Park
P.O. Box 2676
Gaborone
Tel: 391 0180
Fax: 392 2070
Email: dembanai@mega.bw

FRANCISTOWN AND SURROUNDING AREAS
DAMBE JOHANNES ATTORNEYS
Attorneys, Notaries and Conveyancers
Plot 407 Moffat Street
P.O. Box 266
Francistown
Tel: 241 5800
Fax: 241 6019
Email: dambejoannes.attorney@gmail.com

JOSIAH & ASSOCIATES
Attorneys, Notaries and Conveyancers
Blue Jacket Squares First Floor Suite 105
Above Supreme Furnitures
Private Bag F229
Francistown
Tel: 241 9437
Fax: 241 9438
E-mail: jos@botsnet.bw ; richardjsh@yahoo.com

NDAWANA & COMPANY
Plot No. 3986, Mokowe Street, Minestone
P.O. Box 500159
Francistown
Tel: 241 4954
Fax: 241 7519
Email: ndawanaattorneys@yahoo.com

LOBATSE AND SURROUNDING AREAS
NNOI & CHILUME ATTORNEYS
Barclays Bank Suite 12
Plot 4649 Khama 1 Ave

P.O. Box 367
Lobatse
Tel: 533 0221/533 3068
Fax: 533 3214
E-mail: nnoichilume@mega.bw

MAUN AND SURROUNDING AREAS
DAMBE JOHANNES ATTORNEYS
Attorneys, Notaries and Conveyancers
Sethunya House Office No.2, Old Mall
Above Standard Chartered Bank
Private Bag 00284
Maun
Tel: 686 0871
Fax: 686 0871
Email: maddandu@yahoo.com

PALAPYE AND SURROUNDING AREAS
NDAWANA & COMPANY
Plot 1247 Dairy World Complex
P.O. Box 1090
Palapye
Tel: 492 4298
Fax: 492 4510
Email: info@ndawanaattorneys.co.bw

STARTING BUSINESS REGULATIONS

MARKET OVERVIEW

Botswana offers a stable political, fiscal, and macroeconomic environment. Botswana's per capita income of $7,730 makes it an Upper Middle-Income Country according to World Bank standards; however, the country has one of the world's widest gaps between rich and poor with a Gini coefficient of over 0.60. GDP is valued at approximately $14.7 billion and real GDP growth was 4.4% in 2014. Botswana has a small population of 2.1 million; however, it has the potential to leverage its position in the region to serve as a gateway to the southern African market. To do so, it must address air and land infrastructure bottlenecks and streamline customs procedures.

Botswana's export-driven economy is highly correlated with global economic trends. In the aftermath of the global financial crisis, Botswana's economy went into recession, posting a negative GDP growth rate of 4.9%. The country has since recovered, with real GDP growth in 2014 at 4.4%, compared to a 9.3% growth rate in 2013. This was primarily a result of slow positive growth in the mining sector at 6.6%, compared to rapid growth of 12.2% in 2013. The Government of Botswana (GoB) has also indicated that they will continue with prudent management of their fiscal resources given the continued uncertainty over the recovery of the global economy.

Botswana maintains a conservative fiscal policy and low levels of foreign debt. For the year 2013/2014, Botswana reported a surplus of P7.22 billion, significantly higher than the projected surplus of P3.47 billion for the same year. This was due to the better than predicted performance of mineral revenue, coupled by unforeseen high volumes of diamond sales, exchange rate gains, and a 27% underspending rate in government infrastructure projects. Domestic inflation rose from 4.1% in December, 2013 to 4.6% in August, 2014, and remained unchanged at 2.8% in March, 2015 from February, 2015. As of December 31, 2014, Moody's and S&P rate Botswana's sovereign debt as A2 and A-, respectively.

In 2014, movements in bilateral exchange rates increased slightly with the Pula appreciating by 1.7% against the South African Rand compared to the 9.7% increase recorded in 2013, and depreciated by 2.4% against the "Special Drawing Right" (SDR is a basket of currencies comprised of the U.S. Dollar, British Pound, Euro and Japanese Yen) in the twelve months from January, 2014.

Botswana's trade balance is largely tied to the global demand for diamonds, which represent between 70-80% of the country's export revenues. Customs revenue from the Southern African Customs Union and diamonds revenue each contribute about one-third of total GoB revenue. As a result, the government's income, which is subject to global and regional economic trends, is largely outside of the GoB's control. These conditions make for difficult forecasting and place added pressure on policy makers to plan conservatively.

Government spending has traditionally played a large role in Botswana's economy. Botswana's central government expenditures account for one-third of GDP. The government employs about 40% of workers and employees of quasi-public "parastatal" firms make up another 5%. Botswana has been able to keep expenditures higher than the emerging market average because it has combined high diamond revenue with conservative fiscal policies. Diamond revenue has traditionally contributed about 40% to government income, but demand is volatile and has trended downward in recent years, and diamond stores are expected to decline. In 2014, Diamond revenue contributed 34.4% to government income and Southern African Customs Union revenues contributed 29.5%. Botswana must therefore confront the prospect of declining diamond revenues over the medium to long term. Recent studies by the World Bank and IMF have called for stringent control of public expenditure for long term budget sustainability, however, some analysts have questioned the government's political will to rein in spending, raising the possibility that Botswana will suffer a significant contraction in the event of a sudden decline in government revenue.

Botswana's diamond and customs revenue have provided the government with resources to construct and maintain a historically solid infrastructure, including roads, telecommunication systems, hospitals, hotels, and schools. While the presence of a well-maintained infrastructure, complimented by political stability, has tended to encourage foreign investment in certain targeted sectors, poor planning and workmanship has caused several infrastructure problems, particularly in the power and water sectors that are likely continue to constrain growth during the next 12-24 months. As a result, the GoB has introduced water and electricity rationing programs and businesses must contend with additional unscheduled power outages and water shortages. Despite mining's great contribution to the country's wealth, the sector only accounts for about 5% of employment.

The manufacturing sector is small, accounting for about 5.5% of GDP. Agriculture accounts for even less of Botswana's wealth, with only about 2.1% of GDP in 2014. Services represent about 14% of GDP. Travel and tourism account for about 10% of GDP.

U.S. Government trade statistics show total U.S. exports to Botswana of $52.9 million in 2014, down 35.5% from 2013, and consisting of low value shipments ($39 million), machinery ($11 million), vehicles ($9 million), pharmaceutical products ($9 million), and optic and medical insurance ($4 million). U.S agricultural exports to Botswana totaled $500 million in 2013. U.S. imports from Botswana totaled $318 million in 2014, up 12.4% from 2013. As many U.S. products enter Botswana as re-exports from South Africa, the export figure does not represent the total consumption of U.S. goods in the country. Similarly, the U.S. import figure does not include most diamonds, which generally enter the U.S. as re-exports from the United Kingdom.

The major U.S. export opportunities for Botswana continue to be in the area of mining equipment, hospital/medical equipment and supplies, aircraft equipment, pharmaceuticals, telecommunications equipment and services, computer hardware and software, energy equipment, and financial and consulting services.

Botswana is a member of the Southern African Development Community (SADC), a regional intergovernmental organization of fifteen African states. The SADC Trade Protocol provides each member state most favored nation treatment on import and export duties. SADC members have not yet implemented a Free Trade Agreement (FTA) eliminating regional tariffs, although one is in place. FTA negotiations between the United States and the region were suspended in 2006.

Botswana is also a member of the Southern African Customs Union (SACU), which consists of Botswana, Lesotho, Namibia, Swaziland, and South Africa. Customs and excise duties in SACU are pooled and distributed according to a revenue sharing formula. Historically, payments from SACU have represented a large proportion of Botswana's total public sector revenues and it generally represents one-third of GoB revenue. Should member states revise the revenue sharing formula as they are set to do in the near future (South Africa pays the most and has grown frustrated with its role subsidizing the smaller economies), this source of revenue will decline.

The Botswana Democratic Party has ruled the country since independence in 1966. Democratic institutions are in place and function well. Parliamentary elections held in October 2014 were free and fair. The next general election is expected in October 2019.

MARKET CHALLENGES

Due to the country's small population and low supply of skilled workers, Botswana does not have enough experienced managers and specialists to help run many of the companies that would otherwise invest there. According to local and expatriate firms doing business in Botswana, rather than liberalize requirements for work and residency permits for foreign employees, immigration officials have made it more difficult for foreigners to live and work in-country. This recent phenomenon has caused many skilled workers to leave Botswana, and has chilled the appetite for foreign direct investment for many prospective businesses. It remains to be seen whether Botswana will reverse this trend, however, all indications are that government officials do not intend to liberalize restrictions any time soon. With a population of only 2.1 million, 43% of which is spread out over a large, rural area, few U.S. companies have sought to tap into Botswana's domestic market. A free trade agreement between the fifteen Southern Africa Development Community (SADC) member states, and the simplification of laws, regulations and procedures, would reposition Botswana as a transportation and logistics hub the center of a 277 million person free trade zone. However, the slow paces of negotiations within the SADC region have hampered a significant move toward trade liberalization.

Severe water and electricity shortages significantly hamper economic growth, particularly in the mining sector. Other market challenges commonly cited are regulatory constraints in certain sectors which have little or no relationship to the protection of the public interest, excessive red tape relating to licenses and permits, limited access to finance, the high cost of internet, poor customer service, and low worker productivity. The government's increasing number of state-owned enterprises and market holdings crowd out the private sector.

MARKET OPPORTUNITIES

Botswana's mining sector experienced a slow growth in 2014 at 4.5% compared to 10% growth in 2013. The slow growth was attributable to a modest increase of 6.6% in diamond production, compared to 12.2% in 2013. Transport and communications grew by 7.4%, followed by trade, hotels and restaurants 7.1%, general government 5.2% and social and personal services 4.2%. Foreign firms in the heavy industrial sectors face fierce competition from Chinese firms that are underwritten by state-owned Chinese banks.

The government lifted a moratorium on coal licenses in early 2012 after they were suspended in June, 2011. The government is expected to focus on curbing speculation by selectively issuing licenses to firms with the resources to prospect and develop mines and associated infrastructure.

De Beers Co. dominates Botswana's diamond industry. Its mining operation, Debswana, is jointly owned by the Government of Botswana and De Beers, and produces between 20-22 million carats per year. The GoB launched the state-owned Okavango Diamond Company in 2012, a rough diamond distribution company.

Energy remains an important sector to watch for investors. To address the severe shortage of electricity in Botswana and the Southern African Power Pool, Botswana is now seeking to become a net exporter of electricity. Botswana is preparing to facilitate large investments in additional coal-fired power plants and is considering solar power projects. To date, no independent power producer has reached an agreement with the Government of Botswana to sell power, although the legal framework is in place permitting independent power operations.

The rate of growth in the renewable energy sub-sector will depend on government policy decisions such as what rates will be offered for feed-in power agreements and the further development of appropriate standards.

Botswana's political stability and record of prudent fiscal management means that it has potential to become a center for certain niche financial services, but poor regulatory oversight, high internet costs and a poor skills base have hampered strong growth in that area.

Botswana's tourist market is still in its infant stages, with high-end tour operators and hotels representing the majority of the market.

MARKET ENTRY STRATEGY

In Botswana, personal relationships established telephonically, or preferably in person, are essential to establishing effective business relationships. For a large project involving government, meeting partners face-to-face is essential. Investors increase their chances of successfully navigating the bureaucracy to start their projects by partnering with a local firm or a local or central government entity. In order to gain access to government loans and grants, having a local partner is mandatory. Local partnerships are also increasingly necessary to access government tenders and mining procurement contracts. It is also most effective to tie one's project to declared GoB goals and objectives, such as diversifying the national economy away from dependence on diamond revenues, creating employment, and increasing domestic labor market skills and capacity.

The Botswana Investment and Trade Centre (BITC) can facilitate market entry if the investor's project has potential for local employment creation and will facilitate the development of the export market (www.bitc.co.bw). IT or IT-related companies may want to consider a relationship with the Botswana Innovation Hub in order to facilitate market entry (http://www.bih.co.bw/).

Local consultants can source potential business partners and the U.S. Embassy's Economic/Commercial Section can assist American investors by providing general advice on economic conditions and, in some cases, specific market intelligence. The U.S. Department of Commerce's Gold Key partner search, partner matching, and business meeting facilitation services are also available.

The U.S. Embassy offers a service where by U.S. companies interested in bidding on projects in Botswana can have tender documents delivered to them. More information is available here: http://botswana.usembassy.gov/tenders_2013.html

REGISTRATION REQUIREMENTS[6]

	Procedure	Time to complete:	Cost to complete:
1	Select and reserve company name	3 days	BWP 20
2	Sign the declaration of compliance of statutory requirements for incorporation before a commissioner for oaths	1 day	BWP 75
3	Return the complete statutory return to the Registrar of Companies about re-allotment, directors, auditors, company secretary, and registered officers	1 day	BWP 300 by self, and a fee of BWP 2000 where registration is done by agent
4	Register the company with the Registrar of Companies at the Ministry of Commerce and Industry	2-3 weeks	BWP 360 (Registration of constitution)
5	Advertise the intention of applying for a license in the official gazette	3 weeks	BWP 80
*6	Obtain an approval of the working condition after an inspection of company premises	2 days,(simultaneous with procedure 6)	As part of the application procedure the firm's premises will be inspected by the health and environmental authorities to ensure compliance with minimum standards. The cost would be no charge as this Procedure is done by the municipal authorities as part
*7	Obtain an industrial license from the	3 weeks (	BWP 100 for industrial license if applied

[6] The World Bank estimation

	Industrial Affairs Department, Ministry of Commerce and Industry; or obtain a trading license from the local authority	simultaneous with procedure 7)	by self; BWP 1,500 by agent; BWP 60 for trade license if applied by self, BWP 2,000 by an agent
8	Register for Corporate Income Tax number with the Botswana United Revenue Services and obtain the approval from the Commissioner of Taxes for the appointment of a public officer who is in charge of tax return	7 days	no charge by self, BWP1,500 by agent
9	Register for VAT with Director of Customs & Excise	7 days	no charge by self, BWP1,500 by agent
10	Register employees for the work injury insurance	1 day	no charge

* Takes place simultaneously with another procedure.

Registration Requirements Details

Procedure 1.
Select and reserve company name
Time to complete:
3 days
Cost to complete:
BWP 20
Name of Agency:
Comment:
Procedure 2.
Sign the declaration of compliance of statutory requirements for incorporation before a commissioner for oaths
Time to complete:
1 day
Cost to complete:
BWP 75
Name of Agency:
Comment:
Procedure 3.
Return the complete statutory return to the Registrar of Companies about re-allotment, directors, auditors, company secretary, and registered officers
Time to complete:
1 day
Cost to complete:
BWP 300 by self, and a fee of BWP 2000 where registration is done by agent
Name of Agency:
Comment:
The company representative must submit the following forms to the Registrar of Companies: Form 4 (allotment of shares) , Form 2 (list of directors) , and Form 5 (location of office) . The registration is usually done over the counter.
Procedure 4.
Register the company with the Registrar of Companies at the Ministry of Commerce and Industry

Time to complete:
2-3 weeks
Cost to complete:
BWP 360 (Registration of constitution)
Name of Agency:
Comment:
Procedure 5.
Advertise the intention of applying for a license in the official gazette
Time to complete:
3 weeks
Cost to complete:
BWP 80
Name of Agency:
Comment:
Before submitting the application, the new company must advertise, in two consecutive issues of the Official Gazette, its intent to apply for a license.
Procedure 6.
Obtain an approval of the working condition after an inspection of company premises
Time to complete:
2 days,(simultaneous with procedure 6)
Cost to complete:
As part of the application procedure the firm's premises will be inspected by the health and environmental authorities to ensure compliance with minimum standards. The cost would be no charge as this Procedure is done by the municipal authorities as part
Name of Agency:
Comment:
Procedure 7.
Obtain an industrial license from the Industrial Affairs Department, Ministry of Commerce and Industry; or obtain a trading license from the local authority
Time to complete:
3 weeks (simultaneous with procedure 7)
Cost to complete:
BWP 100 for industrial license if applied by self; BWP 1,500 by agent; BWP 60 for trade license if applied by self, BWP 2,000 by an agent
Name of Agency:
Comment:
The trade licensing authorities convene a meeting on the second Tuesday of every month.
Procedure 8.
Register for Corporate Income Tax number with the Botswana United Revenue Services and obtain the approval from the Commissioner of Taxes for the appointment of a public officer who is in charge of tax return
Time to complete:
7 days
Cost to complete:
no charge by self, BWP1,500 by agent
Name of Agency:
Comment:
The company needs to obtain a CIT number (takes 5 days) then the company representative complete and file a taxpayer registration form, which includes the

application for registration of employee withholding tax (pay–as-you-earn tax, or PAYE) (takes 2 days) .

Procedure 9.

Register for VAT with Director of Customs & Excise

Time to complete:

7 days

Cost to complete:

no charge by self, BWP1,500 by agent

Name of Agency:

Comment:

Procedure 10.

Register employees for the work injury insurance

Time to complete:

1 day

Cost to complete:

no charge

Name of Agency:

Comment:

Companies must be insured for workplace injuries. Under the Workers' Compensation Act, they have the option of paying a deposit to the Commissioner as security for any associated claims. Most companies opt to purchase their own insurance.

PROPERTY REGISTRATION

	Procedure	Time to complete:	Cost to complete:
*1	Obtain certificate of compliance at the Lands Department	3 days (simultaneous with procedure 1)	BWP 100
*2	Obtain a rates clearance certificate at the Gaborone City council	3 days (simultaneous with procedure 2)	1 to 5 BWP
3	Notify BURS (Botswana unified revenue services) of VAT payment	5 days	No cost
4	The conveyancer prepares the deed of transfer	1 day	Fees: BWP 7050 + 3*250 + 550 (attorney fees) = BWP 8,350
5	The deed of transfer is lodged at the Deeds Registry	6 days	5% of value or purchase price above BWP 200,000 (transfer duty)

* Takes place simultaneously with another procedure.

Registration Requirement Details

Procedure 1.

Obtain certificate of compliance at the Lands Department

Time to complete:

3 days (simultaneous with procedure 1)

Cost to complete:

BWP 100

Name of Agency:

Lands Department

Comment:

A certificate of compliance is obtained at the Lands Department. It checks the status of the property on any pending compliance issues linked to it, i.e., compliance with conditions of a title deed like zoning and land usage. This is obligatory where the conditions of the title deed require it, such as in this case.

Procedure 2.

Obtain a rates clearance certificate at the Gaborone City council

Time to complete:

3 days (simultaneous with procedure 2)

Cost to complete:

1 to 5 BWP

Name of Agency:

City Council

Comment:

The seller obtains a rates clearance certificate at the Gaborone City Council, showing that there are no outstanding property taxes to be paid.

Procedure 3.

Notify BURS (Botswana unified revenue services) of VAT payment

Time to complete:

5 days

Cost to complete:

No cost

Name of Agency:

Botswana Unified Revenue Service (BURS)

Comment:

As a result of a stronger enforcement of the Value Added Tax Law, additional requirements for all transferor companies to obtain VAT clearance before they can transfer property have been introduced. This requirement was introduced through a Registrar's Circular No 3 of February 20 2009.

If the selling company is not charging VAT in the transaction, a Clearance Letter issued by BURS is required (if the company is not registered for VAT, or claims the property will be used for renting which is VAT exempt) . If the company is VAT registered and is charging VAT, then the conveyancer is required to give an undertaking to BURS that the VAT is accounted for and will be paid to the Seller on transfer. BURS will then issue a letter to Deeds Registry, on confirmation of the VAT details, confirming that the transaction is subject to VAT and advising that the transfer may proceed.

Procedure 4.

The conveyancer prepares the deed of transfer

Time to complete:

1 day

Cost to complete:

Conveyancing fees according to the following schedule:

Property value (in BWP)	Conveyance fees (in BWP)
150,000 to 200,000	3,800
From 200,000 to 300.000	4,300
300,000 to 400.000	4,800
400,000 to 500,000	5,300
500,000 to 600,000	5,600
600,000 to 700,000	6000

700,00 to 800,000 6350

800,000 to 900,000 6700

900,000 to 1,000,000 7050

Formula: 3.800 BWP for the first 200,000 + 500 Pula per 100,000 or part thereof, up to and including 500,000 property value. Where after the fee shall be 350 Pula per 100,000 or part thereof, up to and including 1 million. Where after the fee shall be 250 Pula per 100,000. In this case, fees would be: BWP 7050 + 3*250 + 550 (attorney fees) = BWP 8,350

Name of Agency:

Comment:

The lawyer or notary public must prepare the Deed of transfer. It is mandatory for lawyers to prepare the deed of transfer. The parties cannot do it themselves.
The original deed will be in possession of the seller.
For every transaction there is a disbursement of 550 BWP to the attorney (10% VAT 10% is paid on professional fess) .
The tariffs were gazetted in August 2004.

Procedure 5.

The deed of transfer is lodged at the Deeds Registry

Time to complete:

6 days

Cost to complete:

5% of value or purchase price above BWP 200,000 (transfer duty)

Name of Agency:

Deeds Registry of the Ministry of Lands

Comment:

The deed is lodged at the Deeds Registry of the Attorney General's Chambers (AG) . The Deeds Registry has employed more staff and changed their organization system. There are now internal time limits. If the usual person is absent, then someone else will complete the step, in order to keep the process flowing. The paper will be at his desk for one day, then go to next examiner, then the next and it is then complete. If all is in order (no mistakes or missing documents) , the deed of transfer is endorsed by the Registrar of Deeds (or his delegate) and done in 4 to 5 business days. Once endorsed, one copy is given to the parties' lawyer, the other is kept at the Registry for public reference. Transfer duty in the amount of 5% is payable at the AGs revenue office immediately prior to registration. For citizens, the duty is paid only on the amount above BWP 200,000. Non-citizens pay the whole amount.
Where a transaction is on a commercial basis and the seller raises a VAT invoice, transfer duty is not required for registration, on presentation of the receipted invoice. In this transaction, VAT is treated in the normal way, which is as an input/ output setoff item. The rate of VAT is still 10%.

The Deeds Registry had changed their lodgment times for lodging transactions. It is now between 7:30 a.m to 8:30 am. If the transaction is not lodged before then, it will have to be done the next day.

TRADE REGULATIONS AND STANDARDS

On the regional front Botswana is an active member of the Southern African Customs Union, (SACU) , and the Southern African Development Community (SADC) . Internationally Botswana stands as an Associate member of the European Union (Lome Convention) , it is a member of the World Customs Organization (WCO) and the World Trade Organization (WTO) . Botswana enforces a customs and excise legislation that is in conformity with that of the other members of SACU as well as the WCO convention of Harmonized Commodity Description and Coding System. Opportunities for exports of manufacturing equipment in general have also been enhanced by the enactment of the African Growth and Opportunity Act (AGOA) in 2004.

SOUTHERN AFRICAN DEVELOPMENT COMMUNITY (SADC)

Botswana along with 13 other southern African states (Angola, Democratic Republic of the Congo (DROC) , Lesotho, Malawi, Mauritius, Mozambique, Namibia, the Seychelles, South Africa, Swaziland, Tanzania, Zambia, and Zimbabwe) is a member of the Southern African Development Community (SADC) . SADC was established to promote closer economic, social and political integration in the region. At present, SADC sets policy through protocols which must be ratified by two-thirds of member states to bring them into effect. SADC's most ambitious protocol to date is its Trade Protocol, signed in August 2000 by eleven member states (Angola was absent, DROC and Seychelles joined SADC later) . Angola and Seychelles have indicated they will accede to the trade protocol soon, but the intention of the DROC is unknown. The Trade Protocol calls for the reduction and elimination of tariff and non-tariff barriers between member states. As a progression of the Trade Protocol, SADC launched the SADC Free Trade Agreement on September 1, 2004.

Under the SADC Free Trade Protocol, tariffs will be abolished on 85% of trade between 11 of the 14 states by 2008. The remaining tariffs are scheduled for elimination by 2010. Member states will later agree on a timetable for the elimination of non-tariff barriers to regional trade, such as export subsidies. The SADC Free Trade Agreement will also reduce barriers to imports into the SACU area, as well as provide improved access for exports to the SADC markets. A Trade Protocol Implementation Unit has been set up in Gaborone, where the SADC Secretariat is located, to assist member states to understand and implement the protocol and help them to cushion short term dislocations they might experience as a result of trade liberalization.

SOUTHERN AFRICAN CUSTOMS UNION (SACU)

The Southern African Customs Union (SACU) is an economic block composed of South Africa, Botswana, Namibia, Lesotho, and Swaziland. Historically, the most important trade agreement has been the SACU Agreement, which provides for duty-free trade with Namibia, Lesotho, Swaziland and South Africa coupled with a relatively high degree of protection against imports from the rest of the world. SACU tariffs have been progressively reduced, partly in response to World Trade Organization (WTO) membership. This has increased competition from global imports in SACU countries. SACU acts as a pool for customs duties paid on imports into the SACU countries, and has been the subject of controversy for many years. The structure of SACU is currently under renegotiation. While it is anticipated that the basic provisions ensuring free trade within the SACU area will be preserved, other aspects such as governance, and revenue distribution will be altered.

The SACU states have eliminated duties on goods moving between members with certain strategic exceptions and have imposed a common external tariff on all goods entering the Union. With the exception of certain foodstuffs, import permits are not required for goods entering Botswana from SACU. Duties collected are placed in a common pot and split among member states.

South Africa has proposed a formula which guarantees the other members' revenues remain the same for a year and then slowly taper off. Before agreeing to changes in the revenue sharing formula, all states except South Africa are demanding creation of an accountable SACU Secretariat. Currently, SACU is controlled by the South African Revenue Service (SARS) , an arm of the South African government, which sets tariff rates and oversees disbursements. The other members are demanding that a secretariat with an elected president take over SARS' functions. An agreement on restructuring is probably some time away, but a formula whereby South Africa exchanges control over policy for more equitable revenue sharing seems likely.

VALUE ADDED TAX (VAT)

South Africa may have given new life to accusations of its non-collegial method of managing SACU when it unilaterally announced collection of its VAT at land borders with SACU partners. Previously, goods destined for export to SACU were zero rated, as were goods in transit through South Africa. Goods imported from SACU members had their VAT paid by the South African importer following arrival. SARS announced the cessation of all zero rating as of January 1, 1999, with the exception of those goods consigned for transport on VAT registered carriers. The remaining SACU members claimed the action was taken without adequate consultation, planning, or consideration for the move's effects on their economies. South Africa claimed the move was necessary to eliminate pervasive VAT evasion fraud.

The effect has been that importers and exporters of goods to, from or through South Africa must pay 14.5% VAT upon the goods entry to or departure from South Africa. The VAT can be refunded on export minus a one-and-a-half percent processing fee. Implementation at Botswana's borders has been especially problematic with delayed refund checks, improperly collected processing fees, and long border delays especially at the main Botswana - South Africa border post. While refund issues have been addressed, border delays are likely to remain a serious and costly problem until SARS upgrades its facilities and trains additional personnel or until agreement on longer border operating hours can be reached between Botswana and South Africa.

WORLD TRADE ORGANIZATION

Following its accession to GATT, Botswana became a member of the World Trade Organization (WTO) , which was launched as the official successor to GATT in January 1995. The WTO is responsible for the implementation of the Uruguay Round Trade Agreement. With regard to tariffs and quotas, WTO seeks to: (a) create a market-oriented agricultural trading system - (Botswana and its SACU partners will have to decrease tariffs by 24% over 10 years) and (b) phase out quota restrictions on developing countries' textile exports (which will ultimately benefit Botswana) .

Changes taking place under the WTO and the various rounds of international trade negotiations will have a major impact in the areas of trade in agricultural products and textiles, which have hitherto been subject to various protection agreements. All these developments will have to be taken into account as Botswana considers how to promote diversification. Botswana is hopeful, however, that the stipulations of the WTO, coupled with the interest of some SACU members in seeing trade barriers reduced, should translate into a steady decline in tariff rates.

LOME CONVENTION

Botswana is an associate member of the Lome Convention under which many Africa, Carribbean and Pacific (ACP) states enjoy privileged access to the EU market. The duration of the Convention is coming to an end and is likely to be replaced by a new agreement under which access to the EU for ACP countries will be tied to reciprocal access to ACP markets for EU exporters.

SALES TAX

A 10% sales tax is imposed on items such as fuel, liquor, cigarettes, motor vehicles, computers, domestic electrical appliances and most consumer goods. Importers of such goods are responsible for the collection of the sales tax. Most items of food, construction materials, capital goods, medicines, books and stationery are exempted. Certain services such as hotels, dry-cleaning and hair dressing, also are subject to sales tax. In April 1997, sales tax coverage was extended to selected professional services.

In FY2004 the Government increased sales tax for alcoholic beverages, wines, spirits and mineral water. These rates, which were effectively ranging between 10-15% in 1995, were eroded by inflation down 5-6% in real terms. The government restored the effective rates to their 1995 levels.

VAT

In 1999, the government underscored its intention to replace the existing sales tax regime with a value-added tax (VAT) by April 2001. VAT is supposedly simpler to administer as it is to be imposed on all goods and services. VAT is also expected to broaden the tax base. While a few goods and services will be exempt from VAT, the onus will be on the supplier to establish that the supply falls within the exemption list. In addition, VAT was expected to eliminate the problem created by sales tax, in which taxes paid on inputs were included in the final cost of the product, and was literally a tax on tax.

Botswana's plans to implement its own VAT, originally targeted for FY2001, have however been put on hold due primarily to practical considerations and the system, which is under revision, is expected to be put in place in FY2003.

TRADE REGULATIONS: - IMPORT LICENSES, EXCHANGE CONTROLS, AND DOCUMENTATION

Import permits for goods entering Botswana directly from outside SACU are obtainable from the Department of Commerce and Consumer Affairs in the Ministry of Trade Industry Wildlife and Tourism. The import permits are not transferable. Permits are usually granted upon request, and Botswana's abolition of foreign exchange controls in February 1999 means there is little difficulty in obtaining sufficient foreign currency to cover transactions

Prohibited imports include habit-forming drugs and objectionable literature (pornographic magazines and videotapes) . Importation of certain agricultural products and plants requires approval with the Ministry of Agriculture prior to obtaining the import permit from the Department of Commerce and Consumer Affairs.

There is no tax on exports. Exports from Botswana generally do not require permits. Export controls are however assessed on the following restricted items, which require export permits: radioactive materials, unpolished diamonds, gold, wildlife and wildlife trophies, plants, hides and skins, and agricultural products. An Export Declaration Form (Form CD) must be filed for all goods exceeding approximately USD $370 in value.

Botswana has a "duty drawback" arrangement for the import of goods for processing or assembly followed by re-export.

Documentation required for external trade are: (a) Form CCA I for imports and exports within SACU; (b) Form CE 500 (Bill of Entry) for imports outside of SACU; (c) Form CE 24 (Bill of Entry) for exports of local products and (d) Form CE 23 (Bill of Entry) for exports of imported products.

Customs Officials may be reached at:

Department of Customs and Excise
Private Bag 0041
Gaborone
Tel: (267) 322-855
Fax: (267) 322-781
Contact: Mr. Ken Morris, Director

TRADE AND PROJECT FINANCING

Botswana's banking sector consists of a central bank (Bank of Botswana) , four commercial banks (Barclays Bank Botswana, Standard Chartered Bank Botswana, First National Bank Botswana, and Stanbic Bank Botswana) , an investment bank, Investec Group, and a credit institution, ULC Pty Ltd., operating as a financial lease company. All are geared to arrange finance for new businesses. Development financial institutions, six in number, offer specialized services to specific economic sectors. There are currently no U.S. financial lending institutions or Multilateral Development Banks in the country. Nonetheless, all four major commercial banks operating in Botswana have correspondent relationships with U.S. banks.

The central bank, Bank of Botswana, was established in 1975 and is responsible for monetary policies, central banking services, supervision of financial institutions, issuing of bank notes, implementing exchange rate policies, administering exchange controls and foreign exchange reserves management. The bank's financial statements are in compliance with international standards and Price Waterhouse Coopers and KPMG perform audits, both internationally recognized accounting firms.

Short-term finance, including pre-and-post-shipment credit, is readily available through the commercial banking system at market rates of interest. Export credit insurance is available through Botswana Export Credit Insurance (BECI) .

There are no exchange controls in Botswana. The complete elimination of controls on current and capital accounts allows the free flow of money and capital. The most common method of payment for imports from the U.S. is through Letters of Credit, LC's, bank drafts or bank transfers.

The provisions for U.S. and other foreign firms borrowing in Botswana are liberal while local banks remain highly liquid. The country's commercial banks, however, have difficulty making long-term credit available due to the short maturity nature of their deposits and small capital bases. At present, commercial banks finance only about one-third of the annual investment taking place in Botswana.

Botswana has kept its external borrowing to a minimum. Outstanding public debt is expected to reach approximately P2426.9 million ($485.38 million) by the end of 2004. The current debt service ratio is about 2.3%, while the debt to GDP ratio was about 10.42% in 1999 (down from

15.5% in 1989) . Moreover, the country's favorable balance of payments situation has meant that with one or two exceptions it has not been forced to borrow externally on commercial terms.

OPIC's finance and insurance programs are operable in Botswana, and it has provided finance for U.S. tourism companies' investments and expansions. Export Import Bank financing is available to exporters for exports to Botswana. The Export Import Bank has not, however, been active in Botswana in recent years.

COUNTRY COMMERCIAL AND INVESTMENT BANKS

Organization: Barclays Bank of Botswana Ltd.
Contact Name and Title: Duncan Mlazie, Managing Director
Address: P.O. Box 478, Gaborone, Botswana
Phone: (267) 352-041
Fax: (267) 353-699

Organization: First National Bank of Botswana Ltd.
Contact Name and Title: Mr. John Macaskill, Managing Director
Address: P.O. Box 1552, Gaborone, Botswana
Phone: (267) 311-669
Fax: (267) 302-853

Organization: Standard Chartered Bank Botswana Ltd.
Contact Name and Title: Mr. Andrew Prebble, Managing Director Address: P.O.496, Gaborone, Botswana
Phone: (267) 360-1500
Fax: (267) 351-545

Organization: Stanbic Bank Botswana Ltd.
Contact Name and Title: Mr. Walter Price, Managing Director
Address: Private Bag 00168, Gaborone, Botswana
Phone: (267) 301-600
Fax: (267) 300-171

Organization: Investec Bank Botswana Ltd.
Contact Name and Title: Mr. K.H. Munamati, Managing Director
Address: P.O. Box 49, Gaborone, Botswana
Phone: (267) 581-338
Fax: (267) 581-390

SELECTED LAWS AND REGULATIONS AFFECTING TAXATION[7]

BASIC LAWS

Botswana has a number of laws and regulations governing functioning of the taxation system and the related procedures. Among these laws and regulations are:

Chapter50-01 Customs and Excise Duty
Chapter50-03 Customs and Excise Duty Act
Chapter50-03 Customs and Excise Duty Act Subsidiary Legislation
Chapter50-03 Value Added Tax
Chapter50-03 Value Added Tax Act Subsidiary Legislation
Chapter52-01 Income Tax
Chapter52-01 Income Tax Act Subsidiary Legislation
Chapter52-02 Mineral Rights Tax
Chapter53-01 Capital Transfer Tax
Chapter53-02 Capital Transfer Tax
Chapter53-03 Botswana Unified Revenue Service Act
Income Tax (Ammendments) Act 1999
Income Tax (Ammendments) Act July 2006
Income Tax (Ammendments) Declaration
Value Added Tax Act Amendment Act 2002

CODE OF CONDUCT FOR FOREIGN INVESTORS

This Code of Conduct has been prepared by the Government of Botswana to publicise its attitude to foreign investors.

Botswana expects foreign investors to observe the following code of conduct.

- Foreign investors should regard themselves as full participants in Botswana's economic life and should take a long-term view of their contribution to Botswana. As a consequence of taking a long view, foreign investors should take steps to ensure that their operations in Botswana become as independent as feasible with respect to performing their own technical services, adaptive research, purchasing of inputs, etc. In return, foreign investors can expect to be teated fairly and equitably in regard to such policies as taxation and exchange control, since Government recognizes the requirement for investors to earn a reasonable return on well managed, economiclly viable investments.

- Foreign investors should recognize the need to actively train Batswana for positions at all levels of technical expertise, and should reduce the share of non-citizens in their work force over time. In this effort they must cooperative with the Commissioner of Labour in preparing an agreed training and localization programme. Government has various finacial incentives to assist companies with their training programmes, and Government welcomes suggestions and other contributions from foreign investors on how the public sector can best assist with training and the promotion of opportunities for citizens to

[7] Government of Botswana materials. Please contact ibpusa3@gmail.com for the text of the laws

advance. Foreign companies who are maintaining appropriate levels of training activities and who are moving expeditiously to promote citizens will receive cooperation from the Commissioner of Labour in meeting their remaining requirements for work permits for non-citizens.

- Foreign investors are expected not only to be law-abiding, but also to identify with the development aspirations of Botswana, and its national planning objectives, to assist in the implementation of national development plans, and actively to share Botswana's commitment, to maintenance of a democratic, open, non-racial society.

- Foreign investors are encouraged to offer shareholdings in their ventures to citizens. In some sectors, Government will expect to be a direct shareholder; in others the Botswana Development Corporation will take an equity interest. In most sectors, individual citizens should be sought as investment partners, even if on a modest scale. Government believes that the long-run stability of the economic system will be greater if citizens share ownership of economic ventures in all sectors of the economy. In addition, foreign investors should, if they wish to sell their enterprises, give citizens a fair opportunity to purchase.

EXCHANGE CONTROL

An Act to provide for the control of, dealings in, or possession of gold, currency and securities, to provide for the control of imports into and exports from Botswana and to provide for matters incidental thereto.

[Date of Commencement: 10th December, 1965]

Short title

1. This Act may be cited as the Exchange Control Act.

Interpretation

2. In this Act, unless the context otherwise requires--"currency" includes any notes of a class which are or have at any time been legal tender in any country and any document or instrument intended to enable the person to whom it is issued to obtain currency as defined herein and includes a right to currency in respect of any credit or balance at a bank or with any other person;

"gold" means gold in any form, whether manufactured or unmanufactured, whether in the form of coin, bullion or otherwise;

"securities" means shares, stock, bonds, notes (other than promissory notes) , debentures, debenture stock, units under a unit trust scheme, and shares in any royalty, and shall include--

(a) certificates of deposit;

(b) government bills and Treasury bills;

(c) any description of promissory notes which is for the time being prescribed by the Minister, any letter of allotment, whether renounceable or not, any letter of rights, any warrant conferring an option to acquire a security, any deposit certificate in respect of securities (but not including a receipt which may be required by any regulations made under this Act) , any renounceable certificate, any scrip certificate, any rights coupon, mandate, and such other documents conferring or containing evidence of rights as may be prescribed by the Minister.

power to make regulations

3. (1) The Minister may, by statutory instrument, make regulations prohibiting or restricting dealings in or possession of gold, currency or securities, the control of imports of goods into and exports of goods from Botswana, and for purposes incidental thereto or consequential thereon.

(2) Without prejudice to the generality of the powers conferred by subsection (1) the regulations may--

(a) require any person to make statements or produce documents for the purposes of the regulations;

(b) provide for the entry into any premises and the search of any premises or persons for the purpose of giving effect to any of the regulations;

(c) empower such authorities or persons as may be specified in the regulations to make orders, rules or directions for giving effect to any of the regulations.

(3) Different regulations, orders, rules or directions may be made under this section for, or in relation to, different classes of persons, gold, currency, securities, imports or exports, or different countries, or generally, in relation to anything in respect of which provision is made under this section.

(4) The regulations may provide that any person who contravenes or fails to comply with any provision thereof, or who contravenes or fails to comply with the terms of any order, rule or direction issued or any permission or exemption granted under the regulations, or who obstructs any person in the execution of any power or function assigned to him by or under the regulations, or who makes any incorrect statement in any declaration made or return rendered for the purposes of the regulations (unless he proves that he did not know, and could not by the exercise of a reasonable degree of care have ascertained, that the statement was incorrect) or who refuses or neglects to furnish any information or document which he is required to furnish under the regulations, shall be guilty of an offence and liable to a fine not exceeding P10 000 or the imprisonment for a term not exceeding five years, or to both:

Provided that, where such person is convicted of an offence against any of the regulations in relation to any gold, currency, security or goods--

(i) the fine which may be imposed on him shall be a fine not exceeding P10 000 or a sum equal to the value of the gold currency, security or goods, whichever is the greater, and

(ii) in addition to any other penalty imposed, the court may, if it thinks fit to do so, order that such gold, currency, security or goods shall be forfeited to the State.

Exchange Control (Authorization to Act as Authorized Dealer and Depositary) Order 55:69
Exchange Control (Bankruptcy Notices) Order 55:77
Exchange Control (Branches and Residence) Order 55:74
Exchange Control (Declaration and Evidence) Order 55:75
Exchange Control (Delegation of Powers) Order 55:67
Exchange Control (Import and Export) Order 55:72

Exchange Control (Payments) Order 55:70
Exchange Control (Purchase of Foreign Currency) Order 55:79
Exchange Control Regulations 55:37
Exchange Control (Specified Currency and Prescribed Securities) Order 55:80
Exemptions (From Certain Provisions of Exchange Control Regulations) Order 55:68

S.I. 110, 1976, S.I. 44, 1982.

PART I PRELIMINARY

Citation

1. These Regulations may be cited as the Exchange Control Regulations.

Interpretation

2. (1) In these Regulations, unless the context otherwise requires--

"authorized dealer" means, in relation to gold or any foreign currency, a person for the time being authorized by the Minister, by an order made under regulation 36, to act for the purposes of these Regulations as an authorized dealer in relation to gold, or, as the case may be, that foreign currency;

"authorized depositary" means a person for the time being authorized by the Minister, by an order made under regulation 36, to act as an authorized depositary;

"bearer certificate" means a certificate of title to securities by the delivery of which (with or without endorsement) the title to the securities is transferable;

"certificate of deposit" means a document relating to money, in any currency, which has been deposited with the issuer or some other person, being a document which recognizes an obligation to pay a stated amount to bearer or to order, with or without interest, and being a document by the delivery of which, with or without endorsement, the right to receive that stated amount, with or without interest, is transferable;

"certificate of title to securities" means any document of title whereby a person recognizes the title of another to securities issued or to be issued by such first-mentioned person, and in the case of any such document with coupons (whether attached or on separate coupon sheets) includes any coupons which have not been detached;

"coupon" means a coupon representing dividends or interest on a security;

"foreign currency" has the meaning ascribed to it by regulation 3;

"Government bill" means any bill, note or other obligation of a Government in any part of the world, being a document by the delivery of which, with or without endorsement, title is transferable, and not being an obligation which is or has been legal tender in any part of the world, and includes a Treasury bill;

"policy of assurance" means any policy securing the payment of a capital sum or annuity on the occurrence of a specified event which is certain to happen and includes--

(a) any policy by which the payment of money is assured on death (except death by accident only) or the happening of any contingency dependent on human life; and

(b) any policy securing the payment of an immediate annuity, and the reference in this definition to the occurrence of a specified event which is certain to happen includes the occurrence which is certain to happen, of one of specified events none of which by itself is certain to happen;

"specified currency" has the meaning ascribed to it by regulation 4 as extended by regulation 6;

"unit", in relation to a unit trust scheme, means a right or interest (whether described as a unit, as a sub-unit or otherwise) which may be acquired under the scheme;

"unit trust scheme" means any arrangements made for the purpose, or having the effect, or providing for persons having funds available for investments, facilities for the participation by them, as beneficiaries under a trust, in profits or income arising from the acquisition, holding, management or disposal of any property whatsoever.

(2) Any provision of these Regulations (however worded) the effect of which is to prohibit the doing of any act where a person to or by whom the act is to be done or who stands in a specified relation to any property possesses any specified attribute as to residence or otherwise shall, where the act is done to or by two or more persons or, as the case may be, where two or more persons stand jointly in that relation to the property, operate to prohibit the doing of that act if any of those persons possess that attribute; and any provision of these Regulations imposing an obligation on any person to do an act if he possesses any specified attribute as to residence or otherwise shall, in relation to any act which can only be done by done by two or more persons jointly--

(a) where all those persons possess that attribute, operate to impose a joint obligation on all of them to do the act; and

(b) where only some of them possess that attribute, operate to impose a separate obligation on each one of them who possesses that attribute to do all he can to secure the doing of the act.

(3) Any power conferred by these Regulations to prescribe the declarations which are to be furnished on any occasion shall include a power to require that the declarations shall be made by specified persons and shall be verified in a specified manner.

(4) Nothing in these Regulations shall be construed as requiring the Minister to pay any sum otherwise than in Botswana currency or otherwise than in Botswana, and any provision of these Regulations requiring the Minister to pay any sum to any person shall, where that sum is in a specified currency, be construed as a provision that the Minister shall pay to that person the amount in Botswana currency which he would have received for the specified currency if he had sold i to an authorized dealer in pursuance of an offer made under regulation 4 at the time when the said sum is paid.

(5) The obligations and prohibitions imposed by these Regulations shall, subject to the express limitations contained therein, apply to all persons, notwithstanding that they are not in Botswana and are not citizens of Botswana.

PART II GOLD AND FOREIGN CURRENCY

Dealings in gold and foreign currency

3. (1) Except with the permission of the Minister, no person, other than an authorized dealer, shall, in Botswana, and no person resident in Botswana, other than an authorized dealer, shall, outside Botswana, by or borrow any gold or foreign currency from, or sell or lend any gold or foreign currency to, any person other than an authorized dealer.

(2) Where a person buys or borrows any gold or foreign currency in Botswana or, being a person resident in Botswana, buys or borrows gold or foreign currency outside Botswana, he shall comply with such conditions as to the use to which it may be put or the period for which it may be retained as may from time to time be notified to him by the Minister.

(3) In these Regulations the expression ""foreign currency" includes any currency and any notes of a class which are or have at any time been legal tender in any country outside Botswana, and any reference to foreign currency, except so far as the context otherwise requires, includes a reference to any right to receive foreign currency in respect of any credit or balance at a bank, but does not include any currency or notes issued by the Bank of Botswana.

Surrender of gold and foreign currency

4. (1) Every person in or resident in Botswana who is entitled to sell, or to procure the sale of, any gold, or any foreign currency to which this regulation applies, and is not an authorized dealer, shall offer it, or cause it to be offered, for sale to an authorized dealer, unless the Minister consents to his retention and us thereof or he disposes thereof to any other person with the permission of the Minister.

(2) The foreign currency to which this regulation applies is such foreign currency (hereinafter referred to as "specified currency") as may from time to time be specified by the Minister by order published in the Gazette.

(3) If a person who has obtained the consent of the Minister to his retention and use of any gold or specified currency, and has stated in an application for the consent that he requires it for a particular purpose, no longer requires the gold or currency for that purpose, subregulation (1) shall thereupon apply to him in relation to that gold or currency as if the Minister had revoked his consent to his retention and use thereof.

(4) A person who acquires any gold or specified currency from an authorized dealer shall be treated for the purposes of this regulation as if the Minister had consented to the retention and use by him of that gold or currency (subject, however, to any conditions notified to him in accordance with regulation 3(2)) , and as if any statement made by him in an application for that gold or currency as to the purpose for which he requires it had been made by him in an application for the Minister's consent to his retention and use thereof.

(5) Where a person has become bound under this regulation to offer or cause to be offered any gold or specified currency for sale to an authorized dealer, he shall not be deemed to comply with that obligation by any offer made or caused to be made by him if the offer is an offer to sell at a price exceeding that authorized by the Minister or without payment of any usual and proper charges of the authorized dealer, or otherwise on any unusual terms.

(6) Where a person has become bound under this regulation to offer or cause to be offered any gold or specified currency for sale to an authorized dealer and has not complied with that

obligation, the Minister may direct that that gold or currency shall vest in the Minister and it shall vest in the Minister accordingly free from any mortgage, pledge or charge, and the Minister may deal with it as he thinks fit, but the Minister shall pay to the person who would, but for the direction, be entitled to the gold or currency such sum as he would have received therefor if he had sold it to an authorized dealer in pursuance of an offer made under this regulation at the time when the vesting occurred.

(7) In any proceedings in respect of a failure to comply with the provisions of this regulation, it shall be presumed, until the contrary is shown, that the gold or currency in question has not been offered for sale to an authorized dealer.

Bailees of gold and foreign currency

5. (1) Every person in Botswana by whom or to whose order (whether directly or indirectly) any gold or any specified currency in the form of notes is held in Botswana but who is not entitled to sell it or procure its sale shall notify the Bank of Botswana in writing that he so holds that gold or currency.

(2) The Minister may direct any person in Botswana by whom or to whose order (whether directly or indirectly) any gold or any specified currency in the form of notes is held in Botswana, whether or not he is entitled to sell it or procure its sale, to cause that gold or currency to be kept at all times in the custody of such banker as may be specified in the direction.

Travellers' cheques, etc.

6. (1) This regulation applies to any document of a kind intended to enable the person to whom the document is issued to obtain foreign currency from some other person on the credit of the person issuing it, and in particular to any traveller's cheque or other draft or letter of credit so intended.

(2) For the purposes of these Regulations, the person issuing a document to which this regulation applies, and the person to whom it is issued, shall be deemed respectively to sell and buy foreign currency and where foreign currency is obtained by means of the document to sell and buy that foreign currency.

(3) Any such document not expressed in terms of Botswana currency shall, if it is of a kind intended to enable the person to whom it is issued to obtain any specified currency, be treated also for the purposes of these Regulations as itself being specified currency.

(4) Every person in or resident in Botswana who holds or to whose order there is held any document to which this regulation applies, being a document expressed in terms of Botswana currency, shall encash it or cause it to be encashed in Botswana with the person issuing it or with a banker, unless the Minister consents to his retention and use thereof and, where in his application for that consent he has stated that he requires it for a particular purpose, unless also he still requires it for that purpose.

(5) A person who acquires any document to which subregulation (4) applies from an authorized dealer shall be treated for the purposes of that subregulation as if the Minister had consented to the retention and use by him of that document (subject, however, to any conditions notified to him in accordance with regulation 3(2)) , and as if any statement made by him in an application for that document as to the purpose for which he requires it had been made by him in an application for the Minister's consent to his retention and use thereof.

PART III PAYMENTS

Payments in Botswana

7. Except with the permission of the Minister, no person shall do in Botswana any of the following things--

(a) make any payment to or for the credit of a person resident outside Botswana;

(b) make any payment to or for the credit of a person resident in Botswana by order or on behalf of a person resident outside Botswana; or

(c) place any sum to the credit of any person resident outside Botswana:

Provided that where a person resident outside Botswana has paid a sum in or towards the satisfaction of a debt due from him, paragraph (c) shall not prohibit the acknowledgment or recording of the payment.

Payments outside Botswana

8. (1) Except with the permission of the Minister, no person resident in Botswana shall, subject to the provisions of this regulation, make any payment outside Botswana to or for the credit of a person resident outside Botswana.

(2) Nothing in this regulation shall prohibit the doing of anything otherwise lawful by any person with any foreign currency obtained by him in accordance with the provisions of Part II or retained by him in pursuance of the consent of the Minister.

Compensation deals

9. (1) Except with the permission of the Minister, no person shall in Botswana, and no person resident in Botswana shall outside Botswana, make any payment to or for the credit of a person resident in Botswana as consideration for or in association with--

(a) the receipt by any person of a payment made outside Botswana or the acquisition by any person of property which is outside Botswana; or

(b) the transfer to any person, or the creation in favour of any person, of a right (whether present or future, and whether vested or contingent) to receive a payment outside Botswana or to acquire property which is outside Botswana.

(2) Nothing in this regulation shall prohibit the making of any payment in accordance with the terms of any permission or consent granted under these Regulations.

PART IV SECURITIES

Interpretation of Part IV

10. (1) In this Part--

(a) the expression "registered" includes inscribed;

(b) the expressions "registered in Botswana" and "registered outside Botswana" mean, respectively, registered in a register in, and registered in a register outside, Botswana;

(c) The expression "security which is register" means a security which either--

- is registered in Botswana and is not, and cannot without the necessity for an entry in the register in Botswana become, registered outside, or
- is registered both in Botswana and outside but on a transfer cannot, without the necessity for an entry in the register in Botswana, become registered outside in the name of the transferee; and

(d) the expression "a register" includes any book, file or index in which securities are registered.

(2) For the purposes of any provision of this Part prohibiting the transfer of securities, a person shall be deemed to transfer a security if he executes any instrument of transfer thereof, whether effective or not, and shall be deemed to transfer it at the place where he executes the instrument.

(3) References in this Part to the person holding a certificate of title or coupon shall be construed as references to the person having physical custody of the certificate of title or coupon:

Provided that where the certificate of title or coupon is deposited with any person in a locked or sealed receptacle from which he is not entitled to remove it without the authority of some other person, that other person shall be deemed for the purposes of this provision to have the physical custody thereof.

(4) In this Part the expression "holder"--

(a) in relation to a security transferable by means of a bearer certificate or to a coupon, includes the person holding the certificate or coupon; and

(b) in relation to a security which is registered in the name of a deceased person, or of any person who, by reason of bankruptcy, unsoundness of mind or any other disability is incapable of transferring the security, means the personal representative, trustee in bankruptcy or other person entitled to transfer the security.

(5) The holder of a security or coupon shall be deemed for the purposes of this Part to be a nominee in respect thereof if, as regards the exercise of any rights in respect thereof, he is not entitled to exercise those rights except in accordance with instructions given by some other person, and references in this Part to the person for whom the holder of a security or coupon is a nominee shall be construed as references to the person who is entitled to give instructions, either directly or through the agency of one or more persons, as to the exercise of any rights in respect of the security or coupon and is not in so doing himself under a duty to comply with instructions given by some other person:

Provided that--

(i) a person shall not by reason only that he has a controlling interest in a body corporate by deemed for the purposes of this subregulation to be entitled to give instructions to that body corporate as to the exercise of rights in respect of any security or coupon of which it is the holder, and

(ii) a person shall not be deemed to hold a security or coupon as a nominee by reason only that he holds it as trustee if he is entitled to transfer the security or coupon without permission from any other person.

(6) A certificate of title shall not for the purposes of this Part be treated as in the custody of an authorized depository if either--

(a) the depository has no notice of the nature of the certificate; or

(b) the certificate is deposited with him in a locked or sealed receptacle from which he is not entitled to remove it without the authority of some other person.

(7) Where a certificate of title outside Botswana is by this Part required to be kept in the custody of an authorized depository, it shall be deemed to be in the custody of an authorized depository if--

(a) by his direction or with his assent it is in the custody of some other person who holds it on behalf of and to the order of the authorized depository; and

(b) the certificate is not deposited with that other person in a locked or sealed receptacle from which he is not entitled to remove it without the authority of a person other than himself, and where a certificate of title is by virtue of this subregulation deemed to be in the custody of an authorized depository, references in this Part to the depository parting with the certificate or a coupon belonging thereto shall be construed as references to his permitting the person having the actual custody thereof to part with it otherwise than to the depository, and references to his destroying the certificate or such a coupon shall be construed as references to his permitting it to be destroyed.

Issue of securities

11. (1) Except with the permission of the Minister, no person shall in Botswana issue any security or, whether in Botswana or elsewhere, issue any security which is registered or to be registered in Botswana, unless the following requirements are fulfilled--

(a) neither the person to whom the security is to be issued nor the person, if any, for whom he is to be a nominee is resident outside Botswana; and

(b) the prescribed evidence is produced to the person issuing the security as to the residence of the person to whom it is to be issued and that of the person, if any, for whom he is to be a nominee.

Cap. 42:01

(2) The subscription of the memorandum of association of a company to be formed under the Companies Act, by a person resident outside Botswana, or by a nominee for another person so resident, shall, unless he subscribes the memorandum with the permission of the Minister, be invalid insofar as it would no registration of the memorandum have the effect of making him a member of or shareholder in the company, so, however, that this provision shall not render invalid the incorporation of the company; and if, by virtue of this subregulation, the number of the subscribers of the memorandum, which subscribers on its registration become members of the company, is less than the minimum number required to subscribe the memorandum, the provisions of the Companies Art relating to the carrying on of business of a company, the

number of whose members is reduced below the legal minimum, shall apply to the company as if the number of its members had been so reduced.

Transfer of securities and coupons

12. (1) Except with the permission of the Minister, a security registered in Botswana shall not be transferred, and a security not so registered shall not be transferred in Botswana, unless, in either case, the following requirements are fulfilled--

(a) neither the transferor nor the person, if any, for whom he is a nominee is resident outside Botswana;

(b) the transferor delivers to the transferee at or before the time of the transfer the prescribed declarations as to his residence and that of the person, if any, for whom he is a nominee;

(c) neither the transferee nor the person, if any, for whom he is to be a nominee is resident outside Botswana; and

(d) except where the security is registered in Botswana otherwise than in a subsidiary register, the Minister is satisfied that the requirements of paragraph (c) are fulfilled:

Provided that--

(i) neither the transferee nor his agent shall be deemed to have committed an offence by reason only that the requirements of paragraph (a) were not fulfilled unless the transferee or, as the case may be, his agent, knew or had reason to believe that those requirements were not fulfilled, and

(ii) neither the transferor nor his agent shall be deemed to have committed an offence by reason only that any of the requirements of paragraphs (c) and (d) have not been fulfilled unless, in the case of a non-fulfilment of the requirements of the said paragraph (c) , the transferor or, as the case may be, his agent, knew or had reason to believe that those requirements were not fulfilled.

(2) Except with the permission of the Minister, a security not registered in Botswana shall not be transferred outside Botswana if either the transferor or the transferee, or the person, if any, for whom the transferor or transferee is or is to be a nominee, is resident in Botswana.

(3) Except with the permission of the Minister, no coupon shall be transferred--

(a) in Botswana, if either the transferee or the person, if any, for whom he is to be a nominee is resident outside Botswana;

(b) outside Botswana, if either the transferor or the transferee, or the person, if any, for whom the transferor or transferee is or is to be a nominee, is resident in Botswana.

Issue of bearer certificates and coupons

13. Except with the permission of the Minister, no person shall, in Botswana, and no person resident in Botswana shall, outside Botswana, issue any bearer certificate or coupon or so alter any document that it becomes a bearer certificate or coupon.

Substitution of securities and certificates outside Botswana

14. Except with the permission of the Minister, no person in or resident in Botswana shall do any act with intent to secure--

(a) that a security which is--

(i) registered in Botswana, or

(ii) transferable by means of a bearer certificate in Botswana, becomes, or is replaced by, a security registered outside Botswana or a security transferable by means of a bearer certificate outside Botswana; or

(b) that a certificate of title to any other security is issued outside Botswana in substitution for or in addition to a certificate of title thereto which is in, or is or has been lost or destroyed in, Botswana.

Payment of capital moneys outside Botswana

15. Except with the permission of the Minister, no person resident in Botswana shall do any act with intent to secure that capital moneys payable on a security registered in Botswana are paid outside Botswana, or that where the certificate of title to a security is in Botswana, capital moneys payable on the security are paid outside Botswana without production of the certificate to the person making the payment.

Duties of persons keeping registers

16. Except with the permission of the Minister, no person concerned with the keeping of any register in Botswana shall--

(a) enter in the register the name of any person in relation to any security unless there has been produced to him the prescribed evidence that the entry does not form part of a transaction which involves the doing of anything prohibited by these Regulations;

(b) enter in the register, in respect of any security, an address outside Botswana, except for the purpose of any transaction for which the permission of the Minister has been granted with the knowledge that it involved the entry of that address; or

(c) do any act in relation to the register which recognizes or gives effect to any act appearing to him to have been done with such intent as is mentioned in paragraphs (a) and (b) , whether done by a person in or resident in Botswana or not.

Additional provisions as to nominee holdings

17. (1) Where--

(a) the holder of a security is a nominee and the person for whom he is a nominee is resident outside Botswana; or

(b) the holder fo a security is not a nominee and is resident outside Botswana, then, except with the permission of the Minister, no person resident in Botswana shall do any act whereby the holder becomes his nominee in respect of the security.

(2) Except with the permission of the minister, a person resident in Botswana for whom the holder of a security is a nominee shall not do any act whereby--

(a) the holder, being a person resident outside Botswana, holds the security otherwise than as his nominee; or

(b) the holder, not being a person resident outside Botswana, holds the security as nominee for a person resident outside Botswana.

(3) Where the holder of a security is a nominee, then, except with the permission of the Minister, neither he, if he is resident in Botswana, nor any person resident in Botswana through whose agency the exercise of all or any of the holder's rights in respect of the security are controlled, shall--

(a) do any act whereby he recognizes or gives effect to the substitution of another person as the person from whom he directly receives his instructions unless both the person previously instructing him and the person substituted for that person were, immediately before the substitution, resident in Botswana and not elsewhere; or

(b) do any act whereby he ceases to be a person bound to give effect to the instructions of another person in relation to the security, unless the person who theretofore instructed him is resident in Botswana and not elsewhere.

(4) Where the holder of a security is not a nominee and is resident in Botswana, then, except with the permission of the Minister, he shall not do any act whereby he becomes the nominee fo another person in respect of the security, unless that other person is resident in Botswana and not elsewhere.

Deposit of certificates of title

18. (1) This regulation and regulation 19 shall apply to any security except--

(a) a security which is registered in Botswana otherwise than in a subsidiary register, and on which none of the dividends or interest is payable on presentment of a coupon; and

(b) any such other securities as may be prescribed, and in the following provisions of this regulation and regulation 19 the expression "security", "certificate of title" and "coupon" mean respectively a security to which the said regulations apply, a certificate of title to such a security, and a coupon representing dividends or interest on such a security.

(2) it shall be the duty of very person by whom or to whose order (whether directly or indirectly) a certificate of title is held in Botswana, and of every person resident in Botswana by whom or to whose order (whether directly or indirectly) a certificate of title is held outside Botswana, to cause the certificate of title to be kept at all times, except with the permission of the Minister, in the custody of an authorized depository, and nothing in this Part shall prohibit the doing of anything for the purpose of complying with the requirements of this subregulation.

(3) Except with the permission of the Minister, an authorized depository shall not part with any certificate of title or coupon required under this regulation to be in the custody of an authorized depository:

Provided that this subregulation shall not prohibit an authorized depository from parting with--

(i) a certificate of title or coupon to or to the order of another authorized depository, where the person from whom the other authorized depository is to receive instructions in relation thereto is to be the same as the person from whom he receives instructions,

(ii) a certificate of title, for the purpose fo obtaining payment of capital moneys payable on the security, to the person entrusted with payment thereof,

(iii) a coupon in the ordinary course for collection.

(4) Except with the permission of the Minister, no capital moneys, interest or dividends shall be paid in Botswana on any security except to or to the order of an authorized depository having the custody of the certificate of title to that security, so, however, that this subregulation shall not be taken as restricting the manner in which any sums lawfully paid on account of the capital moneys, interest or dividends may be dealt with by the person receiving them.

(5) Except with the permission of the Minister, an authorized depository shall not do any act whereby he recognizes or gives effect to the substitution of one person for another as the person from whom he receives instructions in relation to a certificate of title or coupon, unless there is produced to him the prescribed evidence that he is not by so doing giving effect to any transaction which is prohibited by these Regulations.

(6) Where a certificate of title which under this regulation should for the time being be in the custody of an authorized depository is not in the custody of an authorized depository, then, except with the permission of the Minister, no person shall in Botswana, and no person resident in Botswana shall outside Botswana, buy, sell, transfer, or do anything which affects his rights or powers in relation to, the security.

(7) Except with the permission of the Minister, no person in or resident in Botswana shall, in the case of a certificate of title with coupons (whether attached or on separate coupon sheets) , detach any of the coupons otherwise than in the ordinary course for collection.

Additional provisions as to deposited certificates

19. (1) Where a certificate of title to a security is by regulation 18 required to be and is in the custody of an authorized depository, the provisions of this regulation shall, except so far as the Minister otherwise directs, have effect in relation thereto until--

(a) there are delivered to him the prescribed declarations as to the ownership of the security and the residence of the owners thereof; and

(b) in the case of a certificate of title which--

(i) would ordinarily be accompanied by coupons (whither attached or on separate coupon sheets) , but

(ii) when it comes into the custody of the authorized depository wants, in order to render it complete, any coupons which would not in the ordinary course have been detached for collection, there have also been deposited with him the coupons so wanting at the time when the certificate of title comes into his custody:

Provided that where the said declarations have been delivered to an authorized depositary and he has parted with the certificate of title, paragraph (a) shall not again apply on the certificate coming into the custody of another authorized depositary or again coming into his own custody.

(2) Except with the permission of the Minister, the authorized depository shall not part with or destroy the certificate of title or any coupons belonging thereto, otherwise than as mentioned in paragraphs (ii) and (iii) of the proviso to regulation 18(3) , or do any act whereby he recognizes

or gives effect to the substitution of one person for another as the person from whom he receives instructions in relation thereto:

Provided that, where the person from whom an authorized depository receives instructions in relation to any certificate fo title becomes bankrupt in Botswana or dies, this subregulation shall not prohibit the authorized depositary from recognizing the person entitled to give instructions in relation to the certificate of title.

(3) The authorized depositary shall place any capital moneys, dividends or interest on the security received by him to the credit of the person by virtue of whose authority he received them, but shall not permit any part of the sums received to be dealt with except with the permission of the Minister.

Special provisions as to dealings in certain securities

20. (1) The Minister may, if in his opinion there are circumstances rendering it necessary or expedient to do so, by order direct that this regulation shall apply to such securities as may be prescribed, being securities on which capital moneys, dividends or interest are payable in a specified currency or as regards which the holder has an option to require payment of any capital moneys, dividends or interest thereon in a specified currency.

(2) Except with the permission of the Minister, no person shall, in Botswana, and no person resident in Botswana shall, outside Botswana, transfer, or do anything which affects his rights or powers in relation to, any security to which this regulation applies.

Validation of certain transfers

21. (1) The title of any person to a security for which he has given value on a transfer thereof, and the title of all persons claiming though or under him, shall, notwithstanding that the transfer, or any previous transfer, or the issue of the security, was by reason of the residence of any person concerned other than the first-mentioned person prohibited by the provisions of these Regulations relating to the transfer or issue of securities, be valid unless the first-mentioned person had notice of the facts by reason of which it was prohibited.

(2) Without prejudice to the provisions of subregulation (1) , the Minister may issue a certificate declaring, in relation to a security, that any acts done before the issue of the certificate purporting to effect the issue or transfer of the security, being acts which were prohibited by theses Regulations, are to be, and are always to have been, as valid as if they had been done with the permission of the Minister, and the said acts shall have effect accordingly.

(3) Nothing in this regulation shall affect the liability of any person to prosecution for any offence against these Regulations.

PART V IMPORT AND EXPORT

Restrictions on import

22. (1) Except with the permission of the Minister, the import of--

(a) any notes of a class which are or have at any time been legal tender in Botswana;

(b) any such other notes as may be specified by the Minister, by order published in the Gazette, being notes issued by a bank or notes of a class which are or have at any time been legal tender in any country; and

(c) any certificate of title to any security, including any such certificate which has been cancelled, and any document certifying the destruction, loss or cancellation of any certificate of title to a security, is prohibited.

(2) In this regulation the expression "note" includes part of a note.

General restrictions on export

23. (1) Except with the permission of the Minister, the export of--

(a) any notes of a class which are or have at any time been legal tender in Botswana or in any other country;

(b) any postal orders;

(c) any gold;

(d) any of the following documents (including any such document which has been cancelled) --

(i) any certificate of title to a security and any coupon,

(ii) any policy of assurance,

(iii) any bill of exchange or promissory note expressed in terms of a currency other than Botswana currency,

(iv) any document to which regulation 6 applies not issued by an authorized dealer or in pursuance of a permission granted by the Minister; and any document certifying the destruction, loss or cancellation of any of the documents aforesaid; and

(e) any such articles exported on the person of a traveller or in a traveller's baggage as may be prescribed, is prohibited.

(2) In this regulation the expression "note" includes part of a note, and the expression "coupon" shall be construed in accordance with the meaning of "security".

Payment for exports

24. (1) The export of goods of any class or description to a destination in any such country as may be prescribed is prohibited except with the permission of the Minister unless the Director of Customs and Excise is satisfied--

(a) that payment for the goods has been made to a person resident in Botswana in such a manner as may be prescribed in relation to goods of that class or description exported to a destination in that country, or is to be so made not later than six months after the date fo export; and

(b) that the amount of the payment which has been made or is to be made is such as to represent a return for the goods which is in all the circumstances satisfactory in the national interest:

Provided that the Minister may direct that, in cases to which the direction applies, paragraph (a) shall have effect as if for the reference to six months there were substituted a reference to such longer or shorter period as may be specified in the direction, or as if the words "or is to be so made not later than six months after the date of export" were omitted.

(2) For the purpose of satisfying himself in the case of any goods as to the matters specified in subregulation 91) , the Director of Customs and Excise may require the person making entry of the goods for export to deliver to the collector or other proper officer together with the entry such declarations signed by such person as the Director may require, and where any such declaration has been so required the goods shall not be exported until it has been delivered as aforesaid.

(3) Where the Director of Customs and Excise is not satisfied in the case of any goods as to the matters specified in subregulation (1) (b) , he shall give his reasons to the person making entry of the goods for export and shall take into consideration any representations made by him.

(4) Any reference in this regulation to the destination of any goods includes a reference to the ultimate destination thereof.

PART VI MISCELLANEOUS

Duty to collect certain debts

25. (1) Except with the permission of the Minister, no person resident in Botswana who has a right (whether present or future and whether vested or contingent) to receive any specified currency, or to receive from a person resident outside Botswana a payment in Botswana currency, shall do, or refrain from doing, any act with intent to secure--

(a) that the receipt by him of the whole or part of that currency or, as the case may be, of that payment in Botswana currency, is delayed; or

(b) that the currency or payment cease, in whole or in part, to be receivable by him:

Provided that nothing in this subregulation shall, unless the Minister otherwise directs--

(i) impose on any person any obligation, in relation to any debt arising in the carrying on of any trade or business, to procure the payment thereof at an earlier time than is customary in the course of that trade or business, or

(ii) prohibit any transfer to a person resident in Botswana and not elsewhere of any right to receive any specified currency or payment in Botswana currency.

(2) Where a person has contravened the provisions of subregulation (1) in relation to any specified currency or payment in Botswana currency, the Minister may give to him or to any other person who appears to the Minister to be in a position to give effect thereto (being a person in or resident in Botswana) such directions as appear to the Minister to be expedient for the purpose of obtaining or expediting the receipt of the currency or payment in question, and, without prejudice to the generality of the foregoing, may direct that there shall be assigned to the Minister, or to such person as may be specified in the directions, the right to receive the currency or payment or enforce any security for the receipt thereof.

Duty not to delay sale or importation of goods

26. (1) Where--

(a) any permission or consent has been granted under these Regulations, subject to a condition providing that, or on the faith of an application stating an intention that, any goods should be sold outside Botswana;

(b) any statement or declaration has been made under any provision of these Regulations that any goods are to be sold outside Botswana; or

(c) any currency has been obtained in, or by any person resident in Botswana on the faith of an application stating an intention that any goods should be sold outside Botswana, then, except with the permission of the Minister, no person resident in Botswana who is entitled to sell or procure the sale of the said goods shall do, or refrain from doing, any act with intent to secure--

- that the said sale is delayed to an extent which is unreasonable having regard to the ordinary course of trade, or
- that, on the said sale, any payment made for the goods is not made in the manner indicated by the condition, statement, or declaration, as the case may be.

(2) Where--

(a) any permission or consent has been granted under these regulations, subject to a condition providing that, or on the faith of an application stating an intention that, any goods should be imported; or

(b) any currency has been obtained in, or by any person resident in Botswana on the faith of an application stating an intention that any goods should be so imported,

(c) then, except with the permission fo the Minister, no person resident in Botswana who is entitled to procure the import of the said goods shall do, or refrain from doing, any act with intent to secure that the import thereof is delayed to an extent which is unreasonable having regard to the ordinary course of trade.

(3) Where in any such case as is specified in subregulation (1) (a) , (b) or (c) or subregulation (2) (a) or (b) --

(a) the goods have not been sold or imported as indicated by the condition, statement or declaration within the time thereby indicated or, if no time is thereby indicated, a reasonable time, or, in either case, within such further time as may be allowed by the Minister; or

(b) it appears to the Minister that the goods cannot be sold or imported as indicated by the condition, statement or declaration, the Minister may give to any person resident in Botswana who appears to the Minister to be in a position to give effect thereto such directions as appear to him to be expedient as to the manner in which the goods are to be dealt with.

(4) Without prejudice to the generality of the provisions of subregulation (3) , the power conferred thereby on the Minister to give directions shall extend to the giving of directions that the goods shall be assigned to the Minister or to a person specified in the directions.

(5) The powers coffered by subregulations (3) and (4) in relation to any goods shall extend to the giving of directions with respect to any goods produced or manufactured therefrom, and, where goods to be sold outside Botswana or to be imported were to be produced or

manufactured from other goods, to the giving of directions with regard to those other goods and any goods produced or manufactured from those other goods.

Property obtained by infringement of these Regulations

27. (1) Where a person--

(a) has made any payment which is prohibited by these Regulations; or

(b) being bound under these Regulations to offer or cause to be offered any specified currency to an authorized dealer, has otherwise disposed of that currency,

the Minister may direct him to sell or procure the sale of any property which he is entitled to sell or of which he is entitled to procure the sale, being property which represents, whether directly or indirectly, that payment or that specified currency, as the case may be, and may be the same or a subsequent direction specify the manner in which, the persons to whom and the terms on which the property is to be sold.

(2) Without prejudice to the generality of the provisions of subregulation (1) , the power conferred thereby on the Minister to give directions shall extend to the giving of directions that the property shall be assigned to the Minister or to a person specified in the directions.

Provisions supplemental to preceding provisions of Part V

28. (1) Where, under this part, the Minister has power to give directions that any right to receive any currency or payment in Botswana currency or to enforce any security for the receipt thereof, any goods or any other property shall be assigned to the Minister; the Minister shall also have power to direct that the right, goods or property shall vest in the Minister, and it or they shall vet in the Minister accordingly free from any mortgage, pledge or charge, and the Minister may deal with it or them as he thinks fit.

(2) Where, in pursuance of directions under the said provisions, any right, goods or property is or are assigned to the Minister or to a person specified in the directions, or, any right, goods or property vests or vest in the Minister in pursuance of directions given under subregulation (1) , the Minister shall pay the net sum recovered by him in respect of the right, goods or property to the person making the assignment or, in the case of any right, goods or property vested in the Minister under subregulation (1) , to the person who, but for the directions, would be entitled to the right, goods or property.

Transfer of annuities, policies, etc.

29. (1) Except with the permission of the Minister, no person resident in Botswana shall transfer to a person resident outside Botswana, or who is to be a nominee for a person resident outside Botswana, any right to the sums assumed by any policy of assurance, so, however, that where the person liable for the sums so assured makes any payment thereof to a person resident in Botswana and not elsewhere, or makes, with the permission of the Minister, any payment thereof to any other person--

(a) he shall not be bound to enquire as to the residence of any person other than the person to whom, and (if it is not the same person) the person to whose order, the payment is made; and

(b) the payment shall, to the extent of the sums paid, discharge him from his liability under the policy, notwithstanding that the payment is made to or to the order of a person who was not entitled thereto otherwise than by virtue of a transfer prohibited by this subregulation.

(2) Regulation 21(2) and (3) shall apply in relation to any transfer prohibited by this regulation as they apply in relation to a transfer of a security prohibited by these Regulations.

(3) In this regulation the expression "nominee" has, in relation to any policy, annuity or insurance, the same meaning as the said expression has in Part III in relation to a security.

Settlements

30. (1) Except with the permission of the Minister, no person resident in Botswana shall settle any property, otherwise than by will, so as to confer an interest in the property on a person who, at the time of the settlement, is resident outside Botswana, or shall exercise, otherwise than by will, any power of appointment, whether created by will or otherwise, in favour of a person who, at the time of the exercise of the power, is resident outside Botswana.

(2) A settlement or exercise of a power of appointment shall not be invalid by reason that it is prohibited by this regulation, except so far as it purports to confer any interest on any person who, at the time of the settlement or the exercise of the power, is resident outside Botswana.

(3) Regulation 21(2) and (3) shall apply in relation to a settlement or the exercise of a power of appointment prohibited by this regulation as they apply in relation to a transfer of a security prohibited by these Regulations.

(4) For the purposes of this regulation--

(a) any reference to settling property includes a reference to the making of any disposition, covenant, agreement or arrangement whereby the property becomes subject to a trust or, in the case of a resettlement, to a different trust;

(b) a person shall be deemed to have an interest in property if he has any beneficial interest therein, whether present or future, and whether vested or contingent, or falls within a limited class of persons in whose favour a discretion or power in respect of the property is exercisable; and

(c) the expression "will" includes any testamentary disposition.

Companies

31. (1) Where there is served on any person resident in Botswana a notice in writing that the Minister wishes any such requirements as are hereinafter mentioned to be complied with by any such body corporate as is specified in the First Schedule (hereinafter in this subregulation referred to as a "foreign company") , and that person can, by doing or refraining from doing any act--

(a) cause the foreign company to comply with any of the requirements;

(b) remove any obstacle to the foreign company complying with any of the requirements; or

(c) render it in any respect more probable that the foreign company will comply with any of the requirements, then, except so far as permission to the contrary may be given by the Minister, that person shall do, or, as the case may be, refrain from doing, that act.

(2) The requirements with respect to which such a notice may be given are as follows, that is to say, that the foreign company shall--

(a) furnish to the Minister such particulars as to its assets and business as may be mentioned in the notice;

(b) sell or procure the sale to an authorized dealer of any gold or specified currency mentioned in the notice, being gold or specified currency which it is entitled to sell or of which it is entitled to procure the sale;

(c) declare and pay such dividend as may be mentioned in the notice;

(d) realize any of its assets mentioned in the notice in such manner as may be so mentioned;

(e) refrain from selling, transferring, or doing anything which affects its rights or powers in relation to, any such securities as may be mentioned in the notice.

(3) Except with the permission of the Minister, no person resident in Botswana shall do any act whereby a body corporate which is by any means controlled, whether directly or indirectly, by persons resident in Botswana ceases to be controlled by persons resident in Botswana:

Provided that this subregulation shall not prohibit any person from selling any securities authorized to be dealt in on any recognized stock exchange in Botswana if the sale takes place in pursuance of an agreement entered into in the ordinary course of business on that exchange.

(4) Except with the permission of the Minister, no person resident in Botswana shall lend any moneys or securities or provide any other form of financial assistance to any body corporate resident in Botswana which is by any means controlled, whether directly or indirectly, by persons resident outside Botswana:

Provided that this subregulation shall not apply where the lender or the person providing some other form of financial assistance, as the case may be, after making such enquiries as are reasonable in the circumstances of the case, does not know and has no reason to suspect that the body corporate is controlled as aforesaid.

(5) In subregulation (4) , "any other form of financial assistance" includes any manner of financial assistance, other than the loan of moneys or securities, and in particular, but without prejudice to the generality of the foregoing, the discounting of any bill of exchange, promissory note, certificate of deposit or similar instrument and any form of leasing, floor plan finance, hire-purchase, letter of credit, acceptance credit guarantee or trade credit.

(6) For the purposes of this regulation and of the First Schedule, persons resident in Botswana or outside Botswana shall be deemed to control a body corporate notwithstanding that other persons are associated with them in the control thereof if they can together override those other persons.

PART VII SUPPLEMENTAL

Exemptions

32. Any provision of these Regulations imposing any obligation or prohibition shall have effect subject to such exemptions as may be granted by order of the Minister, and any such exemptions may be either absolute or conditional.

Blocked accounts

33. Where--

(a) under any provision contained in Part III the permission of the Minister is required for the making of a payment or the placing of any sum to the credit of any person resident outside Botswana; or

(b) any payment falls to be made by an authorized dealer on the sale of any gold or specified currency by any foreign company within the meaning of regulation 31(1) and (2) , being a sale made to comply with any requirement notified under those subregulations,

the Minister may direct that the sum payable or to be credited shall be paid or credited to a blocked account only, and, where such a direction is given, the provisions of the Second Schedule shall have effect in relation to the payment or crediting if the sum.

Contracts, legal proceedings, etc.

34. (1) It shall be an implied condition in any contract that, where, by virtue of these Regulations, the permission or consent of the Minister is at the time of the contract required for the performance of any term thereof, that term shall not be performed except insofar as the permission or consent is given or is not required:

Provided that this subregulation shall not apply insofar as it is shown to be inconsistent with the intention of the parties that it should apply, whether by reason of their having contemplated the performance of that term despite the provisions of these Regulations or for any other reason.

Cap. 46:02

(2) Notwithstanding anything contained in the Bills of Exchange Act, neither the provisions of these Regulations, nor any condition, whether expressed or implied having regard to those provisions, that any payment shall not be made without the permission of the Minister under these Regulations, shall be deemed to prevent any instrument being a bill of exchange or promissory note.

(3) The provisions of the Third Schedule shall have effect with regard to legal proceedings, arbitrations, bankruptcy proceedings, the administration of the estates of deceased persons, the winding-up of companies, and proceedings under deeds of arrangement or trust deeds for the benefit of creditors.

Enforcement and administration

35. (1) The provisions of the Fourth Schedule shall have effect for the purpose of the enforcement of these Regulations.

(2) Persons belonging to the following classes--

(a) bankers, authorized dealers, authorized depositories;

(b) persons to whom any powers of the Minister under these Regulations are delegated;

(c) persons who with the permission of the Minister are in possession of documents which would, but for the permission, have to be in the custody of an authorized depository;

(d) persons concerned with the keeping of any register in Botswana; and

(e) persons entrusted with the payment of capital moneys, dividends or interest in Botswana, shall comply with such directions as may be given to them respectively by the Minister, being--

. in the case of any such persons, directions as regards the exercise of any functions exercisable by them by virtue of, or by virtue of anything done under, any provision of these Regulations, or

. in the case of authorized dealers, such directions as aforesaid or directions as to the terms on which they are to accept gold or foreign currency or directions requiring them to offer their gold or specified currency for sale to the Bank of Botswana on such terms as may be specified in any such directions.

Powers of Minister

36. (1) Any permission, consent or authority granted by the Minister under these Regulations--

(a) may be either general or special;

(b) may be absolute or conditional;

(c) may be limited so as to expire on a specified date, unless renewed; and

(d) shall be published in such a way as, in the opinion of the Minister, to give any person entitled to the benefit of it an adequate opportunity of getting to know of it, unless in this opinion publication is not necessary for the purpose.

(2) Any directions given by the Minister under any provision of these Regulations--

(a) may be either general or special; and

(b) shall be given to such persons and in such manner as the Minister deems appropriate, and if so given shall be valid for all purposes.

(3) Notwithstanding subregulation (2) (b) , a person shall not by virtue of any direction given by the Minister under these Regulations be convicted of an offence, unless the direction was served on him or he knew, or avoided getting to know, of the giving thereof:

Provided that where reasonable steps were taken for the purpose of bringing the purport of the direction to his notice, it shall be for him to show that he neither knew nor avoided getting to know of the giving thereof.

(4) The Minister may, to such extent and subject to such restrictions and conditions as he may deem proper, delegate or authorize the delegation of any of his powers (other than any power to make orders or to give authority to apply for a search warrant) to any person, or class or

description of persons, approved by him, and a reference in these Regulations to the Minister shall be construed accordingly.

(5) Any document stating that any permission, consent, authority or direction is given under any of the provisions of these Regulations by the Minister, and purporting to be signed on his behalf, shall be evidence of the facts stated in the document.

(6) The Minister may be statutory instrument make an order authorizing any person to act for the purposes of these Regulations as--

(a) an authorized dealer;

(b) an authorized depository.

Branches

37. (1) The Minister may be order or direction provide that, for such of the purposes of these Regulations as may be specified in the order or direction--

(a) any transaction with or by a branch of any business, whether carried on by a body corporate or otherwise, shall be treated in all respects as if the branch were a body corporate resident where the branch is situated;

(b) the making of any book entry or other statement recording a debit against a branch of any business in favour of any other branch of that business, shall be treated as a payment to that other branch; and

(c) any property held by or on behalf of the person carrying on the business shall be deemed to be held by such of the branches of the business as may be determined in accordance with the order or direction, and any such order or direction which makes, for any of the purposes of Part IV, such provision as is mentioned in paragraph (c) may contain provisions declaring the circumstances in which a branch is to be treated as nominee for any other branch.

(2) Any reference in subregulation (1) to a branch of a business shall be deemed to include a reference to the head office of that business.

(3) Subregulations (1) and (2) shall apply in relation to any body of persons (whether corporate or unincorporate) carrying on any activity, whether for the purpose of profit or not, as they apply in relation to a business.

Persons leaving Botswana

38. Where a person resident in Botswana leaves Botswana, the Minister may, before, at or after the time he leaves Botswana, direct that, for such period as may be specified in the direction, payments by him or on his behalf and to him or to his credit and transactions in or in relation to securities or secondary securities in which he is in any way concerned shall, whether or not he continues to be resident in Botswana, be subject to such restrictions as may be specified in the direction.

Determination of residence

39. (1) For the purposes of these Regulations, a personal representative of a deceased person shall, unless the Minister otherwise directs, be treated as resident in the country where the

deceased person was resident for the purposes in question at the time of his death and is not resident elsewhere, so far as relates to any matters in which the personal representative is concerned solely in his capacity as such.

(2) The Minister may give directions declaring that for all or any of the purposes of these Regulations a person is to be treated as resident or not resident in such countries as may be specified in the directions.

Prohibitory directions by Minister

40. (1) Where the Minister is satisfied that action is being, or is likely to be, taken to the detriment of Botswana by the government of, or persons resident in, any country outside Botswana, the Minister may give general or special directions prohibiting, either absolutely or to such extent as may be specified in the directions, the carrying out, except with permission granted by or on behalf of the Minister, of any order given by or on behalf of the government of that country or any person resident therein at the time when the directions were given or at any later time while the directions are in force insofar as the order--

(a) requires the person to whom the order is given to make any payment or to part with any gold or securities; or

(b) requires any change to be made in the persons to whose order any gold or securities are to be held.

(2) Where any directions are given under this regulation with regard to any country, a branch in that country of any business, whether carried on by a body corporate or otherwise, shall, for the purposes of this regulation, be treated in all respects as if the branch where a body corporate resident in that country.

FIRST SCHEDULE: FOREIGN COMPANIES

1. The bodies corporate in question are bodies corporate not incorporated under the laws of Botswana in the case of which any of the following conditions in fulfilled--

(a) that the body corporate is by any means controlled, whether directly or indirectly, by persons resident in Botswana;

(b) that more than one-half of the sums which, on a liquidation thereof, would be receivable by holders of share or loan capital would be receivable, directly or indirectly, by or for the benefit of persons resident in Botswana;

(c) that more than one-half of the assets which, on a liquidation thereof, would be available for distribution after the payment of creditors would be receivable, directly or indirectly, by or for the benefit of persons resident in Botswana; or

(d) that more than one-half--

- of the interest payable on its loans and loan capital, if any,
- of the dividends payable on its preference share capital, if any, or

- share capital, is receivable, directly or indirectly, by or for the benefit of persons resident in Botswana.

2. Where the identity of the persons by whom or for whose benefit any sum, assets, interest or dividends are, directly or indirectly, receivable depends on the exercise by a person resident in Botswana of a power of appointment or similar power, the sum, assets, interest or dividends shall, for the purposes of this Schedule, be deemed to be receivable, directly or indirectly, by or for the benefit of person resident in Botswana.

SECOND SCHEDULE: BLOCKED ACCOUNTS

1. In this Schedule the expression "a blocked account" means an account opened as a blocked account at an office or branch in Botswana in favour of any person by a banker authorized by the Minister to open blocked accounts, and the expression "the banker" means, in relation to any person, a banker who opens a blocked account in favour of that person.

2. Where a direction is given that a payment is to be made to a blocked account only, then, subject to the next paragraph following--

(a) the manner in which the payment may be made shall be either--

(i) to the banker, with a direction that it is to be credited to a blocked account of that person (which direction may, in the case of a payment by means of a cheque or warrant, be made by marking the cheque or warrant with the words "blocked account of" (naming the person in question) or words to the same effect) , or

(ii) by a crossed cheque or warrant drawn in favour of that person, marked with the words "payable only to blocked account of payee" or words to the same effect; and

(b) the sum collected shall be credited by the banker to a blocked account of that person.

3. Where a direction is given that a sum is to be paid or credited to a blocked account only, then, notwithstanding the direction, the sum may, with the consent of the person to whom it is to be paid or credited, and subject to the requirements of Part IV of these Regulations, be invested instead in the purchase for that person of any such investments as may be prescribed for the purposes of subparagraph (i) of the proviso to paragraph 4.

4. Any sum standing to the credit of a blocked account shall not be dealt with except with the permission of the Minister:

Provided that, subject to compliance with the requirements of Part III--

(i) the whole or any part of any such sum may, at the request of the person in whose name the account stands, be invested through the banker in such investments as may be prescribed, and

(ii) nothing in this Schedule shall be construed as restricting the manner in which the investments acquired may be dealt with.

5. Where a person in whose name a blocked account is standing becomes bankrupt in Botswana or dies, the baker may, notwithstanding anything in paragraph 4, transfer the account to the name of the trustee in bankruptcy or personal representative, but, except as aforesaid, no change shall, except with the permission of the Minister, be made in the name in which the account stands; and where any such change is made (whether or not the permission of the

Minister is necessary therefor) the account shall remain a blocked account notwithstanding the change, and the provisions of this Schedule shall apply accordingly.

6. Where--

(a) a sum is due from any person to any other person but the Minister directs that it shall be paid or credited to a blocked account only; and

(b) the person to whom the sum is due nominates such an account to the person from whom the sum is due,

the last mentioned person is under a duty to the person to whom the sum is due to cause the sum to be paid or credited to that blocked account, and the crediting of any sum to a blocked account in pursuance of a direction of the Minister shall, to the extent of the sum credited, be a good discharge to the person from whom the sum is due:

Provided that in the case of a sum due under a contract this paragraph shall not apply insofar as it is shown to be in consistent with the intention of the parties that it should apply.

THIRD SCHEDULE: LEGAL PROCEEDINGS, ETC.

1. The provisions of Part III of these Regulations shall apply to sums required to be paid by any judgment or order of any court or by any award as they apply in relation to other sums, and it shall be implied in any judgment or order of any court in Botswana, and in any award given under the laws of Botswana, that any sum required to be paid by the judgment, order or award (whether as a debt, as damages or otherwise) to which the said provisions apply shall not be paid except with the permission of the Minister.

2. Nothing in these Regulations shall be construed as preventing the payment by any person of any sum into any court in Botswana, but the provisions of Part III of these Regulations shall apply to the payment of any sum out of court, whether under an order of the court or otherwise, to or for the credit of any person resident outside Botswana.

3. Without prejudice to the provisions of any written law relating to the making of rules of court, rules of court--

(a) enabling any person who is required by any judgment, order or award to pay any sum, if he apprehends that the payment of that sum is unlawful under these Regulations except with the permission of the Minister, to pay that sum into court;

(b) declaring that payment of a sum into court by virtue of subparagraph (a) , together with the delivery to the other party concerned fo such evidence of the payment as may be prescribed by the rules, shall, to the extent of the payment, be a good discharge to the person making the payment; and

(c) so regulating the process of execution which may issue in respect of any sum required to be paid by any judgment, order or award as to secure that, unless it is shown, in such manner as may be prescribed by the rules, that the permission of the Minister for the payment of the sum is not required under these Regulations or has been given without conditions, the proceeds of the execution will be paid into court, and, so far as is necessary for that purpose, varying the form of any writ of execution or other similar document or the duties of the sheriff or other officer to whom any such writ or other similar document is directed, may be made, as regards the High Court or any other court, by such authority as may be designated in that behalf by the Chief Justice:

Provided that--

(i) the form of any bankruptcy notice shall be such as may be prescribed by the Minister, and

(ii) nothing in this paragraph shall affect the provisions of any written law which requires rules of court for inferior courts to have the concurrence of the rule-making authority for the High Court.

4. In any proceedings in a court and in any arbitration proceedings, a claim for the recovery of any debt shall not be defeated by reason only of the debt not being payable without the permission of the Minister and of that permission not having been given or having been revoked.

5. (1) In any bankruptcy, in the winding-up of any company or in the administration of the estate of any deceased person (being a bankruptcy, winding-up or administration carried on under the laws of Botswana) , a claim for a sum not payable without the permission of the Minister shall, notwithstanding that the permission has-not been given or has been revoked, be admitted to proof as it he had been given and had not been revoked:

Provided that nothing in this subparagraph shall be construed as affecting the application of the provisions of Part III of these Regulations to payments by any trustee, liquidator, personal representative or other person in any such bankruptcy, winding-up or administration.

(2) The provisions of these Regulations restricting the making of settlements shall not apply to any deed of arrangement made for the benefit of creditors generally, and the provisions of subparagraph (1) shall apply in relation to proceedings under any deed of arrangement as they apply in relation to proceedings in bankruptcy.

Cap. 42:02

6. A debt for the payment of which the permission of the Minister is required under these Regulations shall, if in other respects it complies with the requirements of the Insolvency Act, be allowed to be a good petitioning creditor's debt, notwithstanding the said requirement, if and to the extent that the debt can be satisfied either by a payment into court or by a payment to a blocked account.

FOURTH SCHEDULE: ENFORCEMENT

PART I General Provisions as to Evidence and Information

1. (1) Without prejudice to any other provisions of these Regulations, the Minister may give to any person in or resident in Botswana directions requiring him, within such time and in such manner as may be specified in the directions, to furnish to him, or to any person designated in the directions as a person authorized to require it, any information in his possession or control which the Minister or the person so authorized, as the case may be, may require for the purpose of securing compliance with or detecting evasion of these Regulations.

(2) A person required by any such directions as aforesaid to furnish information shall also produce such books, accounts or other documents (hereinafter in this Part of this Schedule referred to as "documents") in his possession or control as may be required for the said purpose by the Minister or by the person authorized to require the information, as the case may be.

(3) Nothing in the preceding provisions of this paragraph shall be taken to require any person who has acted as legal practitioner for any person to disclose any privileged communication made to him in that capacity.

(4) Where a person is convicted for failing to give information or produce documents when required to do so under this paragraph, the court may make an order requiring the offender, within such period as may be specified in the order, to comply with the requirement to give the information or produce the documents.

2. (1) If a magistrate is satisfied by information on oath given by a person authorized by the Minister to act for the purposes of this paragraph either--

(a) that there is reasonable ground for suspecting that an offence against these Regulations has been or is being committed and that evidence of the commission of the offence is to be found at any premises specified in the information, or in any vehicle, vessel or aircraft so specified; or

(b) that any documents which ought to have been produced under paragraph 1 and have not been produced are to be found at any such premises or in any such vehicle, vessel or aircraft,

he may grant a search warrant authorizing any police officer, together with any other persons named in the warrant and any other police officers, to enter the premises upon which the vehicle, vessel or aircraft so specified may be, at any time within one month from the date of the warrant, and to search the premises, or, as the case may be, the vehicle, vessel or aircraft.

(2) A person authorized by any such warrant as aforesaid to search any premises or any vehicle, vessel or aircraft, may search every person who is found in, or whom he has reasonable ground to believe to have recently left or to be about to enter, those premises or that vehicle, vessel or aircraft, as the case may be, and may seize any article found in the premises or in the vehicle, vessel or aircraft which he has reasonable ground for believing to be evidence of the commission of any offence against these Regulations or any document which he has reasonable ground for believing ought to have been produced under paragraph 1:

Provided that no female shall, in pursuance of any warrant issued under this paragraph, be searched except by a female.

(3) Where, by virtue of this paragraph, a person has any power to enter any premises, he may use such force as is reasonably necessary for the purpose of exercising that power.

3. (1) Any article coming into the possession of an executive authority (whether in consequence of the seizure of the article under or by virtue of these Regulations or otherwise) which the authority has reasonable ground for believing to be evidence of the commission of an offence against these Regulations may be retained for a period of three months or, if within that period there are commenced proceedings in respect of such an offence in which the article is, or can properly be, adduced in evidence, until the final determination of those proceedings.

(2) For the purposes of this paragraph, any person to whom any powers of the Minister under these Regulations are delegated or on whom any functions are conferred by or by virtue of these Regulations, including any police officer, shall be deemed to be an executive authority.

(3) For the purposes of this paragraph, any proceedings shall be deemed not to have been finally determined so long as there is pending any appeal in the matter of the proceedings, and an appeal in that matter shall be deemed to be pending during the ordinary time within which

such an appeal may be lodged, and, if such an appeal is duly lodged, the appeal shall be deemed to be pending until it is decided or withdrawn.

(4) The powers conferred by this paragraph in relation to any article shall be in addition to, and not in derogation of, any powers otherwise exercisable in relation thereto.

4. No person in or resident in Botswana shall--

(a) with intent to evade the provisions of these Regulations, destroy, mutilate, deface, secrete or remove any documents;

(b) in furnishing any information for any of the purposes of these Regulations, make any statement which he knows to be false in a material particular, or recklessly make any statement which is false in a material particular;

(c) obstruct any person in the exercise of any powers conferred on him by virtue of this Part of this Schedule.

PART II GENERAL PROVISIONS AS TO OFFENCES

1. (1) Any person in or resident in Botswana who contravenes any restriction or requirement imposed by or under these Regulations, and any such person who conspires or attempts, or aids, abets, counsels or procures any other person, to contravene any such restriction or requirement as aforesaid, shall be guilty of an offence punishable under this Part of this Schedule:

Provided that an offence punishable by virtue of Part III of this Schedule shall not be punishable under this Part of this Schedule.

(2) Where an offence punishable under this Part of this Schedule has been committed by a body corporate, any person who at the time of the commission of the offence was a director, general manager, secretary or other similar officer of the body corporate, or was purporting to act in any such capacity, shall be deemed to be guilty fo that offence, unless he proves that the contravention was committed without his consent or connivance and that he exercised all such diligence to prevent the commission of the offence as he ought to have exercised having regard to the nature of his functions in that capacity and to all the circumstances.

(3) Any person who commits an offence punishable under this Part of this Schedule shall be liable to a fine not exceeding P10 000 or to imprisonment for a term not exceeding five years, or to both; and where the offence is concerned with any currency, security, gold, goods or other property, the court may, if it thinks fit to do so, order such currency, security, gold, goods or property to be forfeited.

PART III IMPORT AND EXPORT

1. The Customs and Excise Duty Act shall, subject to such modifications, if any, as may be prescribed to adapt it to these Regulations, apply in relation to anything prohibited to be imported or exported by any of the provisions of Part V of these Regulations, except with the permission of the Minister as they apply in relation to goods prohibited to be imported or exported by or under any of the provisions of the Customs and Excise Duty Act, and any reference in the Customs and Excise Duty Act to goods shall be construed as including a reference to anything

prohibited to be imported or exported by any of the provisions of the said Part V, except with the permission of the Minister.

2. Any declaration required to be given under Part V of these Regulations shall, for the purposes of the Customs and Excise Duty Act, be deemed to be a declaration in a matter relating to customs.

3. Without prejudice to any of the preceding provisions of this Part of this Schedule, any person who, on any occasion, is about to leave Botswana or arrives in Botswana (which person is hereinafter in this paragraph referred to as "the traveller") shall, if no that occasion he is required to do so by an officer of the Department of Customs and Excise or an immigration officer--

(a) declare whether or not he has with him anything prohibited to be imported or exported by any of the provisions of the said part V except with the permission of the Minister; and

(b) produce any such thing as aforesaid which he has with him, and the officer may examine or search any article which the traveller has with him for the purpose of ascertaining whether he is conveying or has in his possession any such thing, and, if the officer has reasonable grounds for suspecting that the traveller has about his person any such thing, search him, and may seize anything produced as aforesaid or found upon such examination or search as aforesaid as to which the officer has reasonable ground for suspecting that it is prohibited to be imported or exported by any of the provisions of the said Part V except with the permission of the Minister:

Provided that no female shall be searched in pursuance of this paragraph except by a female.

EXCHANGE CONTROL (AUTHORIZATION TO ACT AS AUTHORIZED DEALER AND DEPOSITARY) ORDER

(under regulation 36)

(13th August, 1976)

ARRANGEMENT OF PARAGRAPHS

PARAGRAPH

Citation

1. This Order may be cited as the Exchange Control (Authorization to act as Authorized Dealer and Depositary) order.

Authorized dealer, etc.

2. Any person specified in the Schedule hereto is authorized to act as an authorized dealer and authorized depositary.

SCHEDULE

Bank of Credit and Commerce (Botswana) Limited

Barclays Bank fo Botswana Limited

Standard Chartered Bank Botswana Limited.

S.I. 152, 1976.

EXCHANGE CONTROL (PAYMENTS) ORDER

(under regulation 24)

(12th November, 1976)

ARRANGEMENT OF PARAGRAPHS

1. Citation

2. Interpretation

3. Transfers exempt from provisions of regulation 7

4. Payments exempt from provisions of regulation 7

5. Application of regulation 24

Citation

1. This Order may be cited as the Exchange Control (Payments) order.

Interpretation

2. In this Order, unless the context otherwise requires, "account" means a Botswana currency account with an authorized bank in Botswana.

Transfers exempt from provisions of regulation 7

3. There shall be exempt from the provisions of regulation 7 anything done for the purpose of the transfer to the account of any person of the whole or any part of an amount standing to the credit of an account (being an account with an authorized dealer) of a person resident outside Botswana.

Payments exempt from provisions of regulation 7

4. There shall be exempt from the provisions of regulation 7 any payment made in cash in Botswana to a person resident outside Botswana--

(a) by a person resident outside Botswana if that payment is made out of--

(i) any notes of a class which are or have at any time been legal tender in Botswana,

(ii) any moneys withdrawn from an account (being an account with an authorized dealer) of that person,

(iii) any moneys arising from the sale of gold or any foreign currency by that person to an authorized dealer, or

(iv) any foreign currency so long as that payment is not made as consideration for or in association with the receipt by any person of Botswana currency;

(b) by a person resident in Botswana if that payment--

(i) does not exceed P50 in value, and

(ii) does not form part of a transaction or a series of transactions wherein the aggregate value of the payment exceeds P50;

(c) by an authorized dealer in Botswana acting in the course of its business if that payment is being made from money standing to the credit of an account of a person resident outside Botswana with that authorized dealer; and

(d) by an authorized dealer in Botswana acting in the course of its business if that payment is in respect of the encashment by that person of a travellers' cheque or letter of credit in favour of that person.

Exchange control (Payments) Order

Application of regulation 24

5. For the purposes of regulation 24--

(a) the prescribed country shall be any country outside Botswana;

(b) the prescribed manner of payment shall, in respect of exports to a destination in the prescribed country, be payment either in any specified currency or payment in Botswana currency from an account (being an account with an authorized dealer in Botswana) of a person resident outside Botswana.

S.I. 153, 1976, S.I. 68, 1979, S.I. 91, 1985.

EXCHANGE CONTROL (IMPORT AND EXPORT) ORDER

(under regulation 32)

(12th November, 1976)

ARRANGEMENT OF PARAGRAPHS

3. Items exempt from provisions of regulation 23

4. Further exemptions from provisions of regulation 23

5. Cases in which exemptions do not apply

Citation

1. This Order may be cited as the Exchange Control (Import and Export) Order.

Items exempt from provisions of regulation 22

2. There shall be exempt from the provisions of regulation 22--

(a) the import into Botswana of any notes and coin of a class which are legal tender in Botswana; and

(b) the import into Botswana of the certificate of title to any security which is registered in Botswana and which is not and cannot, without the necessity for an entry in the register in Botswana, become registered outside Botswana, or which is registered both in Botswana and outside Botswana but which on a transfer cannot, without the necessity for an entry in the register of Botswana, become registered outside Botswana in the name of the transferee, or on which none of the dividends or interest is payable on presentation of a coupon.

Items exempt from provisions of regulation 23

3. (1) There shall be exempt from the provisions of regulation 23 the export from Botswana by any traveller on his person or in his baggage of notes and coin--

(a) not exceeding P200, in notes and coin which are legal tender in Botswana; and

(b) not exceeding P200, in the case of notes and coin which are or have at any time been legal tender in any country outside Botswana.

(2) for the purposes of this paragraph, the Botswana currency value of any notes and coin which are or have at any time been legal tender in any country outside Botswana shall be calculated--

(a) at the rate at which they could be sold to an authorized dealer on the day on which they are to be exported; or, if such rate cannot be readily ascertained;

(b) at the rate determined or to be determined by the Minister for the currency concerned.

Further exemptions from provisions of regulation 23

4. There shall be exempt from the provisions of regulation 23 the export from Botswana--

(a) of postal orders in any manner other than on the person of a traveller or in his baggage;

(b) of any bill of exchange or promissory note expressed in terms of Botswana currency, not being a bill or note which is or has at any time been legal tender in Botswana;

(c) of any bill of exchange or promissory note expressed in terms of Botswana currency and issued by an authorized dealer or in pursuance of permission granted by the Minister;

(d) of the certificate of title to any security which is registered in Botswana and which is not and cannot, without the necessity for an entry in the register in Botswana, become registered outside Botswana but which on transfer cannot, without the necessity for an entry in the register in Botswana, become registered outside Botswana in interest is payable on presentation of a coupon;

(e) by any traveller not resident in Botswana, on his person or in his baggage, of any travellers' cheque or letter of credit which has been imported by that traveller.

Cases in which exemptions do not apply

5. The exemptions granted by this Order shall not apply to any person employed or engaged in any capacity on board any train, vehicle or aircraft arriving in or departing from Botswana.

S.I. 154, 1976.

EXCHANGE CONTROL (BRANCHES AND RESIDENCE) ORDER

(under regulation 37)

(12th November, 1976)

ARRANGEMENT OF PARAGRAPHS

PARAGRAPH

Citation

1. This Order may be cited as the Exchange Control (Branches and Residence) Order.

Transactions by branches of business

2. For the purposes of the Regulations any transaction with or by a branch of any business, whether carried on by a body corporate or otherwise shall be treated in all respects as if that branch were a body corporate resident where the branch is situate.

Residence

3. A person or body of persons carrying on in Botswana a branch of any business shall, as respects such business as is carried on by that branch, be treated for all purposes of the Regulations as resident in Botswana.

Branch to include head office

4. References in this Order to a branch of a business shall be deemed to include a reference to the head office fo that business.

EXCHANGE CONTROL (DECLARATION AND EVIDENCE) ORDER

S.I. 74, 1978.

(under regulations 11(1) (b) , 12(1) (b) , 16(a) , 18(5) and 19(1) (a))

ARRANGEMENT OF PARAGRAPHS

PARAGRAPH

Citation

1. This Order may be cited as the Exchange Control (Declaration and Evidence) Order.

Prescribed evidence for regulation 11(1) (b)

2. (1) The prescribed evidence for the purposes of regulation 11(1) (b) to be produced to the person issuing the security shall be evidence that the person to whom the security is to be issued is not resident outside Botswana and from facts known to the person giving the evidence or from enquiries made by that person is not, to the best of his belief, acquiring the security as the nominee of any person resident outside Botswana.

(2) The evidence shall be given by a declaration in writing signed by or on behalf of the person to whom the security is to be issued.

Prescribed declaration of regulation 12(1) (b)

3. The prescribed declaration for the purposes of regulation 12(1) (b) , to be delivered to the transferee at or before the time of the transfer shall be in the form set out in the First Schedule or in a form to the like effect made by an authorized depositary.

Prescribed evidence for regulation 16(a)

4. The prescribed evidence for the purposes of regulation 16 (a) , to be produced to a person concerned with the keeping of a Register in Botswana, shall be--

(a) in the case of the issue of securities, the evidence prescribed by paragraph 2;

(b) in the case of the transfer of securities, the declaration prescribed by paragraph 5 and evidence given by a declaration in writing signed by an authorized depositary that the transferee is not resident outside Botswana and from facts known to the person giving the evidence or from enquiries made by that person is not to the best of his belief acquiring the security as the nominee of any person resident outside Botswana; and

(c) in the case of registration of securities transferable by means of bearer certificates, the evidence prescribed by paragraph 2(1) given by a declaration in writing signed by a depositary.

Prescribed evidence for regulation 18(5)

5. The prescribed evidence for the purposes of regulation 18(5) , to be produced to an authorized depositary. shall be the evidence prescribed in the case of the transfer of securities by paragraph 3(b) .

Prescribed declaration for regulation 19(1) (a)

6. The prescribed declaration for the purposes of regulation 19(1) (a) , to be delivered to an authorized depositary, shall be in the form set out in the Second Schedule or in a form to the like effect made by an authorized depository.

FIRST SCHEDULE

(para. 3)

The holder of the above-mentioned security is not resident outside Botswana and from facts known to us or from enquiries we have made is not to the best of our belief holding the security of a person resident outside Botswana.

SECOND SCHEDULE

(para. 6)

We hereby declare that to our knowledge the security specified in the attached Schedule has not been acquired in contravention of any Exchange Control legislation in force in Botswana since 10th December, 1965, and has not been imported into Botswana in contravention of such legislation.

S.I. 75, 1978.

EXCHANGE CONTROL (BANKRUPTCY NOTICES) ORDER

(under para. 3 of Sched. III to regulations)

(28th July, 1978)

ARRANGEMENT OF PARAGRAPHS

PARAGRAPH

1. Citation

2. Prescription of the form of bankruptcy notice

Schedule

Citation

1. This Order may be cited as the Exchange Control (Bankruptcy Notices) order.

Prescription of the form of bankruptcy notice Cap. 42:02

2. A bankruptcy notice issued in accordance with the Insolvency Act, at the request of a person (or persons) residing outside Botswana being a creditor for an amount due under a judgment, order or award, shall (with such variations as the circumstances may require) --

(a) in a case in which permission of the Minister has not been obtained for payment of the amount due, be in the form set out in Part I of the Schedule;

(b) in a case in which permission of the Minister for payment into a blocked account has been made, be in a form set out in Part II of the Schedule.

SCHEDULE

(paras. 2(a) and (b))

PART I

Bankruptcy notice for use where the permission of the Minister has not been obtained.

TITLE

A.B. (or A.B. and Co.) of

Take notice that whereas C.D. (or C.D. and Co.) of a person (or persons) residing outside Botswana has (or have) obtained judgment against you for the sum of P and whereas permission of the Minister of Finance and Development Planning for payment of the said sum by you to him (or them) has not been obtained, you must within 7 (seven) days after service of this Notice on you excluding the day of such service pay into court in accordance with rules of court made pursuant to the Third Schedule of the Exchange Control Regulations the said sum of P being the amount of the said judgment whereon execution has not been stayed, you must secure or compound for the said sum to his (or her) satisfaction or to the satisfaction of Mr of his (or their) duly authorized agent or to the satisfaction of the court in some manner not prohibited by the said Regulations or you must satisfy this court that you have a counterclaim, set-off or cross demand against him (or them) which equals or exceeds the amount claimed by him (or them) and which you could not set up in the action or other proceedings in which the judgment or order was obtained.

DATED the........day of........19.........

By the Court.

PART II

Bankruptcy notice for use when Minister has granted permission for payment into a blocked account.

TITLE

To A.B. (or A.B. and Co.) of

Take Notice that whereas C.D. (or C.D. and Co.) of a person (or persons) residing outside Botswana has (or have) obtained a final judgment (or order) against you for the sum of P and whereas permission of the Minister of Finance and Development Planning for payment of the said sum by you to him (or them) has not been obtained but the Minister of Finance and Development Planning has directed that the said sum shall be paid to a blocked account and the said C.D. (or C.D. and Co.) has (or have nominated an account in his (or their) name at the Bank of pursuant to paragraph 6 of the Second Schedule to the Exchange Control Regulations, you must within 7 (seven) days after service of this Notice on you excluding the day of such service pay the said sum of P being the amount of the said judgment (or order) on which execution has not been stayed either into the said blocked account or into court or you must secure or compound for the said sum to the satisfaction of the said C.D. (or C.D. and Co.) or to the satisfaction of Mr of his (or their) duly authorized agent or to the satisfaction of the court in a manner not prohibited by the Exchange Control Regulations or you must satisfy this court that you have a counterclaim, set-off or cross demand against him (or them) which equals or exceeds the amount claimed by him (or them) and which you could not set up in the action or other proceedings in which the judgment (or order) was obtained.

DATED the........day of........19..........

By the Court.

S.I. 76, 1978.

EXCHANGE CONTROL (PURCHASE OF FOREIGN CURRENCY) ORDER

(under regulation 32)

(28th July, 1978)

ARRANGEMENT OF PARAGRAPHS

PARAGRAPH

Citation

1. This Order may be cited as the Exchange Control (purchase of Foreign Currency) Order.

Purchases exempt from the provisions of regulation 3(1)

2. There shall be exempt from the provisions of regulation 3(1) the purchase outside Botswana of foreign currency with notes which--

(a) are or have at any time been legal tender in Botswana; and

(b) have been exported from Botswana under the exemption granted by paragraph 3(1) of the Exchange Control (Import and Export) Order,

subject to the condition that the purchases shall comply with such conditions as to the use to which that foreign currency may be put or the period for which it may be retained as may from time to time be notified to him by the Minister.

S.I. 78, 1978.

EXCHANGE CONTROL (SPECIFIED CURRENCY AND PRESCRIBED SECURITIES) ORDER

(under regulations 4(1) and 20(1))

(28th July, 1978)

ARRANGEMENT OF PARAGRAPHS

PARAGRAPH

Citation

1. This Order may be cited as the Exchange Control (Specified Currency and Prescribed Securities) Order.

Specification of foreign currency

2. All currency other than Pula and Thebe is hereby specified as foreign currency to which regulation 4 applies.

Application of regulation 20

3. Regulation 20 shall apply to securities on which capital money, dividends or interest are payable in any foreign currency or in respect of which the holder has an option to require payments of any capital money, dividends or interest therein in any foreign currency.

THE FINANCIAL ASSISTANCE POLICY FOR MEDIUM SCALE PROJECTS

I. WHAT IS THE FINANCIAL ASSISTANCE POLICY ?

The Financial Assistance Policy (FAP) is a programme launched by the Government of Botswana at the beginning of May, 1982. The aim of the policy is to assist businesses so that sore employment is created in Botswana, and so that the economy can expand and become stronger (diversification of the economy away from mining and beef industries?.

II. WHICH BUSINESSES CAN RECEIVE ASSISTANCE ?

Only businesses which are productive activities can receive assistance. Productive activities mean, in the context o" this policy, activities that produce or process goods which can either substitute for imported items or to be exported from Botswana. Two exceptions to this definition are cattle industry including its direct products (however, both tanning and indirect meat processing, such as sausages would be eligible for FAP assistance) and large scale mining. These are excluded because the FAP hopes to diversify Botswana's economy beyond these two sectors. These effectively limits the activities eligible for assistance to manufacturing, small and medium scale mining (i.e less than P 900 000 fixed investment) , and agriculture other than cattle (all other types of agriculture are eligible, e.g poultry, dairy, small stock, forestry, fisheries, horticulture, pigs, etc. Dryland farming is however covered by the policy only at (pandasatenga) .

There is, though, one other type of industry which is eligible for assistance and this is a "linking" industry. Linking industries which provide a marketing or collection function for the above mentioned productive activities say be eligible for assistance, depending on an analysis of the particular case. The same applies to repair and maintenance facilities specifically aimed at maintaining equipment used in productive activities. Generally, linking activities involve support for a large number of small- scale informal or formal sector producers.

Service industries such as internal transport, retail trade. construction, banking, tourism and entertainment are not eligible for assistance. Also the br~~ewing/distillin~g industry is specifically excluded from the Policy.

Both new productive businesses and expansion of existing productive businesses can apply for assistance. An expansion is defined as any increase in employment or output (as measured by scale) . In arable agriculture an expansion must usually involve previously uncultivated land, or, improvements in the infrastructure on presently cultivated areas which will result in greater output. Only businesses which raise the national income and have a reasonable chance of becoming financially viable will receive assistance.

Only persons 18 years of age and over may apply for assistance and only citizens of Botswana may apply for the small scale assistance mentioned in Question III. Medium and large scale are open to non citizens as well as to citizens. Application may also come from companies, partnerships, etc.

III. DOES IT MATTER HOW LARGE THE BUSINESS IS ?

The methods of determining the amount of assistance vary according to the size of the project (business) under consideration. All assistance, though, is in the form of non repayable grants as opposed to loans from banks. Projects are divided into three categories on the basis of investment in fixed assets:

1. Small scale business, investment on fixed assets (machinery, equipment and buildings) is P 25 000 or less;

2. Medium scale business, investments between P 25 000 and P 900 000; and

3. Large scale business, investments over P 900 000.

This booklet is primarily concerned with medium scale projects although much information is relevant to large scale projects. A separate booklet is available for those interested in applying for small scale projects assistance. The method of determining assistance to small scale projects is very different from the procedures described in this booklet and persons interested in small scale projects should obtain the appropriate booklet.

IV. HOW IS THE AMOUNT OF ASSISTANCE TO MEDIUM AND LARGE SCALE PROJECTS DETERMINED ?

There are two packages of financial assistance available to medium scale projects. Projects which represent new investments in the manufacturing sector may qualify for Automatic Financial Assistance (AFA) . Expansions of all productive activities and new industries in sectors other than manufacturing are considered for negotiated or Case-by-Case Financial Assistance.(CFA) . A new industry in the manufacturing sector may opt for the GFA. but expansions of the existing activities and new investments in sectors other than manufacturing may not opt for the AFA.

Since the AFA and CFA are different, they will be considered separately.

A. AUTOMATIC FINANCIAL ASSISTANCE.

An application for Automatic Financial Assistance involves several steps. First, a business must be registered as a company before it will be eligible for AFA (see section VIII below for a more detailed explanation) . Secondly, if manufacturing licence is required, it must be secured in advance of the granting of the AFA (again see below for more details?. Thirdly, at the time of application, the applicant(s) will be required to sign an agreement allowing FAP Officers access to current and past tax records. This will involve tax records of the company, if any, and information on all directors and all principal shareholders. The applicant(s) may also be requested to authorize access to tax records from other countries in the case of non- citizen investors. Fourthly, once an applicant has cleared the above steps, The Ministry of Commerce and Industry will examine the market in which the project will compete. If there is a ready market for the goods to be produced, the application will be approved and grants administered as outlined below. If it is not clear that a market for the goods produced exists (e.g if there is already substantial domestic production relative to the domestic market) , then the project will not receive AFA but may apply for CFA. Thus, not all new investments in manufacturing qualify for Automatic Financial Assistance.

It is possible to get some advance guidance on whether specific projects are likely to be eligible for AFA from the Division of Industrial Affairs, Ministry of Commerce and Industry. This guidance will, of course, not be binding on Government.

The Automatic Financial Assistance has three components. If a project is granted AFA, it will receive all three components together. These components or types of assistance. are discussed below:

1. Type of Assistance : TAX HOLIDAY

(A map showing classification areas is included at the end of this booklet) .

a. Amount of Assistance: (In Urban and Peri-Urban areas) .

100% tax reimbursement for years 1 and 2

75% tax reimbursement for year 3

50% tax reimbursement for year 4

25% tax reimbursement for year 5

In those areas outside the Urban and Peri-Urban areas, the amount of assistance under the Tax Holiday is:

100% business tax reimbursement for years 1,2,and 3

75% business tax reimbursement for year 4

50% business tax reimbursement for year 5

It is important to note that the Tax Holiday applies only on company tax attributable to the specific project being assisted and therefore may not cover all of the company's tax liability. Am such it is better to register a new company to implement the project for which AFA is sought. Also withholding tax on non-citizens profits is not covered nor is any cost incurred in arriving at an assessment of liability.

For tax purposes, straight line depreciation will be practiced.

The new rates are : (These new rates will apply to all new investment regardless of whether or not a project enjoys Financial Assistance?.

Building of Industrial Undertakings on the original value	- Initial Allowance	25%
Building of Industrial Undertakings	- Annual Allowance	2.5%
Commercial Buildings	- Annual Allowance	2.5%
Short-Lived Plant and Machinery	- Annual Allowance	25%
Normal Plant and Machinery	- Annual Allowance	15%
Durable Plant and Machinery	- Annual Allowance	10%

The income to the firm from the below mentioned employment and training grants should be added to the total revenue in the tax year received and treated as part of taxable income. Reimbursements of business taxes under the Tax Holiday grant would not be part of taxable income (exempted as a class of income) .

b. Time of Assistance: The firm files a tax return each year, pays tax liabilities, as assessed, to the Department of Taxes and then later receives a reimbursement from the Financial Assistance Policy (this procedure may be modified to a system of tax credits in the near future) . Any later-assessment resulting in an increased tax liability will not be covered by the FAP. Any later reduction in liability will have to be repaid to the Policy.

c. Monitoring of Assistance: Tax reimbursement will be monitored pursuant to applicable tax laws.

2. Type of Assistance: Unskilled Labour Grant.

a. Amount of Assistance:

An 80% reimbursement of unskilled labour wage bill in years 1 and 2

A 50% reimbursement of unskilled labour wage bill in year 3.

A 40% reimbursement of unskilled labour wage bill in year 4.

A 20% reimbursement of unskilled labour wage bill in year 5.

Unskilled labour is defined as labour earning less than the lowest notch of Industrial Class Group 1 in the Government of Botswana wage scale. (For "piece-rated" employees, their wage hourly earnings should be aggregated to a nine hour day to establish if they should be classified as unskilled) . Only citizen employees may be covered by this grant.

b. Time of Assistance: The reimbursement is paid at the end of three month intervals.

c. Monitoring of Assistance: Claims will be checked against wages books for consistency. It is the responsibility of the firm to ensure that these are accurate and submitted to the National Development Bank on the appropriate claim forms. Government will also inspect premises periodically to measure labour on site etc.

3. Type of Assistance: Training Grant.

a. Amount of Assistance: 50% of the training costs during the first five years of the project will be paid by the Financial Assistance Policy. Only training completed at an institution licensed by the Potswana Ministry of Education is automatically eligible provided total costs do not exceed P 2 500 per trainee per year. Training outside of Botawana, off-the-job training done with the firm and/or training. costing over P 2 500 per trainee per year, must receive special permission if FAP is to fund half the related costs of such training. In house-training- defined here as training which does not take place in the process of production will be eligible if the firm convincingly separate and substantiates the claimed costs. Firms will be required to provide training plans in advance of the prescribed training in writing to the FAP Secretariat, who will review the investors plans and advise accordingly The FAP can cover 50% of the following costs: Tuition, room and board, travel, materials and wages (if not already covered by the other FAP grants?; the costs of a training officer may also be included. The grant applies only to the training of citizens.

b. Time of Assistance: Assistance is provided at three months intervals commencing when training starts.

c. Monitoring~ of Assistance: Presentation of receipts and documentation of the training institution and course content are required.

The above three types of assistance comprise the Automatic Financial Assistance. This assistance is provided unconditionally to any new investment in manufacturing that is deemed eligible by the Ministry of Commerce and Industry.

B. CASE-BY-CASE FINANCIAL ASSISTANCE.

The second type of assistance offered is the Case-by-case Financial Assistance. Available to new and expanding investments, the CFA is slightly more complicated than AFA. As its name implies, the CFA analyses projects one at a time. As with all AFA applications, at the time of application for CFA. the applicant(s) will be required to sign an agreement authorizing access by FAP Officers to their tax records. The analysis for each project is then as follows:

First, the proposed project must yield a real economic rate of return to Botswana of atleast 6%. In calculating the economic rate of return, the investment's projected expenditure and revenues are carefully analyzed Government recognizes that projects should be analyzed from a national as opposed to a private view point of costs and benefits. To this end, the project evaluation process favours projects which use unskilled

labour instead of capital or skilled labour and projects with which profits accrue to Batswana. If a project does not have an economic rate of return of at least 6%, the request for assistance is denied. If, on the other hand, the 6% economic rate of return requirement is met, the case-by-case Financial Assistance is calculated. There are four components of this Assistance. If a project is granted CFA, it may be eligible for all four of these components together (if within the specific limits) . These components or types of assistance are discussed below.

1. Type of Assistance: The grants will be P 1 000 per job created for non-citizen owned or joint venture projects and P 1 500 per job created for 1001 citizen owned projects. The total capital allowable is limited as follows:

Not more than 40% of total fixed investment in Urban Areas.

Not more than 50% of total fixed investment in Peri Urban Areas.

Not more than 55% of total fixed investment in non-Urban primary centres.

Not more than 65% of total fixed investment in rural areas east.

Not more than 85% of total fixed investment in rural areas west.

(A map indicating these areas is included at the end of this brochure) .

b. Time of Assistance: The capital grant is paid before the project commences. It is provided as a bank account which may be used only to cover the purchase of fixed assets. Firms will not be given cash. Instead, NDB which is the disbursing agent pays the suppliers of the assets directly.

c. Monitoring of Assistance: Should a firm fall behind its original projections of employment, the Government will have the option of demanding repayment of that portion of the capital grant (plus interest at above prime rate) that the firm is no longer entitled to (based on the amount of the job originally granted?. The capital grant is part of taxable income, as are all CFA grants. However, the portion of the capital grant actually spend prior to the commencement of a business will be deemed to accrue only to the first day of a business's operation.

2. Type of Assistance: Sales Augmentation Grant.

a. Amount of Assistance : The grant will be made for a maximum of:

8% of sales revenue in each of the first 2 years

6% of sales revenue in year 3

4% of sales revenue in year 4

2% of sales revenue in year 5

(In all years, sales of scheduled agricultural produce are not included in sales revenue) .

b. Time of Assistance: The sales Augmentation Grant is made at three months intervals, starting three months after production begins.

c. Monitoring of Assistance: Payments will be based on sales revenue data i.e

- Sales analysis book
- Cash sales receipt
- Bank deposit slips

It is very important that all these records are in order to avoid delays in processing the claims.

N.B. customs protection, may under certain circumstances, be granted to a project in place of a sales augmentation grant. However, only projects capable of supplying a large portion of the domestic market will be considered, and protection will only be granted when Government is convinced it is in the overall economic interest of the nation to do so.

3. Type of Assistance: Unskilled Labour Grant.

THESE ARE IDENTICAL TO THE UNSKILLED LABOUR GRANT UNDER AUTOMATIC FINANCIAL ASSISTANCE, EXPLAINED ABOVE?.

4. Types~ of~~ assistance: Training Grant

THESE ARE IDENTICAL TO THE TRAINING GRANT UNDER AUTOMATIC FINANCIAL ASSISTANCE POLICY EXPLAINED ABOVE) .

5. Limits to Assistance under the CFA

The total value of Sales Augmentation Grant, plus the Unskilled Labour Grant, plus the Training Grant summed over the five year period, should not be more than:

a) 50% of the domestic value added accruing to Batswana over the five year period. Value added is defined here as Sales Revenue minus tradable inputs minus transfers to non-citizens;

OR

b) A percentage of unskilled wages plus training costs over the same period of time. The percentage varies by location and is determined by the schedule below:

Gaborone - 80%

Other Urban and Peri- - 100%

Urban Areas

Non Urban Primary

Centres - 110%

Rural Area East - 120%

Rural Area West - 130%

(Refer to the map at the end of the brochure) . The maximum assistance is the lower of a and b.

V. IF I CAN CHOOSE BETWEEN APA AND CPA, HOW DO I DECIDE ?

Without completing both application forms, (one for APA and one for CPA) , it is difficult to determine the precise financial difference between the two assistance packages. However, some simple "rules of thumb" can be applied for general guidance. The AFA entails a far simpler and more rapid application process than the CPA. Also, as there are no limits on assistance in AFA, there is greater certainty for the investor at the outset. However. AFA provides no funds whatsoever to help with initial project investment. All AFA grants are in the form of reimbursements (see above for details) .

The CPA involves a fairly detailed application form and procedure. Each project is carefully scrutinized, and because of the limits to CPA, the assistance package is not certain until the end of the process. The CPA can provide some capital at the start of a project, although this is never for one hundred percent of the fixed capital required to launch the project or expansion.

Rural based, labour intensive projects do best out of the CPA (and also do best out of the PAP) ; urban based, capital intensive projects usually do best out of the AFA. Projects that have a ratio of fixed investment to employment of P 10 000 per job or less and for which an urban location is not absolutely essential would be well advised to calculate the extra PAP assistance they would enjoy by locating instead at a rural site. There are many excellent rural industrial areas, in close proximity to urban areas, which offer full services for water, electricity, telecommunications and transport (both rail and tarred roads) . There is also the advantage of a more stable rural workforce. For some projects, the extra FAP assistance offered at a rural location has exceeded P 200 000 over five years. The ultimate decision is of course left to you, the investor. but it ~s important to take account of the financial incentives that we offer to those who opt for a rural site.

VI. AFTER THE AMOUNT OF ASSISTANCE IS DETERMINED, WHAT HAPPENS ?

After it has been determined that a project qualifies for Automatic Financial Assistance, that assistance is available without further analysis. An agreement has to be signed between the applicant and the Ministry of Finance and Development Planning. The contract includes a provision for a bond on the assets of the firm equal to the projected amount of assistance. This bond may be cancelled by Government in the event of non-compliance with the agreement. (However, the bond will not interfere with a firm's ability to raise capital) . The directors and beneficial shareholders will be required to guarantee payment of the bond as part of the contractual process. The agreement will also give Government the right to require an annual external audit of the firm, at the firm's own expense, as well as to provide other relevant information throughout the five year life of the contract. Under the Case-by-case Financial Assistance Procedure. an application for assistance must first pass the 6% economic rate of return to Botswana requirement. Then the amount of assistance must be compared to the maximum allowable assistance, and the amount requested must not exceed passed does the request for assistance go to the Productive Employment Technical Committee (PETC) . The PETC is the body which has the decision making authority for medium-scale. It meets in Gaborone at the Ministry of Finance and Development Planning about once a month. If the application is accepted. a contract is then drawn up between the Ministry of Finance and Development Planning and the applicant(s) (this will contain the provision mentioned above with regards to the AFA contract) .

VII. HOW OFTEN CAN I APPLY ?

There is a limit of one successful application per 12 months period. As a result, firms contemplating several expansions over a 12 month period are advised to aggregate these into one expansion for that 12 month period. No assistance will be granted to expansions retrospectively.

VIII. NOW THAT I UNDERSTAND WHAT THE FAP OFFERS, HOW DO I ACTUALLY APPLY ?

A. To apply for AFA the four steps outlined in Question IV should be followed. First~ in order to register a company you should contact the Registrar of Companies or your Attorney. They will be able to advise you on the requirements and costs involved Second, a licence to manufacture if required by the project, must be obtained in advance of application to AFA. However, the application form for AFA is the same as that for a manufacturing licence (revised version) . The applicant may request both a manufacturing licence and AFA at the sane time on one form. Alternatively, the application may be for a licence or AFA alone the later case would arise if either a licence has already been secured or if a licence is not required for the project) . As part of the application process, the request for AFA will be gazetted in order to allow those possibly affected to enter objections with the Ministry of Commerce and Industry. This is similar to the procedure followed with applications for manufacturing licence and AFA being requested, there will be only one gazetted notice, covering both applications. All objections on AFA for a project will be assessed on their merits. Although, internally within the Ministry of Commerce and Industry, the application for a licence will be processed before considering the request for AFA, the investor will be informed on both at the same time. The length of time required will be the same as that for a manufacturing licence (approximately six to eight weeks) . Should a manufacturing Licence be refused, AFA will obviously not be approved. Furthermore, approval of a manufacturing licence does not guarantee a favourable decision on AFA. Whether an application is for AFA alone, a manufacturing licence alone or both together, the usual gazettement fee (currently two cheques of P 20) , must be attached to the application form. An application will not be processed if payment is not attached. As explained above in Question IV the tax access letters must also be signed by the directors and principal shareholders of the business. The required form letters will be provided (or posted) at the time of submission of the application. AFA application (and gazetted fees) should be submitted to the Division of Industrial Affairs, Ministry of commerce and Industry, Private Bag 004, Gaborone (Attention: Financial Assistance Policy) . Enquiries should also be routed through that address.

B. To apply for UFA, only a manufacturing licence, if required by the project. is needed in advance of application. Registration of a company is not a requirement of CFA, unlike AFA. The CPA application form is a lengthy one but it is not very complicated to complete. All that is needed by the applicant is patience and the same information any bank would require for assessing a loan application. Initial contact should be made with the relevant Ministry in Gaborone (i.e if an agricultural project. with the Ministry of Agriculture; if a mining project, with the Ministry of Mineral Resources and Water Affairs and if a commercial or industrial project. with the Ministry of Commerce and Industry) . Assistance in completing the forms can be obtained from BEDU. Rural Industries Promotions. Botswana Development Corporation. etc. Also most private consulting firms chartered accountants. banks, etc. are in a position to provide guidance for a fee. However, it is important to remember that the resnonsibility for accurate and complete preparation of an application rests ultimately with the applicant. Completed applications should be submitted to the relevant Ministry in Gaborone.

IX. I STILL HAVE QUESTIONS. WHAT DO I DO ?

If, so a potential investor, you still have questions, address enquiries to the relevant Ministry in Gaborone (Commerce and industry, Mineral Resources, or Agriculture) .

K. WHERE DO I GET APPLICATIONS ?

Application forms are obtainable from the Ministry of Finance and Development Planning, the Ministries listed in Question IX, Botswana Development Corporation. Commercial Banks, the National Development Bank, consulting firms, Government of Botswana missions overseas, Rural Industrial Officers in rural areas and Town Clerks in urban areas.

EXCHANGE CONTROL (DELEGATION OF POWERS) ORDER

(under regulation 36 (4))

(13th August, 1976)

ARRANGEMENT OF PARAGRAPHS

PARAGRAPH

1. Citation

2. Delegation of powers

Schedule

Citation

1. This Order may be cited as the Exchange Control (Delegation of Powers) Order.

Delegation of powers

2. All the powers vested in the Minister under the provisions of the Exchange Control Regulations are hereby delegated to the Bank of the Schedule, which are retained by the Minister.

SCHEDULE

regulation 2
regulation 4(5)
regulation 24(1)
regulation 25(2)
regulation 26(2)

regulation 27 and 28
regulation 36(6)

Fourth Schedule, Part I, paragraphs 1(1) and 2.

S.I. 112, 1976, S.I. 113, 1976 S.I. 114, 1976 S.I. 115, 1976 S.I. 92, 1985.

EXEMPTIONS (FROM CERTAIN PROVISIONS OF EXCHANGE CONTROL REGULATIONS) ORDER

(under regulation 32)

(13th August, 1976)

ARRANGEMENT OF PARAGRAPHS

PARAGRAPH

Citation

1. This Order may be cited as the Exemptions (From Certain Provisions of the Exchange Control Regulations) Order.

Interpretation

2. In this Order "regulation" means a regulation of the Exchange Control Regulations.

Landing money to banks, etc.

3. The restrictions imposed by regulation 31(4) on the lending of money shall not apply to the lending of any money or securities by any person resident in Botswana to any office or branch in Botswana of any bank or building society which is by any means controlled, whether directly or indirectly by persons resident outside Botswana.

Gold coins and manufactured gold

4. The provisions of regulations 3, 4 and 5 shall not apply in respect of gold coins and manufactured gold.

Bailees

5. Any banker is hereby exempted from the obligation imposed under regulation 5 to the extent that he shall not be required to notify the Bank of Botswana in any case where he is satisfied that the person for whom or by whose order gold or specified currency in the form of notes is held is not required, by virtue of regulation 4, to offer or cause to be offered that gold or specified currency for sale to an authorized dealer.

Temporary visitors

6. A person who is not resident in Botswana is exempted from the provisions of regulation 4.

Partial exemption

7. Residents of Botswana, including those designated as temporary residents, are hereby exempted from the provisions of regulation 4 up to an amount not exceeding the equivalent of P300 per person in foreign currency.

G.N 292, 1976, G.N. 292, 1976, S.I. 131, 1982, G.N. 288, 1984.

SUPPLEMENTS

MAJOR BANKS

Bank	Contact Address	Telephone
African Banking Corporation of Botswana Limited(trading as 'BancABC')	Private Bag 00303 Gaborone	367 4300
Bank Gaborone Limited	Private Bag 00325 Gaborone	367 1510
Bank of Baroda (Botswana) Limited	P O Box 21559 Bontleng Gaborone	318 8878
Bank of India (Botswana) Limited	Private Bag 00111, Gaborone	392 8513 761 23199
Barclays Bank of Botswana Limited	P O Box 478, Gaborone	391 4521
Capital Bank Limited	P O Box 5548, Gaborone	390 7801
First National Bank of Botswana Limited	P O Box 1552, Gaborone	364 2630
Stanbic Bank Botswana Limited	Private Bag 00168, Gaborone	361 8189
Standard Chartered Bank Botswana Limited	PO Box 496, Gaborone	355 2036
State Bank of India (Botswana) Limited	P O Box 505243, Gaborone	762 74380

CITY AND DISTRICT COUNCILS

GABORONE CITY COUNCIL

Ms. Agnes Serage
City Clerk
Civic Centre, Plot 330, Independence Avenue
Private Bag 0089, Gaborone, Botswana
Tel: +267 3953525, Fax: +267 3900141

FRANCISTOWN CITY COUNCIL

Mr. Kutlwano Matenge
City Clerk
Private Bag 0040
Francistown
Tel: +267 2412363

LOBATSE TOWN COUNCIL

Ms. Gabotlotlane Serage
Town Clerk
Private Bag 028
Lobatse
Tel: +267 5330241/5330392

SOWA TOWN COUNCIL

Mr. Charles Amos
Town Clerk
Private Bag SOW1
Sowa
Tel: +267 6213440

JWANENG TOWN COUNCIL

Mr. Leano Mokete/ Mr Odirile Mabaila
Town Clerk
Private Bag 001
Jwaneng
Tel: +267 5880306

SELIBE PHIKWE TOWN COUNCIL

Ms. Kagiso Molelo
Town Clerk
Private Bag 001
Selebi-Phikwe
Tel: +267 2615772

CENTRAL DISTRICT COUNCIL

Mr. Gaolatlhe Dipholo
Council Secretary
Private Bag 001
Serowe
Tel: +267 4637446

CHOBE DISTRICT COUNCIL

Council Secretary
Private Bag K30
Kasane
Tel: +267 6250896

GHANZI DISTRICT COUNCIL

Mr. Nelson Molepolole
Council Secretary
Private Bag 0015
Ghanzi
Tel: +267 6596211

KGATLENG DISTRICT COUNCIL

Ms. Kesentseng Kebabonye
Council Secretary
Private Bag 0011
Mochudi
Tel: +267 5748039

KWENENG DISTRICT COUNCIL

Mr. Waja Tema
Council Secretary
Private Bag 005
Molepolole
Tel: +267 5920201

KGALAGADI DISTRICT COUNCIL

Mr. Joshua. / I. Maluleke
Council Secretary
Private Bag 005
Tsabong
Tel: +267 6540061

NORTH WEST DISTRICT COUNCIL

Mr. Kwele Puso
Council Secretary
Private Bag 004
Masunga
Tel: +267 2489242

SOUTHERN DISTRICT COUNCIL

Mr. Dick Kalanke
Council Secretary
Private Bag 002
Kanye
Tel: +267 5440163

SOUTH EAST DISTRICT COUNCIL

Council Secretary
Private Bag 002
Ramotswa
Tel: +267 5381226/274

TAX OFFICES

MACCARTHY'S RUST

P/Bag 10,Tshabong
653 0056
653 0055

MIDDLEPITS

Bag M10,Tsabong
653 0060
653 0055

MAKOPONG

P.O.Box 164, Werda
653 0063
653 0064

BRAY

P.Box 103, Werda
6530068 /9

RAMATLABAMA

Border Post
P/Bag 001,Pitshane
540 7170/548 6296
548 6306

PIONEER

Border Gate
P.O.Box 211 ,Lobatse
533 3992 / 533 0382
Fax: 530 11 61

LOBATSE

South Regional Office
P O Box 263 Lobatse
(267) 533 0566
Fax: (267) 533 2477

RAMOTSWA

Border Post
P.O.Box V118 , Ramotswa
539 03 44
Fax: 539 0344

TLOKWENG

Border Post
P/Bag 00102,Gaborone
317 0800
Fax:393 1403

SIKWANE

Border Post
P.O.Box 54, Sikwane
570 0000
Fax: 577 8209

JWANENG

P O Box 5 Jwaneng
588 0695
588 3438

PHITSHANE MOLOPO

P.O.Box 32,
Phitshane Molopo
548 7204

BURS HEAD OFFICE

P/Bag 0013, Gaborone
3638000
3639999

GABORONE

Post office
P/bag 00102,Gaborone
390 1210

SERETSE KHAMA

Airport
P/Bag 00102,Gaborone
395 3022/ 364 3190
391 2506

MAHALAPYE

Central Regional Office
P O Box 240, Mahalapye
4710486
4710873

PALAPYE

Central Regional Office
P.O. Box 97, Palapye
4920388
4920784

MARTINS DRIFT

P.O.Box 100, Sherwood
491 5907 / 491 5913
491 5905

ZANZIBAR

P.O. Box 122, Tsetsebjwe
2646217/2630012
2630009

PLATJAN

Boarder Post
P.O.Box 129,S/Phikwe
264 6333
264 6375

POINT DRIFT

P.O.Box 129 S/Phikwe
264 5260
264 5354

MATSILOJE

Border Post
P.O.Box 93,Matsiloje
248 3275

FRANCISTOWN

Airport
P.O.Box 457,Francistown
241 2065
241 3114

FRANCISTOWN

North Regional Office
P/Bag 38, Francistown
(267) 2413635
2413114/2414267

RAMOKGWEBANA

Border Post
P.O.Box 1,Ramokgwebana
248 92 66
248 9286

SOWA AIRFIELD

P/Bag SOW 55,Sowa Town
621 3219
621 3219

MAUN

Airport
P.O.Box 219, Maun
686 0278
686 0194

KAZUNGULA FERRY

P.O.Box 41 , Kasane
6250420
6250192

MAITENGWE

P.O.Box 174 ,Maitengwe
248 3275

KASANE

Airport
P.O.Box 347,Kasane
625 0175

KAZUNGULA ROAD

P.O.Box 41 , Kasane
6250320 /6251303
6251315

PANDAMATENGA

P.O.Box 95,Kasane
623 2029

MOHEMBO

P.O.Box 197,Shakawe
687 5505
687 5524

MAMUNO

P.o.Box 69, Charles Hill
659 2013
659 2271

POINT DRIFT

P.O.Box 129 S/Phikwe

LIST OF CUSTOMS CLEARING AGENTS PER REGION
SOUTH CENTRAL REGION ACTIVE

NAME OF COMPANY	POSTAL ADDRESS	CONTACT PERSON	E-MAIL	FILE NUMBER	REGISTRATION NUMBER	BOND NO.	LICENSE NUMBER	O/R NNUMBER AND DATE
1.SDV(AMI) Botswana	Private Bag 172 Gaborone	Mrs Kwapa Tel no: 3951961	manager@sdv.co.bw	BURS/CE 5/197	BURS/CE E 01	2 of 2009	64 of 2012	R25115 dd 14.12.12
2.UTI	P.O. Box 726 Gaborone	Sheila Thekiso Tel no: 3913586	sthekiso@uti.co.bw	BURS/CE 5/177	BURS/CE E 06	5 of 2009	114/5 of 2012	R25867/9 dd 27.12.12
3.Manica Freight Services	P.O. Box 1372 Gaborone	Mmatshipi Motsepe Tel no: 3912677	manica@info.bw	BURS/CE 5/142	BURS/CE E 08	16 of 2009	94/95 of 2012	R25632/3 dd 21.12.12
4.Zebra Shipping	P.O. Box 502373 Gaborone	O.D. Makgane Tel no: 3923327	zshipping@botsnet.bw	BURS/CE 5/469	BURS/CE E 09	28 of 2009	5 & 79 of 2012	R21465 Dd 29.10.12 & R24959 dd 13.12.12
5.Royal Freight (Pty) Ltd	P.O. Box 60737 Broadhurst Gaborone	T.Gaelebale Tel no: 3938555	royalfreight@it.bw	BURS/CE 5/424	BURS/CE E 010	33 of 2009	135/6 of 2013	R462 dd 9.1.13
6.BMR Freight Services	Gaborone	Briston Rendo Tel no: 3165301	bmrfreight@mega.bw	BURS/CE 5/557	BURS/CE E 013	15 of 2009	71 & 73 of 2012	R25261 & R25223 dd 17 & 18.12.
7.Clakho Import & Export	P.O. Box 201281 Bontleng	Mrs Clara Dube	clakho@mega.bw	BURS/CE 5/566 A	BURS/CE E 014	3 of 2009	38 of 2012	R23639 dd 28.11/12

8.Moneylink (Pty) Ltd T/A Blue Freight Services	P.O .Box 1751 Gaborone			BURS/CE 5/622	BURS/CE E 015	1 of 2009		
9.Atlantis Clearing & Consultancy	P.O .Box 223 Mochudi	K. Keitumetse Cell: 71666942		BURS/CE 5/624	BURS/CE E 023	23 of 2008	124 of 2012	R25904 dd 28.12.12
10.Hotalot Operations (Pty) Ltd T/A Massyn Moves	P.O. Box 403968 Gaborone	Reuben Tsatsi Tel no: 3957049	reuben@massyn	BURS/CE 5/606	BURS/CE E 025	28 of 2008	40 of 2012	R23919 dd 30.11.12
11.DHL International (Botswana) Pty Ltd	P.O .Box 1077 Gaborone	Mr.Modise Tel no: 3912000	Modise.nengu@dhl.com	BURS/CE 5/605	BURS/CE E 027	32 of 2009	122 & 123 of 2012	R25904/5 dd 28.12.12
12.Hoya (Pty) Ltd	P.O .Box 2227 Gaborone	Andrew Chifedi Tel no: 3951281	hoya@it.bw	BURS/CE 5/587	BURS/CE E 028	37 of 2008	30 of 2012	R232 dd 23.1
13.Elliot Forwarding (Pty) Ltd	P.O Box 2044 Gaborone	Aubrey Bowles Tel no: 3912531	Aubrey.bowles@elliott.co.bw	BURS/CE 5/121	BURS/CE E 029	18 of 2009	88 of 2012	R25 dd 19.1
14.Bulk Freight (Pty) Ltd	P.O. Box 402126 Gabs	M.Ntuane Tel no: 3952192		BURS/CE 5/514	BURS/CE E 019	36 of 2009	134 of 13	R28 7.1.1
15.Imperilog Botswana (Pty) Ltd	P.O Box 10077 Gaborone	K.P. VijayaKumar Tel no: 3186556	imperilog@info.bw or vijaykp@imperilog.co.bw	BURS/CE 5/539	BURS/CE E 021	30 of 2008	50 & 51 of 2012	R24 dd 7.12.
16.Fraser's International (Botswana) (Pty) Ltd	P.O Box 201874 Bontleng Gaborone	Morobi Motswagole Tel no: 3922558	magdelines@agsfrasers.co.bw	BURS/CE 5/550	BURS/CE E 033	10 of 2009	103 of 2012	R25 dd 24.1
17.Phoenix Shipping (Pty) Ltd	Private Bag BR 211 Gaborone	A.R. Mackay Tel no: 3922222	intermodal@info.bw	BURS/CE 5/490	BURS/CE E 036	27 of 2009		
18.Nice Touch Investments	P.O Box 402299 Gaborone	B.S. Kebatlhotse Tel no: 3905954	nicetouch@botsnet.bw	BURS/CE 5/563	BURS/CE E 038	36 of 2008	10 of 2012	R21 dd 5.11.
19.Onketsang Investments T/A Thasi	P.O. Box 602290 Gaborone	M. Ntuane Tel no: 3952192		BURS/CE 5/611	BURS/CE E 039	20 of 2009	105 of 2012	R25 dd 24.1

Transport

20.Mogaka (Pty) Ltd T/A The Courier Junxion	Private Bag 00149/294 Gaborone Plot # 20634 B/Hurst	Batsile Ngwako Tel no: 3936111		BURS/CE 5/564	BURS/CE E 041	27 of 2008	118/9 of 2012	R258 dd 28
21.Jeffs Enterprises (Pty) Ltd	P.O. Box 50821 Gaborone	Jeffis Mpala Tel no:3938847	jeffmpala@yahoo.co.uk	BURS/CE 5/570	BURS/CE E 045	38 of 2008	125 of 2012	R259 28.12
22.Twinco (Pty) Ltd	P.O .Box 501718 Gaborone	Tel: 3104269 Fax: 3104269		BURS/CE 5/661	BURS/CE E 046	38 of 2009	56 & 57 of 2012	R246 R247 10/11
23.One Nation Freight	P.O Box 2997 Gaborone	Henry Wamumi Cell: 71521024/71926023	wamuwihenry@yahoo.com	BURS/CE 5/675	BURS/CE E078	52 of 2009	1 and 2 of 2012	R203 Dd 16.10
24.Tikule Marketing t/a Rite Freight Services	P.O Box 301884 Tlokweng	L.enah Mungale Tel no: 71394761	lenahmungale@yahoo.co.uk	BURS/CE 5/620	BURS/CE E 049	32 of 2008	15 & 16 of 2012	R224 dd 12
25.Vision 2010 Transport (Pty) Ltd	P.O.BOX 1571 GABORONE	Beauty B. Matale Tel:3974225		BURS/CE 5/639	BURS/CE E 053	20 of 2008	117 of 2012	R258 28.12
26.Towdar Co (Pty) Ltd, t/a Dolphine Freight Services	P.O. Box 1333, Mogoditshane	M. Motsumi		BURS/CE 5/600	BURS/CE E 057	4 of 2009	89 of 2012	R255 20.12
27.Clear Future (Pty) Ltd	P.O Box 1697 Mogoditshane	D. Ngakantsi		BURS/CE 5/652	BURS/CE E 060	26 of 2009		
28.Estamok Freight (Pty) Ltd	P.O.Box 746 Gaborone	Koketso Mogale Tel: 3188014		BURS/CE 5/642	BURS/CE E 061	24 of 2008	74 of 2012	R25 18.1
29.Rohlig Botswana	Box 1973 Gaborone	T. Mothei Tel: 3953505 Fax: 3953473	Lief.rohling@botsnet	BURS/CE 5/194	BURS/CE E 066	35 of 2008	91 & 93 of 2012	R25 R25 21.1
30.Pelican Moving Company (Pty) Ltd	P/Bag # 479 Kgale Postnet KgaleView	Gloria Kgalalelo Zhou	gloriaz@pelican.co.bw	BURS/CE 5/508	BURS/CE E069	10 of 2008	144 of 2013	R96 15.1
31.Beryl & Beryl (Pty) Ltd	P.O.Box 202587 Gaborone	Jacob Seiphemelo Tel: 72871162		BURS/CE 5/646	BURS/CE E070	29 of 2008	150 of 2012	R25 14.1
32.Magnum	P/Bag BR	Michael Grant	magnum@accelerate-it.co.bw	BURS/CE	BURS/CE	33 of	43 of	R23

Freight (Pty) Ltd	335 Gaborone	Tel: 3930782		5/522	E071	2008 201		
33.Advanced Computer System (Pty) Ltd T/A Digital Clearing House	P. O. Box 10077 Gaborone	K.P.Vijayakumar	vijaykp@global.bw	BURS/CE 5/654	BURS/CE EO72	21 of 48 o 2008 201		
34.Tops Operations (Pty) Ltd	P/Bag 502157 Gaborone	Galefele Opana Johannes	opanajohannes@yahoo.co.uk	BURS/CE 5/632	BURS/CE E 075	11 of 7 2008 and 8 of 201		
		Tel:5392805 Cell:716605075						
35.Pinnacle Express (Pty) Ltd	P.O.Box 403898 Gaborone	Manson Du Toit Tel: 3935537/89 Mobile: 71895024		BURS/CE 5/ 634	BURS/CE E 077	13 of 2008		
36.Express Link (PTY) LTD		Maitseo J. Makgowe				42 of 2009		
37. Express Cartage	P.O. Box 41008 Gaborone	M.P. Southwood Tel:3922801/392263	Express.cartege@botsnet.bw	BURS/CE 5/359	BURS/CE E02	43 of 2009		
38.One Nation Freight	P.O Box 2997 Gaborone	Henry Wamumi Cell: 71521024/71926023	wamuwihenry@yahoo.com	BURS/CE 5/675	BURS/CE E078	52 of 2009		
39.Consolidations Botswana	P.O. Box 231 Gaborone	Lucas Barreto Tel: 3908236	consol@global.bw	BURS/CE 5/519	BURS/CE E068			
40.Warehousing Services	P/Bag 00146 Gaborone	Modibedi Bonnie Tel: 3922815 Fax: 3922816/3972841		BURS/CE 5/671	BURS/CE E012	49 of 2009		
41.Speedway Freight	P/Bag 00229 Gaborone	Yami Chalira Tel: 3163271	speedway@botsnet.bw	BURS/CE 5/407	BURS/CE E04		107 of 2012	R25830 dd 24.12.12
42 TZ Freight Services (Pty) Ltd	P.O. Box 30509 Tlokweng	Tlhophego Zacharia		BURS/CE 5/619	BURS/CE E 035	58 of 2009	129 of 2012	R28845 dd 12.12.12
43. Kadi Freight Services	P.O.Box 201596 GABORONE	Dikeledi Sebapalo Cell; 71994221		BURS/CE 5/630	BURS/CE E081	61 of 2009	29 of 2012	R23227 dd 22.11.12
44. TriOptium	P. O. Box	Gillman	Michael@triopti.com	BURS/CE	BURS/CE	77 of	26 of	R22967

Logistics CC	2227 Gaborcne	Martin 3957281 3182383		5/ 692	E 94	2009	2012	dd 19.11.12	
45. All About Freight		Brian De Larosa				6 of 2010			
46. Dimotha Ivestments	P.O. Box 405533 B/Hurst Gaborone	Nalih Pontso	Dimotha@botsnet.bw	BURS/CE 5/583	BURS/CE E 052	5 of 2010	13 of 2012	R22098 dd 6.11.12	
47 Grandrish Investments	P.O. Box 2883 Gaborone	Thabo Thobogang Tel: 3901700 Cell: 71808996		BURS/CE 5/707	BURS/CE E 87	15 of 2010	45 of 2012	R22705 dd 14.11.12	
48 Bayusuf (PTY) LTD	P. O. Box 202083 Gaborone	George Nyakure TeL: 3857147 Cell: 71551744	gnyakure@yahoo.co.uk	BURS/CE 5/714	BURS/CE E 89	24 of 2010	4 of 2012	R20752 Dd 19.10.12	
49. Dexter Import and Export	P. o. Box 501089 Gaborone	Harrison mapipo		BURS/CE 5/719	BURS/CE E 91	29 of 2010	155 of 2013	R3326 dd 21.2.13	
50. Vin Kathy Freight Services	P. O. Box 20079 Gaborone	Vincent Phologolo Tel; 3182216 Cell;71447102	ii	BURS/CE 5/732	BURS/CE E 099	61 of 2010	39 of 2012	R23943 dd 30.11.12	
51. Rite Logistics (PTY) LTD	P. O. Box 404070 Gaborone	Tumo Malema Tel: Cell: 71217749		BURS/CE 5/741	BURS/CE E 101	22 of 2011	59 & 60 of 2012	R24965/7 Dd 13.12.12	Plot 20604, Blk 3 B/Husrt Unit 11-2 Oriental Plaza
52. Mex-Link Botswana	P. O. Box 11066 Gaborone	Mabedi Mogapi	mexlink@gmail.com	BURS/CE 5/731	BURS/CE E 103	36 of 2011	148 of 2013	R1189 dd 17.1.13	Plot no.17970 1st Floor Supa Veg Building Gaborone
53.Notch Above (PTY) LTD	P/Bag 129 Gaborone	Osia Jan Tel: 3917083 Fax: 3917064		BURS/CE 5/768	BURS/CE E 108	8 of 2012	104 of 2012	R25530 dd 20.12.12	Plot # 20604, Unit D11 Oriental Plaza Gaborone

54.New Deal Enterprise	P/Bag 00468 Gaborone	Boys Moilwa Tel: 3180284 Fax: 3184899	Newdeal@gmail.com	BURS/CE 5/769	BURS/CE E 109	10 of 2012			Fairgr Mall
55.Paccon Logistics Botswana	P.O.Box 402839 Gaborone	Lucas Barreto Tel:3908236 Fax:3900493		BURS/CE 5/767	BURS/CE E108	07 of 2012	61 & 62 of 2012	R25110/1 dd 14.12.12	Plot #20731,unit 6
56.Skyberry Botswana	P. O. Box 3318 Gabororne			BURS/CE 5/776	BURS/CE E111	15 of 2012	84/151 of 2012	R25509/R1532 dd 20.12.12/23.1.13	
57. Ram Transport						29 of 2012	22 &23 of 2012	R19708 dd 8.10.12 R23087 dd 21.11.12	
58. Spring Falls Holdings (PTY) LTD						35 of 2012	137/8 of 2013	R496/7 dd 9.1.13	
59. Sharpville (PTY) LTD						23 of 2012	83/162 of 2012	R24947 dd 13.12.12 & R3161 dd 19.2.13	

TOTAL: 59 (FIFTY NINE)

SOUTH REGION

ACTIVE

1.Rachel's Consultancy	P.O .Box 1195 Lobatse	Magosi Seope Tel no: 5334652 Cell:74159537	rachelpioneer@gmail.com	BURS/CE 5/657	BURS/CE E 016
2.Reliable Investments (Pty) Ltd	P.O.Box 10027 Ramotswa Station	B.L.Phiri Tel: 5390440 71448688		BURS/CE 5/ 633	BURS/CE E 076
3.Eveready Freight Services (Pty) Ltd	P.O .Box 658 Lobatse	Kentse O. Sesupo Tel: 2442171 Cell: 71606501		BURS/CE 5/573	BURS/CE E 040
4. Tikule Markerting (PTY) LTD	P.O. Box 301884 Tlokweng	Lenah Mungale Cell: 71394761		BURS/CE 5/620	
5. Hyper Transport t/a Hyper Clearing & Forwarding	P.O.Box 164 Molepolole	Goabaone Maikano Tel: 5487192 Cell: 71300424		BURS/CE 5/656	BURS/CE E059
6. Thoto Trading	P. O. Box 575 Lobatse	P. Kesaolpa 713673365	Kesaolopsthbe@gmail.com	BURS/CE 5/709	BURS/CE E 093

7. Kadi Freight Services	P.O.Box 201596 GABORONE	Dikeledi Sebapalo Cell; 71994221	rtt@botsnet.bw	BURS/CE 5/630	BURS/CE E081
8. Olorato Clearing	P. O. Box 10599 Lobatse	Lorato Bakgoeng 72948294 74614832	lolobakgoeng@yahoo.com	BURS/CE 5/727	BURS/CE E 95
9.J & T Clearing & Forwarding	P.O.Box 20256 Gaborone	Tom Magama Tel 71822473 Tel 2417241 Fax 2417240		BURS/CE 5/640	BURS/CE E 056
10.Tops Operations (Pty) Ltd	P/Bag 502157 Gaborone	Galefele Opana Johannes Tel:5392805 Cell:716605075	opanajohannes@yahoo.co.uk	BURS/CE 5/632	BURS/CE E 075
11.Pinnacle Express (Pty) Ltd	P.O.Box 403898 Gaborone	Manson Du Toit Tel: 3935537/89 Mobile: 71895024		BURS/CE 5/ 634	BURS/CE E 077
12.Mod – Mol Investments	P.o.Box AD71ABE Gaborone	Albert Dipatane Tel:3953847		BURS/CE 5/772	BURS/CE E110
13.TLK Clearing	P. O. Box 83 Pitsane	Never Lekgowe 5486300 71460019	Nlekgowe@yahoo.com	BURS/CE 5/777	BURS/CE E 112
14. Tasurfo Investments	P. O. Box 10670 Lobatse	Phillip Ohilwe		BURS/CE 5/77	BURS/CE E 115
15. Black Ice (PTY) LTD		Ramasala Ntwaetsile		BURS/CE 5/796	
16. Slimber Security (PTY) LTD	P/BAG 80 LOBATSE	Thatayaone Lesang Tele/Fax; 5330967 Cell; 72844583/72757417		BURS/CE 5/797	
17. Manica Botswana (PTY) LTD	P. O. BOX 1372 GABORONE	Mmatshipi Mptsepe			

TOTAL: 17 (SEVENTEEN)

NORTH REGION

ACTIVE

1.KYA Sands Transport	P.O .Box 10310 Tati Town Francistown	Paul Tel no: 2410626	kyasands@botsnet.bw	BURS/CE 5/650	BURS/CE E 032
2.Minetech (Pty) Ltd	P.O Box 10701 Francistown	W. Wheeler Tel no: 2412725	minetech@botsnet.bw	BURS/CE 5/651	BURS/CE E 030

3.Clearstory (Pty) Ltd	P.O. Box 420, Francistown	Evelyn Hlant Tel: 2419146		BURS/CE 5/617	BURS/CE E 058
4. Manica Freight Services	P.O. Box 1372 Francistown	Mmatshipi Motsepe Tel: 3912677	manica@info.bw	BURS/CE 5/142	BURS/CE E 08
5.J & T Clearing & Forwarding (Francistown)	P.O.Box 20256 Gaborone	Tom Magama Tel 71822473 Tel 2417241 Fax 2417240		BURS/CE 5/640	BURS/CE E 056
6.Eveready Freight Services (Pty) Ltd	P.O .Box 30504 Francistown	K. Teko Teko		BURS/CE 5/573	BURS/CE E 040
7. Nine One One (PTY) LTD (Ramokgwebana)	P.O. Box 501464 Gaborone	Rebana Mmereki Tel: 3956924/5		BURS/CE 5/572	BURS/CE E 063
8.Unitrans Botswana					
9.J & T Clearing & Forwarding (Ramokgwebana)	P.O.Box 20256 Gaborone	Tom Magama Tel 71822473 Tel 2417241 Fax 2417240		BURS/CE 5/640	BURS/CE E 056

10.J & T Clearing & Forwarding (Matsiloje)	P.O.Box 20256 Gaborone	Tom Magama Tel 71822473 Tel 2417241 Fax 2417240	BURS/CE 5/640	BURS/CE E 056	22 of 2008	36 of 2012	R8654 dd 13.11.12
11. Nine One One (PTY) LTD (Matsiloje)	P.O. Box 501464 Gaborone	Rebana Mmereki Tel: 3956924/5	BURS/CE 5/572	BURS/CE E 063	16 of 2010		

TOTAL: 11 (eleven)

ACTIVE

1.Calida Freight Services	P.O. Box 111 Kasane	Alice Sibanda		BURS/CE 5/	BURS/CE E 024	23 of 2009	81 of 2012	R27052 dd 13.12.12
2.Intertrans Commodities	P.O.Box 616 Kasane	J. Taylor Tel: 6250188/9 Fax: 6250189	ic@botsnet.bw	BURS/CE 5/585	BURS/CE E 055	39 of 2009	166 of 2013	R6438 of 12.4.13

3.Gorata Enterprises (PTY) LTD	P.O. Box 587 Kasane	Willie Miti Mobile:71801117		BURS/CE 5/666	BURS/CE E 047	41 of 2009	82 of 2012	R26613 dd 13.12.12
4. Sishasi Enterprises	P.O. Box 703 Kasane	Peter Sinvula Chika Cell: 71131689		BURS/CE 5/676	BURS/CE E 079	53 of 2009	80 of 2012	R25438 dd 23.11.12
5. First Tours (PTY) LTD	P.O. Box 20909	Pontsho Tirelo Cell: 71445010		BURS/CE 5/690	BURS/CE E O84	72 of 2009		

(Kazungula ferry)	Maun	74286366			
6. First Tours (PTY) LTD (Maun)	P.O. Box 20909 Maun	Pontsho Tirelo Cell: 71445010 74286366		BURS/CE 5/690	BURS/CE E O84
7. SDV Botswana (Kazungula Ferry)	P/Bag 172 Gaborone	Gareth Hugh Lendrum		BURS/CE 5/197	BURS/CE E 01
8. Manica Botswana	Box 1372 Gaborone	Mmatshipi Motsepe			
9.SDV(AMI) Botswana (Mamuno)	Private Bag 172 Gaborone	Mrs Kwapa Tel no: 3951961	manager@sdv.co.bw	BURS/CE 5/197	BURS/CE E 01
10. Daniella Investments (Mamuno Border)	P.O.BOX 130 Serule	Kesebonye Nshatha Tel: 71637643	knshatha@yahoo.com	BURS/CE 5/687	BURS/CE E 083
11. Olorato Clearing (Mamuno Border)	P. O. Box 10599 Lobatse	Lorato Bakgoeng 72948294 74614832	lolobakgoeng@yahoo. com	BURS/CE 5/727	BURS/CE E 95
12. First Tours (PTY) LTD (Mamuno Border)	P.O. Box 20909 Maun	Pontsho Tirelo Cell: 71445010 74286366		BURS/CE 5/690	BURS/CE E O84
13. Twinco (PTY) LTD (Mamuno Border)					
14. Keaz Investments					
15. Mega Solutions					

TOTAL: 15 (FIFTEEN)

CENTRAL REGION

ACTIVE

1.Dimotha Investments (Palapye office)	P.O Box 871 Selebi Phikwe	Nalih Kebadiretse		BURS/CE 5/583	BURS/CE E 052
2.Dimotha Investment (Selebi Phikwe office)	P.O Box 871 Selebi Phikwe	Nalih Kebadiretse		BURS/CE 5/583	BURS/CE E 052
3.Dianella Investments (Martins drift office)	P.O.BOX 130 Serule	Kesebonye Nshatha Tel: 71637643	knshatha@yahoo.com	BURS/CE 5/687	BURS/CE E 083
4. Darwin (PTY) LTD					
5. Onketsang Investments T/A Thasi Transport (Martins drift Office)	P.O. Box 602290 Gaborone	M. Ntuane Tel no: 3952192		BURS/CE 5/611	BURS/CE E 039
6. BMR Freight Services (Martins drift office)	Gaborone	Briston Rendo Tel no: 3165301	bmrfreight@mega.bw	BURS/CE 5/557	BURS/CE E 013
7.Dimotha Investment (Martins drift Office)	P.O Box 871 Selebi Phikwe	Nalih Kebadiretse		BURS/CE 5/583	BURS/CE E 052
8. Repeat Investment (Martins drift Office)					
9. Micronet Innovative Technology (Pty) Ltd (Martins drift Office)	P.O.Box 26552 Gaborone	Prince Michael Danda Tel: 71328971	globaldays@yahoo.com	BURS/CE 5/637	BURS/CE E 051
10.Imperilog Botswana (Pty) Ltd (Martins drift Office)	P.O Box 10077 Gaborone	K.P. VijayaKumar Tel no: 3186556	imperilog@info.bw or vijaykp@imperilog.co .bw	BURS/CE 5/539	BURS/CE E 021
11.Manica Freight Services	P.O. Box 1372 Gaborone	Mmatshipi Motsepe Tel	manica@info.bw	BURS/CE 5/142	BURS/CE E 08

(Martins drift office)		no:3912677			
12.SDV(AMI) Botswana (Martins drift)	Private Bag 172 Gabcrone	Mrs Kwapa Tel no: 3951961	manager@sdv.co.bw	BURS/CE 5/197	BURS/CE E 01
13.One Stop Clearing and Forwarding (M/Drift)	P. O. Box 402282 Gaborone Martins Drift Border Post	Kagiso Bogatsu Cell: 74127107		BURS/CE 5/753	BURS/CE E 105
14.Speedway Freight (Palapye)	P/Bag 00229 Gaborone	Yami Chalira Tel: 3163271	speedway@botsnet.bw	BURS/CE 5/407	BURS/CE E04
15. New Deal Enterprises					

TOTAL: 16 (SIXTEENTEEN)

TLOKWENG REGION

ACTIVE

1.Magnum Freight (Pty) Ltd	P/Bag BR 335 Gaborone	Michael Grant Tel: 3930782	magnum@accelerate-it.co.bw	BURS/CE 5/522	BURS/CE E071
2.Imperilog Botswana (Pty) Ltd	P.O Box 10077 Gaborone	K.P. VijayaKumar Tel no: 3186556	imperilog@info.bw or vijaykp@imperilog.co.bw	BURS/CE 5/539	BURS/CE E 021
3.SDV Botswana	P/Bag 172 Gaborone	Gareth Hugh Lendrum		BURS/CE 5/197	BURS/CE E 01
4.Advanced Computer System (Pty) Ltd T/A Digital Clearing House	P. O. Box 10077 Gaborone	K.P.Vijayakumar	vijaykp@global.bw	BURS/CE 5/654	BURS/CE EO72
5.Profreight Express (Pty) Ltd	P.O.Box 80944 Gaborone	Gillian Rizzo Tel no: 3901535	Gillian@vbnservice.net	BURS/CE 5/618	BURS/CE E 026
6.Estamok Freight (Pty) Ltd	P.O.Box 746 Gaborone	Koketso Mogale Tel: 3188014		BURS/CE 5/642	BURS/CE E 061
7.KTU Express Pty Ltd	P.O. Box 502465 Gaborone	Ndiye Smith Tel;3913331 Cell;72608965	smithktundiye@yahoo.co.uk	BURS/CE 5/730	BURS/CE E 098
8.Multi Phase Investments	P. O. Box 3902326 Gaborone	Alfred Moatlhaping Tel:3903326 Cell:72766210	admoatlhaping@bns.co.bw	BURS/CE 5/722	BURS/CE E092
9.Hoya	P.O .Box	Andrew Chifedi Tel	hoya@it.bw	BURS/CE	BURS/CE

(Pty) Ltd	2227 Gaborone	no: 3951281		5/587	E 028
10.Bayusuf (PTY) LTD	P. O. Box 202083 Gaborone	George Nyakure TeL: 3857147 Cell: 71551744	gnyakure@yahoo.co.uk	BURS/CE 5/714	BURS/CE E 89
11.Kadi Freight Services	P.O.Box 201596 GABORONE	Dikeledi Sebapalo Cell; 71994221	rtt@botsnet.bw	BURS/CE 5/630	BURS/CE E081
12.Hotalot Operations (Pty) Ltd T/A Massyn Moves	P.O. Box 403968 Gaborone	Reuben Tsatsi Tel no: 3957049	reuben@massyn	BURS/CE 5/606	BURS/CE E 025
13.Express Cartage	P.O. Box 41008 Gaborone	M.P. Southwood Tel:3922801/392263	Express.cartege@botsnet.bw	BURS/CE 5/359	BURS/CE E02
14.Mogaka (Pty) Ltd T/A The Courier Junxion	Private Bag 00149/294 Gaborone Plot # 20684 B/Hurst	Batsile Ngwako Tel no: 3936111		BURS/CE 5/564	BURS/CE E 041
15.Rohlig Botswana	Box 1973 Gaborone	T. Mothei Tel: 3953505 Fax: 3953473	Lief.rohling@botsnet	BURS/CE 5/194	BURS/CE E 066
16.Nice Touch Investments	P.O Box 402299 Gaborone	B.S. Kebatlhotse Tel no: 3905954	nicetouch@botsnet.bw	BURS/CE 5/563	BURS/CE E 038
17.Pinnacle Express (Pty) Ltd	P.O.Box 403898 Gaborone	Manson Du Toit Tel: 3935537/89 Mobile: 71895024		BURS/CE 5/ 634	BURS/CE E 077
18.KYA Sands Transport	P.O .Box 10310 Tati Town Francistown	Paul Tel no: 2410626	kyasands@botsnet.bw	BURS/CE 5/650	BURS/CE E 032
19.Perfect Horizon (Pty) Ltd	P.O.Box 45263 Gaborone			BURS/CE 5/645	BURS/CE E 067
20. Frontline Investments	P/Bag BO 242 Gaborone	Baokgethetse Mathe	Frontline courier@info.bw	BURS/CE 5/629	BURS/CE E034
21.Fraser's International (Botswana) (Pty) Ltd	P.O Box 201874 Bontleng Gaborone	Morobi Motswagole Tel no: 3922558	magdelines@agsfrasers.co.bw	BURS/CE 5/550	BURS/CE E 033
22.Manica Freight Services	P.O. Box 1372 Gaborone	Mmatshipi Motsepe Tel no: 3912677	manica@info.bw	BURS/CE 5/142	BURS/CE E 08
23.Dynamic	P.O.BOX	Tel: 3161565		BURS/CE	BURS/CE

Road Services	201113 Gaborone	Fax: 3937264		5/643	E 064
24.Ron Holdings (Pty) Ltd	P.O.Box 301201 Tlokweng	Tebogo Lizzy Bogatsu 3939856/3913586	Tebby bogatsu@Ronholdings.co.bw	BURS/CE 5/635	BURS/CE E073
25.GMR Freight	P.O. Box 1444 Gaborone	Kuli. Tel no: 3952484	gmr@infor.bw	BURS/CE 5/528	BURS/CE E 07
26.Consolidations Botswana	P.O. Box 231 Gaborone	Lucas Barreto Tel: 3908236	consol@global.bw	BURS/CE 5/519	BURS/CE E068
27. Jays Couriers	Plot 4790 Electron House, Gaborone	Jane Kome			
28. Tops Operations (Pty) Ltd	P/Bag 502157 Gaborone	Galefele Opana Johannes Tel:5392805 Cell:716605075	opanajohannes@yahoo.co.uk	BURS/CE 5/632	BURS/CE E 075
29. Zebra Shipping	P.O. Box 502373 Gaborone	O.D. Makgane Tel no: 3923327	zshipping@botsnet.bw	BURS/CE 5/469	BURS/CE E 09
30. DHL International (Botswana) Pty Ltd	P.O .Box 1077 Gaborone	Mr.Modise Tel no: 3912000	Modise.nengu@dh l.com	BURS/CE 5/605	BURS/CE E 027
31.Nine One One (Pty) Ltd	P.O .Box 501464 Gaborone	Rebana Mmereki Tel no: 3956924/5		BURS/CE 5/572	BURS/CE E 063
32. Sprint Couriers		Neo Mmoni Burton			
33. Uti Botswana	P.O. Box 726 Gaborone	Sheila Thekiso Tel no: 3913586	sthekiso@uti.co.bw	BURS/CE 5/177	BURS/CE E 06
34.Mulbridge (Pty) Ltd	P.O. Box 20954 Maun	Delon Van Zyl Tel no: 660636 Fax: 6861113	mulbridge@botsnet.bw	BURS/CE 5/648	BURS/CE E 018
35. Road Transportation Team	Private Bag 351 Gaborone	John Mcpartland 72704487 3930094	rtt@botsnet.bw	BURS/CE 5/686	BURS/CE E 082
36. Multimex (PTY) LTD	P. O. Box 47139 Gaborone	Tshokolo Mmereki Tel: 319139 Cell: 71602566		BURS/CE 5/755	BURS/CE E 105
37. TriOptium Logistics CC	P. O. Box 2227 Gaborone	Gillman Martin 3957281 3182383	Michael@triopti.com	BURS/CE 5/ 692	BURS/CE E 94
38. BMR	P.O. Box	Mohamed Arbi	Bmr_arbi@yahoo.co.uk	BURS/CE	BURS/CE

Agents	999 Gaborone	Tel: 3102217/21		5/677	E031
39.Jeffs Enterprises (Pty) Ltd	P.O. Box 50821 Gaborone	Jeffis Mpala Tel no:3938847	jeffmpala@yahoo.co.uk	BURS/CE 5/570	BURS/CE E 045
40. Minestone Freight		Mr. Richard Tsedi Tel: 3482888/3908333 Cell: 74649677/72113116	Richard@orangemail.co.bw	BURS/CE 5/734	BURS/CE E 100
41. K. K. Square Clearing	P. O. Box 40016 Gaborone	Kaone Kgabung Tel: 3165237 Cell: 74065355	kkgabung@gmail.com	BURS/CE 5/718	BURS/CE E 90
42. KTU Express Pty Ltd	P.O. Box 502465 Gaborone	Ndiye Smith Tel;3913331 Cell;72608965	smithktundiye@yahoo.co.uk	BURS/CE 5/730	BURS/CE E 098
43.Perfect Horizon (Pty) Ltd	P.O.Box 45263 Gaborone			BURS/CE 5/645	BURS/CE E 067
44.Express Link	P.O. Box 202031 Gaborone	Maitseo Makgowe Tel no: 3926997		BURS/CE 5/683	BURS/CE E 050
45. J-KGB Sealand Dealers (PTY) LTD	P.O. Box 50310 Gaborone	T.M. Johwa		BURS/CE 5/673	BURS/CE E 107
46. Hotland (PTY) LTD	P. O. Box 601269 Gaborone	O. W. Thabano. Tel: 3930034	wetoth2004@yahoo.co.uk	BURS/CE 5/750	BURS/CE E 104
47. Ram Transport (Botswana) LTD					
48. Trust Link (PTY) LTD					
49. Mild and Neat (PTY) LTD					
50. Tikule Mrketing					
51. Freight Partners					
52. THB					

TOTAL: 52 (FIFTY TWO)

LIST OF APPROVED SUPERANNUATION FUNDS

	NAME	REF. NO	APPROVED
2	Debswana Pension Fund	IPE 028	10/1/1984
3	Edgar's Pension Fund (Botswana)	IPE 029	7/1/1990
4	Barclays Bank of Botswana Ltd. Staff Pension Fund	IPE 051	10/1/1979
5	Shell Oil Botswana (Pty) Ltd Pension Fund	IPE 060	1/1/1990
6	Botswana Cap and Helmet Man (Pty) Ltd Pension Fund	IPE 093	7/1/1989
7	Standard Chartered Bank (Botswana) Pension Fund	IPE 103	4/1/1975
8	Deloitte and Touche Pension Fund	IPE 110	3/1/1982
9	Botswana cooperative Union Pension Fund	IPE 122	3/1/1980
10	Falcon Bridge Explorations Botswana Pension Fund	IPE 132	1/1/1981
11	Martex Investements (Pty) Ltd Pension Fund	IPE 133	3/1/1980
12	Pep Stores Botswana Pension Fund	IPE 135	9/1/1982
13	ICL Pension Fund	IPE 137	9/1/1990
14	Metro Cash & Carry Botswana (Pty) Ltd Pension Fund	IPE 139	11/1/1984
15	Botswana Cooperative Bank Ltd Pension Fund	IPE 140	1/1/1984
16	J. Haskins (Pty) Ltd Group Pension & Live Assurance Scheme	IPE 141	7/1/1984
17	I.G.I. Botswana Limited Pension Fund	IPE 142	12/1/1986
18	National Development Bank Staff Pension Fund	IPE 143	10/1/1993
19	BP Botswana (PTY) Pension Fund	IPE 147	1/1/1990
20	Ellerines Furnishers (Botswana) Staff Pension Fund	IPE 148	9/1/1990
21	Botswana Diamond Valuation Company Pension Fund	IPE 150	6/1/1986
22	Coopers and Lybrand Pension Fund	IPE 151	3/1/1986
23	Manica Freight Services Botswana (Pty) Ltd Pension & Group Life Scheme	IPE 152	3/1/1987
24	Botswana Housing Corporation Staff Pension Fund	IPE 153	1/1/1985
25	Botswana Power Corporation Staff Pension Fund	IPE 154	01/04/198*
26	Colgate Palmolive Pension Fund	IPE 155	2/1/1990
27	Tati Company Pension Fund	IPE 156	7/1/1986
28	Botswana Eagle Pension Fund	IPE 157	1/1/1990
29	Kettex Botswana (Pty) Ltd	IPE 158	7/1/1987
30	Botswana Liquor Manufacturer Pension Fund	IPE 159	1/1/1988
31	Botswana Telecommunications Corporations Staff Pension Fund	IPE 160	4/1/1989
32	Avis Pension Fund	IPE 161	7/1/1989
33	Botswana Christian Council Pension Fund	IPE 162	6/1/1990
34	Frasers Pension Fund	IPE 163	9/28/1998
35	Botswana Agricultural Marketing Board Pension Fund	IPE 164	9/28/1998
36	CAPS (Botswana) Pension Fund	IPE 165	10/1/1987
37	Botswana Technology Centre Pension Fund	IPE 166	6/1/1989
38	Botswana Vaccine Institute Pension fund	IPE 167	9/28/1998
39	Apostolic Faith Mission of Africa Pension Fund	IPE 168	6/1/1989

40	Botswana Medical Society Pension Fund	IPE 169	1/1/1987
41	Steward Scott NCL Pension Fund	IPE 170	9/1/1990
42	Boswe Construction (PTY) Ltd. Pension Fund	IPE 171	9/1/1987
43	PG Industries Botswana Pension Fund	IPE 172	4/1/1987
44	Glens (Pty) Ltd Pension Fund	IPE 173	2/1/1988
45	Air Botswana Pension Fund	IPE 174	6/1/1988
46	Botswana Railways Staff Pension fund	IPE 175	4/1/1990
47	Protea Furnishers (Pty) Ltd Pension Fund	IPE 176	6/1/1989
48	Kerry Trading Company (Pty) Ltd Pension Fund	IPE 177	1/1/1990
49	First Paper House Botswana Pension Fund	IPE 178	3/1/1991
50	Shashe Mines Pension Fund	IPE 179	1/1/1988
51	Botswana Development Corporation Pension Fund	IPE 180	1/1/1988
52	Botswana Livestock Development Corp. Pension Fund	IPE 181	9/28/1998
53	Water Utilities Corporation Pension Fund	IPE 182	9/28/1998
54	Botswana Insurance Pension Fund	IPE 183	9/23/1998
55	PG Pension Fund	IPE 184	4/1/1990
56	Dulux Pension Fund	IPE 185	2/1/1986
57	Sentlhaga Pension Fund	IPE 186	9/28/1998
58	Botswana Building Society Pension Fund	IPE 187	2/1/1987
59	Bank of Botswana Staff Pension Fund	IPE 188	10/1/1998
60	Caltex Botswana Pension Fund	IPE 189	01/01/199*
61	Univerisity of Botswana Staff Pension Fund	IPE 190	7/1/1989
62	Rusfurn Group Pension Fund	IPE 191	01/07/199*
63	Dutch Reformed Church of Northern Cape Pension Fund	IPE 192	7/1/1988
64	Cashbuild Botswana (PTY) Ltd Pension Fund	IPE 193	7/1/1992
65	Tyre Services Retirement Fund	IPE 196	7/1/1994
66	Tswana Technical Consultancy Services Pension Fund	IPE 197	3/1/1994
67	Total (Botswana) Pension Fund	IPE 198	7/1/1994
68	Evangelical Lutheran Church Pension Fund	IPE 199	7/1/1994
69	Botswana Managed Retirement Fund	IPE 200	11/1/2001
70	Botswana Citizen Pension Fund	IPE 206	7/1/1987
71	New Defined Contributions Sefalana Pension Fund	IPE 207	4/1/1986
72	B.G.I Trading Company (Pty) Ltd Pension Plus Plan	IPE 208	12/1/1987
73	Francistown Milling & Trading Com. (Pty) Ltd Pension Plus	IPE 210	10/1/1988
74	Everest Mills (Pty) Ltd. Group Comp. Pension Plus Plan	IPE 211	4/1/1988
75	Nza Associated Pension Plus Plan	IPE 213	1/1/1989
76	Puthadikobo Museum Pension Fund	IPE 214	4/1/1989
77	Fridgeco (Botswana)(Pty) Ltd (Gaborone) Pension Plus Plan	IPE 216	9/1/1987
78	B.G.I. Limited Plus Plan	IPE 217	11/1/1988
79	Wholesale Centre (Pty) Ltd Pension Plus Plan	IPE 218	7/1/1988
80	Botswana Furniture Manufacturers Pension Plus Plan	IPE 220	1/1/1989
81	Fridgeco (Botswana) (Pty) Ltd (F/Town) Pension Plus Plan	IPE 221	4/1/1988
82	Sedgewich Insuarance Brokers Pension Fund	IPE 223	1/1/1994

83	Institute of Development Management Pension Fund	IPE 225	10/1/1994
84	Mompati Retirement Annuity Fund	IPE 228	7/1/1996
85	Information Trust Company Pension Fund	IPE 229	1/1/1994
86	Botswana National Productivity Centre Pension Fund	IPE 231	11/14/1995
87	Multi Construction Building & Engineering Pension Fund	IPE 232	1/1/1996
88	Kentz Botswana Pension Fund	IPE 233	1/1/1996
89	Transet Limited Pension Fund	IPE 234	10/1/1996
90	Cempak (Botswana) (PTY) Ltd Pension Fund	IPE 235	7/1/1995
91	Botswana College of Agriculture Pension Fund	IPE 237	4/1/1995
92	Metropolitan Staff Pension Fund	IPE 238	2/1/1997
93	Metropolitan Life of Botswana Retirement Annuity Fund	IPE 239	2/1/1997
94	Ntlo Pension Fund	IPE 240	2/1/1997
95	Ntlo Provident Fund	IPE 241	01/02/199*
96	Compass Botswana (Pty) Ltd	IPE 242	4/1/1997
97	Botswana Craft Marketing Pension Fund	IPE 243	4/1/1997
98	Earnest & Young Pension Fund	IPE 244	10/1/1997
99	Gaborone Private Hospital Pension Fund	IPE 245	10/1/1997
100	Botswana Telecommunications Authority Pension Fund	IPE 246	6/1/1997
101	Prehold (Botswana) Pension Fund	IPE 247	1/1/1996
102	Millennium Botswana Insurance Pension Fund	IPE 248	8/1/1997
103	The Tosas (Botswana) Pension Fund	IPE 249	7/1/1997
104	Peermont Global Botswana Pension Fund	IPE 250	7/1/1997
105	RIPCO (Botswana) Pension Fund	IPE 251	7/1/1998
106	Botswana Savings Bank Staff Pension Fund	IPE 252	4/1/1994
107	JD Group (Botswana) Defined Contribution Pension Fund	IPE 253	10/1/1996
108	Engen Botswana Retirement Fund	IPE 254	11/1/1995
109	Old Mutual Group Staff Pension Fund	IPE 255	4/1/1998
110	Breweries Pension Fund	IPE 256	10/1/1998
111	Deferred Pensioners Pension Fund	IPE 257	2/1/1999
112	Score Supermarkets Botswana Retirement Pension Plan	IPE 258	7/1/1999
113	Bank of Botswana Defined Contribution Staff Pension Fund	IPE 259	10/1/1998
114	Global Holdings (Botswana) Pension Fund	IPE 260	7/1/1999
115	Mascom Wireless Pension Fund	IPE 264	9/1/1999
116	Builders Merchants Botswana Retirement Fund	IPE 265	12/1/1999
117	Logical Botswana Retirement Fund	IPE 266	12/1/1999
118	Stanbic Bank Pension Fund	IPE 267	7/1/1999
119	The MacMillian (Botswana) Pension Fund	IPE 269	5/15/2000
120	AIB Umbrella Pension Fund	IPE 270	7/1/2000
121	Metsef Pension Fund	IPE 271	10/1/1999
122	Free Standing Additional Voluntary Contribution Retirement	IPE 272	7/1/2000
123	CCB Benefit Fund Rules	IPE 273	1/1/1997
124	Construction Industry Trust Fund	IPE 275	12/15/2000
125	Botswana Public Officers	IPE 276	2/8/2000

126	Retirement Plan for FSN	IPE 277	3/6/1994
127	Fedics Botswana	IPE 279	11/1/2000
128	Barlow and B and B Retirement Fund Rules	IPE 280	10/1/2003
129	Air Botswana Pension Fund Rules	IPE 281	7/1/2000
130	Profurn (Botswana) Pension Fund	IPE 282	6/1/1989
131	Apex Pension Fund Rules	IPE 283	7/1/2001
132	Motor Vehicle Accident Pension Fund	IPE 284	9/1/1999
133	Alexander Forbes Retirement Fund	IPE 285	7/1/2001
134	Botswana Dev. Cor. Ltd Contributory Staff Pension Fund Rules	IPE 286	3/1/2001
135	Botswana Insurance Fund Man. & Glenrand M.I.B. Ltd (BIFM)	IPE 287	9/28/1988
136	National Food Technology Research Centre Pension Fund	IPE 288	5/1/1999
137	Bolux Group (Pty) Ltd Pension Fund	IPE 289	2/1/2002
138	Botsalo Books Staff Pension Fund	IPE 290	1/1/1994
139	Orange Botswana	IPE 291	5/1/2003
140	Deabocha Investments Pension Fund	IPE 292	2/1/2004
141	New Defined Contributions Sefalana Pension Fund	IPE 293	4/1/2004
142	Botswana Building Society Defined Contribution Fund	IPE 294	4/1/2004
143	Morevest (Botswana) Retirement Fund	IPE 295	12/1/2004
144	Omega Umbrella	IPE 296	6/1/2005
145	Hollard Insurance Botswana Pension Fund	IPE 297	10/1/2005
146	Botswana College of Agriculture Defined Contribution Pension Fund	IPE 299	1/30/2006
147	Khimo Property Asset Management Pension Fund	IPE 300	
148	Botswana Unified Revenue Service Employees Pension Fund	IPE 301	9/1/2006
149	Union Provident Fund Trust in Botswana (Pty) Ltd	IPE 302	7/1/2006
150	Marsh Botswana Pension Fund	IPE 304	
151	Motswere Retirement Fund Rules	IPE 305	
152	Local Enterprises Authority Pension Fund	IPE 306	6/13/2008
153	Citizen Entrepreneurial Development Agency Staff Pension Fund (CEDA)	IPE 307	6/13/2008
154	Botswana Public Employees Union – BOPEU	IPE 308	6/13/2008
155	Majwana Umbrella Pension Fund	IPE 309	
156	Glenrand M.I.B. Orphans Fund	IPE 310	6/1/2008
157	H & A Cutting Works Botswana	IPE 311	8/1/2008
158	Diamonex Botswana Ltd	IPE 312	
159	Capital Bank Ltd	IPE 313	4/1/2008
160	Africa Fifty Three Provident Fund	IPE 314	11/1/2008
161	Botswana Examination Council Pension Fund	IPE 315	2/1/2009
162	AON Botswana Defined Contribution Pension Fund	IPE 316	
163	Botswana Insurance Holdings Pension Fund	IPE 317	
164	AON Botswana Preservation Pension Fund	IPE 318	9/28/1988
165	Lobatse Clay Works Pension Fund	IPE 319	
166	LSC Botswana Pension Fund	IPE 320	
167	Master Farmer (Botswana) Ltd Pension Fund	IPE 321	6/17/2009

168	BIHL Defined Contribution Retirement Fund	IPE 322	6/17/2009
169	G4S Security services Botswana Pension Fund	IPE 323	7/1/2009
170	Centre for Development of Enterprise (PTY) Ltd Pension Fund	IPE 324	9/28/2009
171	Pick n Pay Botswana Staff Pension Fund	IPE 325	11/24/2009
172	Fincraft Retirement Fund	IPE 326	12/8/2009
173	Alredodor Enterprises Staff Pension Fund	IPE 327	12/14/2009
174	Scales Associates Staff Pension Fund	IPE 328	1/6/2010
175	Botswana Bureau of Standards Pension Fund	IPE 329	2/9/2010
176	NBL (Botswana) Staff Pension Fund	IPE 330	3/3/2010
177	Discovery Metals Limited and Subsidiaries in Botswana Staff Pension Fund	IPE 331	3/15/2010
178	Botswana Accountancy College Staff Pension Fund	IPE 332	3/15/2010
179	Choppies Distribution Centre (Pty) Ltd Staff Pension Fund	IPE 333	3/15/2010
180	Orthosurge Botswana (Pty) Ltd Staff Pension Fund	IPE 334	3/23/2010
181	Prefhold (Botswana) Staff Pension Fund	IPE 335	3/23/2010
182	Ellerines (Botswana) Staff Pension Fund	IPE 336	3/23/2010
183	Stobech Facilities Management (Pty) Ltd Staff Pension Fund	IPE 337	3/23/2010
184	William Lee(Botswana) Pension Fund	IPE 338	3/23/2010
185	Kingdom Bank Africa Limited	IPE 339	23/03/2010
186	Trident Holdings (Pty) Ltd Staff Pension Fund	IPE 340	3/23/2010
187	St Joseph's Mission Clinic	IPE 341	5/12/2010
188	Grant Thornton Staff Pension Fund	IPE 342	6/3/2010
189	Golder Associates Botswana (Pty) Ltd	IPE 343	8/24/2010
190	Union Provident Trust (Pty) Ltd	IPE 344	8/24/2010
191	Alexander Forbes Individual Member Retirement Fund	IPE 345	10/8/2010
192	Metropolitan Staff Retirement Fund	IPE 346	
193	Sefalana Group Staff Pension Fund	IPE 347	10/1/2010
194	BCL Staff Pension Fund	IPE 348	6/1/2011
195	Civil Aviation Authority of Botswana Staff Pension Fund	IPE 349	3/1/2011
196	Akani Botswana Umbrella Benefeciary Fund	IPE 350	7/1/2011
197	Botswana Post Pension Fund	IPE 351	11/1/1991
198	Bokamoso Private Hospital Staff Pension Fund	IPE 352	
199	Botswana College Of Distance Open Learning	IPE 353	
200	BOTUSAFE Staff Pension Fund	IPE 354	10/3/2011
201	Botswana Ash Staff Pension Fund	IPE 355	10/17/2011
202	BIC Retirement Fund	IPE 356	

LARGEST LAW FIRMS

- **Armstrongs**
  5th Floor Barclays House, Khama Crescent, Gaborone
  Tel: 267353481 , Fax: 267352757
  Contact: Mr. Neill Armstrong

- **Minchin & Kelly (Botswana)**
  P O Box 1339, Gaborone 0
  Tel: +267 312734 , Fax: +267 308500
  Contact: Mr. Dave Williams

U.S. AND COUNTRY CONTACTS

COUNTRY GOVERNMENT AGENCIES

Organization: Ministry of Agriculture
Contact Name and Title: Mr. Serwalo Tumelo, Permanent Secretary
Address: Private Bag 003, Gaborone, Botswana
Phone: (267) 350-603
Fax: (267) 356-027

Organization: Botswana Agricultural Marketing Board
Contact Name and Title: Mr. Tom Piper, Acting General Manager
Address: Private Bag 0053, Gaborone, Botswana
Phone: (267) 351-341
Fax: (267) 352-926

Organization: Ministry of Commerce and Industry
Contact Name and Title: Ms Connie Moremi, Permanent Secretary
Address: Private Bag 004, Gaborone, Botswana
Phone: (267) 3601-251
Fax: (267) 371-539

Organization: Ministry of Commerce and Industry, Department of Trade and Investment Promotion (TIPA)
Contact Name and Title: Mr. Dihelang Tsheko, Director
Address: Private Bag 00367, Gaborone
Phone: (267) 351-790
Fax: (267) 305-375

Organization: Ministry of Finance and Development Planning
Contact Name and Title: Mr. O.K. Matambo, Permanent Secretary
Address: Private Bag 008, Gaborone, Botswana
Phone: (267) 359-841 or 350-100
Fax: (267) 304-525

Organization: Botswana Development Corporation
Contact Name and Title: Mr. Michael Molefane, Director
Address: Bag 160, Gaborone, Botswana
Phone: (267) 351-811
Fax: (267) 373-539

COUNTRY TRADE ASSOCIATION/CHAMBERS OF COMMERCE

Organization: Botswana Confederation of Commerce Industry and Manpower (BOCCIM)
Contact Name and Title: Mr. Elias Dewah, Director

Address: P.O. Box 432, Gaborone, Botswana
Phone: (267) 353-459
Fax: (267) 373-142

Organization: Botswana Chamber of Commerce and Industry
Contact Name and Title: Mr. Raphael Sikwane
Address: P.O. Box 1402, Gaborone, Botswana

Phone: (267) 300-893
Fax: (267) 359-683

Organization: American Business Council In Botswana
Contact Name and Title: Mr. Bill Scott
Address: Problem Solvers (Pty) Ltd, Private Bag BR 53, Gaborone, Botswana
Phone: (267) 374-134
Fax: (267) 357-433

COUNTRY COMMERCIAL BANKS

Organization: Barclays Bank of Botswana Ltd
Contact Name and Title: Mr. Michael Klinck, Marketing Manager
Address: P.O. Box 478, Gaborone, Botswana
Phone: (267) 352-041
Fax: (267) 313-672

Organization: First National Bank of Botswana Ltd
Contact Name and Title: Mr. Trevor Kelly, Marketing Manager
Address: P.O. Box 1552, Gaborone, Botswana
Phone: (267) 374-370
Fax: (267) 374-368

Organization: Standard Chartered Bank Botswana Ltd
Contact Name and Title: Mr. Les Gibson, Managing Director; Mr. Nathan Kgabi, Marketing Manager
Address: P.O.496, Gaborone, Botswana
Phone: (267) 360-1500
Fax: (267) 351-545

Organization: Stanbic Bank Botswana Ltd
Contact Name and Title: Mr. N. McLeman, Managing Director
Address: Private Bag 00168, Gaborone, Botswana
Phone: (267) 301-600
Fax: (267) 300-171

U.S. EMBASSY TRADE PERSONNEL

Organization: Embassy of the United States of America
Contact Name and Title: Mr. David Hunt, Commercial Officer (as of September 1998) ; Ms. Gifty Oduro, Commercial Assistant
Address: P.O. Box 90, Gaborone, Botswana
Phone: (267) 353-982

Fax: (267) 356-947
E-Mail address: uscomml@global.bw

WASHINGTON-BASED USG COUNTRY CONTACTS

Organization: TPCC Trade Information Center, Washington, D.C.
Tel: 1-800-USA-TRADE
Organization: U.S. Department of State, Coordinator for Business Affairs
Phone: 202-746-1625
Fax: 202-647-3953

Organization: Department of Commerce, Office of Africa, (MAC)
Contact Name and Title: Ms. Debra Henke Rogers, Southern Africa Desk Officer
Address: 14th Street & Constitution Ave., N.W. Washington D.C. 20230
Phone: 202-482-4228
Fax: 202-482-5198
E-Mail Address: drogers@usita.gov

Organization: US Department of Agriculture, Foreign Agricultural Service, Trade Assistance and Promotion Office
Tel: (202) 720-7420

BOTSWANA'S DIPLOMATIC MISSIONS

China
Embassy of Botswana
1-8-1/2, Ta Yuang Office Building, Beijing
Republic of China
Tel: 0086 143 2571

European Community
Botswana Embassy to European Communities
169 Avenue De Tervuren, 1040 Brussels, Belgium
Tel: 32273 5611 012 070
Fax: 32273 56318

Hong Kong
Botswana Investment Promotion
4/F Dina House, Ruttonjee Centre,
11 Duddell Street
Central Hong Kong
Tel: 00882 53 485

Namibia
Botswana High Commission
P.O. Box 20359, Windhoek, Namibia
Tel: 221 942
Fax: 2646 136 034

Sweden
Botswana Embassy
Drottnigatan 56, P.O. Box 420, 0128 Stockholm Sweden
Tel: 4687 230 035
Fax: 4687 230 087
Telex: 11684

United Kingdom
Botswana High Commission
Stratford Place, London W1N 9AE, United Kingdom
Tel: 4471 499 0031
Fax: 4471 495 8595
Telex: 4426 2897

United States of America
Botswana Permanent Mission to the United Nations
103 East 37th Street, New York, NY 10016

Botswana Embassy
3400 International Drive, N.W. Washington DC
Suite 7M 20008
Tel: 2444 990
Fax: 2444 164

Zambia Botswana High Commission
P.O. Box 31510, Lusaka, Zambia
Tel: 26012 50019/250555
Fax: 26012 53895

Zimbabwe
Botswana High Commission
22 Philip Avenue, P.O. 563, Harare, Zimbabwe
Tel: 2634 72 9551
Fax: 2634 70 0459

Foreign Missions in Botswana
Departments & Organisations

Air Botswana,
P. O. Box 92, Gaborone.
Tel.352812 / 351921;
Fax. 374802.

Bank of Botswana (BoB) ,
P. O. Box 712, Gaborone.
Tel. 3606000;
Fax. 371231.

Botswana Development Corporation Ltd.,
P. O. Box 438, Gaborone.

Tel. 351811;
Fax.373539.
Telex. 2251.

Botswana Railways,
P/Bag 00125, Gaborone.
Tel. 300163;
Fax. 374360.

Gaborone Chamber of Commerce & Industry,
P. O. Box 1402, Gaborone.
Tel. 353721

Natural Resources Board,
Ministry of Local Government and Lands,
Private Bag 0068, Gaborone.
Tel. 302055; 302051.

MINISTRY OF COMMERCE AND INDUSTRY,

Director of Wildlife and National Parks,
P. O. Box 131, Gaborone.
Tel. 314577;
Fax. 312354.

Department of Trade and Investment
Promotion (TIPA) ,
Private Bag 004, Gaborone.
Tel: 353881 Fax: 371539

Tourism Department,
Private Bag 0047, Gaborone.
Tel. 353024, Fax. 371539,

The Hotel and Tourism Association of
Botswana (HATAB) ,
P. O. Box 968, Gaborone.
Tel.357144;
Fax. 303201.

BASIC TITLES FOR BOTSWANA

IMPORTANT!

All publications are updated annually!

Please contact IBP, Inc. at ibpusa3@gmail.com for the latest ISBNs and additional information

title
BotswanA "Spy" Guide - Strategic Information and Developments
Botswana A "Spy" Guide - Strategic Information and Developments
Botswana A Spy" Guide"
Botswana Banking & Financial Market Handbook
Botswana Banking & Financial Market Handbook
Botswana Business and Investment Opportunities Yearbook
Botswana Business and Investment Opportunities Yearbook
Botswana Business and Investment Opportunities Yearbook Volume 1 Strategic Information and Opportunities
Botswana Business Intelligence Report - Practical Information, Opportunities, Contcts
Botswana Business Intelligence Report - Practical Information, Opportunities, Contcts
Botswana Business Law Handbook - Strategic Information and Basic Laws
Botswana Business Law Handbook - Strategic Information and Basic Laws
Botswana Business Law Handbook - Strategic Information and Basic Laws
Botswana Business Law Handbook - Strategic Information and Basic Laws
Botswana Company Laws and Regulations Handbook
Botswana Constitution and Citizenship Laws Handbook - Strategic Information and Basic Laws
Botswana Country Study Guide - Strategic Information and Developments
Botswana Country Study Guide - Strategic Information and Developments
Botswana Country Study Guide - Strategic Information and Developments Volume 1 Strategic Information and Developments
Botswana Customs, Trade Regulations and Procedures Handbook
Botswana Customs, Trade Regulations and Procedures Handbook
Botswana Diplomatic Handbook - Strategic Information and Developments
Botswana Diplomatic Handbook - Strategic Information and Developments
Botswana Ecology & Nature Protection Handbook
Botswana Ecology & Nature Protection Handbook
Botswana Ecology & Nature Protection Laws and Regulation Handbook
Botswana Energy Policy, Laws and Regulation Handbook
Botswana Export-Import Trade and Business Directory
Botswana Export-Import Trade and Business Directory
Botswana Foreign Policy and Government Guide
Botswana Foreign Policy and Government Guide
Botswana Immigration Laws and Regulations Handbook - Strategic Information and Basic Laws
Botswana Industrial and Business Directory
Botswana Industrial and Business Directory
Botswana Internet and E-Commerce Investment and Business Guide - Strategic and Practical

title
Information: Regulations and Opportunities
Botswana Internet and E-Commerce Investment and Business Guide - Strategic and Practical Information: Regulations and Opportunities
Botswana Investment and Business Guide - Strategic and Practical Information
Botswana Investment and Business Guide - Strategic and Practical Information
Botswana Investment and Business Guide - Strategic and Practical Information
Botswana Investment and Business Guide - Strategic and Practical Information
Botswana Investment and Trade Laws and Regulations Handbook
Botswana Labor Laws and Regulations Handbook - Strategic Information and Basic Laws
Botswana Land Ownership and Agriculture Laws Handbook
Botswana Mineral & Mining Sector Investment and Business Guide - Strategic and Practical Information
Botswana Mineral & Mining Sector Investment and Business Guide - Strategic and Practical Information
Botswana Mining Laws and Regulations Handbook
Botswana Radio Frequencies and Telecom Operation Licensing Regulations Handbook
Botswana Radio Frequencies and Telecom Operation Licensing Regulations Handbook
Botswana Recent Economic and Political Developments Yearbook
Botswana Recent Economic and Political Developments Yearbook
Botswana Recent Economic and Political Developments Yearbook
Botswana Spy" Guide"
Botswana Starting Business (Incorporating) in....Guide
Botswana Taxation Laws and Regulations Handbook
Botswana Telecom Industry Investment and Business Opportunities Handbook
Botswana Telecom Industry Investment and Business Opportunities Handbook
Botswana Telecom Industry Laws and Regulations Handbook
Botswana Telecom Industry Laws and Regulations Handbook
Botswana Telecom Laws and Regulations Handbook
Botswana Telecommunication Industry Business Opportunities Handbook
Botswana Telecommunication Industry Business Opportunities Handbook
Botswana: How to Invest, Start and Run Profitable Business in Botswana Guide - Practical Information, Opportunities, Contacts

Finland Taxation Laws and Regulations Handbook
France Taxation Laws and Regulations Handbook
Gabon Taxation Laws and Regulations Handbook
Gambia Taxation Laws and Regulations Handbook
Georgia Taxation Laws and Regulations Handbook
Germany Taxation Laws and Regulations Handbook
Ghana Taxation Laws and Regulations Handbook
Gibraltar Taxation Laws and Regulations Handbook
Greece Taxation Laws and Regulations Handbook
Greenland Taxation Laws and Regulations Handbook
Grenada Taxation Laws and Regulations Handbook
Guam Taxation Laws and Regulations Handbook
Guatemala Taxation Laws and Regulations Handbook
Guernsey Taxation Laws and Regulations Handbook
Guinea Taxation Laws and Regulations Handbook
Guinea-Bissau Taxation Laws and Regulations Handbook
Guyana Taxation Laws and Regulations Handbook
Haiti Taxation Laws and Regulations Handbook
Honduras Taxation Laws and Regulations Handbook
Hungary Taxation Laws and Regulations Handbook
Iceland Taxation Laws and Regulations Handbook
India Taxation Laws and Regulations Handbook
Indonesia Taxation Laws and Regulations Handbook
InternationalTaxation Laws and Regulations Handbook
Iran Taxation Laws and Regulations Handbook
Iraq Taxation Laws and Regulations Handbook
Ireland Taxation Laws and Regulations Handbook
Israel Taxation Laws and Regulations Handbook
Italy Taxation Laws and Regulations Handbook
Jamaica Taxation Laws and Regulations Handbook
Japan Taxation Laws and Regulations Handbook
Jersey Taxation Laws and Regulations Handbook
Jordan Taxation Laws and Regulations Handbook
Kazakhstan Taxation Laws and Regulations Handbook
Kenya Taxation Laws and Regulations Handbook
Kiribati Taxation Laws and Regulations Handbook
Korea, North Taxation Laws and Regulations Handbook
Korea, South Taxation Laws and Regulations Handbook
Kosovo Taxation Laws and Regulations Handbook
Kuwait Taxation Laws and Regulations Handbook
Kyrgyzstan Taxation Laws and Regulations Handbook
Laos Taxation Laws and Regulations Handbook
Latvia Taxation Laws and Regulations Handbook
Lebanon Taxation Laws and Regulations Handbook
Lesotho Taxation Laws and Regulations Handbook
Liberia Taxation Laws and Regulations Handbook
Libya Taxation Laws and Regulations Handbook
Liechtenstein Taxation Laws and Regulations Handbook
Lithuania Taxation Laws and Regulations Handbook
Luxembourg Taxation Laws and Regulations Handbook
Macao Taxation Laws and Regulations Handbook
Macedonia Taxation Laws and Regulations Handbook
Madagascar Taxation Laws and Regulations Handbook
Madeira Taxation Laws and Regulations Handbook
Malawi Taxation Laws and Regulations Handbook
Malaysia Taxation Laws and Regulations Handbook
Maldives Taxation Laws and Regulations Handbook
Mali Taxation Laws and Regulations Handbook
Malta Taxation Laws and Regulations Handbook
Man Taxation Laws and Regulations Handbook
Marshall Islands Taxation Laws and Regulations Handbook
Mauritania Taxation Laws and Regulations Handbook
Mauritius Taxation Laws and Regulations Handbook
Mayotte Taxation Laws and Regulations Handbook
Mexico Taxation Laws and Regulations Handbook
Micronesia Taxation Laws and Regulations Handbook
Moldova Taxation Laws and Regulations Handbook
Monaco Taxation Laws and Regulations Handbook
Mongolia Taxation Laws and Regulations Handbook
Monserrat Taxation Laws and Regulations Handbook
Morocco Taxation Laws and Regulations Handbook
Mozambique Taxation Laws and Regulations Handbook
Myanmar Taxation Laws and Regulations Handbook
Namibia Taxation Laws and Regulations Handbook
Nauru Taxation Laws and Regulations Handbook
Nepal Taxation Laws and Regulations Handbook
Netherlands Taxation Laws and Regulations Handbook
New Caledonia Taxation Laws and Regulations Handbook
New Zealand Taxation Laws and Regulations Handbook
Nicaragua Taxation Laws and Regulations Handbook
Niger Taxation Laws and Regulations Handbook
Nigeria Taxation Laws and Regulations Handbook
Niue Taxation Laws and Regulations Handbook
Northern Mariana Islands Taxation Laws and Regulations Handbook
Norway Taxation Laws and Regulations Handbook
Oman Taxation Laws and Regulations Handbook
Pakistan Taxation Laws and Regulations Handbook
Palau Taxation Laws and Regulations Handbook
Palestine Taxation Laws and Regulations Handbook
Panama Taxation Laws and Regulations Handbook
Papua New Guinea Taxation Laws and Regulations Handbook
Paraguay Taxation Laws and Regulations Handbook
Peru Taxation Laws and Regulations Handbook
Philippines Taxation Laws and Regulations Handbook
Pitcairn Islands Taxation Laws and Regulations Handbook
Poland Taxation Laws and Regulations Handbook
Polynesia French Taxation Laws and Regulations Handbook
Portugal Taxation Laws and Regulations Handbook
Qatar Taxation Laws and Regulations Handbook
Romania Taxation Laws and Regulations Handbook
Russia Taxation Laws and Regulations Handbook
Rwanda Taxation Laws and Regulations Handbook
Saint Kitts and Nevis Taxation Laws and Regulations Handbook

Saint Lucia Taxation Laws and Regulations Handbook
Saint Vincent and The Grenadines Taxation Laws and Regulations Handbook
Samoa (American) Taxation Laws and Regulations Handbook
Samoa (Western) Taxation Laws and Regulations Handbook
San Marino Taxation Laws and Regulations Handbook
Sao Tome and Principe Taxation Laws and Regulations Handbook
Saudi Arabia Taxation Laws and Regulations Handbook
Scotland Taxation Laws and Regulations Handbook
Senegal Taxation Laws and Regulations Handbook
Seychelles Taxation Laws and Regulations Handbook
Sierra Leone Taxation Laws and Regulations Handbook
Singapore Taxation Laws and Regulations Handbook
Slovakia Taxation Laws and Regulations Handbook
Slovenia Taxation Laws and Regulations Handbook
Solomon Islands Taxation Laws and Regulations Handbook
Somalia Taxation Laws and Regulations Handbook
South Africa Taxation Laws and Regulations Handbook
Spain Taxation Laws and Regulations Handbook
Sri Lanka Taxation Laws and Regulations Handbook
St. Helena Taxation Laws and Regulations Handbook
St. Pierre & Miquelon Taxation Laws and Regulations Handbook
Sudan Taxation Laws and Regulations Handbook
Suriname Taxation Laws and Regulations Handbook
Swaziland Taxation Laws and Regulations Handbook
Sweden Taxation Laws and Regulations Handbook
Switzerland Taxation Laws and Regulations Handbook
Syria Taxation Laws and Regulations Handbook
Taiwan Taxation Laws and Regulations Handbook
Tajikistan Taxation Laws and Regulations Handbook
Tanzania Taxation Laws and Regulations Handbook
Thailand Taxation Laws and Regulations Handbook
Togo Taxation Laws and Regulations Handbook
Tonga Taxation Laws and Regulations Handbook
Trinidad and Tobago Taxation Laws and Regulations Handbook
Tunisia Taxation Laws and Regulations Handbook
Turkey Taxation Laws and Regulations Handbook
Turkmenistan Taxation Laws and Regulations Handbook
Turks & Caicos Taxation Laws and Regulations Handbook
Tuvalu Taxation Laws and Regulations Handbook
Uganda Taxation Laws and Regulations Handbook
Ukraine Taxation Laws and Regulations Handbook
United Arab Emirates Taxation Laws and Regulations Handbook
United Kingdom Taxation Laws and Regulations Handbook
United States Taxation Laws and Regulations Handbook
Uruguay Taxation Laws and Regulations Handbook
Uzbekistan Taxation Laws and Regulations Handbook
Vanuatu Taxation Laws and Regulations Handbook
Vatican City Taxation Laws and Regulations Handbook
Venezuela Taxation Laws and Regulations Handbook
Vietnam Taxation Laws and Regulations Handbook
Virgin Islands, British Taxation Laws and Regulations Handbook
Wake Atoll Taxation Laws and Regulations Handbook
Wallis & Futuna Taxation Laws and Regulations Handbook
Yemen Taxation Laws and Regulations Handbook
Serbia Taxation Laws and Regulations Handbook
Zambia Taxation Laws and Regulations Handbook
Zimbabwe Taxation Laws and Regulations Handbook

NEW! WORLD OFFSHORE TAX GUIDES

Price: $149.95 each

1. Andorra Offshore Tax Guide
2. Anguilla Offshore Tax Guide
3. Bahamas Offshore Tax Guide
4. Barbados Offshore Tax Guide
5. Belize Offshore Tax Guide
6. Bermuda Offshore Tax Guide
7. British Virgin Islands Offshore Tax Guide
8. Cayman Islands Offshore Tax Guide
9. Cook Islands Offshore Tax Guide
10. Costa Rica Offshore Tax Guide
11. Cyprus Offshore Tax Guide
12. Dubai Offshore Tax Guide
13. Gibraltar Offshore Tax Guide
14. Grenada Offshore Tax Guide
15. Guernsey Offshore Tax Guide
16. Hong Kong Offshore Tax Guide
17. Ireland Offshore Tax Guide
18. Isle of Man Offshore Tax Guide
19. Jersey Offshore Tax Guide
20. Labuan Offshore Tax Guide
21. Liechtenstein Offshore Tax Guide
22. Luxembourg Offshore Tax Guide
23. Madeira Offshore Tax Guide
24. Malta Offshore Tax Guide
25. Mauritius Offshore Business and Investment Opportunities Handbook
26. Mauritius Offshore Tax Guide
27. Monaco Offshore Tax Guide
28. Nauru Offshore Tax Guide
29. Netherlands Antilles Offshore Tax Guide
30. Panama Offshore Tax Guide
31. Seychelles Offshore Tax Guide
32. Switzerland Offshore Tax Guide
33. Turks & Caicos Islands Offshore Tax Guide
34. Vanuatu Offshore Tax Guide

To order and for additional analytical and marketing information, please contacrt
International Business Publications, USA at:
P.O. Box 15343, Washington, DC 20003, USA. Phone: (202) 546-2103. Fax: (202) 546-3275.
World Business Info Catalog: http://www.ibous.com. E-mail: ibpusa@comcast.net

www.ingramcontent.com/pod-product-compliance
Lightning Source LLC
LaVergne TN
LVHW080034210926
848481LV00011B/3187